Undr
W

"Levy continues to explore and unmask the wetiko mind-virus of greed and hubris that threatens the human enterprise but also, with unique force, opens up for us ways of 'undreaming' its power so we can live free from its contamination. This is an indispensable manual for all serious seekers."

ANDREW HARVEY, COAUTHOR OF *RADICAL REGENERATION*

"Paul Levy is one of our clearest visionaries about things that truly matter."

LARRY DOSSEY, M.D.

"*Undreaming Wetiko* is infused with Paul's insights and personal experiences spanning over decades, weaving together quantum physics, Jungian shadow work, shamanism, trauma work, and drawing from various spiritual and esoteric traditions. Paul gives us a comprehensive understanding of why the world is the way it is, while he also brilliantly shows us the way out and what needs to be done before we destroy ourselves."

BERNHARD GUENTHER, PSYCHOSPIRITUAL COACH, WRITER, AND COHOST OF *THE COSMIC MATRIX PODCAST*

"Paul Levy emerges from that ancient prophetic tradition of gnostics with the uncanny ability to transmute the poison of our experience into medicine for the soul. This book is an unflinching look at the underworld all around us, with all of the peril and the promise that implies. It leaves the reader not just with the possibility that enlightenment might exist in and through the ocean of darkness that surrounds and assails us; it offers us a bridge, a boat, and a ship to the other side."

REV. MICHAEL ELLICK, COMMUNITY ORGANIZER AND CHRISTIAN MINISTER

"This book serves as an essential guidepost to help us reclaim our creative power from the insidious grip of the wetiko mind-virus. With this book, Paul Levy seals his role as a master alchemist, serving as the lead spokesperson of an emerging consciousness that not only identifies the root of our collective shadow but also gives us the courage to overcome it. There is no way 'out' but in, and creative imagination is the key to 'undreaming wetiko.' Read this book and you will never be the same!"

"*Undreaming Wetiko* is urgently needed medicine in these perilous times. Paul Levy provides a powerful beacon by which we can recognize the dreamlike nature of our existence and lucidly embody our role as co-creators. His revelations help us to understand the trance of delusion and suffering that pervades the human world and empowers us to transmute this darkness into the light of liberation and knowledge of our intrinsic nature."

"When we look upon wetiko with the light of love, we see the illusion, but it only vanishes when our *heart demands justice of our mind.* Thanks to Paul Levy, *Undreaming Wetiko* has inspired me to live from my heart so that wetiko has no use for my mind."

"Through his wide-ranging, comprehensive research, deep and fearless inquiry, and the direct lived experience of his subject, wetiko, Levy has written a book of such power and conviction that just by reading it I was changed. As if giving a transmission, this book went straight into my heart, ignited the spirit, and imparted in me a grounded sense of responsibility but also of agency. Isn't this the very thing that we all need to experience right now? That even though we are in a precarious condition, we also have everything within us that we need to turn the tide."

"Levy's teachings offer unique, multidimensional medicine for our personal and planetary ills. Reading this book will unquestionably alter your perceptions of what it means to be human and how to navigate these times by reconciling the inner world with the outer world, the personal with the collective, the wound with the healing, the unconscious with the conscious, and the shadow with the light."

Undreaming Wetiko

Breaking the Spell of the Nightmare Mind-Virus

A Sacred Planet Book

Paul Levy

Inner Traditions
Rochester, Vermont

Inner Traditions
One Park Street
Rochester, Vermont 05767
www.InnerTraditions.com

Text stock is SFI certified

Sacred Planet Books are curated by Richard Grossinger, Inner Traditions editorial board member and cofounder and former publisher of North Atlantic Books. The Sacred Planet collection, published under the umbrella of the Inner Traditions family of imprints, includes works on the themes of consciousness, cosmology, alternative medicine, dreams, climate, permaculture, alchemy, shamanic studies, oracles, astrology, crystals, hyperobjects, locutions, and subtle bodies.

Cataloging-in-Publication Data for this title is available from the Library of Congress

ISBN 978-1-64411-566-4 (print)
ISBN 978-1-64411-567-1 (ebook)

Printed and bound in the United States by Lake Book Manufacturing, LLC
The text stock is SFI certified. The Sustainable Forestry Initiative® program promotes sustainable forest management.

10   9   8   7   6   5   4   3   2   1

Text design and layout by Virginia Scott Bowman
This book was typeset in Garamond Premier Pro with Barcelona and Optima used as display typefaces

To send correspondence to the author of this book, mail a first-class letter to the author c/o Inner Traditions • Bear & Company, One Park Street, Rochester, VT 05767, and we will forward the communication, or contact the author directly at **awakeninthedream.com**.

✿ ✿ ✿

This book is dedicated to the great doctor of the soul C. G. Jung. Once I came face-to-face with wetiko, encountering Jung's work helped me get a handle on the overwhelming and potentially crazy-making nature of what I had come in contact with. I feel that I am standing on Jung's broad shoulders as I continually deepen my understanding of wetiko. As I've previously mentioned in my writings, Jung, though not having the indigenous name, was tracking the spore-prints of wetiko as it weaved itself throughout the warp and woof of the human psyche and the world at large. Like myself, Jung was convinced that something drastic is needed in a world headed for catastrophe—in his words, "to wake up the dreamers," which in this case is us.

Contents

Acknowledgments

Just like it takes a whole village to raise a child, it took a whole community of spiritual friends to birth this book. I could write a whole book and then some to acknowledge all of the people over the course of my lifetime who have helped me deepen in my own healing and connect with myself, which, when push comes to shove, is the major prerequisite for being able to write this book. I feel that this book has been dreamed up by the field, and as the author, I am merely the instrument for this to take place. That being said, I'd like to express endless gratitude for the countless people—both embodied and otherwise—who have contributed in one way or another to this present work.

I first want to acknowledge my main teachers of the Dharma: Khenchen Palden Sherab Rinpoche, Khenpo Tsewang Dongyal Rinpoche, Lama Rinchen Phuntsok Rinpoche, and Dr. Rina Sircar. I couldn't—nor would I want to—imagine my life without their love, guidance, and blessings.

I am lucky in that I have a large community of people who love and support me and my work. In thinking of who to thank, the usual cast of suspects comes to mind. I first want to acknowledge my longtime friend Larry Berry, who has always been there, without fail, in whatever way was needed, for the many years of selfless service and loving support I've received from him in getting my work out. I want to express immense gratitude to the incomparable Donna Zerner, for freely sharing her many brilliant gifts in shedding light on the darkness (both out in the world and within myself) in order to help this book—not to mention myself—see the light. I want to acknowledge and express my appreciation for the generous support I've received from Kendra Crossen Burroughs in ways I can only imagine. I want to give a shout out of thanks to my friend Robert Simmons, who went out of his way to connect me with Inner Traditions. And I also want to thank all of the wonderful people at Inner Traditions, who have been incredibly supportive in helping this book see the light of day. I particularly want to thank Richard Grossinger, who coincidentally enough, was the person who helped publish my first book on wetiko and then played the same role for this book in totally different circumstances. I'd also like to thank my editors Emilia Cataldo, Margaret Jones, and my publicist Ashley Kolesnik for their selfless support. I would be remiss if I didn't give a special shout of thanks to my dear friend and co-dreamer Matt Cadenelli for having my back when I needed it most. I also want to gratefully acknowledge the help of a close friend of mine who for years has endlessly contemplated the idea of wetiko with me, who, for reasons of his own, wishes to remain anonymous—you know who you are. I also want to thank Damian Thomas, Mark Hartley, Alex Aris, David Frenette, Julianna Bright, Michael Ellick, Richard Daab, Bob Welsh, Cory Parker, Samuel Freni-Rothschild, Bailey Wayton, Karin Gagnon, Mertie Pateros, Grant Stampfli, Bill Baines, Troy Lush, Seth Lorinczi, Gwen Burns, Ruth Leibowitz and Paola and Vanessa Castaldo for their loving reflection and support.

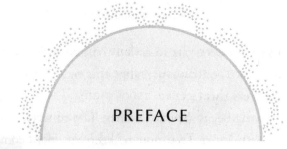

Unmasking Ourselves

This is a time of incredible uncertainty and existential anxiety. Stress seems to pervade the very air we breathe. Fear is being endlessly produced by the mainstream media, infecting the minds of the masses. Propaganda has so insinuated itself into our sources of information that it has become harder than ever before to discern truth from falsehood. There are massive mis- and disinformation campaigns whose purpose is nothing other than to confuse and muddle our minds. We are truly in the middle of a war that, to the extent it is successful, most people don't recognize: a war on consciousness. There is a massive spell being cast all around us by people and institutions that are themselves under the very spell they are casting.

Many among us have become numb and desensitized to the overwhelming nature of our crisis. People are inwardly checking out, becoming more zombielike by the day. It has become challenging to stay connected with our humanity. One of the major problems happening in our world today, amplified by the global lockdowns, is an epidemic of isolation and loneliness. Many people are depressed, despairing, pessimistic, and feeling utterly helpless and hopeless. Mental disorders are trending through the proverbial roof. Diseases of the skin (the organ that expresses the state of the psyche) are on the rise. Widespread homelessness is an undeniable manifestation of the unraveling of our society and our previously held sense of a well-ordered world. It's as if the house of cards that has been our so-called civilization is collapsing in on itself, and whether we consciously realize this or not, our unconscious undoubtedly registers this fact.

The world is aflame, as are our psyches. The collective unconscious is in an uproar. It takes real courage to keep an open, compassionate heart in times such as these. Instead of building more nuclear bombs, we need to develop nuclear compassion. And yet, hidden within the very darkness that has befallen our world is a primordial light. Due to the nearly intolerable pressure in the alchemical vessel of humanity's psyche, never before has there been such a real possibility of mass awakening, a process that always starts with people like you and me.

We are confronted by a darkness that has been living inside of us, a darkness that has been keeping our unconscious wounds, traumas, and unhealed abuse issues alive. We've been able to postpone looking at these shadow energies, but now they are not only in our face, they are behind it as well, which is to say that we are confronted on a soul level by the darkness of the world we live in, a darkness we all share. The question is: do we indulge in our usual coping strategies to keep these seemingly darker, wounded parts of ourselves at bay (food, drugs, Netflix anyone?)—which is ultimately to avoid an authentic relationship with ourselves? Or do we unmask ourselves and unflinchingly face the darker, wounded parts within us?

I can speak for myself. Since the advent of the global pandemic I have felt even more intensely both the light *and* the dark aspects of myself, as if they are interdependent parts of a deeper process wherein one is evoking the presence of the other. Due to the urgent feeling that there's no time to waste, it's as if the creative, light-filled part of me has gotten more vibrant, while at the same time the deepest darkness embedded in my unhealed wounds also seems stronger than ever. The tension between the light and the dark parts of myself has intensified to a practically unbearable degree. As my light increases, the darkness within me is simultaneously coming to the fore, making itself known to the point where it's getting harder and harder for me to look away.

It's as if the light is illuminating everything in me that is not of the light, everything that is dark, which makes sense, as the purpose of light is to reveal darkness. As I more deeply connect with the light of my true nature, my subjective experience is that there is a seemingly dark force within me—wetiko—that wants to prevent me from connecting with the light at all costs. This book is about shedding light on that darkness in order to allow our light to shine.

A Thumbnail Sketch of Wetiko

I've been writing about wetiko in one way or another for over twenty years. I guess you could say that I consider it an important enough topic to devote the rest of my life to trying to capture and elucidate this concept in words. When I wrote my first book, *The Madness of George W. Bush: A Reflection of Our Collective Psychosis,* in the early 2000s, I wasn't overly familiar with what Native Americans call *wetiko,* having just learned about it from writer, scholar, and political activist Jack D. Forbes, in his 1979 book *Columbus and Other Cannibals: The Wetiko Disease of Exploitation, Imperialism, and Terrorism.* I was intimately familiar with its workings, however. That first book was all about wetiko, though I referred to it by a different name, having coined the term *malignant egophrenia,* or ME disease. I remember writing the book as an attempt to keep myself sane in the midst of a world gone mad. That time now seems like the good old days compared to the madness that is now playing out in this wetiko-riddled world of ours some twenty years later. The seeds for all of my future writings on wetiko as well as on quantum physics and the important relationship between the two are found in this first book of mine.

Forbes' book on wetiko is based on the idea that for thousands of years, humanity, which exhibits all the characteristics of a truly deluded species, has been suffering from a psychospiritual disease that is far worse than any physical malady it has ever suffered through: the plague of wetiko. Forbes felt that the real history of the world is the story of the epidemiology of this plague, a history that until now had been left unwritten due to our unawareness of what has actually befallen us. Forbes' exposition on wetiko finally answered the question of why our species has become so incredibly self- and other-destructive.

In his analysis of this mind-virus, Forbes considers wetiko to be the greatest catalytic force of evolution ever known—and I would add *not known*—to humanity. Just like a symbol in a dream, wetiko reflects something back to us about ourselves, if only we have the eyes to see. Wetiko, a form of death that "takes on" life, is at the same time a living revelation, revealing something that is of the utmost importance for us to know at this time.

In dealing with wetiko, we are dealing with a mystery. Wetiko has no intrinsic, independent existence (separate from the mind, that is), which is to say that it has no substantial existence from its own side; and yet it can wreak unimaginable havoc and even kill us. It is amazing—mind-blowing, in fact—that wetiko, by whatever name it is called, has been pointed at by virtually all the world's wisdom traditions as being the very thing that is at the root of our worst troubles, and yet relatively few people have even heard of it (though these days more and more are).

The genesis of wetiko is to be found deep within our minds. It is a dreaming phenomenon, which is to say that it is something that in my language we are dreaming up, both collectively, in the world, and in our individual minds.

When we see our situation as if it's a dream and interpret it as such—which is to say, symbolically—one thing becomes clear: humanity (which is the dreamer of the dream) seems practically uneducable in that we stubbornly persist in doubling down on our unconscious mistakes instead of learning from them. When we don't get the message from a dream, we ensure that the dream will reoccur in a more and more amplified form, until we finally recognize what it is symbolically revealing to us and change our perspective and behavior accordingly. The question naturally arises: what will it take for us to get the message?

It's as if there is something in our unconscious that seems to be intent on preventing us from learning the lessons of our mistakes, as if there is something within us that is invested in keeping us asleep at all costs. The spiritual teacher Gurdjieff pointed out that humanity isn't asleep in an ordinary way, but has fallen into a "hypnotic sleep"[1] in which our state of stupefaction continually regenerates itself within our minds. This situation made Gurdjieff conjecture about whether there was some sort of force (wetiko!) that profits from keeping us entrapped in a mesmerized state, thereby stopping us from seeing the truth of our circumstances and remembering who we really are.

In any case, this mysterious something seems to thwart any deep exploration into its workings. It's as if wetiko has its own propaganda department dedicated to keeping itself hidden. More than anything, wetiko hates to be outed, as it only has power when it works in the shadows of our minds. It avoids the light of awareness like the plague.*

Interestingly, the final verse of the Qur'an (Surah 114), which in Islam is considered to be the voice of God, is warning about wetiko. This holy book refers to the wetiko spirit, depending upon the translation, as "the slinking prompter," "the lurking (or retreating) whisperer," and other similar phrases. The slinking prompter/whisperer secretly and insidiously works through stealth and subterfuge, invisibly creeping into and prompting evil in people's hearts under the cover of the darkness of the unconscious. The Qur'an correlates the slinking prompter with evil, and connects its perfidious presence to

---

*Wetiko is a lucifugous phenomenon, that is, it avoids the light.

when we forget and fail to take refuge in God, which is another way of saying that we unknowingly empower and open the door to this corrupting influence when we don't remember our true nature. This slinking prompter can't stand (nor stand up to) the light of conscious awareness, however, as it immediately retreats—slinking away—when it is seen, which is an expression of its intrinsic feebleness when we are awake to its (and our) true nature.

Wetiko has myriad ways of derailing any serious investigation into its nature. Oftentimes, for example, I'll meet a person or a group of people who seem genuinely interested in wetiko and want to learn more. They'll ask me a couple of questions and then, after hardly any time at all, they think they've got it and feel they sufficiently understand what it's all about—an attitude that short-circuits any deeper inquiry into realizing the endlessly mind-blowing revelation that is wetiko. When this plays out, instead of them "getting" the radical nature of wetiko, wetiko has "gotten" them. I have come up with a name for this syndrome: *premature comprehension delusion,* or PCD.* This is one of multiple strategies that wetiko uses to hide itself from being seen so as to further propagate its phantomlike pseudoexistence throughout the field of human consciousness.

It is not only helpful, but necessary to create new words, phrases, and acronyms to name these unconscious and heretofore invisible processes in order to anchor them in our consciousness so that they can be more easily seen. This is the power of the word in action, as naming something has a seemingly magical effect that bestows on us a power over the thing or process that is named. Language is an ever-evolving medium that continually needs to be updated to keep up with our expanding consciousness. Language is not merely descriptive (describing a world that is separate from us), but is actually creative

---

*See the Glossary of Acronyms in the back of this book for a complete list of acronyms I've invented.

in that it has an effect on creating our experience of both the world and ourselves.

From my point of view, oftentimes these people have less than a 1 percent understanding of the multidimensional, quantum, dreamlike nature of this elusive mind-virus, and yet after only a few minutes of the briefest introduction to it they have already decided and convinced themselves that they comprehend it. If wetiko is seen as an underground creature, it's as if they see its most superficial appendage appearing above ground and think they see the whole beast. In trying to put the mystery of wetiko in a cage of limited understanding, the bird, wetiko, has, so to speak, flown, and their curiosity about this mystery goes out the window with it.

Fitting wetiko in the box of our existing understanding practically ensures that we won't see it, as wetiko, by its very nature, necessarily operates outside our ordinary conception of things. Seeing wetiko necessarily demands that we step out of the limited, partial, fragmented viewpoint of the separate self and see more wholistically; it's a stance in which we recognize our interconnection with the whole, with the rest of the universe. This is to say that seeing wetiko is a transformative experience that radically changes us.

Of course, thinking we apprehend the whole when we encounter only one of wetiko's multiple aspects is a manifestation of the underhanded workings of this mind-virus. Tragically, such a limited and solidified idea about wetiko misses the whole point, not to mention ensures that in our closed-mindedness we are unwittingly becoming a vector for wetiko to insinuate itself even more deeply in our individual minds and in the world.

I've witnessed how some people, after hearing about wetiko, say they don't "resonate" with it. This makes me think that they might not resonate with wetiko, but wetiko is resonating with them. Some simply conflate wetiko with the shadow, with the lower self or with evil (in its simply "bad" aspect). All of these are partial facets of wetiko, but to think this is what wetiko is would be like the proverb about the blind person touching one part of an elephant (say, the trunk) and thinking that an elephant is like a snake. Wetiko has many facets and faces. How it manifests depends on who is looking. Though readily appearing in its most negative, destructive form, wetiko has encoded within it a hidden treasure. It is my hope that this book in some way helps us unlock this treasure.

Though wetiko is a truly multidimensional, many-faceted, and profound idea, its fundamental essence is really simple to understand. In my previous work I've referred to wetiko as *ME disease,* a misidentification of who we think we are. This is to say that the process of identification, of who we *think* we are, is at the root of wetiko.

Who we identify as is oftentimes an unconscious process that when we get right down to it is a made-up construct (a construction) of our mind. We tend to conceive of our sense of identity as a given, as something concrete and written in stone, as nonnegotiable and objectively true, but it is actually anything but. Our sense of identity is not fixed at all, but is rather a creative process that we are participating in, shaping each and every moment.

Who do we *think* we are? This is a real question, one that implies that our sense of identity is related to our thinking, to the mind itself. Our subjective experience of identity is quite malleable and is a function of our mind, which is to say we are actively participating in the moment-by-moment creation of our experience of identity. Not only is our sense of identity a function of our mind, but our mind is a function of our identity. In other words, who we think we are has a radical effect on our mind. Our sense of identity molds us, while we are at the same time continuously crafting our identity. What we don't want is to let wetiko forge our identity for us.

Because wetiko disease basically means to have fallen into a state of mistaken identity, the best medicine for wetiko is to know who we are. When we connect with our authentic self, with our true nature, we discover that our nature is naturally creative. To remember who

we really are is to connect with our creativity; and in a positive feedback loop that generates abundant life, to express oneself creatively
deepens our knowledge of who we truly are and further reveals our
essential nature.

Since the root essence of the wetiko mind-virus is not knowing
one's true nature, not recognizing who we truly are ensures that our
true nature, instead of expressing itself *creatively* in service to ourself
and others, will be channeled *destructively* in a limited and uncre-
ative way that drains our life force. If we don't mobilize our creative
resources, wetiko is more than happy to use our inner assets in a way
that serves its agenda rather than our own true nature. Instead of endlessly tapping into our source and *re-sourcing* and refreshing ourselves,
our own natural reserves get turned against us in a way that creates
a nightmare, just like the one we are currently dreaming up in the
world.

I'd like to introduce the term *nightmare mind-virus* as a synonym
for wetiko. This coinage feels right, as it captures an aspect of this
virus of the mind that adds to and complements the name *wetiko*. The
nightmare mind-virus is the deviant psychic factor that's at the bottom of our unconscious creation of a real-life nightmare in our world.
Finding the name for what is afflicting us is like a deliverance from
a nightmare.

I like how the word *nightmare* refers to and implies dreaming.
Nightmares are an unmediated expression and symbol of the darker
and unintegrated parts of our unconscious having their way with
us. This is precisely what the nightmare mind-virus of wetiko does
when it gains the upper hand in our psyche and in our world, and
runs amok. By teaching us how nightmares work, the nightmare
mind-virus can potentially empower us to transform and stop dreaming up the nightmare we are living through. Multidimensional phenomena like wetiko have inspired many names throughout history,
yet any one name can't possibly capture all of its multiple aspects.
And so to find the name for this parasite of the mind that we are

dealing with is important, for it helps us get a handle on it and how it operates.

Our true nature, our true identity—who we really are—is impervious to wetiko's pernicious influence. Wetiko can't take over, possess, or have any effect on our true nature, which is not an object that can be possessed by wetiko or by anything else, for that matter. For this reason, wetiko's strategy is to set up a counterfeit version—a simulation—of who we are, which it then tricks us into identifying with. Wetiko can't stand it (for it then has no place to stand) when we identify with our true nature, as it then has nothing to sink its fangs into. Wetiko has no creativity on its own, but is a master impersonator—we can conceive of it as aping the Divine.

The Apocryphon of John calls wetiko "the counterfeiting spirit" (the *antimimon pneuma* [Apoc. John III, 36:17]). A master mime, wetiko literally masquerades as ourselves. This counterfeiter plugs into our own innate creativity in order to conjure up a stunted image of oneself as limited, wounded, and beset with all kinds of problems (or the opposite, as inflated and grandiose). This psychic snake-oil salesman then compellingly tells us that this fraudulent representation is who we actually are. If we are not awake in the moment to this fraud, we will be sold a bogus bill of goods; like putting on a garment, we will unknowingly step into—buy into—wetiko's fabricated and impoverished version of who we are. In so doing, in one fell swoop we have given ourselves away, identified with who we are not and have thus disconnected from our creative power. A more perfect recipe for the madness of wetiko to work its black magic within us is hard to imagine.

As soon as we identify with this false self we are a goner, as then, with wetiko's help, we will create experiences that confirm this limited identity in a self-reinforcing, mind-created feedback loop. Wetiko has then fooled us into thinking that a seeming appearance, a display of our mind, a fictitious identity that has no actual reality, is the real deal. We can then be consumed by protecting and defending a make-believe version of who we are that doesn't even exist. We have then stepped out of our right mind and have identified with the mind that wetiko has crafted for us, unknowingly becoming its hand puppet. Behind the scenes, wetiko is manipulating us by pulling our strings, as if we are its marionette, so as to reinforce what it wants us to think instead of us thinking for ourselves. We will then be deposed from the kingdom, from the sovereign position that rightfully belongs to us as part of our inheritance. As sci-fi author Philip K. Dick would say, a usurper has assumed the throne.

Surprisingly (or I should say, *not* surprisingly), any mention of such a counterfeiting spirit was removed from the biblical canon and can only be found in the apocryphal texts—a maneuver that I would venture was inspired by wetiko. Because the Apocrypha are not included in the Bible, its sayings are often thought to be of spurious origin, but the opposite is actually the case: at the time of their writing these texts were accorded the highest respect and veneration. It is as if wetiko itself was on the editorial board of the Bible, doing its damndest to make sure it wouldn't be exposed. And yet in so doing, wetiko reveals one of its main strategies: it does everything it can to avoid being seen, for once it is recognized its cover is blown and its power is then taken away.

In exposing this psychic counterfeiting operation, this book is outing the biggest psyop in the history of the world, an order of magnitude bigger than any psyop that people think might (and may actually) be taking place in our world's body politic. This psyop is taking place within our very minds, and in our unknowing collusion with this operation we are the ones who are perpetrating this nightmare upon ourselves.

A few years ago I had a powerful dream that is relevant to this discussion. In waking life, one of my primary teachers, a Tibetan lama, a truly awakened person who at this time I had known for over thirty-five years and had great love and devotion for, was visiting me for the week. I had offered him my house, and he was sleeping in my bedroom, in my bed. He had just left that day, and this was the first night that I was back sleeping in my own bed. I say this because after having this dream I was left with the feeling that it wasn't unrelated to my teacher's energy permeating my sleeping and dreaming quarters (at least in my imagination). Upon reflection, the dream feels like a form of his blessings, as if he had left me a gift chocolate on my pillow.

In the dream I stumbled upon an inner sanctum that was inhabited by a group of hobgoblin-type entities. These gremlins seemed utterly shocked that I had found my way into their sanctuary, as if hardly anyone had ever discovered their secret abode before. These elflike creatures were not at all happy, to say the least, that I had discovered them. Once they realized that I was seeing them in their element, they immediately shape-shifted and assumed a different form so as to conceal themselves. As the dream unfolded, I would then recognize them in their new disguise, and they would transform themselves again. This process continued a handful of times until I woke up.

Upon awakening I was left with the feeling that in the dream I was having a wetiko sighting, which is to say my unconscious—the dreamer of my dreams—had objectified for me these most elusive, hard-to-see energies. As I processed the dream, I sensed that these mischievous entities didn't exist solely in my own mind, but that they existed deep down in everyone else's mind too. It was as if I had somehow found access to a nonordinary shamanic realm of reality that wasn't merely the product of my fevered imagination, but existed in its own right, with a reality all its own. There was a strange, uncanny sense I felt upon waking up that in seeing these creatures they now knew that I was onto them and would do everything in their power to make me lose their trail.

The feeling I came away with was that these entities were the "bugs" in the system that messed with our minds, whose job is to create havoc, chaos, and misunderstandings galore. And yet, once the darkness of chaos emerges, I've learned that magic isn't far behind if we allow it to reveal itself. Like typical emissaries of wetiko, however, they literally can't stand to be seen, as being seen not only takes away their power, it renders them into the ranks of the unemployed.

This brings to mind other dreams, visions, and insights I've had over the years, all having to do with seeing a hidden, subterranean, dark force that doesn't want to be seen, and then trying (with varying degrees of success) to communicate what I'm seeing in a way that can be understood by other people. My whole body of work over the last quarter of a century or more can be conceived in this way. Over the years I've hopefully become more creative and fluent in my ability to describe these obscuring forces; this book is my latest attempt.

As I've deepened my study of wetiko, in addition to understanding the destructive aspect of this mind-virus I've begun to realize that it is an extremely unusual yet important form of revelation—the inverse of a revelation from on high, it is a revelation that is emerging through the darkness.

I would like to suggest—and this is what this book is about—that our experience of feeling stuck, of seemingly having fallen prey to wetiko, has encoded within it a revelation of the highest order, having to do with discovering who we really are. Though this state in which we feel stuck feels like a curse, it has hidden within it a very real blessing. For once we become conscious of our seemingly damned state, this insight changes everything, for one of wetiko's favorite strategies is to make us think the problem is outside of us while in essence the real problem is our (mis)conception of who we are. Once we realize this, we can turn our attention inward, which is where the source—and the solution—of our problem is to be found.

There is a world of difference between subjectively experiencing that we are stuck (Who can argue with that? It's our experience!) and actually being stuck, which our true nature, which is naturally always free, can never be. We can potentially discover that part of us that feels stuck, the part that seems to be gripped by and struggles with wetiko, isn't who we really are, but is a wetiko-inspired simulation of us, a stand-in for the real thing. To see through this very convincing illusion is a truly liberating experience that can introduce us to our authentic nature, which wetiko can't touch because it is inherently and unconditionally free.

Ferreting out wetiko is like coming across the very thing that is stopping us from attaining our true potential. Discovering the wetiko mind-virus is the requisite doorway that leads, as if uncovering a buried treasure, to the unearthing of something of tremendous value. It will help a person's life beyond measure to get wind of wetiko, but in the greater scheme of things if this realization only affects one person, the overall impact is fairly insignificant. However, when the discovery of wetiko is shared more widely and more and more people get turned on to it—and turned on by it—then it can easily go viral and change everything, and then some.

The series of historical events that is commonly referred to as the Scientific Revolution and the European Enlightenment (also known as the Age of Reason), which led to the founding of the American experiment in democratic governance and the subsequent rise of many other liberal democracies around the world, is often traced back to the influence of philosopher René Descartes. One of Descartes' most well-known and influential works, *Discourse on the Method* and *Meditations on First Philosophy,* came out of his struggles with the deep epistemological problem of self-deception and the vexing question: How can we really know that anything that we think or believe to be true is in fact actually true?

To explore this unresolved philosophical and epistemological question, Descartes imagined that everything he believed to be true, including his sensory impressions of the physical world and all of his thoughts, were being manipulated by an evil spirit or demon, such that everything that he took to be reality was in fact a deception perpetrated by this fiend. It was in assuming that this was his predicament that he then asked the question: Since I'm being utterly deceived about everything by an evil demon, what can I still know for sure to be true? He concluded that even if all of his thoughts were utterly deluded he could still know that he exists by the very fact that he was having thoughts at all, albeit deluded ones. He thus made his famous statement *cogito ergo sum,* "I think therefore I am." It should get our attention that our entire modern scientific and rationally based world of liberal democracies emerged from a deep consideration of the very demonic deception and mind manipulation that is characteristic of the wetiko mind-virus.

That one person who was open enough to even consider the possibility of having fallen under the spell of something that was deceiving his mind (wetiko) helped lay the foundation for the subsequent Scientific Revolution and European Enlightenment, thereby liberating vast numbers of people from the chains of tyranny (which itself was the result of wetiko) in the process, is a powerful historical example of the emancipatory power of seeing and having the courage to face how wetiko deceives us. Descartes' process is an inspiring example of how one person's inquiry and insight into how wetiko operates within their own psyche can unlock a creative power that each of us intrinsically possesses, and this can potentially make a real difference in the world at large.

This book is all about the light. Light necessarily involves illuminating darkness. The time to illumine our darkness is right now, in the present moment, which is the only time there ever is—the eternal singular and creative moment in which everything takes place. To split off from and avoid our present moment's experience is to not realize that each and every moment is the eternal moment, which in a sense is one of the most fundamental qualities of wetiko disease: being dissociated from the here and now. Ironically, checking out of—splitting from—the present moment can be conceived of as being the disease of our time. The activity of stepping out of the present moment is based on the false assumption that there is another moment to escape to, while the truth is that there is no exit from the present moment. The future always grows out of that which is present, but it cannot be wholesome if it grows in morbid soil. If we don't deal with our unhealthiness in the present moment, we will be destined to create a sick future.

In this book I am pointing out, like many others before me, that it is only from a radical expansion in consciousness that real positive change can happen in our world, and this transformation in consciousness can only start with us each one of us in our own lives. Any superficial measures implemented collectively to deal with the great problem of our time, though potentially helpful, will not only tend to postpone our dealing with the problem, it will at most be palliative care; it won't penetrate to the depths of the individual human psyche, where evil has its roots and where it continually regenerates itself.

Being a virus of the mind, wetiko messes with our discernment. In Carlos Castaneda's books, Don Juan, Carlos's teacher, though not using the word *wetiko,* refers to the same idea as "the predator," which he considers "the topic of all topics." This is another way of saying that there's nothing in the world more crucial to understand than what wetiko is revealing to us.

When I say something like this it's easy to think I'm exaggerating, being grandiose or melodramatic, trying to sell more books. There are many people in this world who understandably, from a business point of view, are trying to market their works by claiming how important they are. Many of these self-promoters have deceived themselves into believing their own specialness, inflated with the self-aggrandizement of their own egos. Wetiko, whose middle name is deception, in fiddling around with our ability to discern, makes it hard for us to differentiate between when someone's message needs to be heeded and when it's just so much hot air that should be discounted as such.

In my work on wetiko I feel like Paul Revere warning of an

impending threat to our lives and the world at large. I feel like jumping on my horse (if I had one; maybe my bicycle will do) and yelling, "Wetiko is coming! Wetiko is coming!" More accurately, it's already here, right now, in our midst, inside our minds. Which is the only place, and time, that the solution can ultimately be found.

PART I

Spells, Curses, and Shamans

In this first part we investigate how the wetiko mind-virus works through our relationships, be they with others, with our ancestors, or our inner relationship with ourself. We explore how the process of becoming triggered, wounded, and falling into suffering can help us more clearly understand the workings of wetiko in a way that transforms our struggles into opportunities for healing and awakening. Our inquiry illuminates a major source of wetiko—unhealed multigenerational ancestral abuse and trauma as it gets acted out and propagated through human family lineages. We then contemplate how, to the extent we are unconscious of our true nature, we have unknowingly turned on our authentic self and are colluding with the very evil by which we feel victimized. This section concludes by highlighting one of the primary archetypes* currently activated in the collective unconscious of humanity, that of the wounded healer or shaman, pointing out that we are all wounded healers or shamans-in-training. Recognizing this deeper universal pattern informing our individual lives can help us recontextualize our current situation as we navigate our collective descent as a species into the underworld of the unconscious, a true bardo realm between our past and future worlds.

---

*Archetypes are the invisible, formless blueprints which inform, give shape to, and organize how—both individually and collectively—we perceive, interpret, and react to our experience.

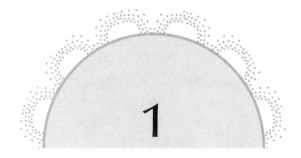

1

Human Family Curse

A number of years ago someone forwarded me an interesting email response to an article I had written about the collective madness that has befallen our species.* It was from well-known author, Alice Miller, who wrote the classic book *The Drama of the Gifted Child.* I was most happy that such an esteemed psychiatrist would take the time to read my work. I quickly became dismayed, however, when I read her reply to my article. Miller roundly criticized the article, dismissing it in one broad stroke by saying, and I quote, that I did not "explain ANYTHING about the CAUSES of this madness," which in her opinion was child abuse.

I immediately thought, how ridiculous—that no matter what anyone would say about any issue, Alice Miller's perspective was that if they aren't talking about child abuse, they aren't dealing with the source of the problem. I remember thinking that perhaps due to her own unhealed abuse issues Miller had clearly gotten triggered by what I had written and was having a knee-jerk reaction, as she could only see the world, I imagined, through her own limited filter. In marginalizing her viewpoint, however, I was unconsciously reacting against something that she was touching on within myself.

---

*The article, titled "The Madness of George W. Bush: A Reflection of Our Collective Psychosis," is the first chapter in my book of the same name.

A mistake I was making was to dismiss Miller's reaction to my article simply because I felt like she was reacting from her unconscious. Just because someone might be projecting their own unconscious process doesn't mean that there might not be some truth in what they're saying. In being triggered by her response and writing off her comments, I might be missing a gift that Miller was offering, as she might be bringing an important message forward. I began to wonder, *What if she's right?*

Child Abuse

What if the source of all the problems in the world—and this includes wetiko—is the age-old tradition of child abuse, which has touched all of us in one way or another? For the sake of clarity I need to define terms, as *child abuse* is so loaded. Many people associate child abuse with physical beating, sexual abuse, and severe neglect of children. But to the extent that our parents were not fully enlightened (and whose were?), child abuse is something we have all suffered from in its more elusive, hard-to-see forms as well as its blatant forms.

When there is conditional love based on our performance or behavior, when we become socialized and are supposed to be a good boy or girl, when our parents vicariously live their unlived lives out through our accomplishments, or when our parents unconsciously act out their own unhealed abuse and tell you it's "for your own good"—these are all forms of very real child abuse. When we receive crazy-making mixed messages from our parents in which they say one thing but their energy expresses something else; when our urge toward emotional independence and autonomy is rejected; when our perceptions are denied; when our expressions of our own unique and creative self are marginalized or criticized—all these are covert forms of child abuse too. All of these actions by adults can potentially obstruct a child in the natural process of growing into who they truly are.

These unconscious *re-actions* by parents can potentially be introjected and internalized into the child's psyche, where they then become the inner oppressive voices that to the extent they aren't integrated, develop a seeming life of their own that can significantly hamper the child's development. Once the child becomes an adult, these internalized voices can stifle its ability to access, express, and embody its intrinsic autonomy and self-sovereignty.

When I first conceived of this chapter, its subject seemed exclusive in that it would only be relevant to parents and their children, but then I realized this includes everyone. We are all metabolizing our ancestral legacy of subtle or overt abuse that has been passed down and propagated through many generations. Maybe the very origin of wetiko is in the unreflected-on, unhealed abuse that exists within each one of us. To the extent that in the present moment we don't become conscious of how we are unwittingly participating in and colluding with the genesis and *re-creation* of our abuse, we are fated to unconsciously act out this abuse on our loved ones and future generations. Evil is thus *re-generated,* spreading from generation to generation. As if under a curse, our species has been suffering from a collectively inherited form of PTSD (post-traumatic stress disorder) that we have unwittingly been transmitting to our next of kin, remaking our victims in our own image. This curse will continue until we refuse to be the link in the chain that propagates the never-ending abuse. To quote theologian Catherine Keller, "Over and over we see the causing of pain—destructiveness and abuse—flowing out of a prior woundedness. . . . This kind of self-damaging and community-destroying and ecology-killing defensiveness tends to proliferate cancerously."[1] Studies have shown that unresolved trauma passed down through the generations is cumulative—to the extent it is not consciously dealt with in one generation, it becomes more severe each time it is passed on to a subsequent generation.

The proverbial idea of the sins of the fathers (and mothers) being visited upon the sons (and daughters) is psychologically true and has found expression in inspired sources as varied as ancient mythology, the Bible, and Shakespeare. We all have a subjective knowing of the validity of this phenomenon based on our lived experience. Every one of us, whether we know it or not, has become who we are, at least in part, as a result of our parents' unconscious, unprocessed trauma. It is not just our bodies that are the offspring of our parents and our ancestry; our psyches are the offspring of our ancestral unconscious as well.

From this perspective, our unhealed wounds are the legacy of intergenerational trauma, which can be conceived of as a spiritual injury, what in Native American tradition is considered a soul wound. The spiritual teacher Gurdjieff counsels us that instead of focusing on the seeming injustice of having to carry these wounds and seeing ourselves as victimized, we should recognize the precious opportunity we have to heal an illness that has threaded itself through the multiple strands of our extended families. When our web of relations is fully extended, it includes all sentient beings, which is to say that our healing has a positive impact on the whole universe. It is Gurdjieff's opinion that we should feel honored and privileged to find ourselves in this role, which simultaneously can serve as a factor for our self-remembering.

Our parents, who Jung suggests we should view as "children of the grandparents,"[2] have been formed by *their* parents, in a lineage that goes back through countless generations. It's not so much our parents but our ancestors who are the true progenitors of our individuality. In this way we are not so much the children of our individual parents, but rather, children of the tribe of our parents. This perspective expands the time frame through which we relate to our family, and ultimately, to ourself.

Psychologically, the central point around which a human personality develops is the place where the ancestors are reincarnated. This is to say that the portal out of which our personality crystallizes into who we are is *in-formed* by the unresolved karma and the unmetabolized trauma of our ancestors. It is as if the ancestral unconscious provides the underlying archetypal structure out of which our personality comes into being. We thus become an open channel for all the unresolved psychic energies in our family line to incarnate in physical form so as to potentially become liberated.

Unlived Lives

Like the moon affecting the tides of the ocean, the unlived lives of the parents have an enormous psychological impact on the children. This acts as an ancestral inheritance that has great weight and gravitas, literally shaping the lives of children, branding them with a particular destiny. The children are thereby driven unconsciously in a direction that is intended to compensate for everything that was left unfulfilled in the lives of their parents. These unlived parts of life—the part of life they have evaded—in all probability are based on a sanctimonious lie that was rendered into the crypt of the parents' unconscious by *their* parents. This process sows virulent psychic germs in a family's unconscious.

The repressed and unlived lives of the parents act like a contagious and malignant psychic virus that infects the surrounding field. Whatever is repressed by the parents is nonetheless alive, covertly working in the surrounding environment, influencing the unconscious of the children. The parents often remain blissfully unaware of how their repression affects other family members, who have to deal with the burden of their repressed contents. This psychological virus is like a nonlocalized bug in the system that creates a *dis-ease* and disturbance in the coherence of the family. This virulent psychic pathogen germinates in and replicates itself through the unconscious of the children, which is the medium it uses to reproduce itself over time, through the generations.

Children see more than the parents suspect or want them to see, as they are empathically tuned in to the unconscious of their parents. The parents' unconscious, which seems to be in the background, is actually in the foreground of the child's psyche, flowing into and *in-forming* the child's psyche. The silent facts in the background have an enormously influential and contagious effect on the children, inasmuch as the parents' relationship to their own unconscious influences the children's unconscious through the collective unconscious, in which both are contained and through which they are connected.

Children sense the underlying spirit of things. The unspoken things that hang in the air and are vaguely felt by the child, the oppressive atmosphere that results from the parents not dealing with their own problems seep into the child's soul, in Jung's words, like "a poisonous vapor."[3] Like a toxic entity, this unprocessed trauma becomes an ancestral spirit that penetrates and insinuates itself into the core of the child's being. This living spirit is the family inheritance, as it patterns, shapes, and *in-forms* the offspring, who become compelled, to the extent they are under the spell cast by the parents, to unconsciously act out and become a living instrument for the incarnation of the ancestral unconscious. They become the unwitting purveyors and living revelation of the "hidden gospel" of the unconscious of the ancestors, creating for their progeny the same psychic atmosphere from which they suffered in their youth.

We don't exist in isolation from one another, but rather, in relation to all members of our human family who have existed throughout history. One's individual life is a blossom on the stem of a thousands-of-years-old family tree. We are continually reaching back through the centuries, living the ancestral life, satisfying the instincts and appetites of unknown ancestors, paying the debts of our forefathers. We are the heirs to this family "fortune," the current karmic fruition of our family tree.

The child is so much a part of the psychological atmosphere of the parents that hidden, secret, unresolved issues between the parents can greatly influence their psychological and even their physical health. The unconscious identification between the parents and the child—what is called participation mystique—causes the child to unconsciously take on and feel the conflicts of the parents and to feel burdened by them as if they were their own conflicts. It is rarely the obvious conflict between the parents that has such a toxic effect, but almost always the parental problems that have been swept under the rug and not consciously dealt with, rendering them into the entire family's shared unconscious.

Participation mystique,[4] is a concept that Jung borrowed from

French anthropologist Lucien Levy-Bruhl. It describes a primitive and unevolved state of consciousness in which we have magically merged with our environment so as to not be able to differentiate between ourself and others on a fundamental level. When participation mystique happens between a parent and a child, it is a state of mutual unconscious identification in which they are codependently entangled with each other and aren't able to experience psychic autonomy and independence from each other, thus reciprocally inhibiting the intrinsic freedom of both.

To the extent that the parents are still fused in a state of participation mystique with the unconscious of *their* parents and haven't psychologically separated and individuated, they themselves will not relate to their offspring as autonomous and independent beings, but rather, as unconscious extensions of their own psyche. Parents who still haven't worked out their parental baggage dream up the kids to be psychic appendages of their own unresolved process, which is a subtle but very real form of child abuse. The author of these real-life dramas, as Jung points out, is the unconscious itself.

The Parental Imago

The parental imago, in psychoanalytic theory the idealized image of the parents in the psyche of the child, contains extraordinary power, influencing the psychic life of the child so profoundly that it is as if the parents are not ordinary human beings in relation to their children, but rather wield a seemingly magical power over the unconscious of their offspring. What gives parents such power over their children is due to the *re-presentations* and animations of the archetype of the divine parents, which exists in the collective unconscious. Parents are thus instruments to play out, embody, and activate the preexisting, numinous divine parental archetype, which lives within the psyche of each of us. Just as a bird's migratory and nest-building instincts are not individually learned, but are inherited from its collective ancestry, the seeming magical power of the parents is derived from a primordial, archetypal image that resonates deep within the psyche of our species.

We don't control the power of the archetype, but rather, are at its mercy to an unimagined degree. Some of us resist its compulsive influence, but some of us identify with its magnetic power. Once we identify with the archetype, we become its instrument—possessed by it—and without knowing it we exercise the same influence on others. Once the parent unconsciously identifies with the parental archetype, the danger is that not only does it exert a dominating influence on the child's unconscious by the power of suggestion, it causes the same unconsciousness in the child. Succumbing to the influence of the parent's unconscious, the child cannot oppose its effects from within. The child's outer process with the parent is thus internalized and becomes an inescapable and compelling inner process that the child will be fated—for good or evil—to deal with for the rest of their life.

In this way parents play a key and fateful role in their children's karmic destiny. When parents repress their unconscious and do not responsibly do their inner work, it radiates out into the family environment and infects the children, who will be compelled to live out the repressed, unconscious, unlived lives of the parents. In this way, unresolved emotional issues get passed down through the generations, like the mythic curse of the House of Atreus, which in Greek mythology symbolizes an ancestral, multigenerational family curse. Either the children fight against their parents' unconscious attitude in silence (though occasionally the protest can be quite vociferous), or else they succumb to a compulsive imitation. In either case they are compelled to act, feel, and live not as they want to, but as their parents want them to.

When parents succumb to the compulsion to turn away from their own darkness and hence avoid a relationship with their shadow, they do not realize that by succumbing to this compulsion, they are passing it onto their children, making them slaves to their parents and to the unconscious as well. In doing so, it's as if the parents have placed a curse on their children, who will live out their cursed condition long after the parents are dead. If the parents have genuinely lived and fulfilled their own lives sufficiently, however, they leave no curse for the future generations to unconsciously live out.

If the parents are in the habit of compulsively avoiding their responsibility to self-reflect, a toxic atmosphere that is very disturbing to the family's emotional body gets conjured up in the family system. "The repressed problems and the suffering thus fraudulently avoided secrete an insidious poison," Jung tells us, "which seeps into the soul of the child through the thickest walls of silence and through the whitest sepulchers of deceit, complacency, and evasion. The child is helplessly exposed to the psychic influence of the parents and is bound to copy their self-deception . . . just as wax takes up the imprint of the seal." The one thing that can save the child from this unnecessary and most unnatural psychic injury is for the parents to choose to not remain, in Jung's words, "artificially unconscious," but rather, to work on themselves, illuminating the dark shadows within their own psyche.[5]

Parents are not asked to be perfect, with no faults or unresolved complexes, which is impossible and would be a catastrophe for the kids. Rather, they should make a sincere effort to not deny and repress their weak points and unconscious areas; they should recognize them for what they are and try their best to work on them, at the very least for the sake of their children. This is an ethical responsibility. It becomes a moral sin when parents are potentially able to shed light on and deal with some unconscious areas in themselves and choose not to, staying artificially unconscious, says Jung. Notably, in one letter, Jung equates remaining unconscious with "serving the devil."[6]

When the unconscious is dealt with responsibly by the parents, however, this relieves the children of a burden that ultimately was not theirs to begin with. Parents can genuinely bless their children to the utmost by stepping into their own authenticity, vulnerability, and transparency. When a parent deals responsibly with their own unconscious, they are modeling and activating the very same process in the child, as parents and children are nonlocally interconnected and intimately co-related through the collective unconscious. Self-reflection by the parents is instantaneously and reflexively received and reflected by and through the child. Occurring in the depth of the psyche, this process of self-reflection mirrors back to both parents and children who they are, and it empowers children to naturally flower and blossom into who they are here to be.

Parents' self-reflection not only helps to heal both parents and children, it nonlocally sends ripples back through time, initiating a process of healing the entire ancestral lineage. It is as if we are the culmination, crystallization, and carriers of a higher-dimensional and multigenerational process of working something out. Potentially, in this very moment, we have the precious opportunity to transmute and liberate these rhizomic strands of ancestral trauma that extend far back in time and equally far into the future, but which also converge and are spread throughout the present, taking the form of the society and culture in which we live. We can be the ones to break the link in the chain and dissolve these insidious, mycelium-like threads, which are literally the warp and woof on which the tapestry of the past, present, and future history of our species is woven. As the current lineage holders of an ancient, ancestral tradition, our task, whether we are in the role of parent or child, is to alchemically transmute the potentially destructive spirit that animates and perpetuates the family abuse (both in our nuclear family and in the greater collective human family), so as to liberate our own creative brilliance, which it seemingly holds captive.

Looking at the bigger picture: realizing how the transmission of child abuse works—in our own lives, with our own parents and children—changes everything, as we are then no longer an unconscious link in the chain, but in touch with our ability to choose how to interpret our experience, place meaning on it, respond to it, and creatively express it. We have then gotten in touch with our creative power, and with how we have a hand in creating our experience of ourselves and our world. Ultimately, we are the ones who are responsible for our fate; we are the composers of our lives, which more than anything ask to be fully engaged with and creatively lived. Expressing our experience creatively as only we can liberates the energy that is bound up in the compulsive and neurotic pattern of recreating our ancestral trauma, freeing the part of our soul that has been imprisoned and paralyzed, thereby dispelling wetiko's curse over us.

I imagine Alice Miller would say that we have finally reached the very root of the problem. In my mind I feel her breathing a sigh of relief, sensing that we are now in a position to truly be of benefit to the world.

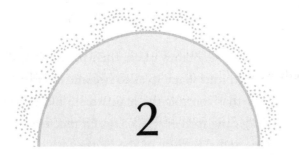

2

Wetiko in Relationships

Being a form of psychic blindness, wetiko, as I can't mention often enough, only has power over us to the extent it is not seen. Wetiko will therefore use everything in its bag of tricks to evade our scrutiny. Wetiko is plugged into and not separate from our process of perception. Wetiko is not something objective, "out there," but rather, is inseparable from the act of perceiving. As quantum physics points out, our perception of the universe is a key factor in the ongoing genesis of the universe.

It is as if wetiko has a radar-jamming device whenever anyone begins tracking it too closely. The mind-virus will use its connection to the nonlocal field to hide from being seen. In a real-world example, the ever-increasing censorship happening in our media today has the fingerprints of wetiko all over it. Whenever anyone tries to shed light on the dark, wetiko-inspired goings-on in our world, if it contradicts the official mainstream narrative—a narrative informed by wetiko—they become victims of attack pieces and are censored and deplatformed.

Crazy as it is, people who unthinkingly subscribe to consensus reality are convinced that they are in possession of the truth, and they are reinforced in this conviction because the overwhelming majority of people in their echo chamber, having also bought into what the powers-that-be want them to think, have a similar take on things. Supporting one another in their deluded state, they insanely believe they are awake, and yet they have become brainwashed, their perceptions managed and their minds massaged into shape so as to become mouthpieces for what the corporatocracy that controls the mainstream media wants them to believe. People under the spell of wetiko find it practically impossible to imagine the extent and extremity of the lie they have fallen under and have naively assumed to be true. Parroting what they have been told is true, towing the party line, they believe they are thinking for themselves, not realizing that their thinking is being done for them. Having drunk the Kool-Aid, their minds are programmed such that they have become unwitting instruments being used to propagate the spell they are under to the world at large.

If we see things differently from consensus reality, we open up to being accused of either being a tinfoil-hat wearing conspiracy theorist, an idiot, evil, a domestic terrorist, under a spell, or any number of unsavory things—basically seen as a threat. We will then be concretized, "otherized," demonized, and marginalized, which basically is to be energetically excommunicated from society in one form or another. We are in turn blocked from reaping the apparent benefits available to those who unquestioningly go along with the collectively sanctioned program. It has become dangerous to espouse a different viewpoint than what the powers-that-be want us to believe. This isn't some paranoid conspiracy theory, but a sober assessment of a very concerning situation that is undeniably happening out in the open for all who have eyes to see (interestingly, in the Bible, having "eyes to see" is equated with being blessed).

Feeling like we have to be a certain way, that one has to form-fit and shrink-wrap oneself into a culturally sanctioned version of who we're supposed to be, opens us up to wetiko's nefarious influence. If we get hooked into believing, for whatever reason, that we have to offer a prefabricated version of who we are, practically tying oneself up in a pretzel so as to feel like we're meeting others' expectations, we are on our way to becoming disoriented as to who we actually are and our true path in life. We are thereby a dream-come-true for wetiko, easy prey to be used for its sinister purposes.

Over the years of studying wetiko I've realized that one of the main ways it works is by shutting down our voice, both inner and outer. The essence of all of the multiple variations on the theme of abuse comes down to the message that it's not safe to authentically and fully express oneself. Hence we have to hide, compartmentalize, or shut down parts of ourself, a process that is both inspired by and feeds wetiko. Once this dynamic becomes internalized within our mind and rendered unconscious, it becomes our subconscious operating system and is hence invisible to us. We then become our own control system, and preemptively, without even realizing it, we shut down without the aid of any external force. We then invariably feel constrained and victimized by the world, without realizing our complicity in killing our own voice so as to stay safe in a world that is perceived as dangerous. This is why the healing of wetiko involves courageously connecting with our authentic voice and expressing oneself creatively.

In the cancel culture that we now live in, there is a sense that it is dangerous to offend anyone, that it's simply not safe to reveal who we are or what we think or believe. Many of us have learned there are certain taboo areas or "no fly zones," even with our closest friends and family members—topics that are off-limits, that are not okay to bring up for fear of triggering someone. Becoming hypervigilant, we fall into the chronic, unconscious habit of monitoring our environment and ourself so as to know what's safe to reveal about ourself—a most unnatural process that further opens the door for wetiko's preternatural influence.

Being Triggered

One of the most important things we can do to depotentiate wetiko in our world is to make sure that we don't contribute to it. There is a strong unconscious tendency in people when encountering wetiko to add more wetiko to the field via our unconscious reactions to seeing it. This is to say that one of the main ways wetiko replicates itself in the field is through our involuntary, automatic, unconscious reactions to it. Though wetiko can seem so esoteric, it is something each one of us is intimately familiar within our interactions with one another in our everyday lives. Not only does it play out in our own mind, it informs, gives shape to, and propagates through our relationships with others. One of the main ways wetiko insinuates itself into our relationships is when we get triggered by something that someone else is doing or saying. I remember years ago I was triggered in one of the Awaken in the Dream groups I facilitate. One of my close friends in the group who had witnessed me being triggered many times before very matter-of-factly said that when I get triggered, my IQ drops thirty points (thirty points might be an understatement). What he said was so obviously true that it elicited no argument from me at all. When we get triggered by wetiko, our rationality, our intelligence, our ability to self-reflect often goes out the window.

Just like seeing the unconscious in someone necessarily activates our own unconscious, seeing wetiko in someone else practically guarantees (money back!) that wetiko will be triggered in us. Being triggered in itself isn't a manifestation of wetiko; it's how we react to being triggered that is the key. If we have a knee-jerk reaction, indulging in and acting out our trigger, then in our unconscious reaction—which is almost always rooted in past unhealed trauma and wounding—we are unknowingly offering ourselves up to wetiko. It will then flourish in the petri dish of our relationship, where it will undoubtedly create misunderstandings and separation. We will then be off to the races, as we reciprocally trigger one another's wounds in a seemingly interminable process that is not just unproductive, but can be hurtful and traumatizing for all concerned.

Operating through individuals, wetiko spreads viruslike through the unconscious masses, replicating itself and bonding people together through their shared wounding, trauma, and unconsciousness. Wetiko thus exploits groups of people—and on a larger scale, masses of people— to propagate its evil.

In Buddhist literature, taking the bait and being hooked (in Tibetan, called *shenpa*), and then acting out our triggered reaction is likened to a highly contagious disease—a virus (sound familiar?) in that it will then activate other people's triggers and wounds, which will then reignite our own. This is a circular process that at a certain point loops back on itself and becomes self-generating; left unchecked, it will spin out of control. All the participants are then swept away in the undertow of the unconscious, dark archetypal forces that are beyond our conscious understanding and drive the whole process, while wetiko rejoices as it inspires these self-generating cycles of chaos, conflict, and wounding.

But if when we are triggered we are able to become aware of and acknowledge that we've gotten triggered and choose to simply notice it and not act on it, we have created space around the triggering event and can thereby become more spacious. In this way we can interrupt our unconscious habitual, compulsive reactions, which takes away the fuel for wetiko. Then we—instead of wetiko—can rejoice. And if we are then able to self-reflectively turn our awareness to the underlying source of our trigger—invariably a wound of some sort—at that moment we will be able to assimilate and transmute that tiny unit of wetiko that is keeping our wound alive in its unconscious state, a process that feeds the light of our own conscious awareness.* This is to say that wetiko, when arising in the field between us, has actually—due to the way we hold it—expanded our consciousness. This is a key characteristic of wetiko: it is the source of incredible conflict between people, and yet, if recognized in the moment that it arises, it can deepen our intimacy and strengthen our connection with one another,

---

*One of the most beautiful teachings in Buddhism is called the "Lion's Gaze." The following example is given as an illustration: If we throw a stick (symbolic of a negative emotion that gets triggered within us) with a dog, the dog runs after the stick. The dog's reaction is symbolic of putting our attention outside of ourselves, relating to what is triggering us as the problem. But if we throw a stick with a lion, the lion will chase after us! Having the "gaze of the lion," this practice entails turning our awareness within when we are triggered and treating the moment as an opportunity to self-reflect, looking at whatever it is within us that has been activated.

as well as feed our lucid awareness. Encoded in the very pathology of wetiko is its own medicine!

The Nonlocal Field

Wetiko is a field phenomenon; we can only start to see it when we recognize the underlying unified quantum field in which we are all contained, of which we are expressions. When someone in a family system becomes a conduit for wetiko, be it an actual family, a group of people, an institution, a nation, or our entire species, it affects and is an expression of the state of the whole nonlocal field, which interfaces with and is not separate from our own mind.

The concept of nonlocality, which has transformed our understanding of the fundamental nature of the universe in a radical way, is a recently proven feature of the universe. Nonlocal connections between distant particles demonstrate correlations that seem to indicate that their separation is an illusion. Such instantaneous connectedness, where one part(icle) in no time whatsoever (that is, outside of time) appears to affect and communicate with another distant part(icle) in the universe in an immediate and unmediated way is called *quantum entanglement*. In a nonlocal quantum universe such as ours, no part of the universe is or can be separated from any other part. Nonlocality thus is an expression of the deep interconnectedness and indivisible wholeness of the universe.

To understand the nonlocal agency of wetiko, we can't just focus on one person in isolation from the rest of the family system, but rather we need to look at how all of the interrelated roles in the system reciprocally co-arise and mutually condition and reinforce one another. In the nonlocal quantum field there are no separate parts interacting; instead, all of the seemingly discrete aspects of the system are ultimately expressions of and inseparable from one another and from the greater whole.

It is only when the whole system and underlying nonlocal field that informs and gives shape to it are brought into focus that we can begin to see—sometimes with the force of a revelation—how wetiko, behind the scenes, choreographs all of the myriad interlocking roles that compose the field to play out the way it does. A spectral, devilish agent, wetiko has a backstage quality that surreptitiously moves among unwitting groups of people, activating their unconscious wounds, traumas, and unhealed abuse issues, each in their own unique way, so as to incite misunderstandings between them. Elusive as hell, no one knows where to find the source of the confusion, so we typically find someone else to blame. Few suspect the culprit is to be found deep within our own mind and in our unconscious reactions.

The abuse, trauma, and wounding that happen in relationships could never play out the way they do—and the person in the role of the abuser could never get away with such abuse—without the field conspiring to enable it. Crucial to understanding the phenomenon of wetiko (and the abuse that it inspires) is seeing how individuals are being dreamed up to pick up interdependent roles in the field that, when seen together as a whole, operate in a way that is analogous to iron filings organizing around an invisible magnetic field. This is how wetiko creates the circumstance through which it is able to propagate itself throughout the quantum field. It is only when the deeper pattern that connects and informs all of the interconnected parts comes into focus that we are able to recognize that wetiko is a field phenomenon, which is to begin to see it.

When abuse (a manifestation of wetiko) and the concomitant wounding that is the inevitable result is enacted in a family system, a field invariably gets conjured up to hide the abuse and protect the abuser. This is an expression of how wetiko nonlocally configures the field so as to perpetuate itself. Typically, one person acts out the role of the abuser, and other people collude with the abuse by turning a blind eye to it or by protecting the abuser by hiding or rationalizing their behavior. The unconscious collaboration between the abuser and the field that is conjured up around the abuser to protect them—what is literally a nonlocal protection racket—further cements and preserves the wound that is the result of the abuse.

There are countless examples where this plays out—in families, intimate relationships, workplaces, politics, spiritual communities, Hollywood, and the Catholic Church. The evil of the abuse ripples out into the surrounding field, creating more potential trauma and wounding of one sort or another in just about everyone, influencing people through their unconscious reactions to what the abuse is touching within themselves. These reactions, which occur beneath our level of conscious awareness, create the tapestry by which wetiko weaves itself through the warp and woof of our relationships.

This dynamic of protecting the abuser is an externalized reflection of a psychological process that exists within each one of us, as we all have a propensity to turn a blind eye toward the darkness within. Each person, to the extent that we are not fully enlightened (and who is?), is unwittingly protecting the abuser in their own way, which means that we are each obstructing a part of ourselves from being illumined. This is where we become complicit in our own abuse. Like an ostrich with its head in the sand, we are keeping ourselves in the dark about what we are unconsciously doing to ourselves. This dynamic also reflects that part of us that, through our willfull blindness, is complicit in the large-scale patterns of oppression that are continually taking place in the world at large, many of them in our name. In turning a blind eye, we are unwittingly supporting and enabling these colossal collective injustices.

Though our current world situation may feel so overwhelming that we feel helpless, we *can* start to access the incredible creative power that lies within us via the process of shedding light on this darkness, which holds our natural creative power captive.

The Magical Effect of Telling Our Story

Some weird things can happen when members of our species try to communicate with one another. Our wounds, unhealed abuse issues, unassimilated trauma, and unconscious triggers and projections can get in the relational field between us so as to create all sorts of misunderstandings and problems. The wetiko bug is at the bottom of most if not all of these experiences, bringing about hurts, frustrations, and anger, causing us to feel separate from and possibly even threatened by one another—unless we recognize the deeper, wetiko-fueled process that is going on and learn to deal with and overcome these wetiko-inspired feelings.

When we've had direct encounters of the wetiko kind (which is to say when we've encountered evil), it can be a bit risky to share our experiences with others. Say, for example, we've had an experience of abuse, which consisted (as it almost always does) of our authentic being and creative self-expression being judged, pathologized, or maybe even shut down by someone in a position of authority, be it a parent, teacher, healer, therapist, or the like. Oftentimes this kind of experience can shake us up so badly that it can completely shatter our sense of the safe world we thought we lived in—which is the very nature of trauma. It can also undermine and debilitate our self-confidence, self-esteem, and our sense of self. This encounter can, depending on its intensity, potentially take a long time, years even, or a lifetime, to be fully integrated.

Imagine we then go to another authority figure and express to them as best we can what our undigested experience of abuse is. Our intent is that if they "get" what we are trying to share with them (playing the role of an enlightened, compassionate witness), it will help us assimilate and come to terms with the trauma of it all. Because we are still in the process of metabolizing the trauma from our direct, unmediated encounter with the dark side, in all probability we will have an emotional charge—a passion—around what we are trying to transmit. Hearing our trauma-ridden and emotionally charged story, however, can easily constellate an unconscious reaction in the listener.

It can then happen that instead of fully receiving, taking in, and understanding what we are trying to transmit (which, in making us feel understood and seen, would help us integrate the toxic aspect of the experience), the authority figure diagnoses and pathologizes us instead. Their judgment is an unconscious reaction to what has gotten triggered within them by the traumatic nature of our story, as well as the way we are passionately trying to communicate it. I call this process *traumatized messenger dismissal syndrome,* or TMDS.

One way to understand this is to see that the unprocessed evil of the abuse that we are trying to share with others, being nonlocal, does get across (in the sense of being transmitted) to them, but in a way that bypasses their conscious mind, thereby activating their unconscious. Like a magician's conjuration, they get dreamed up (by our unconscious, as well as their own) to play out with us a form of the very evil at which we are pointing. The result? They are then unwittingly recreating and literally acting out with us a more subtle, hard-to-see iteration of the very abuse that brought us to them in the first place. By unintentionally mimicking our original encounter with evil with us, a faint echo of the initial unhealed abuse is making itself known through our interaction. Though different in scale and degree, this reenactment consists of the same archetypal form and pattern of our original encounter with evil. And as if by magic—*abracadabra!*—in speaking about our unhealed abuse we then evoke it in the field such that it can then enact itself in a disguised but embodied form. This process shows us how language— the power of the word—particularly when it is imbued with emotional energy, can be a vector for the transmission of wetiko. Likewise, depending on how language is used and its effects processed, it can also liberate us.

This kind of experience has the potential to be incredibly retraumatizing, as now the original trauma is combined with a newer version overlaid on it. But if we have the awareness that the other person's reaction, being a function of their own unintegrated trauma, has more to do with them than it does with with us, we can recognize that they are unwittingly offering us a real-time opportunity to deepen our healing of the unhealed abuse that we have shared with them. In unconsciously reenacting the fundamental structure of our abuse with us, the other person is, without knowing it, offering us an opportunity to have a corrective experience whereby we can stand strong in our truth and our inner knowing and not take on or get hooked by their projection.

In the other person's unconscious reaction to hearing about our abuse, they are dreaming (dreams, it should be remembered, are the unmediated expression of the unconscious). By so dreaming in their waking life, they are unknowingly acting out their—and our—unconscious in and through our relationship dynamics. In other words, as if experiencing a shared dream, the person in whom we are confiding is getting dreamed up to play out with us their unconscious process, as well as our own. The role they are acting out, though reflecting a judgmental voice that we have internalized, is, paradoxically, not personal to us (which means we don't need to take it personally). If we don't buy into their projection (which, not being personal, is simultaneously their projection as well as our own, as it belongs to the field), we can realize that we, rather than they, are the arbiters of our own experience. We can potentially realize that we are the ultimate authority when it comes to our experience of ourself. By not being concerned or affected by what another person thinks of us (and therefore, not taking on their projection), we are, in real time, withdrawing our projection of authority to the outside world, finding it within ourself instead. What can be more healing and in service to our wholeness than that?

By unconsciously taking on the role of the original abuser (albeit in a more subtle, nuanced, easily digestible form), the authority figure in whom we are confiding is unintentionally helping us to potentially deepen our connection to ourself. This whole process shows how our unhealed abuse, which is gestating in the cauldron of our unconscious, literally informs, gives shape to, and flavors the various experiences we have in life. To put this differently: the unassimilated contents of our unconscious can't help but unfold and be enacted via our relationship with the world over the course of time.

This process has the same underlying structural dynamic as how our dreams at night are constructed, wherein our unconscious sculpts the form of the dream as a way of expressing itself. This is one way of understanding what is meant by the dreamlike nature of reality. When we snap out of viewing events in our life from a personal, reductive, and literal point of view, we can recognize that everything that we're experiencing can be seen to be symbolic expressions of a deeper transpersonal, archetypal dreaming process. Realizing that the deeper dreaming process beneath our waking awareness is crafting the underlying dynamics in our relationships with the world opens the door to healing. This is an example of how within the seeming pathology of wetiko is to be found its very cure—one of the primary features of wetiko.

I have coined a couple of terms to describe this seemingly unusual, but truth be told, not that uncommon process: *articulating abuse induces further abuse,* or AAIFA; and *replicating abuse in response to hearing about abuse,* or RARHA. I'm not sure about anyone else, but it certainly helps me to have a name for this potentially maddening process, which I've experienced throughout my life in various guises. Being able to find—and create—a name for this dynamic has enabled me to more clearly see this unconscious process, and this has helped me access the hidden potential healing that has been encoded within the process all along. So instead of this heretofore unconscious process having its way with me, I find my way by using it to create my own path.

Missing Golden Opportunities

Over the years I've been in groups that have been devoted to trying to help heal the world. It is not uncommon that at the same time the members of the group are brainstorming, philosophizing, sharing ideas, theorizing, and envisioning what we can do to help the world, wetiko is playing itself out through the group's unconscious via the relationships and interactions of its members. For example, someone in the group might be triggered by another member, which activates their unconscious such that they react by projecting onto the person who is triggering them something within their own unconscious. Acting out their projection, this in turn activates (and triggers) the person who is the recipient of the projection. Now both people's unconscious are in an activated, charged state—in my language, there is a dreaming process happening in the group that can be an open doorway for wetiko to enter the relational field and create separation and misunderstanding in the field, or if recognized, this can be an opportunity for deepening our realization of the dreamlike nature. When this interpersonal—and unconscious—process is pointed out, oftentimes people seem completely uninterested in what's actually present in the room, relating to it as merely a distraction and wanting to get back to their abstract visionary processes about how to heal the world.

From my point of view, however, this dynamic is the very thing—wetiko—they're wanting to heal being collectively dreamed up in the shared field. Because wetiko's manifestation is not recognized as it gets enacted in the group, its members (albeit with the best of intentions), in imagining how they are going to be healing wetiko in the world, ironically become distracted from the possibility of healing this elusive mind-virus as it plays itself out through them in the present moment, which is the only place it can actually be addressed in reality. Not recognizing their golden opportunity that is right in their midst, they have unwittingly empowered the very malevolent energy they are imagining they are trying to heal! This process can be utterly maddening, or liberating if we recognize it is a revelation of wetiko, depending on our point of view.

Typically, the one who tries to shed light on the unconscious group dynamic does so at their own risk, as this person is often seen as the one who is causing the problem instead of being recognized as the one who, in bringing awareness to what is happening, is helping to dissolve the problem. If you are cast in the role of seeing the potential for wetiko to play out in the aforementioned group, it is important to use skillful means for pointing this out to the people involved.

If you recognize that two other members are triggering each other and acting out their unconscious as a result, you might want to intervene and point out the energetic, relational—and unconscious—process that you are witnessing between the two people. If you discern that one or both of them are in too charged of a state to receive your reflection, that they are too absorbed in and identified with their unconscious complexes and won't be able to self-reflect on what they are unconsciously acting out, maybe skillfull means would entail waiting for the next meeting where both people aren't so worked up and in their unconscious and then pointing out and contemplating with them what had happened in the previous meeting in a way where everyone involved can better understand what played out and extract the blessings that were encoded within the experience. Contemplating their shared experience after the fact, when both people are no longer triggered, can help them look back in a more detached, objective way so as to reflect upon how wetiko was potentially coming through them via their unconscious reactions. They can genuinely learn something about wetiko—and themselves—as a result. This isn't merely an intellectual knowing, but can give them insight into their unconscious process such that it can change their unconscious habitual reactions and behavior and greatly improve their life.

In attempting to shut down the light of consciousness and provide cover for the darkness, wetiko is simultaneously revealing itself by showing us how it works and who it works for—the powers of darkness. In its attempt to snuff out the light, however, wetiko is exposing its dark agenda, which thereby feeds the very light it is trying to destroy (this brings up the thought—is wetiko a double-agent? Does it secretly work for the light?). Whether the light becomes obscured or shines brighter depends on whether we register in our consciousness what is openly being revealed to us. As always, how wetiko manifests depends on how we dream it.

Wetiko Can Exploit the Most Awake Among Us

I recently connected with a very awake person. She had been doing serious spiritual practice for a number of years. A practitioner of dream yoga, this person was having lucid dreams just about every night and was clearly having deep realizations about the dreamlike nature of our reality as well as the nature of her own mind. I was deeply impressed.

Then she said something that really shocked me. Not having read any of my books on wetiko, she expressed her judgment of my writing about evil, saying how dualistic it is, claiming that writing about such an unsavory topic is not using skillful means. She was of the opinion that the ultimate solution to our multiple converging world crises comes down to connecting with compassion (a point of view that I agree with), and therefore there is no need to talk about or shed light on something like evil, which she thought of as being a distraction from what really matters.

I was gobsmacked by her comment, rendered almost speechless— a rare occurrence for me! Because we had just met, I didn't feel safe reflecting her point of view back to her; on the one hand it seemingly was an expression of the nondual state, yet on the other hand it was extremely dualistic. True nonduality, instead of dualistically excluding and demonizing the darkness, embraces it within a higher synthesis in which light and dark are recognized as being inseparable, complementary opposites that help to illumine each other. That she had a judgment about my work yet hadn't even read it (which, to my mind pointed to her unconscious blind spot) was a real head-scratcher. That I was dealing with evil from a nondualistic point of view seemingly hadn't occurred to her.

Her comment made me curious to know if she had any awareness that when we see the dreamlike nature of reality and interpret our waking experience as we would a dream, that this waking dream, in manifesting in such a dark, destructive way, is placing a demand on us to shed light on and expose the darkness. It made me think of how Jung stressed over and over that more than anything else in these dark times we need to shed light on evil, to become conscious of the darkness.

In our conversation I shared with her how her comment made me think of a dream I had a number of years ago. In this dream I was becoming lucid, recognizing that I was dreaming, and was trying to let my fellow dream characters know that we were having a collective dream—a questionable strategy, I might add, one that showed that a part of me wasn't fully lucid, for I was still investing some of my attention in trying to awaken characters in the dream, thinking that they were separate from me. One of the figures in the dream had an interesting reaction, saying that he didn't relate to the word *dream,* as it was a charged word with too many associations. I remember feeling in the dream the bind that his comment put me in, as I wanted to communicate to him that he *was* in a dream, but he didn't want me to use the word *dream* because of what it brought up in him.

The comment from this woman made me feel that I was in a similar situation. We're living in a world where evil (there's no better word for what's happening) is manifesting all around us, but she didn't want me to name it, explore it, understand it, or put my attention on it—all under the guise of being "spiritual." I found that something important was being revealed to me in her comment: that she was embodying and giving voice to a perspective that existed in the field (as well as in all of our minds, including my own) that needed to be factored into the equation of what we are up against.

The experience made me sad, as it brought home how sometimes even the most awake among us, in thinking they are representing the light, are actually, without realizing it, giving cover to the darkness. Unless we are careful, wetiko, which has been described as a "sickness of exploitation,"[1] can fool even those who have attained sublime states of awareness or are going through great awakenings, by deputizing them to be its unwitting minions. We are all fair game for wetiko, which places a demand on us to be mindful and self-reflective as much as we are capable.

Dreaming Wetiko into Relationships

Wetiko, to the extent it is not recognized and dealt with, configures our relationships in all sorts of ways. One of the spore prints of wetiko in a relationship is when often out of the blue there is a weird and seemingly unnecessary misunderstanding between close friends or family members that creates separation between them. If there's an alchemical "container" (in this case, a relationship sturdy and trusting enough to withstand the pressure of "cooking" the prima materia of life) between them, they'll be able to process what is happening in their relationship, dispel the separative energy, and get even closer than before. But if there's no container, their attempt at processing what is happening in their relationship often makes things worse, eventually creating a don't-go-there zone in their relationship, a part of their relationship that is taboo and conversationally off-limits. Over time, this drains trust, intimacy, and connection.

We all have, to whatever degree, our unconscious wounds, traumas, unhealed abuse issues, and shadow content. A good way to understand how wetiko plays out in our relationships is to contemplate how dreams, which are unmediated expressions of the unconscious, work. In a night dream, our unhealed, unconscious parts get "dreamed up," for a dream is nothing other than a reflection of our inner process. If we don't recognize that the unconscious shadow aspects that we're interacting with in the dream are actually inner reflections of parts of us, we will instinctively react and act out what has gotten triggered within us by these unrecognized parts. We will then unconsciously recreate and play out our unhealed wounds in a way that perpetuates them, becoming retraumatized in the process.

In the same way, our unconscious is projected out into the world. We then connect the dots on the waking inkblot so as to create meaning. We dream up and create in fully materialized form our unhealed, unconscious parts, which we will then interact with and act out via our relationships. Like an artist, we sculpt, giving shape and embodied form to our unhealed unconscious inner process in the seemingly outer landscape of our relationships.

If we don't notice the reflective correlation between the inner landscape of our unconscious life and our experiences in the world, as if falling under a spell we will feel victimized by what happens to us through our relationships, not realizing the part we are playing in creating our experiences. Wetiko, it should be remembered, acts itself out through the projective tendencies of the mind. It is as if our unconscious scans the environment for people who, based on their unconscious shadow and wounds, have suitable "hooks" on which we can hang our projections. Once we find someone who can carry our projections, we continually evoke and subtly amplify the shadow aspects of the other person, unconsciously solidifying them to practically embody this shadow quality (at least in our mind) so that they can play out an unconscious shadow part of ourself. Being that this entire process happens unconsciously, it has the same underlying dynamic as how our unconscious crafts our dreams at night. We are dreaming not just at night, but through our waking lives as well, experiencing an instantaneous rendering of the contents of our unconscious through the various forms of our waking experience.

This dynamic underlies the diabolical nature of the repetition compulsion, which is the very pathology of trauma. Our unhealed trauma compels us, beneath our conscious awareness, to *re-create* and play out the original trauma in hidden and not-so-hidden forms, again and again. Encoded within our compulsively acting out our trauma, however, is its potential resolution. Our unconscious, forgotten, dissociated, dismembered, and unremembered parts that inform our trauma are longing to be consciously experienced, which would liberate the unconscious energy that's continually enlivening the re-creation of the original trauma. The frozen energy that animates the trauma is continually taking on physical form so as to act itself out, which is the very medium through which it can be unlocked in order to rejoin the wholeness of the psyche. It is as if our trauma needs something to push up against in order to be liberated. This is another example of that same dynamic that underlies wetiko—that hidden within its pathology is its own cure.

A Wetiko Case Study

Wetiko will oftentimes leverage the slightest misunderstanding between people in order to create as much separation in the field as humanly possible. As a way of illustrating this, let's imagine two platonic friends, Jim and Sally, who are both on the spiritual path, belong to the same spiritual community, and are committed to working on themselves. They are both good, highly intelligent people who genuinely care about each other. Both highly sensitive, they have been tracking each other's unconscious over the course of their relationship.

Let's imagine that Jim has become aware of an unintegrated shadow element in Sally's unconscious. We all have unconscious aspects that live in the shadows of our mind that can come out when they are evoked and called forth by life. Circumstances arose such that Sally acted out an asleep part of herself (I will leave the specifics to the reader's imagination) and Jim saw it. Because of the nonlocality of the unconscious, it is impossible to see the unconscious in someone else without activating our own unconscious too. This is to say that seeing an aspect of Sally's unconscious triggered something in Jim's unconscious such that he starts ever so slightly projecting onto her, subtly skewing his interpretation of what Sally is doing or saying so as to confirm the truth of his projections.

Jim is now in an interesting state of both seeing and not seeing Sally, while Sally is in a unique position of having her unconscious seen while at the same time being the recipient of Jim's projections (and therefore, in another way, she is not seen). The situation Jim and Sally find themselves in is not uncommon—maybe it happens most, if not all of the time, in human relationships. Rarely reflected-on in depth, a dynamic like this can be very challenging—and maddening—to successfully navigate and resolve. Jim is now dreaming up Sally in such a way as to play out with her an inner process of which he is unconscious, while Sally's unconscious is doing the same with Jim. They are co-dreaming.

Because this process is unconscious, Jim will become convinced that how he is experiencing Sally is objectively true, for due to his own unconscious being activated, he is unaware of the slightly distorted lens through which he is now interpreting and placing meaning on the relational dynamics between them. Because this process is playing out through Jim's blind spot, which has become activated by seeing Sally's blind spot, he is not open to having his unconscious process reflected back to him by Sally, for it challenges his experience of what is real. If Sally picks up and reflects back to Jim the unconscious energy that she now feels coming from him, he will invalidate her reflection as simply an expression of the unconscious energy he has been seeing in her.

If Jim's unconscious process is pointed out to him by Sally, rather than considering what is being reflected, he will undoubtedly interpret her reflection of his unconscious as further confirmation of his familiar experience of being victimized and not seen* (an experience that deep down, most, if not all of us, share). This will only feed into and strengthen the seemingly never-ending playing-out of the very unconscious dynamic that was being pointed at by Sally in the first place (whose origin, it is helpful to remember, is to be found in Jim seeing something unconscious in Sally). Wetiko then has a field day, once again turning an opportunity for expanding Jim's and Sally's consciousness into its opposite, where they both can potentially be retraumatized by each other.

This dynamic is complicated by the fact that when Jim views his relationship with Sally through his now-activated projections (which we all do at times, maybe even most of the time), he is, in psychology speak, "in his complex," which ensures that his perceptions will be infused with an emotional charge. This charge is, by its very nature, contagious, which is to say that Sally, the recipient of this charge, due to the inductive effects of the now-activated unconscious in the field,

---

*It is typical that when our unconscious blind spot is seen by someone and reflected back to us, we at first will feel not seen.

can't help but to become triggered and thereby become emotionally charged herself.

If Sally, in recognizing how Jim might be slightly altering and misconstruing what he is seeing in her through his unconscious filter, insists on trying to point this out to him, Jim, instead of receiving her reflection, will undoubtedly feel, focus on, and react to the nonverbal emotional and energetic charge that he is experiencing coming from Sally (a charge, it is helpful to remember, that was activated by Jim's original charge). If Jim now tries to reflect back to Sally the unconscious part of her that he originally saw, she will not be able to hear him either, as she is mostly experiencing Jim's unconscious charge, which renders the (very real) content of what he is pointing at invisible to her. Sally's inability to take in Jim's reflection will not only strengthen Jim's perception of her being the one with the blind spot, but will also feed into and amplify Jim's charge (which, in a mutually reinforcing feedback loop, will feed back into and strengthen Sally's charge), thereby putting more fuel on the fire of misunderstanding that is beginning to ignite between them. This results in both of them, to the extent they are identified with and playing out their unconscious process, missing the potentially helpful reflection that the other is offering them. Once again, wetiko feasts on the smorgasbord of misunderstanding that has gotten conjured up between them.

Jim, in being triggered by Sally's reflection, might begin to access suppressed emotions that underlie and inform the unconscious and unhealed complex that is at the root of his process in the first place. Jim might, for example, get angry at Sally (who, in her mind, was only trying to offer what she thought was a helpful reflection). In his anger, Jim, in externalizing and acting out his inner process via the medium of his outer relationship with Sally—as if his inner dreaming process is being materialized and played out in his actual life—might even feel like he is confronting the figure of an abuser. On the one hand, it can be really healing for Jim to stand up and set a boundary to the imagined abuser (Sally) and be able to access and express his suppressed anger. In doing so, Jim is enacting, giving voice to, and potentially liberating a latent unconscious process that has haunted him from within—which can be truly healing for Jim.

On the other hand, Sally, the recipient of Jim's anger, might feel hurt by being the recipient of this anger, but if Sally can cultivate a meta-awareness of the deeper process that is playing out between them, she can decide to not take it personally and realize that she is being dreamed up to play a very unpopular, painful, but strangely beneficial role in Jim's process. Sally has then found herself in the role of the wounded healer or shaman who can potentially be helpful to Jim if she doesn't get further hooked by what is playing out between them, but rather, can hold Jim's process nonreactively so that it can optimally unfold.

It would serve Sally (and indirectly, Jim) if she could self-reflect on what within her has been triggered via her exchange with Jim. It would further serve both of them if at a certain point they each could step out of identifying with the roles they are playing out with each other and self-reflect on what they were unconsciously acting out via the medium of their relationship. To do so would be to conjure up an alchemical vessel within their relationship in which the shadowy, unconscious contents in each of them that have gotten activated and were at the bottom of their conflict can potentially become conscious, transformed, and integrated into their growing self-awareness.

However, if Sally takes the bait and gets hooked by Jim's outgassing of his suppressed anger, it can create further separation between them. Mirroring Jim's experience, Sally can then easily feel unfairly victimized, not seen, and unfairly attacked, and might even become angry herself. Now both parties feel attacked and not seen by the other, which is superfood for wetiko to further propagate itself in the field. This dynamic might even end the relationship. The point is that encoded within this dynamic, which is laced with both unconsciousness as well as the possibility for a burgeoning new consciousness, is the potential for healing and/or separation, depending on whether one or both of them recognize the deeper dreaming process that is giving shape to their relational dynamics.

Though this process seems to have had a beginning in linear time (maybe one of them initiated it by acting something out unconsciously), when this dynamic is traced back through time it reveals itself to be beginingless, that is, without a specific causal event that started the whole process. In other words, this is a reciprocally co-arising process that both people, in the timeless domain of the unconscious, were mutually dreaming up.

This process might not end with the two of them; it could spread into the surrounding environment, creating fault lines there as well. If the two parties aren't able to work things out and get to the bottom of what's informing their process—wetiko—but instead let what is playing out between them create separation, either one can feel hurt by the other, and can solidify their friend in a negative way. For example, if Jim becomes fixed in his viewpoint that Sally has treated him unfairly, he might share his experience with a mutual friend in their shared community, who then supports and gets into alignment with Jim's negative view of Sally. And maybe Sally is doing the same regarding Jim. It can easily happen that each of them will recruit allies in support of their version of what took place between them.

Once we become convinced that our experience in a relationship with another person is what has objectively happened to us, without any awareness of the part we have played in the experience, it will happen that when we describe our subjective experience to our mutual friend, our story will be completely convincing. When we have become convinced of the truth of our experience, we will have a very convincing effect on others. Hearing a person's rendition of their experience is typically convincing, particularly if it feeds into the part of us that unconsciously has issues with the person in question, such that it is easy to forget that there are two sides to every story.

We all have an unconscious tendency to be convinced that our *subjective* experience is what has *objectively* happened, forgetting that we are creatively conjuring up our subjective experience via the inner filter through which we are interpreting and placing meaning on our experience. We are deeply involved, whether we know it or not, in creating the very experiences we are having in our relationships.

This is analogous to how our thinking mind operates: we often-times create an inner experience via our thoughts, and then forget our agency in creating our experience, relating to our experience as if we have nothing whatsoever to do with creating it, as if we are merely passive victims of an experience that is happening to us.*

The inevitable and tragic result of this kind of relationship process is that it creates unnecessary fragmentation and polarization within the previously unified community. The mutual friend might share whatever version of the story they have heard with other members of the community, who, filtering this through their own unconscious projections and wounds, will take sides. Instead of merely creating separation between Jim and Sally, the wider community then gets dreamed up to play out the separation between its two members on a larger scale. Some people become aligned with Jim, others with Sally—which splits the community into opposite camps. Wetiko, which is at the bottom of the whole process, rejoices as the fracture widens. This is an example of how wetiko exploits our unconscious projections to create division in as many ways—and on as many scales—as possible.

Though the specific details of the above fictionalized dynamic differ from my own story, a similar end result—the breaking apart of my family—ultimately manifested. I've written a book about this, *Awakened by Darkness: When Evil Becomes Your Father,* so I won't go into the details (which for the purpose of this chapter aren't important). In my family of origin, my father, based on his own unhealed abuse, acted out the role of the abuser, with me as the recipient of his

---

*Notably, physicist David Bohm felt that practically all of the problems of humanity can be traced back to the fact that thought is not what he called "proprioceptive," that is, aware of what it is doing. Thought creates something, forgets that it did so, and then *reacts* to its own self-creation as if it exists objectively. In this, Bohm was tracking wetiko.

abuse. He's been dead for over twenty years, but his diabolical impact on the family system lives on today as if he had never left. Because of his position of power in the family, my father wrote the family's history. The outcome is that the remaining relatives have become allied to—entranced by—my father's version of what played out between us and are all convinced that I'm crazy, while I think of them as being incredibly asleep and ignorant. Our differences in perspective have created seemingly irreconcilable differences between us, destroying any possibility of us having an authentic relationship.

What played out in my family shows how when one person in a family system becomes a channel for wetiko, its nonlocal energy will infect the entire family, such that if what has gotten stirred up between the family members is not consciously dealt with, misunderstanding and separation will get conjured up between its members. Though on a superficial level wetiko seems to have won by destroying my relationships with my remaining family members, on a deeper level the fact that I've been able to recognize and thereby transform the nightmare that broke apart my family into a revelation that has informed my work is to say that the jury is still out on whether what destroyed my family is a curse or a blessing. Time will tell.

Wetiko Dis-Relations

Wetiko can inspire us to create problems in our relationships where none exist. A personal example: a few years ago a friend of mine accused me and another friend of talking about him behind his back. We were doing no such thing. His charges were a fiction, the result of his paranoid imagination. But once we got wind of his accusations, my friend and I of course began talking about our friend, which strangely enough proved his accusation to now be true. As if by magic, he conjured up the very thing he was afraid of out of thin air.

How often do we, in one form or another, unconsciously enact this same process? Like the sorcerer's apprentice who is out of their depths, we call into reality the very thing we don't want. A collective version of this process of creating the nightmare we don't want is currently playing out on the world stage, in living (and dying) flesh and blood. Hence the name "the nightmare mind-virus."

Here's another example of a different sort. A number of years ago I was close friends with a man who was a number of years younger than me (like a father to his son). He purposely moved into my neighborhood to be close to me. He would sit next to me every morning at the café where I wrote my books, feeling like my creativity was contagious. He'd come over to my house every day to visit, calling me on the phone multiple times a day. I was happy to have him as a trusted friend.

Then at a certain point he got a girlfriend. We've all experienced what comes next—it was as if I had dropped off the face of the earth, and I didn't hear from him for months. His reaction was typical (particularly, I think, for guys) and not overly problematic (except for being a bit sad for having temporarily lost a friend). I was familiar with this process and understood. Once I got wind that he wasn't calling me regularly like he had been doing, I wasn't going to go running after him, but following his lead, stopped reaching out to him as well, which felt natural, as if this was the role that I was being dreamed up to step into.

After months and months of this going on, with neither of us hearing from the other, we finally got together, and I brought up what had been happening between us. I tried pointing out that he had initiated this process, but he got angry—actually going into a rage—and was very defensive at the thought of this, denying it to the max. He kept on pointing out that I wasn't calling him either, claiming that our separation was mutual. I right away realized that this was a hot-button topic that we weren't going to be able to talk about, so I dropped it. From then on I didn't feel safe bringing up this issue, so I never broached the subject with him again.

Over the years, my friend and I have become distant. This is typical when there is a "don't go there" zone in a relationship, as if this taboo area over time secretes its poison and invariably creates separation. To this day I'm sure that in his mind it has been a natural process of drifting apart, a mutual separation. It feels to me that as a father figure I was symbolically "killed" by my friend as a part of his individuation process. I understand this and am willing to play this role in my friend's process of growth, though it's a drag for me to lose his friendship.

It's interesting to me that my friend seems unable to look at or own the part of him that wanted to separate from me, projecting his impulse to do so as belonging to both of us. I imagine that he felt his unconscious desire to separate from me existed outside of himself, that this gave him permission to act out what probably seemed to be a forbidden impulse. It catches my attention that by not calling him I got dreamed up to step into a role in his dreaming process, a role that in his mind confirmed to him that our separation was mutually created.

Disregarding the specific details and content of this example, how often do we play out something similar to this situation that arose with my younger friend? How often do we not own our own impulses, but instead project them out to someone else—outsourcing them, in effect—dreaming up the field in order to play out something so that we can justify our own unconscious actions? Just like a dream, the unconscious informs, at least in part, all of our behavior. This in itself isn't problematic, for acting out our unconscious is the way we become conscious. But if we insist on doubling down on our unconsciousness once we meet its reflection in the world, refusing to look at and receive the gift that our unconscious is dreaming up for us through our experiences in life, we remain artificially unconscious, and then we miss the gift of it all.

Since writing this there's an update on this story: This person recently came over to help me move, which was the first time I've seen him for close to five years. On the surface everything seemed normal, as if we had seemingly picked up our friendship right where we left off. The whole time I was with him I had the feeling that if I brought up the unresolved issue between us he would get very upset and would immediately see me as the one who was creating a problem out of thin air, when he was simply wanting to help me move. So I didn't bring anything up, which resulted in our "friendship" staying on the superficial level.

A general example of how wetiko can disrupt a relationship occurs when in an intimate relationship one person feels that they're under the other person's "spell" in that they feel overly influenced, manipulated, and even controlled by that person. This process always involves both parties, however, as it is never just one person casting a spell on the other, who is a passive victim. Rather, the person who is subject to and falls under the spell being cast gets hooked through a blind spot in their unconscious, which is to say they are colluding with the spell—keeping it cemented in place—just as much as the spell-caster. Their two processes fit together like a lock and key, as the spell in their relationship is a deeper process that doesn't exist solely in either of their individual processes, but is getting mutually dreamed up and animated through their coming together and being in relationship with each other.

In such instances, the person under the spell has an intuitive sense that they need to leave the relationship, but they find it hard, if not impossible, to do so due to the compelling power of the spell that's been cast. I imagine that what I am describing sounds familiar—it certainly does to me. In any case, this is yet another example of the endless variations of how wetiko can lay waste to our relationships.

One final example: A number of years ago it came to light that someone in one of my Awaken in the Dream groups, unbeknownst to the other group members, had been secretly acting out—and actively hiding—an aspect of his shadow in the group. The specifics aren't important other than to say that he had been violating people's boundaries in a way that, to put it mildly, was not okay. In his actions it was beyond debate that he had dishonored the sacredness of the group's container.

After finding out what he had been caught doing, I called him on the phone to get more understanding of what he had played out before he came back to the next week's group. I reflected back to him that what he had done and (it came out later) had been consistently doing for the years he had been in the group was a transgression of people's boundaries. He reacted by challenging me to explain how what he had done was a boundary violation. I kept on trying to explain this as best as I could. What he had acted out was the epitome of transgressing boundaries, but no matter how much I tried to reflect this back to him he wouldn't take in what I was trying my best to communicate, continually reacting by saying I hadn't sufficiently explained how what he had done was a boundary violation. As he continually challenged me, I was getting more and more "charged," until finally I got angry. As soon as I got angry, he immediately responded by saying, "Stop yelling at me." I immediately recognized that he was now going to portray himself as the victim who was being abused by me, which is exactly how he presented what happened in our phone call at the next week's group. He had somehow turned the tables on me; more accurately, wetiko had.

Upon reflection, it doesn't feel like he did this as a conscious strategy, but rather, his unconscious, informed by wetiko, set things up so as to allow him to conceal from himself a part of his shadow. Instead of self-reflecting and seeing an unconscious shadow aspect of himself as it was being reflected, wetiko flipped the switch, enabling him to see his own darkness as being separate from himself, which he then projected onto another person—me.

Most of us have experienced this kind of situation playing out in our lives in one form or another. If, for example, someone is not in touch with their anger, oftentimes they will provoke (dream up) someone in the field to get angry at them, and as soon as this happens they will judge the person who has gotten angry (who had in all likelihood unconsciously picked up, at least in part, the dissociated anger in the person's unconscious). Judging the other person's angry display is a reflection of how this person condemns their own suppressed anger.

They have consequently dreamed up their inner situation to play out in the outer world. Unless they have some degree of lucidity they will feel that they have absolutely nothing to do with the other person being angry at them and will feel victimized by that person's anger—which reflects how they feel victimized by their own unexpressed and unintegrated anger.

The point of this discussion is to shed light on how the wetiko mind-virus is not some esoteric, occult, abstract idea, but is something that each of us experiences regularly in the midst of the daily grind of life. The multiple forms wetiko takes in relationships are legion. This mind-virus creates misunderstandings and separation on all scales—between family members, lovers, friends, communities, nation states, as well as between different parts of oneself. And yet if we wake up and shed light on how wetiko is fueling the disharmony among us, we are on our way to alchemically transmuting the very poison of wetiko into an agent of healing. It is the grit in the oyster, after all, that makes the pearl.

Fleeing Wetiko

We all have a blind spot in our vision that corresponds to the place in our eye where the retina and the optic nerve meet. Unless we do certain exercises to show us our blind spot, we aren't aware of—are blind to—our blind spot. This same situation is mirrored in our psyche. We fill our blind spot in with our projections, a process that is done beneath our conscious awareness, the result being that we think we are seeing clearly when we still have a blind spot. We then relate to our projections, whose source is within our own mind, as if they objectively exist in the outside world—which is to become blind to the true nature of our situation.

Being that wetiko works through our psychological blind spot, if we see that someone is afflicted with wetiko and we reflect their blindness back to them, they will in all probability feel not seen. In seeing wetiko as it operates through another person (which, it should be added, is a reflection of how it covertly operates through us), we are seeing the part of them that not only doesn't see and has become blind, but is possessed by something that is acting itself out through their unconscious. How to skillfully deal with this in order to help the other person snap out of their spell while not creating separation in the relationship is a tricky business that involves the utmost discernment, self-reflection, and compassion.

Being a mercurial trickster, wetiko can trick us out of our right mind through our mind's projective tendencies in a multitude of ways. Wetiko is slippery, elusive, and devious. Sometimes when we reflect a person's projections back to them, they will do everything they can to avoid an encounter with what's being pointed out. As if having figured out what we want to hear, the person can then very convincingly appear to own their projections, demonstrating the "proper" response by saying the right words ("Yes, I see what you're saying, I own that I am projecting"). In doing so, they simultaneously fool us—and themselves as well—into believing that they have owned their projections, while in fact they are doing nothing of the sort. I call this *fake ownership syndrome,* or FOS.

As if chanting a magical incantation, they are casting a spell on the very person who is trying to help them break free of their projections. Convincing us that they have owned their projections when they are simply mimicking this realization deceives us into believing that something is happening when it is not. What has actually happened is that wetiko, the sponsor of the projections in the first place, now has more cover for its deceptive antics to be acted out. Wetiko then has two people under two different spells, which enables this mind-virus to further proliferate in the field without being seen. Having multiple people under multiple spells provides fertile soil for wetiko to run rampant.

Wetiko can use language adroitly to both hide and replicate itself. Language is designed for communication, so we can understand

and connect with one another. But once wetiko gets ahold of our language, its connective purpose becomes inverted. In the hands of wetiko our language creates misunderstandings, polarization, and separation. When language is used unconsciously, we can easily fall under the spell of the unconscious by believing in our own verbal pronouncements.

When someone is unknowingly caught by—and becomes a host for—wetiko, it is *as if* an entity, both metaphorically and literally, has gotten into the driver's seat of their vehicle. When this seeming entity gets wind that another person is seeing how it is influencing its host, it will make sure to steer the person away from the situation in which it is being seen. Even though the person so afflicted might not consciously realize that another person is seeing how wetiko is "working" them, the wetiko spirit within them is very attuned to being seen and recognizes when it is being tracked by someone. The person taken over by wetiko will then come up with the perfect excuse and rational reason for why they need to create distance in the relationship. Due to wetiko's connections to the nonlocal field, oftentimes the environment will conspire with this process. For example, the perfect art class will be offered on the very night during which the person stricken with wetiko would ordinarily be spending time with the person who is seeing their inner condition.

When wetiko is in the field of a relationship, what really determines how things will unfold is whether or not there is a container that has been cultivated in and through the crucible of relationship. One of the key factors that helps build a strong container is understanding that relationships with the people closest to us is the vehicle by which wetiko most directly plays itself out. The more intimate the relationship, the deeper, darker, and more unconscious will be the (inter)play of wetiko. If the people so involved understand that a wetiko outbreak between them is an opportunity to make the darkness within each of them more conscious, they will value these challenging moments as the doorway that can introduce them to their authentic selves. If, however, they don't recognize the potential blessing encoded within the difficulty, they will metaphorically run the other way as fast as they can. I call this the *wetiko fleeing process,* or WFP. If we flee when we encounter our shadowy parts that are under the influence of wetiko, we are avoiding a relationship with a part of ourselves.

On the other hand, if we resist the urge to flee when we come face-to-face with what inside of us has been living in the dark, we will find that we can recognize heretofore unconscious aspects of ourself, expand our knowledge of who we authentically are, and potentially integrate the split-off parts that have been having their way with us. Encountering our dark side challenges us down to the very core of our being. Self-reflection, a buzzword in spiritual circles, involves not just reflecting on our divinity and wholeness, but also reflecting on— adding light to—the dark and wounded parts within us as well. One of the dangers in doing this is to identify with this dark side and think it's the totality of who we are, which can lead to despair, instead of realizing that it's just a previously unknown aspect of ourselves with which we can cultivate an increasingly conscious relationship.

Another danger that many of us who are committed to doing our inner work can fall prey to is to turn our encounter with our wetiko-laced shadow—a potential coming-to-grips with it—into a mere intellectual idea instead of an experience that needs to be lived through and actually felt on a visceral level. If we avoid this living encounter with our own darkness through a trick of our mind, we have then, right at the point of confronting wetiko, given ourself over to it. Then, with our collusion, the wetiko cycle—the endless cycle of samsara, of never-ending suffering—regenerates, repeating again and again until it is eventually seen for what it is.

The Buddhist notion of samsara (as juxtaposed with nirvana, or enlightenment) can be helpful in deepening our understanding of wetiko. Samsara, like wetiko, continually feeds off of itself in a self-perpetuating, seemingly never-ending cycle (known in Buddhism as *cyclic existence,* referring to the endless cycle of death and rebirth). From an exoteric and dualistic point of view, samsara and nirvana are conceived of as being opposites—samsara equated with "bad," nirvana with "good." And yet the highest Buddhist teachings point out that samsara *is* nirvana, that they are actually inseparable allies that are ultimately one. All of the most profound wisdom teachings throughout the ages have pointed to a state of mind in which such opposites are recognized to not just be related, but rather, to be inseparably united as aspects of a greater whole.

This is reminiscent of Jesus's statement that "the kingdom of heaven is spread upon the earth [which, based on appearances, seems to be the opposite of any kingdom], but men do not see it [because of our mind-blindness]." In other words, the determining factor between experiencing samsara or nirvana, or the kingdom of heaven or hell on earth, is to be found within our own mind. This relates to how the present-moment manifestation of our wound is either an obstacle to our realization or the way to its liberation, depending on how we view our experience.

The esoteric conception of samsara as being inseparable from nirvana can help us further understand how encoded within the manifestation of wetiko is its own medicine, a medicine that not only heals wetiko but offers us an additional gift, by helping us realize the dreamlike nature of reality and remember who we are. From this more expanded perspective, wetiko (equivalent to samsaric consciousness), in potentially introducing us to that part of us that transcends it, is at the same time mysteriously itself and an expression of the part of us that is wetiko-free (equivalent to nirvanic consciousness, which is our true nature). Just like the way samsara, which is ultimately a state of mind, evaporates when its deceptive and phantomlike nature is seen through, the same is true for wetiko. The seeming darkness of wetiko has no power over us when it is seen and recognized for what it is— and for what it is not—by the light of clear-seeing awareness.

It is helpful to remember that there is no time like the present— the only time there really is—to recognize our role in the seemingly interminable process of samsara/wetiko, and break the cycle. We have

it within our power to accomplish this. The main obstacle is thinking that we can't, which, it is worth noting, is a thoughtform inspired
by wetiko, which through its reality-creating power convinces us of
the truth of its viewpoint. Knowing who we are in our depths necessarily involves becoming familiar with how wetiko works within us.
Though seemingly being the obstacle that stops us from truly knowing who we are, wetiko can actually be the very tight passage through
which we actually deepen our realization of who we are.

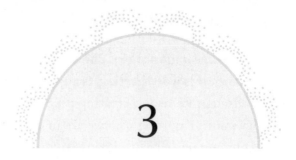

3

Wilhelm Reich's
Murder of Christ

It feels like my fate to continually come across unique and creative articulations of humanity's primordial sickness. As I was finishing up this
book, I revisited Wilhelm Reich's classic *The Murder of Christ,* a book I
had read many years ago, and realized that Reich was pointing at wetiko
in a unique way that could help us see it. As a result, I've decided to
include a few words about Reich's groundbreaking work in this book,
as the more creative articulations of this elusive mind-virus, the better.

Reich starts off by contemplating the fact that human beings are
born free, yet we somehow live our lives as if we were slaves. For centuries, maybe since the beginning of time, there has been something at
work within human society and within the human mind that renders
impotent any and every attempt, no matter how ingenious, to solve our
collective malaise, with all of its myriad problems. Sound familiar? Over
the years, not a single attempt to deal with, shed light on, and heal our
collective misery has been successful. We are left endlessly searching for
a solution to this nightmare.

Reich pointed out that the great problem of life is "a psychiatric one,"[1] one that is to be found within the depths of the psyche.
He focused on what he called "the character structure" of humanity,
believing that the fundamental problem of humanity, what he called

"the most dangerous enemy of mankind," is that we "evade the essential."[2] In other words, we are attached to the nonessential and are overly focused—practically addicted—to superficial, trivial matters because they distract us and provide us with a refuge from the ever-present existential factors that pertain to the unfathomable mysteries of our very being. People in general are afraid of the depths; many will choose a familiar form of suffering if it will help us avoid the long, hard work that necessarily accompanies the kind of self-examination that descending into the depths requires. As a result, we human beings have not been able to get at what we most want: the truth of who we are. All of these thousands of years have not brought us one iota closer to understanding who we truly are. How have we managed to hide from the truth of ourselves for so long and so effectively?

Reich realized that there is something within us and in our world that not only obstructs the resolution of our self-created problems, but stops us from asking the right questions so as to know where to even begin. Something well-hidden is covertly at work beneath our conscious awareness. Whatever this "something" is, Reich realized that it is extremely elusive and seems to know how to protect itself from being exposed by disabling the immune system of the human psyche, whose job it is to monitor such threats to its ecology. Reich is pointing at wetiko.

Reich called this "hidden something" the "emotional plague"[3] of humanity. This plague kills the unobstructed, free-flowing life force, what Reich equates with the love of God (which he refers to as "the Christ") within our bodies. When we dam up the wellspring of life, the free-flowing Christ force that lives within us, we become one of the damned. To the extent we suffer from this emotional plague, we've become chronically and unconsciously armored against both the world and the creative life impulse within ourself, with the unfortunate consequence that we've become split-off from the truth of who we are. This is a diabolical emotional affliction that drives us apart, dividing and separating us from one another. When we fall under its thrall, it renders invisible and makes inaccessible what we all have in common with one another: both our humanity and our Christlike divine essence.

If we live in a dark cellar for too long we will begin to hate the sunshine. Our eyes might even lose the ability to tolerate light, and we will develop an aversion to the light, which we will avoid like the plague. We will then feel threatened by the light, which can make us unconsciously act out in ways in order to exterminate the light—both in ourselves, as well as in the world (a process in which we are playing out our inner process in the external world). Becoming split within ourself, we both secretly yearn for the light and hate it at the same time. Such is our plight, says Reich. This split within us is both the result of—and the breeding ground for—the plague of wetiko.

The Dark Powers Dig Their Own Grave

This perverse inner process in which we destructively turn against our own inner light (and ultimately ourself)—the essence of the emotional plague of humanity—is what Reich calls "the murder of Christ,"⁴ with Christ, "the lamb of God," symbolizing life itself. *In-forming* the murder of the grace-filled, uncontracted, and innocent Christ is a hatred of the free-flowing life force of the human organism, a hatred of the wild spontaneity of life itself. It is life turning against itself. The question naturally arises: Why do human beings kill the life within themselves?

The answer to this question is to be found in the word *adversary,* which is a literal translation of the word *Satan.** The devil, whom Christ called "a murderer from the beginning" (John 8:44), is the personification of an energy both out in the world and within us. Reich is describing wetiko to a *T* when he says this energy opposes the holy, opposes our wholeness, and opposes life itself.

Yet there is a revelation encoded in the murder of Christ that can

---

*"Satan" literally means "adversary" or "opponent/accuser" (in ancient Hebrew, "ha-satan" as in an adversary of God).

be accessed by contemplating the Crucifixion symbolically, seeing it as a dreaming process that expresses the unconscious covert operations of how evil works deep within the collective human psyche. Seen symbolically, God uses his innocent son's murder to serve as the disclosure and revelation of the very unconscious process within the human psyche that inspired this evil act in the first place.

With the Crucifixion, the forces of evil, in murdering the truth-teller who was shedding light on their covert operations, believed they were protecting the power structure of their earthly kingdom by preventing us from accessing our true intrinsic power that Christ was reflecting back to us. But their sinister actions actually brought about the opposite of what they intended. In their violent silencing of the whistleblower Christ, the dark forces of the Antichrist unwittingly exposed themselves and revealed their nefarious workings. In trying to kill the light that was revealing their evil, the darker forces acted out for everyone to see the very evil behavior they were trying to conceal. Unwittingly "outing" themselves in the process, they blew their cover by trying to maintain it. Seen symbolically, the powers of darkness were unknowingly playing out their preordained role in the divine plan of, ultimately speaking, bringing forth the light.* In murdering the one who was publicly exposing their evil, the darker forces were revealing their darkness, which was unwittingly serving the very light they were trying to eradicate.

It is an archetypal idea that evil, which is imbued with the worst of intentions, inevitably brings about the opposite: a higher good that never would have manifested without its appearance. Goethe's masterpiece *Faust* is but one creative expression of this dynamic.

Similar to that crucial moment in a myth or fairy tale when the hero finds the name of the demon, it can be helpful for us to come up with the name of this diabolical process. Naming a process objectifies

---

*In this discussion I'd like to acknowledge the work of cultural anthropologist René Girard.

it, helping us see something to which we had previously been blind. I'd like to coin the term *revelation through suppressing exposure,* or RTSE (pronounced "ritzee"), to describe how suppressing the light actually reveals the darkness, thereby ultimately serving the light. We normally think of illumination as seeing the light, but seeing the darkness and gaining insight into how it operates is a form of illumination as well.

To quote the Bible: "None of the rulers of this age understood it [the wisdom of God], for if they had, they would not have crucified the Lord of glory" (1 Corinthians 2:8). If the dark powers knew that they were digging their own grave by crucifying Christ, they would have vehemently opposed his murder. Though on the surface the Crucifixion appeared to be a triumph of the dark forces, this act revealed their hidden agenda and set the stage for their ultimate defeat.

Satan, the personification of wetiko, is extremely cunning when it comes to inciting conflict, scandal, and the like, but he doesn't comprehend—is blind to—divine love. Only Satan could have set in motion the process of his own destruction without realizing anything was wrong. The sponsor for and inspiration behind the Crucifixion, Satan, as if suffering from a form of blindness himself, was duped by the cross and fell into his own trap. Though brilliant (a dark genius!) in one way, Satan lacks divine intelligence and, due to his blindness and disconnection from the light, is ignorant—stupid, actually—for in trying to destroy the truth, he unwittingly and freely offers it to humanity, making it possible to expose and thereby overturn his lie.

It is noteworthy that blindness plays a key role in this whole process, be it from our side or from the side of the powers of darkness. Wetiko, after all is said and done, is an all-around form of psychic blindness in which neither its perpetrators nor its victims are spared. This is why the cure for wetiko is to *see* it.

It should be noted that RTSE, the process of revelation emerging as a result of suppressing the exposure of the lies that are intrinsic to the darkness, is playing out all around us in our current moment. Anyone who diverges from the corporate media's narrative of what's happening in the world and sheds light on its lies and propaganda is attacked, deplatformed, and cancelled. The massive censorship going on in the world today may be a less murderous form of RTSE than the murder of Christ, but it is the same underlying dynamic, differing only in degrees. Why are the powers-that-be so intent on silencing the voices that point to their lies? The answer is obvious—censoring the whistleblowers confirms that there is something important at which the whistleblowers are pointing.

With the Crucifixion, the very workings of evil were exposed and stripped naked, as was recorded in the gospels for all to contemplate. There was nothing Satan could do to prevent this revelation, for he—and his actions—are not only the inspiration for the revelation, he *is* the revelation. And the Crucifixion, being the supreme revelation that it is, was the price Christ was willing to pay to reveal the hidden unconscious psychological dynamic that holds all humanity captive, thereby offering us the key to unlock the trap we are in.

The murder of Christ is an act that, to the extent we remain unconscious, we are complicit in to this day. This internal dynamic enslaves us because it is invisible, which is to say we are unable to identify it, and hence, are blind to what keeps us imprisoned. The symbolism of Christ's selfless sacrifice, an act of pure love, can heal our blindness so that we can see and become conscious of the role we are playing in our own imprisonment. By joining with Christ, we can realize our own intrinsic freedom, a freedom that was seemingly obscured with the Crucifixion, but was actually revealed—provided we have the eyes to see.

The Spell Has Been Broken

"Evil," to quote Reich, "*is being created by man himself.*"[5] Reich is saying that as a result of our willfull blindness, we have a hand in investing evil with power over us. Reich realized that the evil we know as wetiko is a *dreamed-up* phenomenon (as are all phenomena), which we have unwittingly passed down through the generations. To the extent that we are asleep to the participatory role we have been playing in co-creating our experience of this reality, we are complicit in unconsciously dreaming up the worldwide wetiko epidemic.

The murder of Christ, otherwise known as wetiko, imprisons humanity as it informs and gives shape to a world made in its own false image. A world under the sway of this murder will reflect the perfect illogic (wetiko ill-logic) of the evil which inspired the murder in the first place. A world ruled by wetiko is a world where the irrational seems perfectly reasonable. As it says in numerous places in the Bible, the devil is "the ruler" of our world. The Gnostic equivalent for wetiko are called the *archons,* a word whose literal meaning is "ruler."

Reich points out that evil is a perversion of the divine in that it grows out of the suppression of (and armoring against) the sacred. In turning away from our wholeness/our holiness, we are contracting against our intrinsic light, and in so doing we are unwittingly colluding with the forces of darkness. As the Christ event clearly reveals, it is humanity itself that has killed Christ. Our empty and armored souls, in trying to fill the insatiable void within us in a way that *a-voids* our true essence, has become an unwitting culprit in hatching the evil of wetiko.

Ironically, as Reich realized, the murder of Christ is protected by those who suffer the most from its ill effects. This is one of the chief features of people who have fallen under the spell of wetiko: they fanatically support what is against their own best interests. This is an outer reflection of a wetiko-riddled psyche getting dreamed up into material form through the medium of the outer world in a destructive way.

We live in an age of misinformation and lies. There is something very powerful at work that obstructs the truth from working its empowering and liberating magic. It is the emotional plague that keeps the seed of truth from blossoming and yielding its beneficent fruit. The plague reigns where it is not possible for the seed of truth to live; the living truth is kryptonite to it.

Christ is a mirror—he simultaneously reflects both our spiritual nature and our most depraved shadow aspects. If we see Christ as a being who is separate from us, he becomes unreachable and unknowable, and the divine aspect of ourselves becomes inaccessible to us. Reich points out that the character structure of humans, which is a form of armor, is set up such that we are not able to take in the very truth that could save us. Our character armor arose as a result of our terrifying initial encounter with the truth of our intrinsic freedom. When the limited human ego encounters the truth of our open-ended and free nature, it is experienced as the ultimate threat that must be avoided, silenced, or killed at all costs. The intrinsic freedom of our true nature is paradoxically the very thing that can dismantle the character armor that it itself has set in motion. Christ embodies the qualities that act on the armored character structure endemic to those under the sway of the emotional plague like the effect of the color red on a bull.

Proclaiming the truth by itself will never work, Reich realized, until we find the secret pathway to realizing and actually embodying the salvific nature of the truth within us. Otherwise, when we hear the truth we will compulsively be driven to kill it, which is to unconsciously enact the murder of Christ. We will then unknowingly act out our inner process of murdering the light of truth within us in the outside world, lest it remind us of the grievous tragedy of our own self-betrayal, of what we have killed within ourselves.

Reich felt that to create projects that bring in the light without first comprehending the dark forces that are at odds with it—the very forces that have been murdering humanity for ages—would not only fail, but would inevitably be usurped by the unillumined, death-creating forces of the plague. He felt that a thorough investigation into the unconscious dynamics within us that continue to compel the murder of Christ was the single most important issue facing humankind.

It is noteworthy that in one of the worst examples of censorship in U.S. history, Reich's books were burned by our government. When books are burned, fascism is not far behind. Reich's books were burned not that many years after the Nazis' notoriously burned any books (including Reich's) that were contrary to their insane and murderous worldview. It makes one wonder why the powers-that-be were so threatened by what Reich was saying. Compare that to all the internet censorship that is happening in the world today, and there is no doubt we are experiencing a modern-day digital book-burning that is reminiscent of the Nazis.

It is the nature of evil that it destroys everything in its vicinity, including, ultimately, itself. It is only by shedding light on the darkness of evil that we can spare ourselves from being brought down by it. Reich realized that it is our task to protect life/light at all costs from what he considered to be the evil plague we know as wetiko. In order to safeguard what is most sacred—life itself—we need to know what threatens it. There is no getting around this.

The murder of Christ is as true today as it was two thousand years ago; it is both a historical event and a living symbol of how the emotional plague that infects humanity kills life and truth. This tragedy is so moving because it is a universal myth; it is everyone's tragedy. The murder of Christ is the true story of humanity.* It is, to quote Reich, "the tragedy of Man under the reign of the well-protected Emotional plague."[6]

The disease of wetiko is infectious; its presence can potentially activate the latent plague in ordinarily decent people. We all have our emotional plague impulses, just as we all have pathogenic as well as healthy organisms in our bodies. It is our responsibility to deal with these energies within us so as to limit their destructive fallout. There is an emotional plague "chain reaction" analogous to the way a nuclear chain reaction works, spreading radiation uncontrollably. Even healthy, well-integrated people can at first be paralyzed by the shock that results from a close encounter with this noxious mind-virus before they are able to metabolize, integrate, and make sense of what they've come in contact with.

It is not by happenstance that one of the main features of our

---

*Even if, as some people assert, this never happened historically, it is true symbolically.

culture's myth of the incarnation of God is a murder in which humanity is participating. Might this be shedding light on something within our collective unconscious? The answer is yes. Just like the way all characters in our dreams are aspects of ourself, we are simultaneously the Christ (the light within us) who is being murdered, while also being the murderer. Like in any form of self-abuse, we are simultaneously the victim and the perpetrator, unknowingly enacting the very evil we are fighting against.

Once we internalize the abuser, we unconsciously shut down our own light without even knowing what we're doing. In light of this, Christ's words as he *consciously* experienced the brunt of this unconscious process are revealing: "Father, forgive them, for they know not what they are doing" (Luke 23:34). In his infinite love for us, Christ, who, after all, was love itself in human form, was letting himself be murdered so as to reveal to us the very unconscious process within us that seemingly keeps us separate from this love.

To the extent that humanity apparently doesn't recognize the revelation that comes as a result of Christ's sacrifice of himself, we remain in bondage, unknowingly participating in his murder while, as Reich points out, moaning about our plight and dreaming of the coming Messiah. How insane! The recognition that this biblical event is but a mirror that reflects what is going on deep within us is the doorway through which we can begin to see the madness that we are blindly enacting. This realization helps restore us to our basic sanity.

Once this murderous internal process gets rendered unconscious and becomes chronic, however, it camouflages itself in a multitude of ways. We then become a secret to ourselves, which opens the door for wetiko to further manage our perceptions and behavior without our conscious awareness. It is the very essence of the plague to conceal its murderous nature and the lie that covers it at all costs, lest the truth get in, for this destructive dynamic only has power over us if it surreptitiously does its work in the dark, that is, remains unconscious. This violent murder is ahistorical and atemporal in that if left unconscious, it regenerates again and again in the present moment as it informs and gives shape to our human experience. Once it is made conscious, though, it loses its power to perpetuate itself in the human unconscious, becoming undone in the light of consciousness, as we heal our mind-blindness and begin to see.

The "good news" is that the murder of Christ is truly in its death throes today. This helps us recontextualize the dark goings-on that are happening in our world today. When demons are on the verge of being vanquished is when they make their greatest outcry. Once we recognize the unconscious murderous process that we are all complicit in, the end of the murder of Christ is truly at hand. Acknowledging this, Reich says, "But the spell has definitely been broken. The ENDING of the murder of Christ is at hand."[7] With these words, Reich gives voice to the fact that in waking up to our complicity in the murderous process that has been unconsciously informing our species all along, we have broken the curse we have fallen under as we begin to realize our creative agency in putting a stop to this ongoing self-murder. This is not a passive understanding, but a living, ongoing, vital realization—that we ourselves are playing a crucial role in embodying and thereby bringing into our world the end of the murder of Christ. This is truly cause for celebration that brings with it a profound responsibility—the ending of the murder of Christ is not only at hand, but is in our hands. To realize this is to begin to break the spell of the nightmare mind-virus.

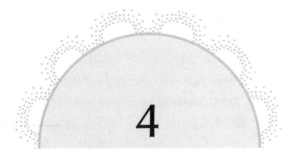

4

Shamans
to the Rescue

Note: I completed this chapter on shamanism immediately before the global pandemic came upon us. Little did I realize at the time how prescient I was in pointing out that our species is collectively going through a death and rebirth experience.

Human civilization is currently in the throes of a collective nervous breakdown. Institutions and corporate structures that are supposedly serving us but are in actuality keeping us asleep are breaking down as their underlying corruption is being exposed. Analogous to what can happen within an individual psyche, only writ large on the world stage, we are going through a collective shamanic initiation, a genuine near-death or death and rebirth experience in which our world is turning upside down and inside out. Something within us, reflected by events in the external world, is falling apart and dying, potentially to be reborn and recreated in a new, more coherent and integrated form. The more immanent the death experience, the greater the possibility for transformation.

Historically, shamans have been the first physicians, psychotherapists, artists, spiritual emissaries, prophets, translators, mediums, magicians, entertainers, culture heroes, and storytellers. Shamanism is the oldest form of healing in the world. Just as dreams are the unconscious's way of balancing a one-sidedness in an individual's psyche, the shamanic archetype is the dynamically evolving pattern of healing that is catalyzed in the collective unconscious as a compensatory response to the ongoing violence, suffering, and trauma that is being acted out on the world stage.

As Jung repeatedly warned, if we don't understand the powers of darkness within the unconscious that are emerging in our world and deal with them, we will be fated to suffer the consequences of our blindness. Encountering the dark forces of the unconscious invariably activates the shamanic archetype within the collective unconscious. The dark powers demand that we contend with forces that are alien to and outside of the control of our conscious egoic self, thereby animating the underlying patterns of response that inform the shamanic archetype to become operative. We as a human species as well as individually are making a shamanic descent into the underworld, the netherworld of the unconscious, the shadow within our psyche, where we must face our own dark side.

We all have shamanic abilities, whether we know it or not. These gifts are an intrinsic part of human nature. Though it is dangerous for the uninitiated and naïve Westerner to engage in the shamanic realm, Michael Harner, one of the most accomplished Western shamans, was of the opinion that "one of the biggest dangers connected with shamanism is to be ignorant about the unconscious shamanic abilities we all have."[1] It is a narrow passage between these two extremes—participating in the shamanic realm unawares, or being asleep to our natural shamanic gifts. By being unconscious of the intrinsic shamanic gifts that are our birthright, we are fated to act them out unconsciously in a way that endangers ourself and others. We are at the point in human history where we have all gotten drafted into an archetypal shamanic initiatory process, and the sooner we wake up to this and try to understand our role in this process, the better.

When someone is called to be a shaman, there is no external shaman who can heal them. The would-be shaman has to find the resources they need within. They need to call forth from within a totally unique and creative way that applies only to them. The path of healing that they discover, though an iteration of a deeper, archetypal, universal pattern, is not already known in the collective and therefore does not follow a prescription; it has to be each person's own way. This is another way of saying that through the shamanic initiatory process the apprentice is required to discover their own unique, creative self. This is the deeper pattern that *in-forms* the shamanic process on the individual level and reflects back to us what we are each called to do as we consciously embody and live this activated archetype.

"Shamans," philosopher and historian Mircea Eliade writes in his classic book *Shamanism,* "are pre-eminently the antidemonic champions."[2] This is to say that the shaman is the figure both in the world and within our individual psyche who has it out with the forces of darkness that threaten the larger ecosystem. In confronting evil, we often find ourselves in a double bind, forced to choose between the lesser of two evils; there seems to be no way out. This is a sign we are in a numinous situation, where there is no logical, rational solution. This type of conundrum is how the principalities, the primordial powers, approach humanity.

The problems in our world on the surface certainly appear to be insurmountable. Psychologist and author Arny Mindell writes in *The Shaman's Body,* "Shamanism is an archetypal form of behavior that appears in you when you are faced with unsolvable problems."[3] Though Mindell is talking about the individual, the same is true for the collective. The myriad seemingly unsolvable world crises humanity is facing catalyze the shamanic archetype deep within the core of our very being to become activated. Therefore it behooves us to get to know this "archetypal form of behavior," as it is how the higher powers are making their acquaintance with us.[4]

A Sacred Calling

Shamanism is a sacred vocation in that the would-be shaman is "called" by the voice of their inner true nature. How our life turns out depends on whether we hear this call and how we respond. If the person so summoned by the spirit of the unconscious refuses the call, they typically become neurotic, sick, and possibly even psychotic, and will probably die an early death. Assenting, saying "yes!" to our deeper shamanic calling, activates the universe's support of our initiatory ordeal, as the universe is the agency that has sponsored our calling in the first place.

Due to being wounded and traumatized by life itself, the shamanic archetype can become spontaneously activated in us whether we consciously know it or not.* Instead of cursing our brokenness (or our abusers), we can instead recognize this as a numinous event, an archetypal, creative, and potentially redemptive moment that seeks to make us participants in a divine, eternal happening.

We are at a moment in our species' history where each one of us is being called by something deeper than ourselves. In indigenous cultures, the figure of the shaman was a role in the field that was dreamed up by the community to serve a healing function for all of its members.

---

*A friend asked me what resources (books, outside authorities, research) I used to write this chapter. I responded by saying I based what I wrote here on my own inner experience. She responded by saying that it sounded like I channeled, which didn't sound right to me (unless I can claim to have channeled myself, as compared to some alien entity). I am certainly no shaman (I joke with my friends that I am only a shaman in my wildest dreams), but the shamanic archetype has been activated in me for years. When I think about it, I realize that over the decades I have gone so deeply into my own personal version of what I've written about that I have reached an archetypal, impersonal, universal level of experience. I realize that this has given me a confidence and certainty that what I'm writing about, though coming from the insights gleaned from my own personal experience, is universally true for everyone. As is always the case for me, it is through the very process of writing about what's going on inside of me that deepens my realization of what I'm writing about (and it wouldn't be as interesting for me to write if this weren't the case). To read more of my writings on shamanism, see my book *Awakened by Darkness*, chapter 20, a chapter aptly titled "Shamanism."

In our current day and age, our postmodern civilization—we could even say the universe itself—is dreaming all of us up in order to step into the role of shamans. Instead of our ritual implements being drums and rattles, however, our accessories might be something like the keyboard of a computer or the tools of multimedia, as we work to inspire change in the underlying consciousness of the field by a simple keystroke or with the creative use of a video camera or website.

Harner opines, "I think that almost everybody is a potential shaman."[5] We are all potential shamans-in-training, as our wounding dissociates us from our wholeness, which in turn catalyzes us into starting the shamanic hero's journey in search of the split-off parts of ourselves. The inner archetype of the shaman, the latent shaman within us, becomes particularly animated in people who are highly sensitive to the underlying contradictions, cognitive dissonance, double binds, and psychospiritual illness that characterize wetiko and pervades the unconscious social and cultural fabric of the human community.

The shamanic experience is inherently resistant to being politicized, bureaucratized, or incorporated into mainstream, corporate culture, as it is antihierarchical at its core, an expression of the wild spontaneity of nature herself. The shamanic vocation is truly democratic in that it is available to anyone who is open to receiving its call. The shamanic journey needs no external authority such as a church or priest, as it is based on direct, unmediated experience.

The person who is called to a higher destiny sacrifices themselves to their vocation. If their uniquely personal calling were to be mimicked and lived unconsciously by the collective, however, it would invariably lead to disaster on a massive scale. Oftentimes the person who is called to follow their own inner guidance is seen by people who subscribe to consensus reality (itself a form of collective madness) as having gone mad. The insidious and seemingly built-in madness of our world can make us feel crazy, and yet something in the service of true sanity is potentially available to us through our sensitivity to this madness. Though oftentimes seen as being crazy, shamans are actually the secret agents who bring sanity into the lunatic asylum that is our world, since they are usually the healthiest members of a community.

Typically highly empathic, shamans are very sensitive to the unconscious, both in themselves and in others. Existing in a liminal space, at the gateway between two different worlds, the shaman has very permeable boundaries between their conscious mind and the unconscious. It's as if within a shaman's psyche there is a bridge that allows the contents of the light and dark realms of consciousness to easily pass through, intermingle, and reciprocally co-inform each other. Through sympathetic resonance, shamans have an ability to feel into what is happening *outside* of themselves (be it in another person, a group, or the nonlocal field) *inside* of themselves. Finding the outside world reflected within them, they go within and become truly vulnerable, turning themselves inside out to creatively express what they find.

A key part of the shaman's work is their ability to travel into the spirit world and contend with the seeming entities who inhabit this realm. Seeing the spirits, in essence, is being able to recognize and develop a relationship with the forces of the unconscious. Wetiko can be thought of as being a spirit in its own right, which is why it is important to see how the spirit of wetiko operates nonlocally, out in the world, in our relationships, through our reactions, and inside our own minds. The process of becoming conscious doesn't banish the unconscious, but rather helps us develop trust toward its spirit, thereby allowing us to surrender to the unconscious time and again as we learn to access and receive its gifts of wisdom.

The Demon of Sickness

It is an age-old archetypal idea that a person who is sick or troubled can transmit their condition to a healthier person such as a healer or shaman, who is then able to absorb the sickness and subdue its harmful effects, but not without endangering and impairing, at least temporarily, their own well-being. An essential aspect of shamanic work is that the shaman "takes on" (which has the double meaning of "to confront" as well as "to take within oneself") the sickness that has infected the field around them. The shaman takes the illness within themselves—so as to "suffer with" the other, which is one of the meanings of genuine compassion.

In his writings, Jung mentions the figure of the "demon of sickness,"[6] an equivalent term for wetiko. Due to its *dis-integrating* (evil, anti–life) effects, it is a primordial, age-old idea that sickness is represented as an evil demon. Our subjective experience of the demon of sickness is an encounter with a seemingly autonomous, life-destroying entity whose intent is to take us down.

Both Freud and Jung recognized that there is a daemonic element within the psyche, and once it gains a certain momentum and seeming autonomy, it can constellate negatively and become demonic, continually keeping neurotic, unproductive suffering alive. One of Freud's deepest discoveries is that there is something within us that he called "thanatos," the death instinct, which demands our destruction. Freud realized that this internal force—what can be conceived of as a shadow of the will—actively resists and opposes the recovery of our wholeness in every way it possibly can. Jung refers to this same disintegrative factor as a "morbid" fragment of the personality, which inspires a "will to be ill."[7] The danger is that this sick part of the personality can devour and replace the normal functioning ego. Hidden within us is an unconscious part of us that actually *wants* us to remain sick. This morbid aspect of the psyche is firmly resolved to hold on to our state of illness and suffering, no matter what the cost. It should get our attention that Freud and Jung were both tracking the life-negating aspect of wetiko, each in their own way.

Wetiko can simultaneously be the cause and the effect of trauma. Inherently overwhelming and unable to be integrated into the wholeness of the psyche, trauma splits the psyche. If one is sufficiently severed from one's intrinsic wholeness, this split-off part of the psyche can potentially develop a seeming autonomy. This can become, in psychology speak, an "autonomous complex"—what indigenous cultures call a *demon*—that can go rogue and become an antilife force, an agent of death, a part of us that wants to destroy us. This internalized element fosters unfeeling, destructive, even murderous acts within us, which are directed inward, toward the self, as well as outward, toward others.

Continually and chronically promoting psychic disintegration, this internalized agency is as close as we can imagine to evil incarnate—the dark side of God—existing within the personality. This understanding can help demystify what Jung meant by the "psychological" (as compared to the metaphysical or theological) reality of evil.

Jung considers humanity as a whole to be in the developmental stage of adolescence. Due to our level of unconsciousness, he says we are not that much different from our earliest ancestors in many ways, in that the subterranean processes in the unconscious influence we modern people just as much as they did "primitives." To quote Jung, "We are possessed by the demons of sickness no less than they."[8] We are just as much in danger of being negatively affected by unconscious psychic forces or falling under a spell as were people in the distant past; whereas those early ancestors might have interpreted these deleterious effects as coming from demons, we modern, sophisticated people refer to the forces of the unconscious. Only the names are different.

A word of clarification: the idea of the demon of sickness connotes the immaterial essence, the very spirit of sickness that informs disease on all levels—physical, emotional, mental, and spiritual. When a shaman takes on someone's sickness, the essential idea is that the shaman is taking on the *spirit* that is animating and is at the root of the sickness. The spirit of sickness has two main aspects: the personal and the archetypal/transpersonal. In becoming intimate with the particular sickness that has afflicted the person, the shaman might acquire insight into the uniquely personal traumatic event and psychospiritual dynamic that initially opened the door for the sickness to invade the person's mind-body. In seeing the personal dimension of the sickness, the shaman can then place this sickness in its larger, transpersonal context.

This is to understand that this particular version of sickness is one of countless variations of the archetypal sickness of wetiko that afflicts our species. Through their own uniquely personal and particular experience of having internalized the collective sickness, what the shaman finds by going within provides them with the key to understanding the greater collective malaise from which their community and the whole world is suffering.

The Wounded and the Healed Healer

In taking on the sickness of a person, the shaman subjectively experiences the malady "from the inside," literally falling sick themselves, thereby becoming personally acquainted with the nature of the *dis-ease*. This can be conceived of as being a creative illness as well as a wounding experience, hence the shaman is an iteration of the wounded healer archetype (Chiron in Greek mythology). The archetype of the wounded healer has to do with carrying the wound (reminiscent of carrying one's cross), which always necessitates a descent into the underworld to discover the healing encoded within the wound—in other words, finding the light that is hidden within the darkness.

Only the wounded physician can heal. According to the myth of the wounded healer, it is their ability to be *vulnerable* (the Latin word *vulnus* means "wound") and hence capable of being wounded, and then bringing consciousness to their wound, that bestows on the wounded healer or shaman the power to heal. The wounded healer has to suffer through the sickness in order to be able to cure it. This brings to mind the universal truth that only those who have truly suffered and thus know suffering can relieve others' suffering. Only those who bear sickness as an existential possibility within themselves can constellate the healing process in others. Because the wounded healer personally knows the experience of being wounded, they are able to bear others' experience without the compulsive need to fix them. Healers have healing abilities not in spite of their wounds, but *because* of them.

In her book *Shamanic Voices,* anthropologist and Zen Buddhist roshi Joan Halifax writes, "Balanced between worlds, the shaman teaches by powerful example that illness can be a passageway to a greater life. . . . The healing image that the shaman projects is of disease as a manifestation of the transformative impulse in the human organism."[9] In other words, by going through the experience of illness, the shaman epitomizes how illness itself can potentially be a spiritual vehicle leading to a life more in touch with who we actually are.

Sometimes the shaman is permanently scarred and marked by the experience, destined to carry and suffer an indelible wound throughout their life. The wounded healer archetype, after all, has to do with carrying an incurable wound. In the wounded healer, to quote mythologist Carl Kerényi, author of a classic book on the subject, there is "the knowledge of a wound in which the healer forever partakes."[10] The resultant scar, with its associated vulnerability, is a reminder and a testament to a wound that must be consciously suffered. Our perpetual woundedness bestows on us an intimate, first-hand knowledge of evil, and this can potentially be our saving grace.

It is noteworthy that Christ, who epitomizes the archetypal wounded healer, still bore the visible marks of his wounds in his resurrected body of glory. Our wounds, afflictions, and scars have something—maybe everything—to do with the resurrection. According to the Book of Revelation (5:6), Christ will be worshipped in the form of "a Lamb looking as if it had been slain." Christ symbolizes our lamb-like innocence, the core of our spiritual nature consciously experiencing and assimilating over-the-top trauma. It is not for nothing that our culture's mythology of the incarnation of God on Earth is an abuse drama. A clearer symbol of the sacredness of being wounded through our innocence is hard to imagine.

Radically different from any self-created, neurotic suffering, *authentic* suffering, the purifying suffering that the Christian mystics envisioned as coming from God, belongs to our innocence, not our guilt. As long as we try to escape the nightmare of this suffering, our resentment insidiously and continuously generates more suffering, keeping us inextricably caught in a trap in which we are unwittingly colluding. It is only by not recoiling, but instead accepting and voluntarily allowing our innocent parts to consciously experience this suffering, that the hell that seemingly imprisons us is broken open. Consciously experiencing our innocence can be the elixir that can transform this hellish dynamic, opening up an energetic pathway to that part of us that is unconditioned and hence free.

The biblical Jacob, suffering for the rest of his life from a wounded hip as a result of his wrestling with the "Angel of God," is an example of being wounded through an encounter with the darker side of the numinosum. The wound then becomes the portal through which the wounded healer, or shaman, accesses a deeper dimension of their being (the *plenum*, the pure, unmanifest potential that is the fundamental nature of reality). This numinous experience is the origin of their ability to heal others. In the myth, as a result of living through his encounter with the dark Angel, Jacob's name was changed to Israel, "he who has wrestled with God," which symbolizes that his nature was changed by the experience.

The figure of the wounded healer was the precursor to the luminous divine physician. In Tibetan Buddhism, this figure is represented by the radiant Medicine Buddha (also known as the Healing Buddha). There are occasions when the shaman, by going through the process of taking on the demon of sickness, becomes even more in touch with their wholeness than before the ordeal (the alchemical image used to portray this is when a peacock eats poison, its plumage gets even brighter), as they step into the role of "healed healer." This is similar to how scar tissue that has formed over a wound can become even tougher and stronger than the surrounding normal tissue.

In ancient times, when the myth of the wounded healer first emerged, the idea was that sickness was the result of a divine action that could only be cured by another divine action. This is a homeopathic concept—a divine sickness cast out by a divine remedy (like cures like).

Because the sickness was vested with a royal dignity, it lent itself to a new attitude that saw it as also being laden with great healing power. Commenting on the figure of the divine physician, Jungian analyst Carl Alfred Meier writes, "*He* was the sickness *and* the cure. These two conceptions were identical. Because he was the sickness, he himself was afflicted . . . and because he was the divine patient he also knew the way to healing. To such a god the oracle of Apollo applies: 'He who wounds also heals.'"[11]

There is a great danger in "catching" (which has a double meaning of to be "infected by a contagion" as well as "to contain/capture") the sickness: when the shaman is "taken down," will they eventually rise up to recover their health, or stay stuck in a diseased state? Once the shaman introjects the sickness that is in the field, the sickness becomes an "inside job." This is to say that the sickness perversely attempts to interfere with, enlist, and usurp the shaman's inner resources in order to sustain and generate itself within the shaman's mind-body over time, as if the sickness wants to make the shaman its new host.

Once taken within, the demon of sickness doesn't have an intrinsically independent, objective existence separate from the shaman, but rather, it depends on the shaman's participation for its continued survival. Once introjected, the sickness is not just happening to the shaman merely as its passive victim, it also becomes part of the shaman's internal landscape such that they have an active hand in its generation. In essence, the shaman's process becomes that of discovering the role they are playing in nourishing the sickness within his or her own person in order to find the strength and creative ability to stop feeding it.

The demon of sickness can only put down roots and become lodged within the psyche of the would-be shaman if they unwittingly collude with and accommodate the sickness through their unconscious reactions to it. The shaman therefore needs to find the unconscious hooks that are keeping the demon alive within them and uncouple from these hooks.

Our wounds are semistable resonance patterns of vibratory energy to which we have become accustomed as existing in a particular, seemingly objective way. They are ongoing events or processes, held in place by how we pay attention to and interpret them, and so awareness is the key to how we experience them. It is in intentionally attending to our wounds in a new and creative way that we, as shamans-in-training, change their resonance pattern and the way these wounds manifest.

Though the moment(s) of our wounding happened historically, sometime in the past, our *experience* of these wounds takes place in the present moment. When we get right down to it, our wounds are not a hangover from the past, but are freshly constructed, with our full participation, in each and every moment. And it is only in the present moment that they can be healed.

If we can imagine that dark forces exist within the fabric of our universe, one of the ways these dark forces operate is to seduce us into getting hooked by, and identifying with, our wounds. On the other hand, if we fall into the habitual pattern of avoiding our wounds, we are unwittingly granting them an unwarranted and substantial existence in which we reinforce their reality (for if they weren't real, we wouldn't need to avoid them). In avoiding a relationship with our wounded parts—which is, ultimately speaking, to be avoiding relationship with ourselves—we unconsciously collude with our wounds so as to sustain and perpetuate them over time, thus keeping them alive. A wounded healer, a shaman, is someone who has overcome this unconscious tendency to avoid a relationship with these wounded parts within his or her own person, in order to alchemically transmute and rechannel the energy that is informing these wounds in such a way that serves the creative spirit within them.

Paradoxically, the spirit enlivening the demon of sickness can serve to reveal to the budding shaman what in their unconscious is unknowingly complicit with the sickness. This enables the shaman to stop creating—to *undream*—their sickness. By unwittingly helping the potential shaman deepen their realization of their true nature, the dark forces of wetiko can connect them with a higher form of light—

expressing a more expanded consciousness—that transcends the dual-istic notion of light and darkness opposing each other. In this way, transforming the dark forces into secret allies deputizes the shaman-in-training to be a true healer for others.

Penetrating to Our Vitals

The spirit that lives within the sickness can potentially light up the shaman's awareness so as to illumine those unconscious parts of the shaman's psyche that resonate with the sickness. Becoming aware of all of these unconscious aspects can help the shaman further see and integrate their unconscious, greatly enlarging their ability to cre-atively engage with the unconscious in the field. Assimilating their own unconscious—to whatever degree—is thus a crucial step in opening the doorway to an immense array of inner healing resources. Though their unconsciousness allows the sickness to take root in the shaman, it must be noted that after all is said and done, the uncon-scious is also a repository of inexhaustible riches and practically infi-nite creativity, and this is the ultimate source of healing. And so the unconscious can either feed the sickness or heal it, depending on one's relationship to it.

It is the reciprocal interplay between the sickness and the shaman's unconscious reactions to it—how they relate to it, what meaning they place on it, how they bear the *dis-ease* and the suffering that it brings—that causes the sickness to take the particular form it does within them. Etymologically, *to bear* has to do with giving birth;* the point is that how we bear, that is, how we carry the sickness, can potentially give birth to a new version of oneself. The shaman is thus adding their *conscious* awareness—as best as they can—to a process that happens to most of us *unconsciously.*

---

*From the old High German word *beran* comes the word *gebaren,* meaning "to carry, to gestate and give birth."

It is a very tricky business, however, when we have a living encounter with the demon of sickness. It is important to *not* keep it separate from ourselves by rationalistic, intellectual, or *apotropaic* (warding off evil) means. The whole point of the process is to be affected—actually touched—by the demon, to feel it within oneself. When we "have it out" with the demon of sickness, if we do not at least partially succumb to it, letting it touch us, nothing of its apparent evil will enter us, and this precludes the possibility of any regeneration or healing taking place as a result of our encounter.

The darkness encoded in the demon of sickness, according to Jung, is "meant to penetrate to a man's vitals."[12] We must be affected by it, otherwise its full effect can't reach us. Without a period of being taken over and possessed by an unconscious psychological complex such that it is "lived out," we would not be able to integrate the complex into conscious ego functioning. We can only understand something, really grok it, if we experience it inwardly. We need to succumb to the sickness and let it penetrate us to our core or we won't be sufficiently impacted by it within our own subjective experience; but at the same time we must, to at least some degree, retain some independence from the experience. This can enable some measure of meta-awareness of the process while one is still in it, turning it into an object of knowledge.

When we are touched by the demon of sickness, wetiko, it is imperative that we become aware of what has impacted us. To put this differently: it is crucial to learn what has affected us (as well as, I might add, what within us has been affected); this is to turn something unconscious into conscious knowledge. The result of this gnosis is twofold: what has afflicted us has been transformed by adding consciousness to it, and we have thus been transformed—we've expanded our consciousness—through our encounter.

However, if we succumb completely to the demon, we will be swept away by the blind flux of psychic events, and perhaps even psychologically destroyed. If we haven't developed a strong enough sense of self in order to be in relationship with these powerful archetypal energies, we can be taken over so completely by the demon that we become possessed by it, such that we would lose our ability to snap out of our state and self-reflect and then, losing ourself, we could fall into psychosis. And so there is the possibility of great danger when the shaman takes on the illness: they can identify with it and become absorbed in it, hence taken over by it such that they not only cannot help anyone else, they then become just another person who needs help. This would, tragically, be a failed initiation.

Knowing Our Limits

There are different ways of dealing with the demon of sickness, wetiko, depending on where we're at in our development. It's important to know our limits and not take on more than we can handle, or we can get in over our heads. If we take on more than we can chew or metabolize (which evokes the image of turning the demon of sickness into bite-size bits that are easier to digest), we will be unable to assimilate it into the wholeness of our being. We then suffer from psychic indigestion, as if an alien substance that can't be integrated has entered our system. For people who are unconsciously identified with and deeply suffering from these negative energies, it can be a relief—helping them feel not so crazy—to recognize that these energies are alien, separate, and other than themselves.

There is a danger of prematurely realizing that wetiko is a part of us, the risk being that we can easily become overwhelmed when we unexpectedly find violent, immoral, and criminal impulses within us. If we identify with these energies, this becomes deeply problematic and dangerous. If we prematurely try to "own" the demon of sickness and we haven't developed a strong enough sense of self, the danger is a negative inflation, as we begin to identify with, and act out, these impulses. We can then easily fall into despair and depression, which can then further feed our lack of self-worth. This doesn't help anyone and is in fact an obstacle on the path.

And yet there is real benefit available if we can genuinely own these negative energies as belonging to us, but not identify with them, as we realize they are not who we are. So rather than feeling like sinister energies are attacking us (which can foster fear and paranoia), recognizing that wetiko is part of us can be very empowering and help us take responsibility for our life. Instead of feeling helpless, thinking we have no ability to deal with these dark energies, this realization bestows on us a greater agency, for by doing our inner work we can address these energies creatively.

And so our strategy regarding how to deal with wetiko is determined by where we're at in our psychospiritual evolution and our degree of self-realization. This whole process is not linear, but more circular—a circumambulation—which is to say that at any given moment we might be relating to certain aspects of wetiko "out there" as being separate from us, while at the same time (or the next moment) recognizing other (or the same) parts as reflections of something within us. Typically, we go back and forth between these levels all the time as we become integrated with our nature.

This inner psychological process is symbolized in myths and fairy tales. If the hero encounters the monster prematurely, before they have developed enough ego strength, and they try to fight the monster, they will be destroyed due to their lack of inner development. In this instance, to run away, mythologically represented as "the magic flight," instead of being cowardice would be the path of wisdom. But later on, after having gone through a series of initiatory events that have fostered the hero's inner development, when they next meet the monster, if they flee they are indeed acting out of cowardice and avoiding their fate, as they have been called to have it out with—and vanquish—the monster.

One thing our wounds teach us are our limits. In alchemy there are certain elements that are so poisonous, called the *terra damnata* (accursed earth), that if they are allowed into the alchemical work they will corrupt and ruin the whole operation. A key part of an awakened, all-embracing attitude is accepting that there are certain things that are not to be embraced because they are toxic to our psychological ecology.

A real-life example of this phenomenon is when someone sufficiently awakens and realizes the unity and oneness of all existence and feels the divinity of all that is, they can feel an enormous amount of love and feel so all-embracing towards everyone such that they dissolve all sense of boundaries and invite people into their life, some of whom feed off of their light and vampirically drain their energy. Instead of solely being an expression of their lucidity, this process is also an expression of their unconsciousness around boundaries, showing them their growing edge where they can learn something.

Though the ego is not who we actually are, it is important in matters such as these to not demonize our ego—our imagined sense of self—thinking that it is just an illusion that we need to kill—a common misconception in spiritual circles. Despite having a bad reputation, the ego has an important role in our evolution. If we haven't developed a strong enough ego, a healthy sense of self, we won't be able to stand strongly in our individuality so that we can distinguish ourselves from and be in relationship with these dark forces; in that case we'll either dissociate when we encounter them (becoming dissociated ourself), or we'll become possessed by them. In either case we become disoriented, deranged, and out of touch with who we really are.

It is helpful to remember that the divine light within us is never stronger than when it has to struggle against the invading darkness. If we succumb only in part to the darkness and are able, by our own self-assertion, to protect the little flame of light of our conscious awareness from being completely swallowed by the threatening darkness, then through this ordeal there is the possibility of gradually reasserting oneself so as to metabolize and alchemically transmute the sickness in a way that feeds our wholeness and connects us with a newfound inner agency.

Distinguishing Ourself

Relating to the demon of sickness as if it is other than ourselves is at the same time to relate to ourselves as other than the sickness. Shamanically-inclined people have a capacity for *ecstatic* states (to be *ec-static* is to be beyond "stasis," i.e., to not be static or stuck), which involves stepping outside of our limited identity patterns and to be "beside ourselves" (in a good way). In *objectifying* the demon of sickness (having it be *beside,* i.e., outside of ourselves), we are simultaneously *dis-identifying* from it (remember—identifying with it is the great danger!) while at the same time creating ourselves distinct from and relative (and in relationship) to it.

When we are unconsciously identified with something, we can't see it. It then becomes the lens through which we see everything, flavoring all of our perceptions, which renders us blind to it. We do not con-sciously choose to identify ourselves with such and such content, but rather, we subjectively experience our identity with it as if it is the way things are. When we identify with a content of the unconscious, we weaken our consciousness, which is dangerous, because when we are unconsciously identified with certain contents and perspectives of the unconscious, we are possessed by them.

In the conscious act of *dis-identifying* with something, we are let-ting go of our tight hold on it, changing our relationship to it. Once we *dis-identify* with something, it is no longer equated with us, no longer at the center of our identity. It becomes only a part of us, no longer defining us. We then step into the position of defining *it.* In psycho-logical language, this is the process of ego-differentiation; in religious language it is the process of detachment (the opposite of attachment/ identification/possession).

What initiates the shamanic process in the first place is typically an overwhelming trauma in which the psyche dissociates. This is the very wounding that activates the shaman within to start the journey of going in search of the lost parts of oneself. The psyche is by nature dissociable; this is either a defense mechanism that protects us, a potential pathology that splits us in two (becoming, in psychological terms, a dissociative disorder), or an incredible gift.

The ability to *consciously* dissociate from a part of oneself can be a true superhero power, for to project a part outside of oneself and then to objectify it so as to relate to it as other than who we are is the very psychological mechanism that saves us from being swallowed by the trauma of it all. To consciously dissociate from a part of oneself is to disconnect, disentangle, and disidentify from this part. This allows us to potentially see it and develop a relationship with it, whereas if left unseen, it would keep us stuck in a neurotic (or possibly even psychotic) state. Thus built into the pathological aspect of dissociation is the means to overcome it. This is another example of how encoded in a psychological process is both the poison and the medicine, combined in a quantum superposition. How things will ultimately manifest depends on how they are carried within us.

By consciously *dis-identifying* from the demon of sickness, we are able to step out of experiencing it solely from the inside (subjectively), as we can then cultivate the ability to witness and reflect on it from the outside (objectively). Embracing these paradoxical perspectives and becoming omniperspectival cultivates the ground for understanding and wisdom to grow. Going back and forth between these two viewpoints serves our integration and individuation, and is a way of characterizing the archetypal shamanic journey between the worlds. The trajectory of this journey brings the subjective and objective points of view closer together, until (at least in theory if not in practice) they come together as one, producing lucid awareness in the process.

Paradoxically, recognizing the demon of sickness as other than who we are is the very thing that allows us to eventually own, embrace, and integrate it as part of ourselves. On the one hand, we need to not see the sickness as being separate from us, and instead feel into it so as to get on intimate terms with it. On the other hand, we do need to *distinguish ourselves* from the sickness, objectifying it—for example, through the practice of active imagination—which allows us to not identify with it. In doing thus we create ourself anew, finding that part of us that is always transcendent to and untouched by the sickness. Realizing this, we can then give ourselves over to the sickness, allowing ourselves to become possessed by it. The whole ordeal is an initiation that introduces us to that part of ourself that can't be possessed, which is our true nature.

Allowing oneself to be taken over like this is a form of death, as it involves passing beyond our normal egoic identity, which can potentially result in being delivered from—dying to—aspects of a limited self that no longer serve us. Eliade writes about how the shamanic process is equivalent to "re-entering the womb of this primordial life, that is, to a complete renewal, a mystical rebirth."[13] This is to submerge oneself in the power of creativity that lies at the very foundation of our being; moment-by-moment, we can create ourselves anew, assuming a new, more healed and whole identity.

By going through a shamanic *dismemberment* (in which the parts of oneself that have become rigid and no longer serve us are dissolved back into their source), we heal our amnesia and *re-member* who we are (putting our *members* back together), as we retrieve the lost and split-off parts of our soul. Individuation, after all, involves a gathering, a *re-collecting* of all the disowned parts of oneself that we have projected out into the world.

While experiencing the demon of sickness, we can at the same time connect to, witness, and identify with that part of us that is healthy. Though sickness and health are typically conceived as being opposites, the shaman uses sickness as the way to deepen their experience of health. As we identify more and more with our wholesome, whole, and holy nature, the demon of sickness typically tries to hook us through our weak points and blind spots so that we will identify with *its* version of who we are. This seems to be a real obstacle to our wholeness until we realize that the entity inhabiting the sickness, acting *as if* it is a demon, is actually helping us (though at times forcing us) to get further established in our true nature so as to become immune to its seductions. It's as if the reflections in the mirror are teaching the mirror to not identify with and be caught up by them.

The shaman is only able to avoid being caught by the illness because of their strong connection to the all-pervasive, spacious, ever-present wholeness of the Self, a wholeness that is both transcendent to and untouched by the illness. In other words, the shaman brings the radiant healing light of their true nature to bear on and reassert its salutary presence on the illness in such a way that heals the disease.

The shaman's ability to heal and facilitate healing in the field depends on their ability to access the omnipresent underlying field of abundant potential and open-ended creativity—the plenum. Linking to the intrinsic numinosity of the plenum is therapeutic down to its core— what Jung calls "the real therapy"—as it releases us from what he calls "the curse of pathology."[14]

Therapist as Shaman

Jung felt that shamanism was the earliest forerunner to the depth psychology that he developed. The function of ancient shamans is in fact very much like that of a modern-day psychotherapist in that both have direct experience of the unconscious, in both its light and dark aspects. Marie-Louise von Franz, Jung's closest colleague, conceived of the training of a psychotherapist, wherein the candidate follows a higher calling that leads to their vocation, as analogous to a shamanic initiation. When I reference therapy, I conceive of it as a noble and sacred art that deals with issues pertaining to the human soul, rather than the debased, flatland version of therapy widely practiced nowadays in our materialistic culture, a form of therapy that is primarily concerned with behavior modification and the use of brain chemistry–altering medications.

In freeing the soul from its enchantment by and identification with its unconscious complexes, the therapist is performing a modern-day reenactment of the shamanic practice of soul retrieval. In helping their clients open up and gain access to the collective unconscious, the therapist is introducing the person to the shamanic realm of gods and demons that live within each of us. The best therapists are those in whom the shamanic archetype is activated in their work with their clients.

The deep energetic interaction between the shaman and the person being healed maps onto what happens in the realm of the psyche in psychotherapy (when seen as a genuine art form) between the psychotherapist and the client. This is to say that we can gain insight into how a shaman helps heal a person (and, perhaps, the larger community) by understanding how something similar happens in the sacred, ritualized space of therapy.

Jung was of the opinion that therapists are only effective when they allow themselves to be open and vulnerable so as to be affected—even potentially wounded—by their client's problems. If the therapist hides behind their alleged authority like a suit of armor, they foreclose on their ability to constellate healing in their client. The shaman/therapist can exert no influence on their client unless they become susceptible to being influenced by them. If the therapist is only influenced unconsciously, there is a blind spot in their field of consciousness that makes it impossible for them to fully see the person. So a field of what Jung refers to as "mutual influence" needs to be constellated between them.

A mysterious alchemical reaction happens when two people authentically interact with each other. It's like mixing two different chemical substances. As the alchemists were well aware, if there is any combination at all, both parties are transformed. Being truly present with the client can't help but bring about changes in the therapist's unconscious. Jung uses the term *psychic infection* to refer to when the highly sensitive, empathic therapist, through the inductive effects of the activated unconscious, shares with and sometimes even takes over the sufferings of their clients.* In the art of psychotherapy there is always the

---

*For the interested reader, Jung talks about the many aspects of this process in *The Practice of Psychotherapy,* Collected Works vol. 16.

real yet necessary risk of the client's psychic illness being transferred to the therapist. This evokes the therapist's shamanlike function of *taking on*—having it out with as well as taking within themselves—the demon of sickness from which the client is suffering.

Once the underlying spirit and dynamic of the illness is transmitted and "transferred" via the act of *transference** to the therapist, this evokes unconscious reactions and projections, known as *countertransference*, within the therapist's own unconscious, which are then projected on the client. Jung felt that the transference/countertransference is the crux, the most crucial part, the alpha and the omega of therapeutic work. In essence, the transference/countertransference is based on the undeniable fact that projections have an effect on the unconscious of the recipient, evoking counterprojections. Instead of unwittingly projecting onto the client countertransference reactions, it is the therapist's responsibility, like the shaman's, to consciously deal with and assimilate the unconscious reactions triggered in them by the countertransference.

Jung was interested in the purpose of this living dynamic, as he sensed that hidden within the phenomenon of transference/countertransference are the seeds of further development for both parties involved. Jung points out that the success of therapy depends on whether the therapist is able to make conscious, integrate, and skillfully deal with the unconscious contents that have been stirred up as a result of the transference/countertransference dynamics.

Once the transference/countertransference becomes activated, this leads both the therapist and the client to a direct—and indirect—confrontation with the transpersonal daemonic forces of the unconscious. When there is the intention to channel light, we are sure to invite a guest: the unconscious. Due to the transference/countertransference, the unprocessed shadow aspect of the unconscious becomes constellated

---

*The illness is not the only thing transferred (through the transference) to the therapist. There are numerous projections put on the therapist, some of them extremely positive such as a positive father or mother figure, healer, or guru.

in a negative and *diabolic* (the inner meaning of diabolic is that which separates and divides) way via the relationship between the therapist and the client such that it can create all sorts of projections and misunderstandings, yet this is the very *prima materia** out of which the sacred medicine is born.

It is as if the unconscious manifests in an elusive, deceptive, shape-shifting entity—what can be conceived of as being the third party in the therapist-client relationship, which flits about from client to therapist and then back again. This seeming entity can cause all sorts of disconnects between the therapist and the client, and yet, if the therapeutic container is strong enough, they can potentially decode and assimilate the unconscious contents that are encoded within the diabolical goings-on between them.

The alchemists personified this impish and wily figure as Mercurius. Though they often lamented how this figure endlessly hoodwinked and bamboozled them, they still held it in the highest regard, considering it as practically a deity. Mercurius is akin to the godhead, but paradoxically he also has an exceedingly shady character, with many connections to the dark side. It is noteworthy that Mercurius is a close relative of wetiko, who likewise has both sublime and sketchy characteristics. The consulting room is a sacred vessel in which (*Deo concedente,* "God willing," as the alchemists never failed to add) the therapist and client are able to contain, add consciousness to, integrate, and transform the powerful forces of the unconscious that have been unleashed due to their work together, in order to derive the healing that is hidden within these forces.

Transference and countertransference are forms of the projections and counterprojections that all of us typically cast on one another via our psychological exchanges in normal, day-to-day relationships. What

---

*"Seen alchemically, wetiko is related to the prima materia of alchemy. The 'famous secret' and the basis of the entire alchemical opus is the unique prima materia, which is the chaos and raw material out of which the refined substance or 'gold' is revealed." (Levy, *Dispelling Wetiko,* 316.)

makes the transference/countertransference unique is that the therapist and the client are playing prescribed roles, and their dynamic is happening in a hermetically sealed container, a sanctified space, which is similar to the shaman creating a sacred space in which to work. The therapist, as if fulfilling a sacred contract, is cast in the shamanic healing role of taking on, working with, and bringing the light of consciousness to the unconscious that's been constellated in the therapeutic container, in a way that's helpful to the client.

The dynamics that happen in the therapist's office also occur in our everyday relationships: all the projections that go back and forth, the acting out of unhealed abuse issues, the misunderstandings that arise as a result of these dynamics, and, hopefully, as in the therapeutic setting, the healing and transformation that emerge when in our relationships we add consciousness to this process. All human relationships that have any level of intimacy will constellate transference phenomena, which will manifest as either helpful or disturbing factors in the relationship. Whether or not we successfully navigate this psychological terrain that is naturally dreamed up in the course of our relationships with one another depends on whether we have created a proper container in which to metabolize what has gotten triggered within and between us from the subterranean depths of the unconscious.

Oftentimes the client isn't able to directly confront their inner evil, but through the transference might unconsciously project onto the therapist the evil they are wrestling with. Under these circumstances it is the therapist's role, as consciously as they are able, to carry the client's projection without identifying with it (in which case they would unwittingly act it out, thus reinforcing the client's trauma). As Jung never tired of pointing out, what we are unconscious of approaches us from the outside; it gets projected into the external world, dreamed up through life itself.

Projections are a tricky thing: they can either hurt or help us, either keep us asleep or wake us up, depending on our relationship with them. When we unconsciously project onto another person, we do not clearly see the person we're projecting onto, as we're merely seeing our own unconscious, split-off part mirrored in them. In this case we are not in a genuine relationship with that person. Yet encoded within the projection are our unconscious parts yearning to be integrated into our wholeness, provided we can recognize the projection as belonging to us.

Once the unconscious contents of the client sufficiently impact the therapist, the therapist finds themselves cast in the role of potential shaman taking on the now-activated unconscious contents of the client. Once the client shares their hidden emotional vulnerabilities and secrets with the therapist, it's as if the therapist, in taking in and connecting with the person's process, can help them metabolize it. When the transference is fully activated in what is referred to as *shamanic transference,* instead of just the client's isolated psyche wrestling with the demon of sickness, there are now two psyches, the client's and the therapist's, united in their healing intent, chewing on (making it easier to swallow) these unconscious contents so as to digest (assimilate) them into consciousness.

In a book on Navaho healing, Jungian analyst Donald Sandner writes, "The medicine man [the shaman] identifies with the patient in his confrontation with evil, and in almost all the prayers handles the evil so closely that he nearly identifies with it himself. In certain of the prayers he does finally identify himself with it, thus risking all the effects of evil upon himself in order to banish it from the patient."[15] Similar to how a shaman has to confront the evil that their client is struggling with, the therapist often has to *have it out* with the evil that the client is suffering from.

Once the therapist makes conscious what has gotten activated in their own unconscious so as to metabolize and integrate it, the therapeutic task now becomes how to pass the *medicina* over to the client. In essence, the healing influence of the therapist comes via their embodying their integrated state, which is nonlocally transmitted to the client through the many subtle psychic capillaries that run through the interactive field between them as a result of the transference/countertransference. This can only take place because of a psychic bridge or pathway that has opened up between them due to both the client and the therapist being sufficiently open to being influenced by each other.

Thanks to the therapist, who faces within themselves what the client cannot yet face within their own psyche, the client, consciously or unconsciously, recognizes in the living person of the therapist how someone else (who is actually reflecting this latent part in the client) has transformed and integrated the very unconscious affliction with which the person has been wrestling. Even if the client doesn't consciously recognize this process of inner transformation in the therapist, the eye of the unconscious of the person "sees," and is affected by, the therapist's transformation.

In a very real sense, this interactive relational dynamic between therapist and client models and is a blueprint for the natural shamanic process of healing that can take place between anyone in whom the shamanic archetype is activated. The deeper patterns *in-forming* the shamanic experience are encountered repeatedly throughout the world, as they are part and parcel of the human condition.

No therapist can heal a client; the therapist's role is to constellate the inner healing that exists in potential within the person's soul. The therapist can only do this if they are in touch with that, just as the client has an inner healer, the therapist also has an inner wounded part. These two seemingly opposite figures—the wounded and the healer aspects of us—are two interconnected parts of a greater archetype (which are always bipolar, or two-sided).

If, however, the therapist sees the sickness as only residing within the client without recognizing that the person is reflecting the wounded part of the therapist, then the therapist has split the archetype (as well as their own soul) and is unconsciously projecting out one of its poles (the wounded aspect) onto the client. Solidifying the patient in the role of being the sick one—often with the best of intentions—the therapist literally casts a spell, unwittingly helping to keep the client sick. In addition, if the therapist is not in touch with their own wounds—and hence, with their equality with their client—this opens the door for the therapist to unconsciously abuse their power. If, on the other hand, the therapist is aware of their own woundedness, they will not monopolize the healing aspect of the archetype, but rather, in their vulnerability, will increase the probability that healing becomes constellated within their client.*

The question naturally arises: what constitutes true healing? In Jung's work it is clear that he doesn't equate healing with the allevia- tion of symptoms. Etymologically, *healing* is related to the word *whole- ness;* becoming healed has to do with getting in touch with our intrinsic wholeness. Jung (and I imagine many shamans/wounded healers would agree) felt that real healing has to do with understanding whatever les- son is hidden within an illness, as well as deepening the person's insight into their suffering and possibly even getting closer to understanding the very meaning and preciousness of life. This understanding can lead to a genuine transformation in which the person more fully steps into simply being who they authentically are. Hence real healing only hap- pens when we step into, own, and embody who we are meant to be.

From this perspective, there would be no real healing unless the cli- ent developed a truly religious attitude, not in the dogmatic sense of being a believer in any particular religion, but in the sense of continu- ally opening up to and cultivating an ever more profound relationship with something to be found deep within—what Jung calls "the Self," or the God within, that which is beyond and greater than the limited egoic self. In other words, the person would become more spiritual in the true sense of that word: more in touch with and connected to the spiritual side of things.

To the extent that the shaman/therapist is able to move through the

---

*I'd like to thank Jungian analyst Adolf Guggenbuhl-Craig for his insights into this process. Please see his book *Power in the Helping Professions.*

illness and connect with their own intrinsic wholeness, they are nonlocally helping the whole universe by lightening the shadow and dissolving the sickness in the collective field ever so slightly. In their work, the therapist isn't solely helping the client's soul, but their own soul as well, not to mention laying a miniscule healing granule on the scales of the soul of humanity itself. As insignificant as their offering may seem to be, both therapist and client are participating in the *magnum opus* (the great work) of alchemy, accomplished in a dimension where the source of humanity's fundamental problems is to be found.

Any one person integrating their inner darkness could be, as Jung says, "the makeweight that tips the scales,"[16] catalyzing a phase transition in the collective psyche of all humanity—what's popularly known as the hundredth monkey effect. Jung correlated this process to how symbols spontaneously precipitate out of the unconscious. One of his favorite examples of describing this dynamic is when we dissolve granules of sugar in a glass of water. Each additional grain of sugar will dissolve in the water until it reaches its saturation point. If we then add one more granule of sugar, a crystal will spontaneously manifest in the water. Jung likened this to humanity's situation: any one of us who is self-reflecting, realizing the dreamlike nature of reality and owning our shadow, could be the grain of sugar that tips the scales of the collective unconscious of our species, catalyzing a worldwide evolutionary expansion of consciousness. The realization that this is truly possible can be the very inspiration we need to continue our spiritual journey just when the darkness seems so overwhelming.

No Distance

All of the stages of the shaman's journey seem paradoxical, contradictory, and utterly mysterious, but when seen from a metaperspective, a deeper pattern begins to emerge. The inner experiences that the shaman lives through during their initiatory ordeal are reflections of the archetypal process of individuation that we all are destined to go through. The intrinsic wholeness of our nature, which we connect with through the individuation process, contains something very mysterious, if not mystical.

Matters such as these don't easily lend themselves to language—they have an inherent contradictory quality, which points to the trickster-like nature of what we're dealing with. Expressing in words what a shaman does is challenging and practically impossible due to what's implicit in our Western two-valued logic* and the limited grammar of language itself. Whereas the shaman operates in the nonlocal, atemporal, open-ended expanse of mind itself, the English language is rooted in the more localized third-dimensional space-time continuum. The limited and limiting ways of thinking built into two-valued logic stultifies the natural creative brilliance of our minds. Two-valued logic is the structural grammar for the operation of the wetiko virus, which is why this form of logic can itself be considered a virus, what I call the *two-valued virus,* or $2V^{2}$, pronounced "2Vsquared."

The shaman's mode of operation brings to mind the complementarity principle of physics, where seemingly contradictory and mutually exclusive states can both be true at the same time. Expressing only one aspect (that the demon of sickness is not who we are, for example), though true in and of itself on one level, is only a partial description of the situation and hence, incomplete. As it is incomprehensible from within the perspective of two-valued logic, in order to wrap our mind around this absurd idea (that we are both other than the demon of sickness while at the same time being inseparable from it) involves a higher form of logic—what is called *four-valued logic* in Buddhism. As compared to the two options intrinsic to two-valued logic, four-valued logic has two additional possibilities: something can be true (and true only), false (and false only), both true and false, or neither true nor false. Four-valued logic provides a more complete picture of reality than two-valued logic. Four-valued logic is the logic of interdependence, wholeness, and

---

*Basic to Western analytical thought, in two-valued logic there are two options—for example, things are either true or false. It can be thought of as either/or logic.

the unity of all things. An example of four-valued logic has to do with the nature of light. It is well known that sometimes light appears as a particle, and other times it will manifest as a wave, depending on how we are observing it. Is light a wave or a particle? This question is not amenable to two-valued logic, but is better addressed by four-valued logic—light is both a wave and/or particle and neither a wave nor a particle. It is not one or the other.

Four-valued logic, the logic that characterizes the interconnectedness of the universe, is also the logic required by quantum physics, which has unequivocally revealed the oneness of our universe, which is to say that our universe is not composed of separate parts interacting, but is a seamless whole. Truly subversive from the point of view of mainstream thought, this higher form of logic helps us let go of our clinging to whatever particular viewpoint we hold, as it undermines any fixed view of reality that we are seemingly caught in. Instead of doing away with differences, four-valued logic embraces distinctions, as it both encompasses the realm where things are either true or false, but goes beyond this limited viewpoint, where the notion of something being true or false doesn't apply. Expanding the dimensionality of rational thought, four-valued logic can potentially introduce us to the timeless dimension of our experience, which is the realm that informs our dreaming.

This higher form of logic is an expression of a more expanded consciousness that is in touch with the wholeness of our true nature. The archetype of the shaman/wounded healer symbolizes a type of consciousness that can simultaneously hold the seemingly mutually exclusive and contradictory opposites of being consciously aware of both the sickness within themselves as well as their wholeness. As if simultaneously inhabiting two (or more) parallel universes (which, at least on the surface of things, have no intersection), the shamanic temperament can see through either of the different viewpoints without solely identifying with—and hence, being caught by—any one of them.

The shaman's enacting two seemingly opposed processes—distancing from the demon of sickness, which is to relate to it as other than themselves while at the same time realizing that it is not separate from themselves—seems on the surface to be utterly paradoxical, and yet it is a perfect example of four-valued logic. What the shaman is doing—or rather, being—is not paradoxical from their perspective, however, for in the atemporal, nonlocal domain that is their workplace, there is no time or distance. In realizing that there is no distance between themselves and the demon of sickness the shaman gains access to a means of connecting with and hence transmuting the demon within their own person. This is their inner sanctum, the secret workplace of the shaman, the only place where they can affect real change in the outside world of space and time.

There is a danger in implementing four-valued logic without fully understanding it. Wetiko is more than happy to usurp anything that is in the service of expanding our consciousness in order to enlist it into serving its dark agenda. For example, holding the creative tension that is required in seeing omniperspectivally, through four-valued logic, does not preclude the possibility that one or more viewpoints might actually be true, which is to say it might be what is actually happening. This might mean that the other point of view could actually be false, an illusion made up of misinformation by which we can easily deceive ourself into thinking something is true when it is not.

It would then be a mistake to overly identify with the seemingly more expansive metaperspective that four-valued logic provides us with, which holds that all possibilities are true. In so doing, we might marginalize, ignore—and not see—what is actually happening. Seeing through the lens of four-valued logic and not taking sides, though seemingly an enlightened approach that doesn't want to become fixed in a particular viewpoint, can be appropriated by wetiko to serve its agenda. Viewing our world from this more expansive perspective does not mean that we never take a viewpoint as being true—at certain points it literally demands that we do so. Someone recently asked me if four-valued logic is similar to the "doublethink" of George Orwell's classic book *1984*. Doublethink, which, for example, proclaims that "war is peace," though superficially resembling four-valued logic in its seeming uniting of opposites, is a way of thinking that literally fractures the mind, disables our ability to think critically, and splits us in two. Doublethink collapses the distinction between opposites in a way that blurs opposites and creates confusion; it's an example of how wetiko transforms four-valued logic into doublethink to fit its agenda in order to prevent us from accessing our inner light. Instead of creating an inner dissociation, four-valued logic actually helps us to access our intrinsic wholeness such that we remember who we are, thus helping us to access our creative agency to move through—and move—the world.

The Shamanic Shift

Through a deep maneuver of—and in—awareness, the shaman potentiates healing energies to radiate throughout the nonlocal field, which can help the sick person. Through a shamanic shift in consciousness, instead of relating to the outer and inner worlds as separate and independent realms, the shaman becomes lucid to the dreamlike nature of reality and recognizes that the physical world and all the beings in it are not only not separate, and not merely reflecting their inner world, but are arising within their own awareness.

A good way to think of this is to envision a torus. Imagine if we draw a circle on top of the donut-shaped torus that encircles the hole. If our consciousness existed on the line of the circle and we looked out toward the outer edge of the torus, this can be conceived of as representing the outer world. If we turn our attention 180 degrees and look toward the inner edge of the torus, this can be thought of as representing the inner world. On the surface, the two worlds, inner and outer, seem separate and discontinuous, with a clear boundary between them; this corresponds to the limited and partial perspective of a person who's not awake to the dreamlike nature of reality. An accomplished shaman, on the other hand, sees and feels the whole figure of the torus from a

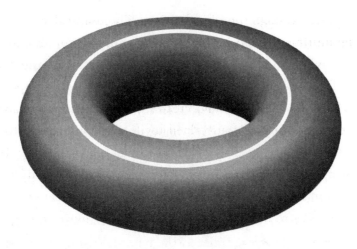

A torus provides a beautiful geometric image of how what
we typically call our "inner" and "outer" experiences (or the "subjective"
and "objective" realms) only appear to be separate but are
in fact not ultimately separate at all. See text on previous page.

metaperspective and realizes that if we explore either the inner or the
outer worlds deeply enough, we will recognize that they are not separate but are ultimately continuous with and indistinguishable from each
other, as they truly are one.*

Another symbolic representation of the oneness of the inner and
the outer is a Klein bottle. At first glance, a Klein bottle looks like it
has an inside and an outside, but this is merely the way it superficially
appears when we only have a partial view of it instead of seeing it as a
whole. A single-sided bottle with no edge or boundary (which would
separate its seeming inside from its seeming outside) to be found anywhere within it, its inside *is* its outside. The geometry of our psyche
is analogous to a Klein bottle in that the psyche appears to have an
inside (the world within our head) and an outside (the external world)

---

*This can help us understand the revelations emerging from quantum physics, which,
by deeply exploring the microstructure—the building blocks—of the outer world,
discovered that it is inseparable from the inner world of consciousness.

when we are only attending to a part of it, but when we see our whole nature, we realize that the psyche and the world are ultimately insepa-rable. The psyche infuses (and is fused with) the world such that the world is indistinguishable from and exists within the psyche, just like the psyche exists within the world. In other words, the psyche is not simply contained within our skull, but rather, we are contained within the psyche. This is another way of saying that we are having a collec-tively shared dream.

Christ said in the Gospel of Thomas (Saying 22) that we enter the kingdom of heaven, "when we *make* the inner as the outer and the outer as the inner." Making the inner as the outer isn't simply a passive act of recognizing a state of already existing affairs (for the inner and the outer, being inseparable, are always one and reflect each other, but are oftentimes not recognized as such); it is rather an active act of doing and then living out of and from this realization. In other words, the shamanic intervention is a combination of being receptive (feminine) and active (masculine) at the same time. Interestingly, another anal-ogy Christ uses to express this paradoxical state in the same Gospel of Thomas is "to make the male and the female into a single one."

If someone in their world is suffering from an illness, the shaman recognizes this to be a part of themself that is sick and out of bal-ance. The shaman is able to use their own ability to restore and bring themself back into balance in order to affect a change in the under-lying field, which increases the probability that the sick person can more easily find their way back to health too. This shamanic practice is at the root of healing traditions throughout the world. It's as if the shaman's self-regulating psychospiritual immune system expands from the personal to the transpersonal, from the local to the nonlocal, as it extends outside of its individual physical organism to include oth-ers, as well as the entire environment (which is potentially the whole universe).

In the big picture, once humanity arrived on the scene and our consciousness developed to the point that we became somewhat aware

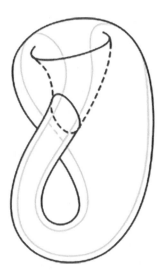

A Klein bottle can be considered to be a three-dimensional version
of a Möbius strip (a seemingly two-sided strip that actually has
only one side) in that it appears to have an inside and an outside
but upon closer inspection it actually has only one side. Just like
the psyche, what initially seems to be the "inside" and the "outside"
of the Klein bottle are actually one and the same side.

of ourselves, self-conscious relative to the world around us, it served
the evolution of our species to think of the outside world as being
separate from us. This helped protect us from becoming overwhelmed
with too much empathy in dangerous situations, which could become
problematic when what was needed was fight or flight, such as when
predators were attacking us. This adaptation, seeing ourselves as separate from the rest of the world, though a survival advantage in prehis-
toric times, is now antiquated and no longer serves our best interests.
Over the ages, by reifying our sense of separateness from one another,
we have deadened our empathic resonance with all living things, and
this, in an ever-more complex and interdependent global community,
is increasingly killing us.

The survival of our species depends on answering the shamanic
call of a deeper spiritual imperative that is pulsing through the veins
of humanity for us to see through the illusion of thinking that we are

separate, both from the world and from one another. The reason why shamanism is so efficacious is because we are ultimately all connected with one another. Recognizing our interconnectedness with all of life, the shaman realizes that we depend on one another for our very survival. This deeper evolutionary impulse that is organically emerging from the universe is *in-forming* the potential spiritual awakening of humanity—depending, of course, on whether we listen to the call of our inner voice.

Einstein says we are all interconnected parts of the whole universe, yet we somehow experience ourselves as being separate from it and from one another. He calls this an "optical delusion of consciousness. . . . This delusion is a kind of prison for us. . . . Our task must be to free ourselves from this prison by widening our circle of compassion."[17]

The thinking that we are separate from one another and from the universe is what a shaman or a genuine spiritual practitioner can see through and dispel through their compassion for all those who are still suffering under this self-created delusion.

Most of us have become conditioned to passively accept our imprisonment in this dualistic state as being normal, such that we aren't even aware that there is an actual state called freedom, having become so accustomed to our confinement that we conflate it with freedom. The first and most crucial step in breaking free from this self-created prison is to cultivate the awareness that we are in it. Freeing ourselves from this prison, as Einstein suggests, must become our main task.

The accomplished shaman can see through the primordial duality between dreaming and waking, inner and outer, and spirit and matter. To a shaman, there is ultimately no difference between helping others and helping oneself, as the illusory self-other duality is dissolved in the light of consciousness. The gift of the shaman is the ability to light up what others perceive as darkness; the journey of the shaman, when we get right down to it, is all about helping a humanity that is perilously close to losing its way.

Shamanism in Everyday Life

We are all potential healers and dreamers; our very nature is shamanic. We all have shamanic abilities that knowingly or unknowingly we use every day. We tend to think of shamanic gifts as being very esoteric and supernatural, but these abilities are, in addition to being celestial, in actuality very down-to-earth and therefore easy to miss. We oftentimes think of shamans as being adorned in feathers, wearing sacred beads, shaking rattles, and banging drums, but modern-day shamans can just as easily wear ordinary clothes and have normal mainstream jobs and seemingly mundane lives.

Young children are natural shamans. Oftentimes kids will unknowingly act out the unconscious parts of their parents. Kids are so attuned to their parents' psyches that if a part of the parents' psyches is not integrated, but rather, is compartmentalized, left in the shadows and not being dealt with consciously, the highly sensitive kid will feel this. It's not uncommon for the naturally sensitive child (which all kids are) to get dreamed up to either trigger this unconscious part of the parent or to play it out for them.

This is why when a child who was in psychological distress came to Jung for therapy, he would first want to do therapy with the child's parents, for he realized that oftentimes the problems of the child originated in the psyches of the parents. In the bigger picture we are all getting dreamed up to pick up certain roles in other people's processes, be they our parents, an intimate partner, or the larger human community. There is a natural shamanic function that exists within the psyches of all of us.

Many of us, unfortunately, have become conditioned by our educational system and the broader culture to split off from, become numb to, and marginalize our intrinsic shamanic abilities. We are all being dreamed up by the shared unconscious in the family system—which in this case is all of humanity—to act out and give full-bodied form to the marginalized part of the collective group's unconscious.

An accomplished shaman is someone who unfolds this unconscious process by adding consciousness to it, whether it be within their own mind or within the shared container of the community. They typically "make light" of the unconscious shadow they are picking up in the field, which carries a double meaning: to create light by alchemically turning the darkness of the shadow into light, as well as to add humor to the heaviness of the shadow—to not take it so seriously. This is why the shaman is often associated with the archetype of the trickster, the Divine Fool; Mercurius, a kin of wetiko, is a trickster par excellence.

One of the chief features of the shamanic aspect of ourselves is to be able to see through so as to see beyond—and step out of—our limited sense of who we imagine we are. Here's an example of something I do as a writer that is very shamanic. Say I've written an article and I begin to wonder what a particular person whose perspective I value would think about what I've written. I will then read the piece, consciously imagining I'm them, stepping into imagining what *they* would think as I read it. Even though I've read my piece countless times, whenever I do this exercise I always have new insights that never occurred to me when I was reading my piece as the one who has written it.

What makes me refer to this as a shamanic process is that by doing this I've stepped out of my habitual identity pattern and am seeing the world—via my creative imagination—through another's eyes, stepping into their shoes, so to speak. Through sympathetic resonance I have stepped out of myself and my limited point of view, and by traveling on the wings of the creative imagination I have stepped into another identity and corresponding worldview in a way that is helpful to me (it improved my article, for example).

We enact processes like this every day, mostly unconsciously. For example, many of us see ourselves through the lens of how we imagine other people see us, which then conditions and affects our actual behavior. In essence, instead of simply being who we are and seeing the world through our own eyes, we will see ourself through the imagined eyes of others, which severely constricts our freedom to simply be who we really are. We have then given away our power to the outside world, to which we become enthralled. We then try to behave in ways that fit our carefully constructed self-image of who we imagine we are according to the eyes of the world. Becoming blind to our own authentic nature, we have disconnected from—and outsourced—our own vision.

This, too, is a shamanic process in that we step out of our own point of view and via our creative imagination assume an imaginary other's perspective of who we are, but in a way that suffocates our true creative expression. Notice the difference between these two examples: the first scenario (of consciously imagining that I'm reading my writing as someone else) inspires my creative expression and expands my sense of self; the second example constrains our creative expression and constricts our idea of who we are. We are truly magicians who knowingly or unknowingly wield creative power beyond measure. It makes all the difference in the world whether we use our shamanic gifts consciously or not.

It's No Time to Be "Normal"

These times of "the new normal" are not normal times at all. To connect with our underlying shamanic identity is to have the courage to step out of appearing to be normal. We are all inhabitants of two realms simultaneously: ordinary, mundane, mainstream consensus reality, and the nonconsensus shamanic reality of dreaming that is enfolded within our day-to-day lives. As we become integrated within, we can fluidly navigate between these two seemingly opposite realms and manage to skillfully assume whatever role we are being asked to step into by circumstances in the moment.

Psychoanalyst Joyce McDougall uses the term *normopathy* to connote an excessive and pathological attachment and adaptation to conventional social norms. English psychoanalyst Christopher Bollas uses a word with a similar meaning, *normotic*,* which seems to be a play on the word *neurotic*. Not having developed a sense of self, people who are normopathic or normotic have a neurotic obsession to appear normal, to fit in. They are abnormally normal. At the bottom of this malady is an insecurity of being judged and rejected. Normotics are overly concerned with how others view them, which makes them afraid to creatively express their unique individuality, which results in them being reticent to participate in the call of their own individuation. As Jung counsels, we should be afraid of being too healthy-minded, as ironically this can easily become unhealthy. Overly healthy-minded people are what Jung refers to as being "pathologically normal."

Families, groups, and societies can all be afflicted with normopathy (according to whatever the group's rules are regarding what is considered "normal"), such that it is considered normal to be normotic. The strange thing is that if almost everyone in the group is normotic, this pathology is seen as normal and healthy—which makes the person in the group who isn't subscribing to being normotic appear to be abnormal, the one with the pathology. Insanely, in a case of projecting their own craziness, the ones with the pathology then pathologize the one who doesn't have it. Something of this nature is going on in our world at present.

To the extent that we are not in touch with ourselves and want to appear normal, we are susceptible to taking on other people's version of the agreed-upon consensus reality. Our willingness to become a card-carrying member of the prevailing consensus viewpoint of the group disconnects us from our true power and agency. We are then easily manipulated by external forces that control the collective narrative about what is happening in the world.

---

*One of my readers informed me that this idea was originally presented in the book *Normose: A Patologia de Normalidade*, authored by Pierre Weil, Jean Yves-Leloup, and Roberto Crema. Though my Spanish is not very good, the translation of the title, *Normosis: A Pathology of Normality*, clearly points to how being overly normal can be pathological. They refer to this condition as the pathology of modernity.

Whichever term we use, *normopathic* or *normotic,* there are many of us who derive our self-worth through external validation by others. Being social creatures, we have an unconscious undertow that pushes us to want to belong to a group, which can disconnect us from our natural urge to individuate. Instead of seeing the world through our own eyes, we then see the world and ourself not through the eyes of others, but how we *imagine* others see us. We're still using our creative imagination, but the difference is we're giving our power away to others. To connect with our own sovereignty we have to find the source of our true creative power within.

In the challenging times that we are living in, it is crucially important that we *not* fit in. Instead, we must express the creative spirit that more than anything wants to come through us and find its place in the world. Instead of passively subscribing to "the new normal," let's create "the new abnormal," in which we engage in the radical act of being our naturally creative shamanic selves. Whereas repressed and unexpressed creativity is the greatest poison to the human psyche, creativity that is given free reign to express itself is the greatest medicine imaginable.

The Shaman as Artist

The shamanic trip is a spiritual and alchemical art form. By submerging into the depths of the unconscious and creatively symbolizing what they experience during their encounter with the dark and light forces there, the shaman is an artist par excellence.

As we willingly succumb to and embrace the demon again and again, instead of feeding it, we feed our creative expression and get in touch with who we really are. By creatively expressing what moves us, the *demon* in the sickness reveals itself to be a *daemon,* our inner voice and guiding spirit. Assenting to our natural shamanic calling helps us to become our own best allies. Our daemon, the source of our genius, is the inspiration for the most sublime creativity imaginable. A shaman, after all is said and done, is none other than a creative artist of the spirit.

Similar to how a shaman/wounded healer takes the suffering of the entire community within, Christ—the very embodiment of this archetype—descended from the heavens, so to speak, to experience firsthand (from the inside), and then *re-present* and creatively express, both literally and symbolically, what it is like to be a limited, suffering human being. Paradoxically, the moment of experiencing what it is to be a finite human being is when God actualized the infinitude of his divinity. This is why Jung referred to the shaman as an "approximation of the savior."[18]

Vincent Van Gogh regarded Christ as an extraordinary artist who didn't make paintings, but rather, through his intimate experience of taking on the proverbial suffering of humanity, worked in living flesh and blood to transform human beings into immortal, eternal souls. Similarly, artist, poet, and visionary William Blake wrote that "Jesus and his Apostles and Disciples were all Artists—A Poet, a Painter, a Musician, an Architect: The Man or Woman who is not one of these is not a Christian."[19] To offer oneself as an instrument for something beyond us to come through and creatively express itself is to be truly following in Christ's footsteps.

Christ was the supreme artist and shaman; his life exemplified this archetype in human form. Obeying the inner call of his vocation, Jesus chose to voluntarily expose himself to the assaults of what Jung called "the imperialistic madness"[20] that ruled the day. Instead of being suppressed by this onslaught of wetiko, he consciously let it have its way with him, thereby assimilating it into his wholeness. By having it out with wetiko and taking the archetypal form of the madness and evil of his day within, but then adding consciousness to this process, Jesus was able to integrate it into his divine light. The nature of the psychic power that Jesus encountered was the power-intoxicated devil of that time, the will-to-power of the unintegrated shadow—a mindset as rampant today as it was two thousand years ago.

A Semblance of Evil

In our shamanic encounter with evil—depending on what we make of it—we can potentially realize, in Jung's words, that it is "only a semblance of evil,"[21] and is actually a Luciferian bringer of light in the true sense of the word. In his writings on Mercurius, Jung describes this figure as an "adumbration,"[22] a foreshadowing and preconfiguration of the primordial light-bringer. It is noteworthy that by assimilating the demon of sickness, we can potentially return to a greater state of health than before. And so what convincingly *seems* to be evil in actuality could be a bringer of some greater good that wouldn't have been able to arise without its arrival on the scene—a precise description of the underlying workings of wetiko.

Being archetypal, meaning it pervades the nonlocal field and exists deep within the collective unconscious, the demon of sickness, wetiko, can potentially make us conscious of the evil and sickness from which the whole community is suffering, be it the nation or the whole human race. This darkness is presented to us and subjectively experienced in a unique form particular to each one of us, which makes it easy to assume that it is only an individual characteristic that belongs to us personally rather than realizing that it is a characteristic enfolded throughout the nonlocal field.

It is a key moment in our healing when we snap out of interpreting our experience of wetiko sickness from the merely personal and reductive point of view that leaves us in a state of despair, where we feel disillusioned, resigned, and victimized. When we instead see it as being our personal share in a wider archetypal experience that is encoded throughout the whole universe, we can step out of pathologizing ourself—liberating us from Jung's "curse of pathology"—and recontextualize our personal share in the *dis-ease* of being human as being part of a wider transpersonal pattern holographically enfolded throughout the global field of human experience.

The shaman suffers from the plight of their people (which in our modern-day global village is all of humanity) and the spirit of their age.

By making the sickness and evil from which the whole of humanity is suffering conscious, the shaman carries the practically unbearable creative tension of balancing, holding, and mediating within themselves the unconsciousness of humanity as a whole. The shaman's sacred vocation—their cross to bear—is to carry the weight of our species' collective psychosis without going permanently crazy in the process.

The journey of the shaman invariably involves stepping out of the illusion that we exist as a separate self as we *re-member* our interconnectedness and realize that what we are experiencing within our individual life is a unique instantiation of something that pervades the universe, and which everyone else, in their own unique way, is also experiencing. As if an iteration of a deeper fractal, our personal experience of the demon of sickness is, in condensed form, the localized signature of the impersonal collective sickness from which our species is suffering. This realization allows us to step into our shamanic garment so to speak, as we realize that whatever aspect of the collective sickness we are experiencing on a personal level, though it is ours to deal with and take responsibility for, doesn't ultimately belong to us, but being transpersonal, is something that everyone is feeling and dealing with in their own way.

Notably, the healing, radiant light of their true nature that the shaman brings to bear on the illness is likewise not theirs in the sense that they don't own, possess, or control it. It is a power that is beyond them. It is the spontaneous expression of the creativity of their—and our—nature. Like an app that's been installed in the operating system of our very being, this is a latent superhero power that we all unknowingly possess. It's an innate part of our nature. The healing that is available to us via our ability to respond to the call of the shamanic archetype is built into the design of being human. Once our intrinsic healing power is recognized by us and goes psychically online, there is nothing else to do but to creatively share it with others, as this healing power belongs to all of us and only increases in power the more it is shared with others.

PART II

Angels, Demons, and Rebirth

As humanity deepens in its process of awakening, there is no getting around a showdown with the forces of darkness. To help us in this encounter, in this section we are introduced to the inner guide, the daemon/angel, an archetypal form that lives within us as a necessary ally in our coming to terms with the equally daemonic energy of wetiko. Analogous to how a symbol in a dream is created by our activated unconscious in order to transform the psyche, the creative tension emerging from our inner neurotic split can be likened to being pregnant, in that the psyche wants to birth something new. We explore the nature of symbols—symbols being the language of dreams—and the importance of cultivating symbolic awareness, which is to interpret events in our lives symbolically, just as we would a dream. We reflect on the idea that by viewing Christ, who symbolically speaking, represents the Higher Self, and the events that transpired through him symbolically (a way of seeing that Christ himself, as revealed in the apocryphal texts, was trying to get across to his disciples), we can transmute the poison that is wetiko into the medicine we need today. We then explore the crucial role that connecting with our creativity plays in a deeper cosmic dreaming process to potentially bring about the redemption, liberation, and incarnation of the Higher Self. This section concludes with reflections on a work of genius, a short but highly controversial essay by Jung about how we can connect with the light when we find ourselves in a time of darkness. Jung was pointing at wetiko.

5

The Battle
for Our Angel

There is a particularly powerful practice in the Islamic tradition that was specially crafted to dissolve the pernicious effects of wetiko. Similar to the way we reflect on images in a dream to discover their deeper symbolic nature, in esoteric Islam the practice of *ta'wil* leads us back to the hidden, inner source of our experience. The sacred art of ta'wil is designed to transmute the sensory data of the physical world into symbols, thereby transfiguring our experience of the world around us, as well as ourselves. Ta'wil, an Arabic term which is fundamental to the spiritual hermeneutics of the Qur'an but can be conceived of as being the central task of any spiritual discipline regardless of tradition, leads beyond a literal understanding of the world so as to recover and reveal the hidden world encoded within our sense perceptions.

In Western tradition, the art of ta'wil is known as *epistrophe*, which comes from the Greek and means a *re-version* (telling a different version of the story). It is the practice of returning a common, everyday phenomenon to its deeper archetypal source. The process of epistrophe is based on the neoplatonic idea that all psychological phenomena have a similarity and correspondence with the deeper archetypal pattern and mythic substrate with which they resonate, to which they belong, and of which they are an emanation.

The art of ta'wil amplifies Jung's practice of cultivating symbolic awareness as far as it can go. Ta'wil is based on the idea that there is not just one level of interpretation, but rather, there are multi-layered levels of symbolic meaning encoded within the fabric of our dreamlike world, and as we unfold these multiple levels of meaning, we are led back to the very source of our soul. Our practice of ta'wil is ever-deepening, similar to how we can continually recognize deeper dimensions within a dream we are having. The art of ta'wil is similar to being in a night dream while—as part of our experience in the dream—we are reflecting upon our dream experiences so as to decipher the symbolic nature of the dream we are having. This process leads us to deeper levels of lucidity until we access the creative source of our dream experience, which is not just our ego, but the dreamer of the dreamer: the Self. Interpreting events in the world literally, "by the book," is a form of blindness, as this way of seeing the world, imagining it exists objectively, separate from ourselves, can deflate, sterilize, and demythologize the sacred dimension of the world and can be considered to be the true Fall of humanity. Thinking we see the world objectively turns *us* into seeming objects as well, an operation that ultimately immobilizes our human potential and literally is in the service of killing the soul.

Seeing life through the eyes of literal-mindedness, which is a form of blindness that interprets events in our world literally, disables our ability to practice ta'wil, which is based on the realization that there is no such "thing" as an objective world separate from the observer. This is to realize that our world isn't a given whose meaning is etched in concrete, and that our experience is in fact akin to a dream whose deeper meaning can only be found from deep introspection and self-reflection. Recognizing the dreamlike nature of the world is to realize that our world is literally thirsting to be interpreted. This is where we—and the spiritual practice of ta'wil—comes in.

The art of ta'wil can be thought of as a gift from our dreamlike universe, but it is a unique type of gift that will only bestow its blessings if we accept its invitation to actively participate in its practice.

In the practice of ta'wil, it is as if the dreamlike universe is coming to our aid, offering us a sacred practice to more deeply engage with and realize its—and our—nature. Once we cultivate the art of ta'wil, the wetiko mind-virus has no foothold, no place to stand, as wetiko's manifestation in our world itself becomes an object of our ta'wil, which not only takes away wetiko's power over us, but deepens the realization of our true nature at the same time. In light of this realization, the present inquiry in which we're shedding light on wetiko is a form of ta'wil.

The art of ta'wil is not accomplished by our mind or intellect, but is a vehicle for a deeper, higher, and more true part of ourselves to make itself known to us. In the same way that the process of individuation is inspired by the Self (rather than the ego), the practice of ta'wil is inspired by the guiding spirit that lives inside of us, what can be thought of as our angel. Our angel doesn't just serve as inspiration for the practice of ta'wil—once we accomplish this art, we become introduced to, familiar with, and in relationship with our angel. It is as if the angel is using our ta'wil to lead us back to itself, which ultimately brings us back to our true home. Just like the Self needs the co-operation of our ego to fully individuate, our angel by itself can do nothing for us—it needs our willing engagement with it in order to accomplish its divinely-sanctioned mission of bringing us back to ourselves.

In modern times, to quote the great Islamic philosopher, theologian, and mystic Henry Corbin, there is a "battle for the Soul of the World,"[1] which is in essence a spiritual battle for the human soul, the dwelling place within us of the Divine Presence. As Corbin points out, this is ultimately a battle for our celestial guiding spirit, who takes the form of our angel. Corbin maintains that we are battling together with our angel against the dark forces that obscure the light of the world from shining; we are also battling to *re-claim* and unite with our angel, who represents none other than our true and perfect nature.

Hermes/Mercury

The universe is a primordial and endlessly unfolding revelation that speaks symbolically, which is the language of dreams. The world is a living symbolic scripture, the literal and symbolic book of life. The whole of creation is a cosmic text thirsting for interpretation, a living embodiment of "the Word" manifesting the various names of the Divine, so everything depends on our interpretation of this very moment. Realizing that all things speak inspires us to develop a hermeneutics, or method of interpretation, that reflects back our realization that the sacred Word becomes materialized in each moment; everything is theophany, a manifestation of the Divine in form, a *reve(a)l-ation* of God.

The art of hermeneutics has to do with interpretation and meaning-making, which are creative processes. The word *hermeneutics* is related to and derived from the Greek god Hermes, also known as Mercury (or Mercurius), who is the god of alchemy. Symbolically speaking, Hermes/Mercury is the god of interpretation and language, among many other things as well. Wetiko is a semantic syndrome, a phenomenon that is related to how we use language and thereby place meaning on, interpret, and hence create our experience. This is one of the many ways that wetiko is akin to Hermes/Mercury. This is why the art of interpretation that is fundamental to the practice of ta'wil is related to dissolving the negative effects of wetiko.

In Mercurius, both Jung and the alchemists were tracking an essential feature of wetiko but calling it by a different name. The alchemists never ceased to point at Mercurius's psychic nature, which is to say that like wetiko, it exists within and operates through the psyche. Jung realized that whatever it is, Mercurius intrinsically possesses the very qualities that we so desperately need to heal the psychic split in ourselves. An alchemical text states, "Whatever the wise seek is in mercury."[2] The same could be said about wetiko: what we, in our wildest dreams, are all looking for is actually to be found in wetiko. This is because Mercurius, that is, wetiko, can be conceived of as a process that appears at first to be evil and ends up bringing about good. Being quantum in nature, in which the whole universe is forever "in process," either of these outcomes, good or evil, are potentialities. How the figure of Mercurius/wetiko manifests is a function of whether we can comprehend what it is revealing to us. How a thing turns out—and the real effect it has upon us—depends upon how we interpret it, how we dream it—this is where we access our creative power, and this is where ta'wil comes in.

Hermeneutics, the practice of interpreting sacred texts, has as its task the transfiguration of the world by means of unveiling the Word in all things. Corbin writes, "If the true meaning of the Book is the interior meaning, hidden under the literal appearance, then from the instant that men fail to recognize or refuse this interior meaning, from that instant they mutilate the unity of the Word . . . and begin the drama of the 'Lost Speech.'"[3]

The function of ta'wil as spiritual hermeneutics is to restore the unity of the Word and recover the lost speech. The lost speech means losing the deeper esoteric meaning of words by interpreting them only literally, while not recognizing the deeper, symbolic interior meaning from which they are derived. Recovering the lost speech refers to restoring the deeper symbolic meaning that is lost when we put things in words. The lost speech also arises from a literal interpretation of our world, a perspective which doesn't recognize that the world is a living oracle that is speaking symbolically. Recognizing the symbolic dimension of reality invites us to carry back the symbols that come our way— whether in our waking or sleeping dream—to the source of their deeper meaning. When we mutilate the unity of the Word and fall into the drama of the lost speech, we become out of phase with ourself and out of integrity with our soul, and then our creative self-expression isn't in alignment with our true nature. Recovering the lost speech in essence means to find our inner voice and inner author-ity, a voice that is ultimately not separate from, but inspired and author-ized by our angel.

Words contain multiple levels of meaning encoded within them. We can say that something—let's call it wetiko—is getting *dreamed* up into the world, is *playing* out in our world, is getting *acted* out on the world *stage*. These words are subtly suggesting and evoking a sense of dream-like theater—that we are acting something out on the stage in a theater, and we are being dreamed up to do so. These words also imply that the whole thing is a play. Encoded in this way of talking is its own lucidity stimulator. Hidden within the words is a subtle power to awaken us, to remind us that we are dreaming. Remembering the dream is to remember the truth of our situation, which is to realize that we have more options at our disposal than we have been imagining. This discovery is a profoundly healing and freeing experience. It's as if these words are emanations of the dreamlike nature of life signalling to us in order to help us remember the dream. Such words are like ciphers bringing us to another dimension, but only if we decipher them and allow ourselves to be led back and carried to their source. In performing our own ta'wil on these words, we retrieve a piece of our soul.

To recover the lost speech requires that our words, and thus our world, be born anew. The creation, discovery, and expression of our own authentic voice results in freedom from the compulsion of the demonic aspect of wetiko. The power of clearly articulated and inspired speech is one of the greatest of humanity's divinely sponsored powers. To find our authentic voice and speak is to translate our experiences into creative expression, which is to say that speaking with the voice that is truly ours is itself a primordial hermeneutic art, a creative, sacred Art with a capital *A*.

It is significant that one of the key things that happens when we suffer an overwhelming trauma or experience abuse is that we become internally fragmented and dissociated, such that we aren't able to access our inner voice. Therefore, in finding our authentic voice we are tapping into the magical, imaginative power of language to *re-create* ourself and our world anew. Language is not merely a way of describing and communicating our ideas about the world; its nature is essentially creative, as language is a tool for bringing the world into existence in the first place. As we find a fitting expression for our experience that arises out of a deep listening, we refine, *re-find*, and "found" our own language, *art-iculating* our world on our own terms, becoming a poet of our own psyche.

Ta'wil

The practice of ta'wil alchemically transforms the impersonal archetypal forces of our nature that can limit us and force us to act compulsively into qualities that feed and nurture our one-of-a-kind individuality, helping us creatively express and give voice to our true nature in our own unique way. When we are unconsciously identified with these impersonal forces—which is to be possessed by them—these powerful transpersonal forces drive us to act them out in our life. Through the practice of ta'wil, we add awareness, symbolize, creatively express, and thus differentiate ourselves from these transpersonal forces such that we are then able to more consciously relate to them and thereby consciously choose our behavior. Ta'wil connects us with the particular angel who looks after us, who can be thought of as our guardian angel whose one-of-a-kindness has the quality of "singularizing" us, animating our own inner voice, making each one of us the unique individual that we truly are. The more we connect with what could be called our "angel of individuation," the more we become who we truly are. It is only in connecting with our true nature, that our angel is the emissary for, can any real healing take place. In helping us remember ourselves, the art of ta'wil, which is inspired by our angel, is continually in service to us. In helping us find our unique voice, the voice that belongs to us, our angel, who *is* our true inner voice, is assisting us to find and articulate the lost speech. The figure of the angel is the archetypal hermeneut, or interpreter, whose speech, as our authentic inner voice, is the lost poetry of creation. Instead of the story of our life being rendered in non-negotiable prose, our angel is inspiring us to become artists and poets of life itself.

In plumbing the depths of meaning beyond the literal, the art of ta'wil enables us to see through the illusory objectivity of the world, inducing the transcendent meaning hidden within the seemingly superficial dimension of our world to reveal itself. Instead of becoming entranced by the seemingly solid and predetermined forms of the world, when we see through its images—whether these images be the world itself, painted images, or images in our mind—they are transformed into sacred icons through which the numinous, hidden reality of the soul shines forth and reveals itself. The act of ta'wil reveals the world to be a transparent see-through medium that allows us to see beyond it by seeing through the illusion of its objectivity. It is only in seeing through ourself that we are able to recognize the transparency of the world, which is merely reflecting our own state. It's as if the forms themselves become windows, inviting us to explore what lies beyond their surface appearance. Paradoxically, we find that what is hidden can only be seen through what is apparent. It is as if in the manifestation of our world the soul is simultaneously revealing itself through its veiling of itself. Acting as a bridge, the art of ta'wil reveals the correspondence between the hidden and the visible.

The practice of ta'wil engages the depths of our soul. It traces back and leads a thing to its source, to its principle, its archetype, to its true reality; in the process it carries us back to our own origin, to the creative source of ourselves. We are participating in a double cosmic movement— genesis and return, descent and ascent to the origin. First there is the act of revelation: sending down a sacred "text," written as the forms of the world all around us. Then there is the act of ta'wil: putting this "text" in its true *con-text* and thus returning it to its source. Ta'wil, or esoteric exegesis, to quote Corbin, is an operation that "properly consists in 'bringing back,' re-calling, returning to its origin, not only the text of a book but the cosmic context in which the soul is imprisoned. The soul must free this context, and free itself from it, by transmuting it into symbols."[4]

The art of ta'wil not only sees the world symbolically, it *recon-text-ualizes* and thereby carries the symbol back to the divine ground from which it ultimately derives. In carrying back the symbol to what it symbolizes, the practice of ta'wil connects the symbol with what, in Corbin's innovative phrasing, it "symbolizes with." The energies that drive the *re-version* to the source carry not only the symbol but also, in one unified movement of awakening and revelation, the soul of the interpreter as well. To quote Corbin, "Transmutation of the sensible and imaginable into symbol, return of the symbol to the situation that brought it to flower—these two movements open and close the hermeneutic circle."[5] The ta'wil of the symbol re-produces and is a "re-citation"—a speaking—of the ta'wil of the soul itself, as the circulation of the hermeneutic circle closes on itself.

Due to the impossibility of interpreting a text without transforming the reader/interpreter, the art of hermeneutics becomes a liturgical act of transfiguration, conferring sacramental gnosis on the participant. The soul can't restore a text to its truth unless it returns itself to its own truth, that is, awakens to its true nature. The practice of ta'wil thus transforms the soul, as the experience and recognition of the deeper meaning of a symbol is always an individual, individuating, and transformative event that profoundly changes us ontologically, in the very core of our being.

The practice of ta'wil has nothing to do with rational intellectual deliberation of ideas or manipulating concepts. Ta'wil is neither a mental nor a linguistic exercise, but rather its opposite, as it takes intellect and language back to their source as true spirit. The act of ta'wil doesn't involve forming new concepts; rather, it unveils and renders transparent what makes us develop these concepts in the first place. In essence, the process of ta'wil is the uncovering of what is happening deep within us, behind the surface operations of the mind. Going beyond conformity, beyond collectively accepted opinions, beyond being slaves to the letter of the law, the art of ta'wil connects us to our own intrinsic authority to author and consciously create our experience of ourself and our world, and it does this by intentionally and consciously engaging in the creative act of interpretation and meaning-making. In this way we write and live the genuine story of our life. This requires no external authority for validation, no middle man for mediation other than our true and authentic self. The art of ta'wil puts any institution that dictates "official" interpretations and attempts to interpose itself between us and Spirit out of business in a heartbeat.

The practitioner of ta'wil recognizes that nature itself is speaking, that our world is itself an oracle and never-ending divination of itself, and thus it takes a special kind of attention to hear and "read" it. Ta'wil's mode of interpretation is not an "anything goes" type of thing, as it doesn't arbitrarily construct meaning out of thin air, but simultaneously creates and discovers meaning that is implicitly encoded in the fabric of the multidimensional, dreamlike nature of the world as it intersects with our mind. Whether we are able to find that deeper meaning woven into the multiple levels of reality depends on whether we have cultivated sufficient access to the variety of internal dimensions within ourselves.

The universe is an ongoing creation, recreating itself and emerging anew out of the plenum of infinite possibilities every nanosecond. Our dynamic, ever-evolving universe is continually speaking to us as it constantly evolves into different versions of itself, hence it is in need of a perpetual ta'wil. When we recognize the dreamlike nature of reality, all things call for a hermeneutics; everything demands to be carried back from its outer surface appearance to its real, essential but hidden form. Continually unfolding our ta'wil ensures that we don't fall prey to a dogmatic certainty, become absorbed in righteous delusions of absolute knowledge and fixed meanings, and hence, become rigidly entrenched in a viewpoint, all of which are signs of wetiko at work. The world is never explained once and for all, but must be continually deciphered, just as a musical score is never deciphered once and for all, but calls to be played again and again in ever more nuanced, refined, expressive, and novel forms. In the act of ta'wil, we are bearing down into the spiritual truth of things, thereby dissolving the authoritarian influence of the mind-virus that imputes a fixed meaning on things. In the art of ta'wil we connect with our own intrinsic authority as we step into becoming the author, instead of the victim, of the story of our life.

The practice of ta'wil renders the world transparent to the indwelling light invested within it, as the forms of the world are raised to incandescence, the hidden meaning of its forms shining through their outer covering. The primordial light inherent to the nature of the soul ultimately allows it to accomplish the ta'wil and perceive the light shining through the world, an inner light that is recognized to be of the same nature as the light of the soul itself. As long as we remain opaque to ourselves, however, we will become immobilized in fixed interpretations that seem to be written in stone, unable to see the light shining through all things. However, in this co-operative contemplation of the process of ta'wil that we are mutually creating and discovering in the writing and reading of these very words in this very moment, we are performing our own ta'wil.

The Angel

An imaginative reading of a text, of the world, or the soul, is as much an act of writing as reading, as much creation as discovery, for it requires us to work in concert with the Divine. Author Tom Cheetham, a contemporary interpreter of Corbin's work, writes in *All the World an Icon: Henry Corbin and the Angelic Function of Beings*, "The ta'wil is that cosmically unique process by means of which a divine figure, an Angel, meets with, struggles for, and transforms *with* an incarnate human soul. The conjunction, the 'coupling,' produces the eternal individual."[6] Our angel needs the co-operation of our soul for it to fulfill its destiny. Only through the union of these two figures can the potentially eternal, greater personality within us be made actual. The Paraclete, the Holy Spirit, is considered to be the unveiler and discloser of what is hidden; it is the initiator, guiding spirit, and sponsor of the ta'wil.

Our challenge is to become whole, and this requires not only assimilating our shadow, but also recognizing, stepping into, and uniting with our light. We are always yoked—in a syzygy—with our angel, who exists as an untapped potency within us, whether we know it or not. "The soul discovers itself to be the earthly counterpart of another being with which it forms a totality that is dual in structure," says Corbin.[7] It is as if in our earthly manifestation, we are a lower-level reflection of a higher-dimensional, intra/extraterrestial counterpart. This is our angel, whose "job" is to not only help us see our light, but to help us see and integrate our shadow into the light of conscious awareness in order to attain our wholeness.

Uniting with our angel completes our being, for without mingling and connecting with our celestial guiding spirit we are not fully authentic as a human being; it is as if our soul, in its seeming inaccessibility, has gone off-line. Without the ta'wil that effects this union, divine creativity has no "place" to express itself in our human realm, as the Divine and humanity then have no place in which to meet. A disjunction is thus produced between these two realms, and a chasm opens up within the wholeness of being. In a very real sense, this very inquiry into the nature of the angel is inspired by the angel itself, as we, both writer and reader—both angel and the human recipient of its messages—collaboratively tease out the angel so as to allow it to reveal itself through our co-contemplation.

The point of any spiritual initiation process in indigenous cultures is to introduce and connect the initiate with his or her personal guardian spirit. Wisdom traditions worldwide have considered that we have a higher-dimensional guide, a heavenly witness and divine alter ego, a transcendent counterpart and celestial partner (our eternal other and better half) who accompanies us on our life journey and with whom we co-create our life, knowingly or not. For Jung, the real goal of psychotherapy is to find and connect with the unconscious guide that dwells within us. This is the same goal of a successful shamanic initiation.

Our angel is the eternally active source of our being. Our guide of light has a multiplicity of names, having as many as can be imagined, which is emblematic of its miraculous-seeming nature. Its very presence bears witness to the reality of the invisible. Oftentimes our angel announces its presence in and through events in our life, as if it arranges events in the outside world so as to express itself.

We are essentially a bi-unity, what Corbin refers to as an "unus-ambo"[8] (one-both). It makes no sense to even think about who we are as being separate from our angel, as the two of us go together always and everywhere, never one without the other. To quote Psalm 23, "For thou art with me . . . all the days of my life." We are never alone. Each of us—ourselves and our Angel—would not, and could not truly be ourselves without the other.

Jung considered the "treasure hard to attain" to be our companion, the being who goes through life at our side who can inspire us to the most sublime creativity. The philosopher's stone, the goal of alchemy, is a living stone that is equivalent to this companion. An ancient alchemical text personifies this precious stone as saying, "Protect me; I will protect thee. Give me my life, and I will help you."[9] These words are reminiscent of the reciprocally reflective relationship between the conscious and the unconscious in which the attitude we take toward our unconscious is mirrored back to us via its relationship to ourself. For example, if we honor our unconscious as a source of wisdom, it will send us dreams that will serve as evidence to validate our perspective.

Our angel is ultimately who we are in that it is the same as us, a higher aspect of us, while paradoxically, at the same time it is different from and other than who we've been conditioned to think of ourself (a limited ego). We are invited to step out of any unconscious identification with our celestial guiding spirit, differentiating ourself from it as we establish a conscious relationship and enter into dialogue with it. To quote Corbin, "This *unus-ambo* can be taken as an alternation of the first and second person, as forming a dialogic unity thanks to the identity of their essence and yet without confusion of persons."[10] Being the same as our angel, we share in its divine nature, which paradoxically allows us to be fully human. As if distinct beings, however, we and our angel are in relationship with each other while sharing the same essence ("forming a dialogic unity"), and yet we (as an ego) must not unconsciously identify with it, which would create confusion, as well as inflation. Being both the same as and different from is a classic example of the four-valued logic of Buddhism. We can think of our angel as the transcendent part of our personality that connects us to something greater than our limited version of who we imagine ourself to be, while at the same time introducing us to what it is to be fully ourselves and truly human. This essential bi-unity of our nature doesn't easily lend itself to the realm of rational thought or language, which are contained within and constrained by the limiting categories of time and space.

We've All Experienced Angels

We've all experienced angels: we have a lucky hunch, an inspired thought seemingly falls into our head out of nowhere, we have a healing dream, we find the perfect book at just the right time, we synchronistically meet precisely the right person who changes the trajectory of our life—all are examples of encountering a higher-dimensional guiding intelligence that seemingly choreographs our life from behind the scenes. Whether as artists, musicians, scientists, spiritual practitioners, or writers—however we commune with the divinely inspired creative spirit—there is no one who has not at certain moments in life had an experience of being guided and inspired by something beyond oneself.

And yet, *strAngely** enough, in our modern society it is practically taboo—we can be easily marginalized and seen as crazy—if we speak

---

*Much to my surprise (and delight), as I was proofreading this chapter, I noticed that the word *strangely* was spelled *strAngely*. I had already read over the chapter numberless times when I found this. My first thought was, did someone get into my manuscript and play a joke on me? I had never before noticed that the word *strangely* had the word *angel* hidden within it. I interpret this event as the play of my angel. When I put the asterisk after *strAngely* so as to write this footnote, my computer immediately autocorrected the mistake and put the *A* in lowercase, thereby taking out the seeming magic at which I was pointing. Needless to say, I changed the *A* back to being capitalized in order to keep the magic from escaping.

about such things. Our hyperrational, intellectual, scientific, materialistic culture has written angels off relegating them to Hallmark greeting cards) and out of the script of our lives. In our postmodern age, angels have become second-class citizens, practically an endangered species, as if our present-day "enlightened" rationalism has erased angels from our collective memory.

Oftentimes our angel makes its appearance when we feel like a stranger in an estranged world. Archetypically, experiences of angelic presences oftentimes get constellated at times of intense crisis, extreme darkness, or great distress, when we hit bottom. A perfect illustration of this is the book by Gitta Mallasz, *Talking with Angels*. Interestingly, Mallasz doesn't consider herself to be the author of the text, but merely its scribe. This book is a compelling account of four close-knit friends' encounter with a seemingly supernatural angelic force that took place in Hungary during the late stages of the Second World War. To quote from the preface, "That 'the unexplainable,' this 'numinous event' came just at the darkest hour of their lives is surely significant: it shows that possibilities for new ways and for transformation *do* come to us where there seems to be no way out—if only we are open to them."[11] The angel's essential message as related by Mallasz is relevant to our current discussion, as well as being hard to argue with: "What could be more natural than our talking with each other?"[12]

Each of us experiences subtle interventions from our angel every day that easily escape our notice or are just taken for granted. Examples of encounters with nonphysical beings who guide, teach, befriend, and help us abound. Jung writes of such an encounter in his autobiography, *Memories, Dreams, Reflections*. He began having personal experiences of a seemingly autonomous and self-created figure that lived inside of his psyche whom he called Philemon. He didn't treat Philemon as literally real, but as metaphorically real, *as if* he were a real person. In some mysterious way Philemon was both a part of Jung while being other than him. Jung felt that when we fathom an inner figure such as Philemon, this is in the service of fathoming our own depths, a way of deepening our connection with our own vastness. Philemon played the same role in Jung's process that Zarathustra played for Nietzsche and that Virgil assumed for Dante.

Jung entered into dialogues with Philemon and was shocked to realize that this inner figure was teaching Jung things that he himself didn't know. Philemon and the metaphorical reality that he represented taught Jung the crucial insight that became the basis of his entire life's work, what he calls "the reality of the psyche,"[13] an insight so profound—Jung considered it the greatest discovery of psychology in the twentieth century—that it is still in the initial stages of being understood by and integrated into the field of psychology. For example, Philemon revealed to Jung that Jung didn't create his thought's forms (such as Philemon). Not created by Jung, beings such as Philemon can be conceived of as creating themselves as if they had their own type of existence. This insight is hard for many of us to realize due to our habit of identifying with the thoughts that arise in our minds, such that we naively assume we have made them. It took Jung a long time to get used to the idea that there was something that existed in himself that was not him. Based on his inner subjective experience Jung concluded that there was no getting around the fact that there were aspects of his mind that were independent of him and appeared to have an autonomous, seemingly objective existence all their own, and the same is true for all of us. This is why Jung also referred to the reality of the psyche as the autonomous objective psyche, in that it seems to operate autonomously, and is subjectively experienced by us as if it objectively exists. Existing within Jung's inner psychological landscape, the figure of Philemon wasn't just subjective, a mere figment of a wild imagination, but rather it existed in its own realm.

Healing our inner state of dissociation involves the unusual experience of recognizing an alien "other" that exists within us that seemingly has a will of its own. It's a strange and disconcerting experience to first become aware of the existence of a being within our own mind—whatever name we call it—that is not us. This can lead us to a world we hadn't yet imagined that lies within the depths of our being. The reality of the psyche is a realm of experience that is neither objective (existing independently on its own) or subjective (just our imagination/hallucination), but is an amalgam of the two that has an ontological reality all its own. This is the shaman's realm of dreams and visions. Jung makes the point that spiritual statements have to do with the reality of the psyche rather than physical reality.

An example of an encounter with a celestial guiding presence is the book *A Course in Miracles,* which many people consider to be a profound wisdom text of the highest order. Helen Schucman, a psychologist and professor in New York City and an avowed atheist, one day began hearing a voice that instructed her to write down what it was saying, and as if taking dictation, she did as told. The result is a book that has helped and inspired countless people all over the world. Thankfully, neither Schucman nor Jung were pathologized for "hearing voices" (although many of Jung's psychiatric colleagues thought he was "going schizophrenic") and then medicated, as typically happens today in such cases, which at the time would have aborted their encounters with these angelic presences.

The Angel as a Reflection of Who We Are

Our angel is a wholly imaginal* reflection of ourself, a living image that has a reality such that it can help us recognize who we are. Instead of being merely a product of our imagination, we can discover that it's the other way around—*we* are the projection of our angel. Turning our rationalistic, causal conception of things on its head, Jung realized through his inner experiences that instead of these inner figures being derived from our psychic conditions, the psychological state we find ourself in is a function of our relationship to these inner figures.

---

*The imaginal is not imaginary, in that it is quite real. Please see the section "The Imaginal Realm," a few pages ahead.

The Buddha says that we create the world as well as ourselves with our thoughts.* In the long run, we are as we think; thought is creative of real being. In contemplating the angel, Corbin writes that it "endows the soul with the aptitude for thinking it. . . . He is the 'destiny' of that soul . . . causing the soul to be what he himself is."[14] In endowing the soul with the capacity for thinking thoughts, the angel makes us— at least in potential—in the image of itself. Corbin adds the following footnote to his previous thought: "In thinking this thought the person who thinks it is thought by the Angel, or on the contrary by a demon, for the alternative can only be the person 'without an Angel.'"[15] Here, Corbin is contemplating the power of thought to create our universe as well as our experience of ourselves.

Depending on our relationship with our own mind, we can create a living hell on earth or heaven on earth. Heaven and hell are not just states of mind, but "places" created by the mind, by the imagination, which take on a reality. Corbin offers a succinct definition of someone in thrall to the demonic: a "person without an Angel."[16] The implication is clear: if we want to vanquish the demonic aspect that is wetiko, we need to find and connect with our angel, and the sooner, the better.

We can only know our true self by finding, knowing, loving, and having a personal connection to our angel; or to say it differently, we only know ourself when our soul walks in company with our angel. Our angel helps us see ourself by looking at us through our own eyes. Being a mirror, our angel is the very figure that helps us truly see our divine nature. As Corbin points out, the divine being and the being in, through, and to which it reveals itself are all interrelated aspects of one process, for God cannot look at an "other" or be seen by an "other." A real eye-witness, the eyes of the person having a revelation of the Divine, are the same eyes through which the Divine looks. Our heavenly witness assumes our own countenance, as it is the mirror of our own face.

---

*The very first words in the Dhammapada, the wisdom sayings of the Buddha, are as follows: "All that we are is the result of what we have thought."

At the same time we often catch glimpses of our Angel out of the corner of our eye.

Interestingly, when we see a reflection of ourself in a mirror in a night dream it often symbolizes and is a reflection of a split-off part of ourself that we are projecting outward, and which is being reflected back to us through the mirror of our own mind. Being that dreams are reflections of our mind, when we see a reflection of ourself in a dream we are actually seeing a reflection within a reflection. This is an invitation for us to *speculatively* (note: the word *speculate* etymologically derives from the word *speculum*, which is Latin for "mirror") reflect on the image, as well as on ourself, so that we might *re-cognize* and integrate this previously unconscious part of ourself. Similarly, our inner vision of our angelic counterpart is a reflection of a heretofore unknown part of ourself. Connecting with our angel helps us lighten up, to not take ourself so seriously, to let go of our self-importance.

Meeting our angelic guide marks the dawning of consciousness. The soul's knowledge of itself *is* its consciousness of the angel. The human soul is composed of the very light of consciousness that illumines and dispels darkness. Once the soul's light is reflected back to it and it is recognized, it needs no outside source for reflection, as it then becomes the source of its own light. The soul, by its very nature, just like the orb of the sun, then effortlessly and unceasingly self-generates, secretes, and radiates its own light, lighting up the world in the process. Light doesn't just shine and illuminate; it transforms everything it touches.

The angel, whose nature is light, can only be seen by the part of us that's of a similar nature; this is an example of the alchemical notion that "like can only be seen by like." Speaking of coming face-to-face with our angel, Corbin writes that we see "a face of light which is your own face because you are yourself a particle of Its light."[17] In this face-to-face encounter between the human "I" and the celestial "I," the soul sees itself. The soul reveals its—and our—light by revealing its light to us through its reflected form, which we then recognize as our own. As if a reflection in a mirror, every mode of understanding corresponds to the mode of being of the interpreter. Like a mirror, to quote Corbin, "My image looks at me with my own look; I look at it with its own look."[18]

We normally think of light and a mirror as being two different things, but the primordial light becomes its own mirror in order to reflect on and see itself. The inner light is sentient, intrinsically endowed with a primordial cognizant awareness enabling it to experience its own radiant, luminescent nature. It's as if the primordial, uncreated light, a light that empowers our ability to see and creates the act of seeing itself, creates an eye in order to be seen; the eye, being solar (light-based) in nature, owes its very existence to light. The creative and immaterial aspect of light has called forth and precipitated out of itself, in fully materialized form, a physical organ reflecting itself so it can reveal itself and be seen and known.* This light can be thought of as the visionary aspect of the soul: it makes seeing possible while at the same time being the light which is seen.

Similarly, the Divine has created human beings so as to be known by and through us, and so as to know itself and be made real in time. Corbin writes about the Divine's "desire to reveal Himself and to know Himself in beings through being known by them."[19] This brings to mind the verse from the great Sufi mystic Ibn 'Arabi, who in contemplating his Lord, writes, "I created perception in Thee only that therein I might become the object of my perception."[20] Compare this to the Divine's statement, "I was a hidden Treasure, I yearned to be known. That is why I produced creatures, in order to be known in them."[21]

The angel embodies the light of truth that casts no shadow, which is to say that the more we receive and take on the luminous body of

---

*This same idea is expressed in Plotinus (Ennead, 1, 6, 9): "For one must come to the light with a seeing power akin and like to what is seen. No eye ever saw the sun without becoming sun-like, nor can a soul see beauty without becoming beautiful."

light of the angel, putting on its garment of light, the less need we have to project the shadow out into the world. The angel, and increasingly, we ourselves, become a source of never-ending light, of "light upon light" as it says in the Qur'an. No longer *out-sourcing* our own light, we become the source of our own light.

Though seemingly an idealized state that is never attainable, this state is, nevertheless, still within the realm of the possible, which is to say there is no reason in the world why we should not continually aspire towards it. To think that uniting with the light is impossible to accomplish and therefore to not even try to imagine or achieve it is a debilitating thoughtform inspired by the wetiko virus. In such a case we have then fallen under the spell of and unwittingly become complicit with the powers of darkness that are fully invested in our not realizing who we are. As we step into our light, however, the outer world reflects back this inner realization. As more of us withdraw our shadow projections—discovering, owning, and taking responsibility for the shadow within us—there is less need for the *seemingly* outer world to get dreamed up to play out our shadow destructively in living flesh and blood. We can then co-create a world reflecting and expressing the light we have found within us.

As we look upon the angel, so does the angel look upon us. It is said we are made in the image of God, but it is our image of God that ultimately makes us. We are in essence contemplating ourselves as we contemplate the heavenly witness, our angelic counterpart—a situation wherein the contemplator becomes the contemplated, and vice versa. Speaking of the reciprocity of this seeing and being seen by God, Meister Eckhart says, "The eye through which I see God is the same eye through which God sees me."[22] When the angel is our witness, it is because we are present both to the angel as well as to ourself. To quote Corbin again, "For he contemplates you with the same look with which you contemplate him."[23] When we look in a mirror, the image that is reflected is both what sees and what is seen.

Uniting with Our Angel

When we enter into an intimate, conjugal relationship with our angel, it is a reciprocal relationship in which both parts of us benefit—the guide and the guided simultaneously give birth to and nurture each other's unfoldment. In his book *The Man of Light in Iranian Sufism*, Corbin quotes a Sufi devotional poem to the angel that perfectly illustrates this reciprocity: "Thou art the Spirit who gave birth to me, and Thou art the Child to whom my spirit gives birth."[24]

The more we become a polished mirror for our angel, the more we are able to reflect on and see it. Seeing our angel acts as a bridge that allows us to deepen our relationship with it, such that we more and more take our angel into ourselves. As we step into our angel, it reciprocally steps into us. As we incorporate the angel into ourself, we are more able to exemplify and more deeply embody it, becoming blessed— "angelicized" in the process. Our angel is continually summoning us to perpetually transcend our self-imposed limitations and become more our true self. And the more we become an instrument for our angel, the more we help it fulfill its dual mission of influencing and incarnating into our third-dimensional world while helping us at the same time. To quote Corbin, "What occurs in and by the person of each adept also affects the being of the angel who is their archetype and who finds his exemplification in them."[25]

This increasing human embodiment of the higher-dimensional, archetypal angelic form that exists in the soul in a state of formless potential leads the soul back to its origin. Each time we, as human souls, unite with our angels to whatever degree we do, we are enacting an archetypal process, becoming deeper embodied representatives of the light-filled world of the *pleroma* (equivalent to the aforementioned plenum), the boundless luminosity that is the essence of who we are.

We are not merely "in" or connected to the pleroma; rather, we are the pleroma itself. The pleroma pervades every aspect of our being, just as sunlight pervades the air or sesame oil pervades every part of a sesame seed. Who we are at our very source is the boundless light of the plenum/pleroma. We are in a process of approaching and uniting—and who knows, maybe one day fully becoming and embodying—our luminous nature.

To the extent that we are battling for our angel, we find ourselves drafted into and playing roles in a deeper, atemporal, endlessly recurring cosmic drama, a recursive iteration of our primordial return from a state of exile. We find ourselves to have gotten drafted into playing roles in a divine drama so as to, shamanlike, potentially retrieve and heal not only our own soul, but the soul of all of humanity, the soul of the world.

Choice

As if inhabiting a Tibetan bardo, we are situated in-between realms, as our very being is itself metaphorical, existing on two levels at once. We are living in close proximity to another world, existing at a threshold where there is a permeable boundary between consciousness and the limitless, mysterious world of the unconscious. We are citizens of two realms simultaneously: the outer consensus, physical reality, and the inner imaginal realm of dreams, visions, and psychic reality. These realms interpenetrate each other such that they are different yet the same, a condition that demands that we cultivate a binocular vision in which we simultaneously have one eye turned outward, toward the material world, and the other eye turned inward, toward our inner landscape. The art of ta'wil creates the bridge for these two realms to *respirate* together (which is the deeper meaning of the word *conspire*) and *in-form* each other.

We are each potential angels or demons, not a composite of the two. Our true nature is not a mixture of divine light and demonic shadow. Who we are when we are most ourselves—when we are one with our human nature—is not a summation of antithetical elements, but a union, a coincidence of opposites, where something that contains and is greater than either/both of the opposites is revealed through us.

Being intermediate beings, we are in suspense between two mysteries—light and darkness, the angelic and the demonic, being and nonbeing. We are responsible for, respondent to, and resplendent in both sides. Our angel is the go-between of these two realms. Angels are typically portrayed as being part human, part nature, and part supernatural; they are a hybrid, just like we are. It is ultimately up to us, through our free will, which side—the angelic or the demonic—we will feed and bring to life.

Our task as a soul is to travel toward the angel from whom we emanate. It's as if we and our angel have made reciprocal pledges to each other in a realm outside of linear time. Our angel is inclined toward us; we just have to remember our intention and be inclined toward our angel so as to *re-forge* (and not *forge*-t) the bond between us. Connecting with our angel is often done in the form of a dialogue. This brings to mind the alchemical definition of *meditatio:* "an inner colloquy with one's good angel."[26] At the very least, angels are the personified transmitters of unconscious contents that are seeking expression in our conscious minds.

Our guiding spirit, our angel, rules over us like a governing star whose invisible hand guides our destiny. This suprasensory personal guide directs us toward our own center. This center, to quote Corbin, is "a place filled with Darkness which comes to be Illuminated by a pure *inner Light*."[27] The two of us, we and our Angel, are situated relative to each other, as if two interdependent, coextensive foci of the same ellipse.

Our soul and its corresponding angel are not a given or guaranteed, but rather something to be won via our own efforts. Whether or not we connect with our angel depends on a crucial existential decision that we are called to make during the course of our lifetime. If we consciously choose to enter into an ever-deepening relationship with our angel, then as we take a step toward it, it reciprocally takes a step toward us. If we engage in sincere, heartfelt prayer and devotion to our angel, being that it is fluent in the language of the heart, it will respond in kind. As we take a step in the direction of our angel, our soul flowers, elevating itself as we ascend to our divine nature, to what is truly real. At the same time, as a result of our choice, the Divine is able to incarnate into our earthly self. Like a bridge that connects the two banks of a river, it is the practice of ta'wil, whereby we transmute the sensory data of our world into symbols, that effects this potential meeting of the two worlds. The soul becomes resuscitated in the process.

Our longing and reaching out to our angel and our angel's reaching back to us are really one and the same movement. Our passion for our angel is not separate from our angel's compassion for us. Both passions ultimately spring from the same source: the Divine wanting to know itself more deeply and reveal itself to itself through us. As we yearn for our own transformation, the angel—as if a greater, more perfected version of ourself (the platonic ideal of ourself) existing as a living reality in the archetypal dimension beyond conventional space and time— becomes engaged with us in a living transformational dynamic within our very soul so as to bring itself into fruition through us.

However, if we turn away from our angel, we are ultimately betraying and abandoning our true self. Degrading our own standing, our soul then falls below our human condition, and, as if spiritually regressing, we've become a fallen angel. We then become confused and disoriented, as we've lost our celestial counterpole, our spiritual magnetic north, our moral compass, and hence, have nothing with which to make our unique personhood. Cut off from our celestial guidance system, we would then be guaranteed to become an isolated unit in a totalitarian nightmare, whether in the greater body politic of the world or within our own mind. Buffeted by the winds of karma, we find ourselves completely at the mercy of the prevailing worldview. The daemonic, instead of leading us to our angel, then transforms into the demonic, becoming self and other destructive. This is to be taken over by and become fodder for wetiko. We have then fallen into a spiritual abyss in which we endlessly incarnate in cyclic existence, seemingly trapped in a never-ending world of suffering, the world of samsara. This is to have lost our soul.

Darkness

Wetiko is a daemonic archetypal energy that is more powerful than any one person; it can possess not just an individual, but a whole group of people, compelling them to unwittingly act out its energy and become its instrument of incarnation. The *daemon** has to do with a determining factor that comes upon us from somewhere seemingly outside of ourselves, like providence or fate, though in the end the ethical decision is always left to us. Hidden within the daemonic is the creative spirit, a spirit that originates from somewhere beyond ourselves that empowers us in our roles as co-creators and dreamers of this world.

The daemonic energy that animates wetiko, when turned away from and not consciously related to, becomes demonic, taking over through our unconscious blind spots as it compels us to destructively act out its dark energy in the world.† The demonic darkness of the times we live in is an expression of the unrealized and unexpressed creative spirit in all of us. Conversely, when honored and entered into conscious relationship with, this same daemonic energy can become the doorway to connecting with our guiding angel, who empowers us to dispel the evil effects of wetiko, awakens us to the dreamlike nature of reality, and helps us discover who we truly are. The demon/daemon is our greatest danger and most invaluable helper at one and the same time; how this energy manifests depends on our relationship to it.

The revelation of divine light always comes through the mediation of angelic figures; our job is to render ourselves fit vessels so as to receive

---

*Plato uses the word *daimon* (an alternate but equivalent spelling of *daemon*) in *The Republic* to describe a soul companion who guides us during our time on earth. Also, the word *daimonizomai* is used in the New Testament; its meaning is to be possessed by a demon.

†When the daemonic is not consciously related to, it creates a symptom that becomes pathological and can obstruct us from our true nature. Sometimes, however, the daemonic—in the form of our angel—creates symptoms and pathologies to get our attention and to keep us on track with our deeper destiny.

the angel and its light. We need to become hospitable to its call. We shouldn't have a limited idea about what our angel might look like, as our myopic vision might make us miss it when it reveals itself in one of its many forms. If we aren't able to see our angel, it's our own darkness which we are seeing as well as providing the lens we are seeing through, as it obscures our clear vision. By superimposing our own darkness onto the angel, we make this figure of light invisible to us, *dis-figuring* it, as well as ourselves. We then become a person without a connection to our angel, unable to imagine anything but a caricature of this figure, likewise becoming a caricature of ourselves. Whatever the soul sees— light or darkness—testifies to its own spiritual condition, to the reality it is creating for itself. And if we are without our angel, we are highly susceptible to falling prey to the seductive, entrancing, demonic spell of wetiko.

The person under the spell of wetiko is unconscious of their igno- rance, as if asleep and not knowing they are asleep. Speaking of this state of somnambulism, Corbin comments, "To free himself from it, he must pass through the Darkness; this is a terrifying and painful experience . . . a true 'descent into hell,' the hell of the unconscious."[28] Like a shaman descending into the underworld of the unconscious, we are each called to make the darkness conscious, thereby creating con- sciousness in the process. If we want to wake up there is no getting around the darkness; we can't know who we are without opening up to the darkness of the unknown.

The same energy that animates the darkness, once it becomes inte- grated into our wholeness and rejoins the unity of the psyche, becomes available to inform the heights of our creativity, as it then feeds our light. Until then, to the extent that we haven't fully connected with our body of light, we are an admixture of light and dark that obscures the light of our soul; our own obscurity to ourselves renders our angel transparent such that it doesn't register in our consciousness—we sim- ply don't recognize it.

In addition to owning the shadow that belongs to us, we also need to separate out from the darkness that is not ours. This is symbolized in alchemy by the process known as *separatio*. I imagine we've all had experiences of having a negative perception of something or someone and then realizing that this is not how we actually feel. In this moment we are realizing that we're taking on someone else's (in this case, wetiko's) perspective on the world that is not our own. Many of us suffer from overly identifying with the personal or the collective shadow, thereby blocking our inner light from shining forth (as well as stopping the light of the universe from being taken in and nourishing us).

Distinguishing ourselves from the darkness that does not belong to us is to cast off its shadow, which welded itself to our soul through the blindness of our own unconscious identification with it. The alchemical treatise *Corpus Hermeticum* admonishes us, "You must tear off this garment which you wear—this cloak of darkness." Taking off the dark garment that has covered up our essential nature helps us to begin to commune in sacred partnership with the light that is our true nature. Owning our own shadow while concurrently separating ourselves from the shadow that doesn't belong to us allows us to connect with our angel and its light. Connecting with the light of our angel, the darkness that has been holding us down falls back into the nothingness of its nature. At this point we have then left behind, overcome, grown out of, and transcended our lower self, which can no longer hold us captive. Uniting with our angel empowers us to spread our wings and freely fly, "winging it" in the divine realm of the creative imagination, rising above—and getting over—ourselves in the process.

The Imaginal Realm

Being an imaginal figure, the angel can introduce us to the world-transforming power of the creative imagination. The very same imaginal organ of perception that is necessary for perceiving and interacting with our angel is necessary to engage in the practice of ta'wil. Ta'wil is accomplished in the imagination, but it is not a flight away from reality.

On the contrary, it is a birth into the world of the truly real. It is to be spiritually born, to come into the real world, to experience Jung's aforementioned "reality of the psyche." Corbin makes a distinction between the word *imaginary*, which is akin to fantasy and connotes "unreal," and the word *imaginal*, which describes an intermediate realm that is fully endowed with its own unique form of reality. He points out that the imaginary is innocuous, but the imaginal never is, in that it affects us profoundly, in the very core of our being.

If psychic reality isn't acknowledged, we become victims of a one-sided belief in the primacy and power of the light of consciousness, which invariably leads to an acute tension within our psyche. This invariably will lead to catastrophe because, with all of our consciousness, the darker powers of the psyche have been marginalized. Our materialistic culture suffers from a monomania of consciousness—overly identifying with the conscious intellect—at our (and the biosphere's) great expense. When the unconscious isn't honored, its darker side constellates destructively, as we are seeing all around us in the world today.

The imagination is a divine creative agency; in a real sense it is the primordial power of the universe. The creative imagination is simultaneously an organ of both perception and creation. The imaginal realm is as ontologically real as the world of the senses, and its contents have a living reality all their own. It is an expression of the extent of our ignorance, our state of dissociation, and the depth of the psychic catastrophe to which we have succumbed, that our culture regards the imaginal realm as mere fantasy.

The imaginal realm, what Corbin refers to as the *mundus imaginalis*,[29] exists in its own right and is its own category of existence. It is as real as we, as psychic entities, are real. The dreams and visions of prophets, shamans, and mystics take place in the imaginal realm. The figures and events of the mundus imaginalis are not perceived with our physical eyes; rather, they themselves are the eyes through which we see the world. Having its own open-ended sphere of seemingly unlimited influence, the effects of the imaginal realm are so real that they mold the psyche, casting it in a form we can only imagine.

To recognize the fundamental role that the creative imagination plays in our experience of our world, to quote Corbin, "is to be delivered of the fiction of an autonomous datum; it is then alone that the eternal companion of the soul will cease to be the counterfeiting spirit bearing witness against it."[30] To realize that our experience of this world is a function of the divine creative imagination is to see through the fiction of an objectively existing universe, filled with empirical, historical data unalterably written in stone.

The realization that the creative imagination plays a key role in creating our experience dispells and evicts the counterfeiting spirit (wetiko), whose task is to deceive us from recognizing the truth of ourselves. This realization simultaneously invites the real companion of our soul, our angel—who bears witness "for" us—to take its rightful place at our side. It requires a higher faculty of consciousness to "see" the imaginal realm and recognize that our dreamlike universe is manifesting in the form of a living, breathing symbol, and this higher-dimensional organ of perception is our divine creative imagination. This is the suprasensory organ that alchemically transubstantiates the mundane sensory data of this world, resurrecting it into its real but hidden form as symbolic epiphany. This, then, allows the universe to fulfill its revelatory and theophanic function.

The art of alchemy realizes that the imagination is a divine body living in every person, a refined and subtle body that is not of human origin but rather is divinely implanted in us from a source beyond us. The imaginative faculty of the soul is not merely a human attribute, but is a higher-order divine activity of the soul in which the human imagination participates and bears witness. The human imagination is enveloped in and suffused with this unconditioned, divine creative imagination, the very imagination that is creating the whole universe—including us—in this very moment. The imaginal nature of our angel necessarily throws us into an imaginative style of discourse. In the practice of ta'wil, we are working with the imagination, speaking to and from it, as well as listening to how it responds.

Prayer

The act of prayer is a continual dialogue, a relationship and exchange with the Divine. Corbin says, "Prayer is the highest form, the supreme act of the Creative Imagination."[31] Prayer evokes a mutually created, shared space that reconstitutes, renews, and recreates the intrinsic interdependence and reciprocal communion between the human and the Divine. Speaking of the angel, Corbin writes, "Prayer in turn is activated by his invisible being, that is, his transcendent dimension, the celestial counterpart of his being."[32] Our impulse to pray is inspired by the very angel to which we are praying. In turn, responding to our prayer is our angel's deepest wish, as this ultimately fulfills its own impulse and raison d'être.

Genuine prayer is an invitation for the angel to visit us, as the angel, though dying to help us, is not able to coerce us in the least, as it doesn't want to get in the way of our free will. The only coercion our angel practices is to force us back into ourselves. Praying from the heart is speaking in the language of the angel, which precipitates an ongoing conversation and *trans(cendental)-action* with the divine." Thus creative prayer is the epitome of the archetypal creative act. Corbin comments that this view of prayer as being creative, "takes the ground from under the feet of those who, utterly ignorant of the nature of the theophanic Imagination as Creation, argue that a God who is the 'creation' of our Imagination can only be 'unreal' and that there can be no purpose in praying to such a God. For it is precisely because He *is* a creation of the imagination that we pray to him, and that He exists.[33]

Corbin is expressing the primacy of the divinely inspired imagination to create our world; we pray to the imagined God because the imagination itself is divine.* Theophanic prayer is the creative in action, used for the benefit of the whole, a unified quantum field that we are not *apart* from, but rather *a part* of.

We shouldn't take the existence of our angel too literally, for thinking that it literally exists leaves it no place to inhabit. Angels can pass through walls, but a world explained by our reason is impenetrable to them. Explaining them away short-circuits them; angels lose their place in a world without mystery, and this is contrary to the spirit of ta'wil, which seeks the hidden in the manifest. Taking them too literally has a hardening effect on them, as to concretize them makes them fall from the realm of the imagination. Taking on too much weight, they are no longer able to help us ascend.

Angels don't have an independent, objective existence any more than we do. When we see through the illusion of the separate self, we realize that we are interconnected with the whole universe in a dynamic way in which everything interpenetrates everything else in an infinitely complex, interdependent co-arising web of interbeing. We only exist as an individual person through and relative to others, who themselves exist relative to others, such that there is no independently existing reference point anywhere in the universe. In the same way, angels don't objectively exist separately from us; the nature of their dreamlike existence mirrors our own.

Though our angel ultimately has no independent, objective existence separate from our own consciousness, if we treat it as if it objectively exists, then it will manifest as if it actually does exist. In other words, if we conceive of and relate to our angel as if it were real, we will experience its blessings in as real a way as we can imagine. This shows us something really profound about ourselves: the incredibly vast,

---

*For example, William Blake comments, "The Eternal body of Man is the Imagination, that is God himself."[34] Blake refers to Jesus as "Jesus the Imagination."[35] Christ, from the alchemical point of view, is the revelation of the divine imagination itself, referred to as the "Imagined God." Alchemically speaking, this is the highest compliment and greatest praise.

yet mostly untapped creative potency of our own imagination. Once we suspend our disbelief about our angel's seemingly *imaginary* nature and overcome the overly rational tendency to categorize as unreal anything that is not a physically measurable object, recognizing instead our angel's *imaginal* nature, our celestial cohort takes on a living body of light such that its effects can literally transform our life. The angel is a personification of a higher order of being, a mode of perceiving and receiving the world based on the living reality of the imagination—a reality through which we can change the world.

An Event of the Soul

The root meaning of the word *psychology* is the study of the soul. We can conceive of the soul as the vital animating core of luminosity, sentience, and aliveness, the very thing that links us to the Divine, to one another, and to that part of us that is most human and most ourselves. Matters of the soul are processes of experience. The soul can't be explained—it is the soul itself that is the principle informing every explanation—but we know the soul when we experience it, like when we meet people who are connected with their soul. We can conceive of the soul as being a perspective rather than a substance; it informs our way of seeing rather than being something seen. Our ta'wil will succeed or fail depending on whether or not it leads back to the symbolic archetypal event taking place in the soul, of which and with which it symbolizes. This "event" is the primary underlying numinous spiritual reality that is ontologically prior to the manifestation of any particular symbol while being the source from which the symbolic dimension emanates as well as being where the symbol leads. When we ask, "To what source does ta'wil return us to?" this contemplation invites a deeper inquiry. To quote Corbin, "The question implies another: *whom* does it lead back, and *to whom* does it lead back?"[36] These are profound questions into the very nature of who we are and the nature of our angel, questions that the act of ta'wil asks and invites us to answer.

Symbolic events flower in the soul to announce something that cannot be expressed otherwise, as if these events are an annunciation of the soul and its corresponding angel. In these experiences, the soul is not witness to an objective, material, external event, but is itself the medium and context in which the visionary event takes place. The soul can never have knowledge of objective reality, for it, and we, are not objects. The soul can only know what it is. When the soul reads and comprehends the deeper meaning of the psychic event that is taking place within it, which is to say when the soul discerns and *re-cognizes* its own story both within itself and out in the world, it lives this event, fully making it its own. Transforming both itself and ourself in the process, the soul simultaneously stamps and *in-scribes* its deeper reality into us. Then the meaning of the event blossoms as the inner life of the soul, as the event is taking place within our soul itself, a "place" that cannot be found within the coordinates of third-dimensional space and time.

When earthly substance becomes spiritual fare and we transmute the sensory data of our experience into symbols through the act of ta'wil, it is not an ordinary event, but rather, to quote Corbin, "essentially *an event of the soul,* taking place *in* the soul and *for* the soul. As such, its reality is essentially *individuated* for and with each soul; what the soul really sees, it is in each case alone in seeing."[37] Our angel can only appear in a unique, personal form to each human soul, as our angel is symbolic of and symbolizes with the soul's most intimate depths. This is similar, I imagine, to the idea that a lifelong Buddhist practitioner will have visions of Buddhas in the after-death state, while a devout Christian will see Christ; each will see the Divine in their own way, depending on what speaks most directly and potently to their soul. This is analogous to how the form that our angel takes so as to manifest to us in our life is utterly unique, as it is based on, conforms to, and is a function of our soul.

In its encounter with the angel, the soul is brought back to its primordial origins. In its speculative reflections on the world, the theophanies that the soul experiences are of the nature of a mirror in that they reflect our true nature. Everything in the universe is a mirror reflecting the supreme light. It is its own image of itself that the soul rediscovers and meets in this act of reflection. As Jung points out, seen symbolically, Christ is a symbol of the Self, of our wholeness, of our perfect true nature. Christ, as the Angel Christos, is the primordial revelation of the angel, a revelation that is an endlessly rich and forever inexhaustible event of the soul. The Angel Christos is a nonlocal, atemporal spirit existing outside of space and time; it has existed forever and manifests in various guises through countless people as it weaves itself through the warp and woof of history.

The Angel Christos is available to anyone, anywhere, anytime, and has infinite ways and a multiplicity of forms in which it can appear, depending on the soul's aptitude for seeing and recognizing a divine figure. The paradox is that though the single, unique, supreme God can only appear by means of a multitude of individualized theophanic forms, we can only see the particular form that God reveals to us. The form of the vision is custom-tailored for each soul depending on its state of development. For example, in the apocryphal Acts of Peter, the apostle Peter, referring to the transfiguration of Jesus on Mount Tabor, says "I saw him in such a form as I was able to take in."[38] Others present saw a boy, a youth, or an old man. In the apocryphal Acts of John, John and his brother James both had a vision of supposedly the same person after returning from a night spent at sea: one saw a young child, another a man. Origen, an early Christian biblical scholar and Neoplatonist who was the first to undertake the study of the Apocrypha, in speaking about the Transfiguration, declares that the Savior existed not only in two forms—the one in which he was commonly seen, and the other in which he was transfigured—but that "he appeared to each one according as each man was worthy."[39] In each situation, people did not see Christ as he was himself, but rather, as he chose to appear to each person.

This is analogous to how the unconscious shapes, forms, and creates dreams that are custom-tailored to the particular situation and state of the dreamer. The dreamer and the dream, being inseparable reflections of each other, mutually reflect and affect each other in a synchronistic, cybernetic feedback loop, reciprocally *in-forming* each other and thus mutually co-arising. The unconscious takes the raw material (the alchemical prima materia) of psychic life and shapes it into communicable symbolic form so as to resonate with a latent story within us. Once we are touched by and change in relation to whatever part of the dream speaks to us, the unconscious, in turn, will *co-respond* and *reflex-ively* transform—changing its form—relative to us. The integration that we've achieved as a result of the dream is instantaneously relayed back to the unconscious, which then reworks and retransmits new mythopoetic reflections of itself back to us. In this process we are simultaneously creating, witnessing, living, and assimilating an ever-novel, dynamically unfolding *drama-tic* revelation of ourselves.

As if intimate partners, we are always having a dialogue and *convers(e)-ation* with the unconscious, as we both work in concert with each other to create symbolic meaning. To say it differently, we are always dreaming in, through, and as our life. Revelation as theophany has no fixed form: it is life, not death; it is not a thing, but a continually unfolding, dynamically evolving, self-referential autopoietic process without end. For the words *dream* or *unconscious,* substitute the word *angel,* and we begin to appreciate the reflective visionary process that we are all participating in and co-creating over the course of our lives, whether we know it or not. It helps immensely if we consciously know it, however.

In these encounters with its angel, the soul is not witness to an external, objective event that exists outside of itself, but is itself reflected through and reciprocally affected by the visionary event. This is what is meant by these experiences being an event of the soul. The Angel Christos can only come into contact with humanity by transforming the latter. The symbolic script of our universe is not something that we are passively watching, but is truly a revelation that is being collaboratively dreamed up and co-created by all of us in the present moment. Corbin writes, "Your contemplation is worth whatever your being is worth; your God is the God you deserve; He bears witness to your being of light, or to your darkness."[40] The truth of our individual vision is proportional to our fidelity to ourself. The God we bear witness to is a reflection of the judgment we pronounce on ourself. When we recognize the dreamlike nature of the universe, we realize that the universe is a living oracle, that there is only revelation, that everything is theophany, that this universe is a continual epiphany, and this is what we are called to see.

An A Priori Image

We each carry within us an archetypal image of our world as well as ourself. This is an innate image that precedes all perception, an image that expresses the deepest part of our being—our very soul. It is an imprint the soul eternally bears. We are answerable to this internal image by how we create and fill out our own living biography. To the extent that this image is unconscious, it gets projected outside and into the world. The world then becomes the stage on which the drama of our unconscious and our destiny plays out. If we are not conscious of this process, we will feel victimized by life and experience the circumstances we meet in life as externally imposed on us. This *a priori* image of the soul that we project out into the world is at the same time the image that enlightens the soul as to its divine nature, for the face that the soul projects onto the mirror of the world is ultimately recognized as being its own reflection.

Once the image of reality that we have so carefully constructed is seen through and recognized to be a product of the soul—the soul's own projection of its (and our) own innermost reality—the world is then recognized in its transparency to be our projection. We realize that not only is the psyche within our brain, but that we are also living inside of the psyche, which is now recognized as being nonlocal, existing everywhere, both inside and outside of ourselves at the same time.

The dreamlike nature of reality, in which the inner situation of the dreamer (ourself) is expressed through the seemingly outer dreamscape, could not be more apparent in its transparency.

Commenting on this situation in which the deepest, innermost reality of the soul is to be found in the most obvious place imaginable, the outside world, Corbin writes, "But an odd thing happens: once this transition is accomplished, it turns out that henceforth this reality, previously internal and hidden, is revealed to be enveloping, surrounding, containing what was first of all external and visible."[41] Corbin is describing exactly what happens when we become lucid in the waking dream of life. The world as well as ourself appears to be turned inside-out and outside-in at the same time, as if the terms *inside* and *outside* have lost their difference in meaning relative to each other. It is as if the interior world of the soul encircles the external world, making the world ensouled.

In making the inward journey of ta'wil, the microcosm (the infinitely small), turns out to be a reflection of the macrocosm (the infinitely large), and vice versa. Corbin says, "Henceforth, it is spiritual reality that envelops, surrounds, contains the reality called material."[42] The events in our world are a thin skin wrapped around the enormous cosmos of pure spirit. The material world is the illusory fringe that both veils and reveals the underlying spirit that animates and *in-forms* our world. The practice of ta'wil connects spirit and matter such that the soul attains incarnate reality. Each soul is therefore not only at the center of the universe, it is a universe in itself.

Realizing that the world lives within us interiorizes the cosmos, which makes us truly integrated and "at one" with ourself. But to integrate the world, to make it our own, we first need to emerge from it. We have to step out of being unconsciously contained by and identified with the world in order to take it within us. Instead of being a stranger in a world of metaphors* that are mistaken for literal reality, what we

---

*Interestingly, the root meaning of the word *metaphor* is "to carry over."

take for reality can now be recognized for what it is: a metaphor for the truly real.

The encounter with our angel is by its very nature an *ec-static* experience that changes us, as it can't help but propel us out of whatever state or identity pattern we've been imagining we're stuck in. It displaces us, helping us to simultaneously inhabit and depart from ourself. The meeting with our angel is a release, an opening, a process of undoing, a continual unfolding, a relaxation into what had previously been closed to us. Connecting with our angel can help us recognize that we are, by our very multidimensional nature, continually in an ecstatic state, which is to say that we are a being who is always beyond ourself.

There is no external criterion for the manifestation of the angel other than the manifestation itself. Meeting our angel is a self-validating experience, as the corresponding change in our state is intrinsically self-authorizing and self-empowering; we thus become our own confidant, the author of our own creative experience of life. Our ongoing encounter with the angel pierces the granite of doubt and skepticism that doesn't believe in ourself or fully trust our own experience. It disables and paralyzes what Corbin refers to as our "agnostic reflex," and breaks through the reciprocal isolation of consciousness and its object, as seeing the symbolic dimension of the world, remembering our soul and connecting with our angel brings together and couples the two realms of subject and object.

Conspiring with our angel dissolves the distinction between our thinking and our being, as we recognize that our experience of ourself is fundamentally a function of our creative imagination, an imagination whose source is to be found in our angel. More and more stepping into our light, we can then get increasingly out of our own way and let our light shine, a light that by its very nature dispels wetiko. This is the message from our angel, or so I imagine, and the very thing we can do to be of real benefit to the world. Not just messengers, angels are themselves the message.

6

Rudolf Steiner on
the Greatest Spiritual Event
of Our Time

Almost a hundred years ago, as if peering into a crystal ball, spiritual teacher and clairvoyant Rudolf Steiner* prophesied that the most momentous event of modern times is what he referred to as the incarnation of the etheric† Christ. By "etheric Christ,"‡ Steiner was referring to

---

*Steiner lived from 1861 to 1925. This prediction was made in 1924, but wasn't made known till 1991. The word *clairvoyant* literally means "clear-seeing"; a clairvoyant is therefore a "clear-seer."

†The word *etheric* derives from *ether*, a term that was once widely used in physics (during Steiner's lifetime) to refer to the medium of space itself. The word *etheric* thus implied a presence co-extensive with space and thus something that completely pervades and is fully present in and as the material forms of the world. There is nowhere where space is not; it is omnipresent and everywhere. As if a higher-dimensional substanceless substance, space is the one element in which all the other elements in the universe exist and take on their form. Ether's presence was therefore conceived as not being explicitly material, but like space in that it is more hidden and implicit, and that it doesn't assume any specific form but instead provides the underlying basis and nonphysical context for all physical forms to arise in the first place.

‡Other noteworthy examples of the manifestation of the etheric Christ are the apostle Paul's encounter with Christ in his etheric form on the way to Damascus, and the highly revered gnostic document known as the *Pistis Sophia*, in which Christ appears to some of his disciples, including Mary Magdalene, in his transfigured, resurrected body of light, giving them teachings for eleven years.

a modern-day version of Christ's resurrected body, which can be conceived as a creative, wholesome and holy spirit that inspires human evolution as it acts on the body of humanity not through the flesh, but via the collective unconscious.

A radically new understanding of a timeless spiritual event known as the Second Coming by Christians, the etheric Christ, instead of incarnating in full-bodied physical form, is approaching via the realm of the spirit—as close as this immaterial spirit can get to the threshold of the third-dimensional physical world without incarnating in material form. The approaching presence of the etheric Christ influences events in both the physical world as well as within the psyche. To quote Steiner, "Christ's life will be felt in the souls of men more and more as a direct personal experience from the twentieth century onwards."[1]

A spiritual event of the highest order, Steiner felt that the incarnation of the etheric Christ is "the most sublime human experience possible"[2] and "the greatest turning point in human evolution."[3] In his talks, Steiner refers to the etheric Christ as "Christ in the form of an Angel."[4] Christ can be seen as the primordial revelation of the archetype of the angel (angels, after all, are messengers), the Angel Christos (see Chapter 5). The Angel Christos is a nonlocal, atemporal spirit existing outside of space and time, and he is immersed in and expressing himself through events in our world. Christ as an angel reveals himself for those who have eyes to see and ears to hear, as over time he weaves himself not only through the flow of world events, but also through our minds, hearts, and souls.

To quote Steiner, "In the future we are not to look on the physical plane for the most important events, but outside it, just as we shall have to look for Christ [up]on His return as [an] etheric form in the spiritual world."[5] The most important spiritual events of any age often remain hidden from the eyes of those who are entranced by the materialistic conception of the world. It greatly behooves us to not sleep through, but rather, to consciously bear witness to what has been up until now taking place mostly unconsciously, subtly hidden beneath mundane consciousness. If this epochal spiritual event, to quote Steiner, "were to pass unnoticed, humanity would forfeit its most important possibility for evolution, thus sinking into darkness and eventual death."[6] And if it is not understood, this potentially liberating event will transform into its opposite: the demonic.

Steiner felt that the Second Coming is the greatest mystery of our times. He believed that the incarnation of the etheric Christ is the deeper spiritual process that is *in-forming* and giving shape to the numerous crises (and opportunities) that humanity presently faces. The never-ending wars and conflicts taking place all over the globe are shadows cast by spiritual events occuring in a higher dimension, which are animating earthly happenings. One of the main reasons why these multiple crises are so dangerous is because their deeper spiritual origin remains largely unrecognized.

The veil that once concealed the spiritual world from what we call "the real world" has fallen away, now making it possible to bear witness to how physical events are an external reflection of a parallel archetypal process taking place on the spiritual plane—as if the spiritual dimension envelops and is expressing itself through material reality. The seemingly mundane physical world and the spiritual world are revealing themselves to be ultimately inseparable and in fact indistinguishable, as life is revealing its revelatory function. More and more of us are beginning to recognize the emergence of the etheric Christ; our realization is a crucial part of the incarnation process. The dawning recognition of the unity between matter and spirit is not merely an awareness of this original unity, but is the very act that completes and perfects this unity.

The higher order of light encoded in the etheric Christ is bringing to light the darkness that is seemingly opposed to it, which further helps the light nature of the etheric Christ to be seen. The radiance of the light can only be seen and appreciated in contrast to the depth of darkness it illumines. It's as if the revelation of something happens through its opposite—just as darkness is known through light, light is known through darkness. A fundamental principle of creation appears to be that when one force—in this case, light—begins to emerge in the universe, a counterforce that is opposed to the light arises at that same moment. This principle of the mutual and simultaneous co-arising of opposites expresses itself as a fundamental state of balance throughout creation.

Just as shadows belong to light, these light and dark powers are interrelated, reciprocally co-arising, inseparably contained within and expressions of a deeper unified and unifying process. These opposites belong together precisely because they oppose each other, and their seeming antagonism is an expression of their essential oneness. The brightest light and darkest shadow mysteriously evoke each other, as if they are secretly related. In essence, spirit is incarnating, and it is revealing itself not only through the light of its presence, but also through the very darkness that it is making visible.

The Beast

Commenting on another aspect of the Second Coming, Steiner chillingly notes that an encounter with "the Beast"[7] was necessary before the etheric Christ could be understood by humanity. He says, "Before the Etheric Christ can be properly understood by people, humanity must have passed through the encounter with the Beast." By "the Beast" he means the apocalyptic beast,* the radically evil: wetiko. The Beast can be conceived of as being the guardian of the threshold through which we must pass in order to meet the lighter, heavenly part of our nature.

When I read Steiner's prophecy I felt the truth of his words. I recognized how what Steiner was saying mapped onto what is happening in our current world-gone-crazy, as well as within my own mind. The everincreasing darkness that has descended like a plague on humanity and is compelling us to race toward our own self-destruction is hard to face, let

---

*Steiner said that an incarnation of the Beast will first arise in 1933, which is when Hitler came to power.

alone fathom. The evil of our times has become so gigantic that it has virtually outstripped our ability to symbolize it; it has become autonomous, unrepresentable, beyond comprehension, and practically unspeakable.

I also recognized the truth of what Steiner was saying based on my own experience. I have noticed that the more I connect with the light within myself, the forces of darkness seem to become more active and threatening. Every clarification and differentiation of the God image brings about a corresponding accentuation of its unconscious complement, the powers that oppose it. And so the figure of Christ can only be fully understood and appreciated relative to its adversary, the Beast. It's as if there is something in me and in everyone else, too (which is to say that this situation isn't personal), that desperately doesn't want us to recognize and step into our light. To quote the great Buddhist sage Shantideva, from his classic text *The Way of the Bodhisattva*:

> I am as if benumbed by sorcery
> My mind reduced to total impotence
> With no perception of the madness overwhelming me
> Oh what is it that has me in its grip?[8]

Shantideva is describing wetiko to a *T*. Like a black magician, wetiko is a psychic anesthetic that numbs our awareness and degrades our mind (which has undreamed-of power) such that we feel powerless. Once under its spell, we become oblivious to the madness that through our unconscious blind spot has taken over. Any would-be bodhisattva* has to answer Shantideva's urgent question, "What is it that has me in its grip?" If we want to connect with our light, we need to become conscious of what is stopping us from doing so.

This internal process is taking place within the subjectivity of countless individual human psyches and is being collectively acted out—in my language, "dreamed up"—in the outside world. The creative tension

---

*A bodhisattva is a being in the process of awakening, which is each of us in potential.

of the cosmos (the macrocosm) in the form of the conflict between the opposites of dark and light is mirrored both in the collective body politic as well as in the psyche of each person (the microcosm). It greatly serves us to recognize this.

Along similar lines, Jung points out that the Antichrist was "provoked" by God's incarnation as Christ. With the advent of Christ, opposites that had been latent until then became differentiated and incarnate. The Antichrist is the counterpart of God in the sense that he is God's antithesis. More than chance, Christ's encounter with Satan was an inexorable psychological law, where one of the opposites taking on full-bodied form reciprocally evoked the other. In short, as we connect with our light it is our destiny to encounter and come to terms with the forces of darkness.

In his prophecy, Steiner says that our encounter with the Beast is initiatory, a portal that can potentially introduce us to the Christ figure: "Through the experience of evil it will be possible for the Christ to appear again."[9] It is noteworthy that these opposites appear together; coinciding with the peak of evil is an inner development that makes it possible for the etheric Christ who is always present and available* to be seen and felt more fully as a guiding presence that can become more embodied in humans, both individually and collectively. In the extreme of one of the opposites is the seed for the birth of the other.†

The Mystery of Golgotha

Steiner felt that because Christ was destined to appear in an etheric body, "a kind of mystery of Golgotha is to be experienced anew."[10] The mystery of Golgotha to which Steiner refers is Christ's Crucifixion, his

---

*Speaking about what Paul saw during his Damascus experience, Steiner says "that Christ is in the Earth-atmosphere and that he is always there!" (Steiner, "Christ Impulse"). Implicit in this statement of Steiner's is the equivalence between the etheric Christ and the omnipresence of the element space, or ether.

†The yin/yang symbol represents this pictorially.

descent into the underworld, and his subsequent Resurrection. Steiner refers to this mystery as "the central, pivotal event of Earth-evolution."[11] He conceives of this mystery as a moment in linear time when the gods opened a window in heaven, allowing humanity to gaze into an atemporal realm that until then was invisible.

As a result of what happened at Golgotha over two thousand years ago, which Steiner considers an act of divine grace bestowed on humanity from above, Christ established himself in the unconscious depths of humanity's collective soul. Christ's emergence as part of the social evolution of humanity is, in Steiner's words, "being prepared in the subconscious." The "Christ-impulse," he says, "was to penetrate to the dark depths of man's inner being . . . to the deepest part of man's nature."[12]

Like an iteration of a deeper fractal, this archetypal, timeless mystery now "is to be experienced anew" in a modern-day version. In Steiner's words, "We shall the better understand the real nature of the events of today and especially of the immediate future if, from a spiritual angle, we see them as the continuation of the events which took place during the early years of Christianity." Mainly dealing with the more superficial aspects of what is happening in our world, humanity today "fail[s] to perceive the deeper impulses, the deep underlying forces that are at work in contemporary events." These impulses, he concludes, "are often a continuation, a resurgence of certain impulses that were manifested especially in the early centuries of the Christian era."[13]

In no other realm than the physical can we learn the true nature of the mystery of Golgotha. To quote Steiner, "Not in vain has man been placed in the physical world; for it is here we must acquire that which leads us to an understanding of the Christ-Impulse!"[14] Though seemingly the polar opposite of the spiritual realm, the world of matter is the place of spirit's incarnation and thereby its revelation in a new, more tangible form. Spirit needs the material world in order to incarnate and reveal itself.

Unlike the first mystery of Golgotha, however, in the culmination of this renewed mystery, humanity becomes engaged as active participants, playing a decisive role in the cosmic drama. This is a kabbalistic insight as well: humanity co-partners with the Divine so as to complete the creative act of God's incarnation.

The modern-day coming of the Messiah is through the transformed and awakened consciousness of humanity as a whole. In a very real sense, we are the very Messiah we have been waiting for. "By a strange paradox," Steiner says, it is "through the forces of evil" that "mankind is led to a renewed experience of the Mystery of Golgotha."[15]

The mystery and drama of the Christ event is now located and consummated in humanity, who becomes its living carrier. The events that were formulated in dogma are now brought within range of our direct psychological experience to become an essential aspect of the process of individuation. Whether we know it or not, we have been drafted and are being assimilated into a divinely sponsored process of incarnation and transfiguration. Not an effortful, intentional straining after imitation, this is an involuntary and spontaneous personal experience of the reality symbolized by the sacred myth. It greatly behooves us to recognize this.

Psychologically, the archetypal process of the incarnation of God symbolically *re-presents* the individuation process of an individual human being. In individuation, the archetype of the Self (the God within) seeks to realize itself. The individuation of a person and the incarnation of the Divine through humanity are one and the same event, expressed in different languages and from two different perspectives. The individuation process of an individual person *in-forms* and continually iterates through the individuation of humankind as a whole. This is why Jung felt that the real history of the world, instead of being based on historical events, is the progressive differentiation and incarnation of the deity both individually and collectively, writ large on the world stage.

Discerning between Good and Evil

The brightest, most radiant, and luminous light simultaneously casts and calls forth the darkest shadows. Through this process of Christ manifesting in the etheric realm, humanity is exposed to evil in a way never before experienced, such that we may potentially be able to find the good and the holy in a more real and tangible way than was previously possible. Through the process of encountering evil, we become more able to appreciate the inestimable value and preciousness of the good.

There are certain moments in time when humans, individually and collectively, are pulled down, submerged in dark powers, and brought below a certain level against their will. This shamanic descent can be envisioned as a test for humanity, so that through our own efforts we may learn how to lift ourselves up. But we raise ourselves not without the help of God, who paradoxically is the sponsor of our descent in the first place.

The descent into the underworld, as depicted in the mythic hero's journey, reveals that only in this region of danger can we find the alchemical "treasure hard to attain." Commenting on what he refers to as "the Descent into Hell," Steiner says, "When this has been experienced, it is as though the black curtain has been rent asunder and he [the hero] looks into the spiritual world."[16]

The mystery of humanity's higher nature is inseparable from the mystery of evil. No realization of the light would ever occur without first getting to know its opposite. Whoever wants to support the sacred must be able to protect it, and we can only do so when we know the forces that oppose it. The question is not whether we believe in evil, but whether or not we are able to recognize and discern, in the actual events of life, that dimension of experience that the ancients called evil, and then take effective action to overcome it. Unless we recognize evil, name it, and deal with it, we will never be able to convert its tremendous energies to good.

Evil is the central problem of our time. We are at a point in human evolution where we are forced to come to terms with it. To quote author and philosopher Laurens van der Post, "Evil is really a challenge of life for us to transform the thing that evil represents."[17] That "thing" is to be found within us. It is beyond debate that in our current age we are called to deal with evil; only those who choose to stay asleep or who are overly identified with the light (and hence, project out and dissociate from their own darkness) are blind to this.

It is of the utmost importance to recognize evil. This means developing an ability to perceive differences and distinctions by cultivating one's discernment. Evil has an intense desire to remain incognito, below the radar, as its power to wreak havoc depends on not being recognized. If we don't recognize evil we will surely succumb to it, thereby unconsciously acting it out. And so we are offered a choice: to come to terms with evil or continue to avoid it (which ineluctably makes us complicit in it). Recognizing and confronting evil means getting to know its operations within oneself without fully succumbing to it.

Recognizing the evil within us is a moment of great peril, as we don't want to fall into paralyzing despair at seeing the shocking depth of our own entanglement with darkness. Another danger is to unconsciously identify with the evil we see, thinking we are that. The key is to see this impersonal dark force within oneself, recognize that we share it with all humanity, and then demarcate ourselves from it. We must see these dark forces as paradoxically both belonging to us while being other than who we are. Becoming conscious of this dark force takes away its power, liberating us from being under its thrall. It is a genuine spiritual event when we confront the dark force within—it's as if we're meeting a whole other being.

Without being exposed to and challenged by evil, we remain helpless to overcome it. The Beast is a higher-dimensional and supersensible (beyond our five senses) being that reveals itself in historical events in our world as well as within the inner landscape of the psyche. A human body and soul can unwittingly (or consciously) become the vessel for acting out these powerful and destructive archetypal powers in ways that further extend these forces into the world at large. In modern times, the centralized, power-based state is the agency of this dark force on a collective scale. Yet any one of us, often with the best of intentions, can unwittingly become an unconscious instrument through which evil enacts its dark impulses.

Encountering, recognizing, and experiencing the depth of potential evil within ourselves helps us develop the ability to get free of it, and in so doing, become acquainted with that part of us that is beyond evil's reach. This enables us to become sovereign human beings and inoculates us against its pernicious influence. Paradoxically, it is only by knowing the Beast in ourself that we can become truly human. So it is to our advantage to know that our worst adversary resides in our own heart, rather than falling for the all-too-common delusion of thinking that we are completely pure and innocent and that the enemy is outside of us.

Withdrawing our shadow projections from the outside world enables us to not only own and come to terms with the darkness within us, but also allows us to withdraw our projections from an outer historical figure and instead discover the living Christ within. This is to realize that Christ, the "Pearl of Great Price" who is symbolic of the wholeness of our true nature, has always lived in us, rather than being an external figure separate from us.

Seeing the etheric Christ necessitates the acquisition of a newly awakened faculty of perception that enables us to recognize that this spiritual presence is revealing himself through the mundane physical world. The etheric Christ has an infinitude of ways and a multiplicity of guises in which he can reveal himself. Just like a symbol in a dream, the form of this vision is custom-tailored for each soul, depending on one's state of evolution. As we each see the etheric Christ in the unique form that is appropriate to our soul, we ascend toward Christ in his etheric body. To quote Steiner, "Those who raise themselves—with full ego-consciousness—to the etheric vision of Christ in His etheric body, will be 'God-filled' or blessed. For this, however, the materialistic mind must be thoroughly overcome."[18] To this he adds, "When this power has permeated the soul, it drives away the soul's darkness."[19] This is similar to when sunlight, which is considered the best disinfectant, enters a room, darkness is immediately dispelled. No darkness can stand up to light, and so darkness has no choice but to yield to the light.

As we stabilize our vision of the etheric Christ, we recognize that we are seeing our own mirrorlike reflection. Christ in his etheric form says in the apocryphal Acts of John, "A mirror am I to thee that perceivest me . . . behold thyself in me who speak."[20] On the one hand, this mirror reflects our own temporal, limited, subjective consciousness; on the other hand, it reflects the transcendental aspect of ourself that is already whole, healed, and awake. These juxtaposed reflections invite us to cultivate the ability to distinguish them as well as to recognize that both seemingly distinct reflections are inseparably united, thereby showing us different aspects of who we are. In so doing, we effect the requisite transformation of consciousness that feeds our individuation.

Our Soul's Image

In our soul's subjective experience of the etheric Christ, it is the image of itself that the soul rediscovers and meets in this reflection. Being a quantum system, the etheric Christ's radiance doesn't shine separately from humanity—its luminous clarity is our own. Humanity invariably becomes transformed when it encounters the etheric Christ, due to becoming aware of an essential aspect of its nature that has been dissociated and thus relegated to the unconscious. That so few people see the Risen One in his resurrected body points to the fact that it is no small feat to *recognize* the newly transformed value that has arisen out of the darkness of the unconscious.

When Steiner envisioned the operations of the etheric Christ, the etheric Christ was operating through Steiner's eyes. The same can be true for us. When we see the etheric Christ, we begin to assimilate and become the thing we are seeing. To quote the gnostic Gospel of Philip, "Some indeed see him and realize that they are seeing themselves." In Buddhism, the image used to express this is when a child recognizes his or her mother, there is no hesitation or doubt—the child immediately jumps into her lap, as mother and child unite, becoming one. In our apperception, the etheric Christ within us naturally recognizes itself, which enables us to step into who we've always been. Humanity is the vessel through which the etheric Christ—the spirit of Christ—takes on human form.

Steiner's description of the incarnation of the etheric Christ implies a progressive transmutation of the underlying etheric substructure of our world, a change in the energetic fabric of space-time itself. His notion of the coming of the etheric Christ has striking similarities to the idea of the noosphere, the mental-etheric envelope that embraces and pervades the living biosphere of our planet, whose growth supports and catalyzes the evolution of human consciousness—a concept eluciated by Russian scientist Vladimir Vernadsky and philosopher Pierre Teilhard de Chardin.

As we genuinely inquire into who we are, we invariably find ourselves playing a key role in a cosmic drama. We are not just passive witnesses, but active participants in a momentous, world-transforming spiritual event. In Steiner's words, "The human being is not a mere spectator that stands over against the world . . . he is the active co-creator of the world process."[21] Steiner's statement is completely in alignment with the perspective of Jung, who emphasizes that we are not merely the passive observers and sufferers of our age, but its makers. Steiner and Jung are both pointing out that by our very nature we are creative beings. What Steiner is describing in terms of the incarnation of the etheric Christ and the emergence of the apocalyptic Beast is in some mysterious way related to—and reflects—the current stage of our collective psychospiritual development.

The worst illness is the one that goes unrecognized, as it therefore cannot be treated. According to Steiner, awareness of the covert operations of the dark forces is the only means whereby their aims can be counteracted.[22] The etheric Christ's light can help us break through our massive inner resistance to seeing the extent to which the overwhelming forces of illness and death have insinuated themselves into our organism and corrupted our soul. The same light that kindles consciousness—the etheric Christ—also illuminates the deadening and rigidifying forces that exist within humanity.

If we can consciously experience the powerlessness that characterizes the deadening forces in our soul, this sense of powerlessness, like an alcoholic hitting bottom, can lead us to an experience of the etheric Christ, which is the revivifying light of awareness that enabled us to recognize our powerlessness in the first place. Speaking about how the divine spirit took on the likeness of the man Jesus over two thousand years ago, Steiner comments that spirit "had endured that moment of utmost, divine powerlessness in order to bring forth the Impulse we know as the Christ Impulse in the further evolution of mankind."[23] Consciously seeing the withered soul of our times intellectualized and materialized to death is the crucial step that initiates the process of resuscitating and resurrecting the soul, bringing it back to life.

Hiding the Light in the Darkness

As if pouring the very essence of his being into the existential abyss, Christ concealed his light by incorporating within himself humanity's deadened life force—as if the Higher Self is clothed in the evil qualities of humanity. To quote a contemporary student of Steiner, the philosopher, scientist, and social activist Jesaiah Ben-Aharon, "The Christ is *seen* through the metamorphosed forces of death, and is *experienced* through the mystery of man's evil."[24] The life-enhancing etheric Christ arises out of the devitalizing forces of death that imprison and obscure the eternal Christ within us. Christ's resurrected body is created and forged through his descent into hell. It is an alchemical notion that it is by means of putrefaction and decay that the glorified body of the resurrected Christ is achieved. The very fabric of the darkness are the celestial threads from which the etheric Christ is woven.*

In the Christian myth, much emphasis is placed on the Crucifixion and the Resurrection, but there is a missing step that connects the two events that is often overlooked: Jesus's three-day journey into the underworld after he died on the cross. In this journey, so reminiscent of the shaman's journey, I imagine that Christ encountered all the souls imprisoned in Hades, and through his love he took on, fully felt, and merged with their experience of being stuck in hell, such that their experience became his own. This is clearly a very dangerous experience for an ordinary, naturally empathic person (like most of us), who would run the risk of identifying with these captive souls such that we too would become trapped in the underworld along with them. But being who he is—the embodiment of the light—Christ was able to experience what it's like to be in hell, but was not caught up in this experience because he was fully integrated with the light of his true nature.

Through this experience of becoming one with the souls who were imprisoned in hell, Christ, out of his unconditional, limitless love for humanity, liberated them. This became the portal by which he attained his resurrected body. Seen as a dream, Christ was the lucid dreamer who, recognizing he was one with the dream he was having, was emancipating those parts of humanity (who were not separate from him) that were imprisoned in Hades.

Christ's descent into the underworld can be recognized as a symbolic reflection of our experience in the world today as, both individually and collectively we journey through a modern-day version of the psychic underworld. It is so easy for us to unconsciously identify with this state,

---

*The dark force within us continually persecutes the Christ in us, creating chronic opaqueness, ossification, and a deadening. This is symbolized in Paul's Damascus experience when he encounters the etheric Christ, who says to Saul/Paul (Acts 8:4), "Saul, Saul, why persecutest me?" This confrontation with the etheric Christ, who reflects back to Saul these deadening forces that were unconsciously at work within him, resulted in Saul having a spiritual epiphany and conversion experience, symbolized by him changing his name to Paul.

thereby—reminiscent of the archetypal idea of spirit becoming imprisoned in matter—getting caught up in it to the extent that we feel hopeless, like we're stuck in the darkness with no way out. This is why it's
crucial for us to connect with the light of our true nature, as symbolized
by Christ—a realization that is always available to us. Doing so allows us
to simultaneously experience the darkness while not getting caught by it.

The question naturally arises: when we are seemingly taken over by
darkness, who is experiencing this? Having the courage to experience
our own darkness, which is analogous to Christ's journey through the
underworld, is the path that empowers us to deepen our connection
with Christ, who is none other than our Higher (and true) Self. A symbolic manifestation in time of a timeless archetypal process, the effects
of Christ's journey into the underworld are nonlocally available to us in
this very moment. In a mysterious way, Christ's descent into the infer-
nal regions of our universe—into the depths of our worst nightmare—
broke the spell of wetiko, the nightmare mind-virus.

And yet, since the time of the Crucifixion and Resurrection there
has been the Inquisition, the Crusades, modern-day holocausts of various peoples, the genocide of Native Americans, the horror of slavery, and
on and on. How do we reconcile the fact that Christ broke the curse of
evil while history gives us overwhelming evidence to the contrary?

Christ's descent into the underworld was an atemporal event, a journey that happened outside of linear time, in the realm of the collective
unconscious. By enacting this journey, he established a new morphic
imprint in the nonlocal field that had not previously existed.* By over-

---

*Or, if this morphic pattern did exist in the collective psyche of humanity, it existed
unconsciously, in potential, and Christ consciously incarnated to reveal it, making it more
easily accessible for the rest of us to tap into. There are other beings and mythologies that
represent this universal dynamic in a different guise, because it's a deeper archetypal pattern
that continually reiterates and symbolically *re-presents* itself over time in different forms. The
Christ event, seen symbolically, is the iteration of this deeper archetypal process that most
deeply resonates with the collective unconscious of our current Judeo-Christian culture and
psyche. It's similar to how the unconscious crafts a living symbol that will have the most
resonance with the state of the unconscious of the dreamer, which in this case is us.

coming the power of evil over him and within him, he made it possible for all humanity to share and partake in this accomplishment—if we so choose.

Christ's experience of descending into the underworld is not something that we can passively, in an uninvolved way (like we're sitting in the audience) simply receive the benefits from by doing nothing (or by just mouthing some prayers by rote). Rather, it is an emotionally engaging archetypal process that demands our conscious involvement—and real passion—in whatever way we are each uniquely called to participate. Our assent to this process—saying "yes" to our calling—activates the support of transpersonal forces, forces more powerful than our personal ego, the very forces that Christ represents and that animated him.

As each of us, through our own process of individuation, connects with the underlying archetypal morphic field that Christ forged and enlivened by consciously living it, our experience strengthens the morphic field nonlocally, making it more easily accessible for other people to become conduits for this deeper transformational process as well. As we become instruments through which a deeper, more coherent field incarnates in our world, this becomes a positive, ever-amplifying feedback loop that increasingly enhances the morphic field. In this way we bring the higher power of love that Christ embodied into living, breathing embodiment in our world. This power is none other than our true nature—the very power that breaks the curse of evil.

Through his descent into the underworld, Christ united with the core of humanity's evil, becoming one with it, thereby initiating an alchemical process of transformation deep within the universe. After his death on the cross, Christ had to journey to hell or his ascent to heaven would have been impossible. In his descent, Christ had to merge with and become one with the forces against him—in Jung's words, he "had to become his AntiChrist," his "otherworldly brother."[25] In *dying livingly* into the abyss, Christ freely offered his life-giving heart to darkness's infinite void. The result of Christ's sacrifice is that his eternal being germinates and grows on behalf of humanity from within the core of all evil. The toxicity of the darkness becomes poisoned by the light that has entered its heart. It's as if once poisoned, the poison becomes medicine.

Christ's Crucifixion is an alchemical dismemberment by which God becomes nonlocally disseminated so as to be made available throughout creation. With the Crucifixion, it appears as if the forces of darkness have overcome and vanquished the light which in its descent into the underworld has disappeared from view. Yet in surrendering to the darkness, the light penetrates the darkness and enters its very heart. Since the light, by its very nature, is imperishable, the darkness can't destroy it; on the contrary, it is an archetypal conception that the light transforms the darkness from within, and the light emerges from the darkness in a transfigured form.

As Jung points out, this same idea is represented in the Christian sacrament of Communion, wherein Christ is supposedly eaten. This can be understood as a symbolic act in which the light is ingested in order to penetrate the darkness of humanity, initiating a process of transformation such that the light can then reappear in an illumined humanity. *Re-cognizing* the light's emergence through the darkness can help us to *re-member* ourselves, as we bring our *members,* the split-off parts of ourselves, back into the wholeness of our being, thus healing our former amnesia. Our remembering ourselves in this way is the direct result of and the resolution of the alchemical dismemberment process.

When this archetypal process is translated into the psychology of an individual, Christ's descent into the underworld correlates to accepting that which is the most despicable and lowest in oneself. In this act we plant, in Jung's words, "a seed into the ground of Hell,"[26] from which grows the Tree of Life, and which eventually results in the conjoining of above and below, inner and outer.

Through Christ's descent into the hell realms, a mutual interpenetration between the lower and higher selves of the universe has taken place. Light has *taken on* darkness, which has a double meaning: to encounter darkness as well as to become it. Light transforms into darkness so as to know and illumine the darkness from the inside as well as to reveal itself. Evil, which on one level obscures the light, has also encoded within it its opposite, such that it now has the power to become the revelation of the very light it seems to be concealing.* If we don't recognize this, however, the darkness will continue to manifest destructively and eventually destroy us.

Being the most problematic element in the life of our species, evil demands our deepest sobriety and most earnest reflection. It behooves us to become conscious of the ways we are unknowingly colluding with the dark forces. The etheric Christ illumines not only the existence of evil as a reality found in the depths of the soul, its light also reflects our complicity in this evil to the degree that we turn a blind-eye to it.

The radiant, luminous light of our true nature effortlessly and instantaneously dissolves the powers of darkness, and yet our true nature can only be accessed by going through the darkness. The truth is out: our true nature and the darkness are in cahoots with each other. And we, in our unconsciousness, are ineluctably in cahoots with the darkness. It is a key insight to see that we collude with the very darkness we are fighting against.

Instead of blindly living our lives, by self-reflecting we constellate the deeper archetypal healing powers of the psyche. To quote Jung, "If ever there was a time when self-reflection was the absolutely necessary and only right thing, it is now, in our present catastrophic epoch."[27] Self-reflection, which is intrinsic to human freedom, is a

---

*In medical terminology, evil can be conceived of as being a kind of cosmic carcinoma, where encoded within it is its own medicine. Containing not just its own cure, this malevolent disease actually bears hidden within itself life-enhancing gifts beyond measure. How this disease manifests, in either its cursed or blessed aspect, depends on whether we recognize what it is revealing to us.

quintessential spiritual act—essentially, the act of becoming conscious. In self-reflection, we recognize ourself via the mirror of the world. In essence a shamanic retrieval of the soul, self-reflection has an integrating effect, as it gathers together and *re-collects* what within us has previously been projected out, divided and separated by the *disintegrating* effects of evil. The true leaders of humanity are not the ones with the biggest bully pulpit or most lethal weapons; they are the ones who are capable of self-reflection.

Thus from all of the evidence it is highly likely that there is some unrecognized purpose for evil to exist. If we become conscious of the evil within us, in our expansion of consciousness, the very evil that has prompted our self-reflection has catalyzed our spiritual development. We have then, through our realization, alchemically transmuted evil into becoming a sponsor for our evolution. To quote Steiner, "The task of evil is to promote the ascent of the human being."[28] Once we realize our collusion with evil by making an unconscious part of us conscious, evil has fulfilled its mission of promoting our ascent. Evil is thus a catalyst for expanding our consciousness.

The question naturally arises: Does evil play a crucial role in the divine plan? Upon careful inspection, it certainly appears that evil is a secret partner or ally of the very light that exposes and thereby transmutes it. This is in alignment with the Kabbalah, which conceives of evil as an essential component of the deity, woven into the very fabric of creation. Evil, according to both Steiner and the Kabbalah, co-emerges along with the possibility of humanity's freedom. It's as if God could not create true freedom for humanity without providing a choice for evil, or as Steiner says, "For human beings to attain to full use of their powers of freedom, it is absolutely necessary that they descend to the low levels in their world conception as well as in their life."[29] Steiner and the Kabbalah both state that evil is created by and for freedom, and it is only through the conscious exercise of freedom of choice, which evil challenges us to develop, that it can be overcome. "This is the great question of the dividing of the ways," says Steiner: "either to go down or to go up."[30] Will we choose life or death? Will wetiko wake us up or take us down? As sovereign beings, the choice is truly ours; we can't blame anyone else.

Answering this question involves a new way of translating our experience. This way of seeing can only be attained if we are not stuck in a fixed viewpoint and dualistic thinking. The price of admission to this new perspective is being open to seeing that the seeming opposites of good and evil are not irreconcilably opposed to each other in the way that we've been imagining. This involves a deeper level of integration so that we can hold these seeming opposites in a new way that recognizes their complementary nature. This represents an expansion of consciousness that not only supports the incarnation of the etheric Christ, but *is* the incarnation of Christ.

How are we to live in such close proximity to evil? Steiner's prophecy, expressed in the language of Christianity, suggests that a complete spiritual renewal is urgently needed. Every cultural crisis—and we are clearly in the middle of one—produces a corresponding spiritual crisis. We need to connect with and rediscover the life of the spirit, not based on outside authority or dogma, but based on our own living experience. Connecting with our spiritual life in whatever way speaks to our soul breaks the spell of wetiko.

As Steiner indicates, no spiritual transformation is possible without coming to terms with the Beast, the inescapable evil encountered in ourselves and in the world. No old formulas or techniques can fit the bill; the way to deal with such darkness is only to be found in the depths of the human heart.

The aim of the Beast is to close, harden, and seal off the human heart with its negative energies. There is no greater protection against the Beast—and no better way to invite the approach of the etheric Christ—than to assiduously strive to cultivate a good heart overflowing with love and compassion—what in Buddhism is called "the precious bodhicitta." Genuine compassion is unconditional; by its nature it is meant to be shared with all beings throughout the universe, *especially* with the Beast within us. Compassion is the only thing in the world that can vanquish the seemingly infinite black hole of evil, as compassion, due to its boundless nature, has no limits. The more we give our compassion, the more we have to give. The etheric Christ is all about compassion, which is its true name.

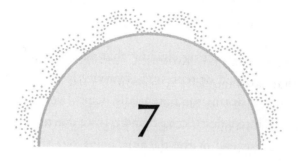

7

Nicolas Berdyaev's Epoch of Creativeness

What all of the world's wisdom traditions point out in their own unique way is that we are creators; we are creative beings. Creativity is an essential part of our nature. These wisdom traditions consider our creative power to be our greatest gift, both to the world as well as to ourselves. Quantum physics, which is still in the beginning stages of being decoded and understood, is revealing to us that we are not just passive observers of this world, but are active participants who are involved, whether we know it or not, in creating our experience of the world and ourselves.

If we aren't actively involved in expressing ourselves creatively, we are unknowingly allied with and become a secret outpost for wetiko. A creative person—and we are all creative—must create. Nothing is more poisonous to our psyche than an unexpressed creative impulse; it can destroy not just our emotional and spiritual health, but our physical health as well. Because the creative function creates the greatest value, it is very dangerous to interfere with it, for if we destroy the creative impulse, we destroy the intrinsic value and self-worth of the individual. "But," as Jung said, "you can still live on as a wall decoration."[1]

Creativity that is not given a suitable form of expression can be envisioned as an obstructing shadow that veils the light of divinity within us. Unexpressed or repressed creativity feeds the evil aspect of wetiko, which transforms the potentially helpful voice of the daemon, our inner guide, into a destructive demon. If we don't honor the creative light within us, instead of the daemon being our trustworthy guide, its demonic counterpart will deceive us and mislead us into all sorts of trouble. When we are deprived of the power of creative expression, we will express ourselves in the drive for power.

Creatively expressing what moves us—as well as what stops us from moving—is the very act that liberates us from the unconscious compulsion of having to self-destructively *re-create* our unhealed wounds, trauma, and abuse. Our undealt-with and unintegrated wounds get lodged into us and fester, growing by accretion, becoming radioactive with wetiko. Genuine creativity, however, consumes and incinerates the remnants of our unprocessed abuse, turning them into ashes.

Creatively expressing what we are experiencing transforms us down to our core, as we create ourselves anew in the process. The creative process is not of our own doing; it takes possession of us and uses us for its own realization. In a real sense it is something that is beyond us, and we are merely its instrument. When we are truly creative we step out of our limited self and become a conduit for a deeper, unknown part of ourself, something transcendent and powerful, to come through us.

Berdyaev's Ideas on Creativity

True creativity is a continuation and *re-iteration* on a human scale of the ongoing act of cosmic creation. The Creator created humanity in his own image, as a free being gifted with creative powers. Humanity was created so that we, too, would create; being creative is our divinely sanctioned vocation. God waits for a response to his call, as humanity is called to actively participate in revealing and engaging our innate creative nature.

Russian philosopher and theologian Nicolas Berdyaev (1874–1948) said, "Man, made by God in His own image and likeness, is also a creator and is called to creative work."[2] In our creative nature God placed within us a mark of his image, for expressing ourselves creatively is to fulfill God's secret wishes. Berdyaev writes, "God's desire is to see in man the creator, reflecting His own divine nature."[3] God wants to see his own free, creative nature reflected back and expressed through the mirror of a creative humanity. I've only recently discovered Berdyaev's work; I particularly love the way he talks about how the Christ event is ongoing in our present day via the creative tension pulsating through the veins of humanity.

Expressing ourselves creatively is the revelation of the image of God within us; it is to partake in our godlike freedom. It is in humanity's creativity that our freedom is revealed, liberated, and actualized. This freedom bestows on us a godlike dignity. Creatively expressing our god-given freedom comes with a great responsibility to have our actions informed by wisdom, as we are ultimately the ones accountable for the consequences of what we create.

Berdyaev writes, "We cannot merely passively await the coming of Christ, we must go up and go toward Him."[4] When any of us actively engages our creative nature we are preparing the ground for and going toward the etheric Christ. The coming Christ will never appear to one who has not, in Berdyaev's words, "accomplished the daring act of revealing his own creative nature."[5] We aren't meant to indulge our weakness and cowardice, passively waiting for the Second Coming (which would be the modern-day fall of humanity), but are called to have the courage to engage with and actively express our creative nature.

There is a direct correlation between the mystery of our creative nature and the coming Christ. If we haven't become a creative person in our lifetime, we have betrayed our true nature. The meaning of the Second Coming lies in the transfiguration of human nature and the formation of a new breed of creative humanity. Our creativity, whose original source is beyond the ego, becomes the medium through which

Christ (who embodies and is symbolic of our Higher Self) incarnates in our world.

Creativity is a healthy response to the *dis-ease* of wetiko at the core of our being. In wrestling with our demons, we are asked to creatively give shape and form to the dark energies that animate our sickness, transforming these demons into something useful, in service to the good, and potentially into allies. It is in overcoming our illness that we access the creative spirit.

In our creativity it's as if we are (perhaps unknowingly) in possession of a magic wand that is powerful beyond measure. But not only do many of us not know how to use it to benefit ourselves and the world at large, most of us don't even suspect that we have such great creative power. Many of us are unconsciously wielding our creative genius to entrance ourselves into thinking that we're not in touch with our creativity. This is then immediately confirmed by the experiences we create for ourselves—which, ironically, demonstrates the enormity of our creative powers. Not knowing that we possess undreamed-of creative powers, our power to create then possesses us from beneath our conscious awareness, which then fuels our worst nightmares, both of the sleeping and the waking variety.

In genuine creativity, the potential for demonic evil within us is alchemically transmuted into creative ecstasy. The demonic evil is raw material, the prima materia, for the most sublime creativity, a creativity that recreates us and the world anew. Creativity is our true, essential spiritual nature as human beings. If we don't alchemically transform this raw material through creative acts, however, it will kill us. The darkness calls on us to creatively intervene by changing the overall context that gave rise to it in the first place, thereby transmuting the darkness into fuel that feeds the creative fire of the human soul.

Divinely inspired creativity and archetypal evil exist juxtaposed in a state of superposition within the daemonic; which one actually manifests depends on whether we respond creatively or not. Jesus's saying comes to mind: "If you bring forth what's within you, what's within you will save you. If you don't bring forth what's within you, what's within you will destroy you" (Gospel of Thomas, saying 70).

Wetiko both spurns and spurs our natural creativity. The mind-virus is a creativity destroyer when not seen; when recognized, though, it unleashes our creative nature beyond imagination. Creative artists are somehow able to synthesize their most sublime, transcendental impulses within the darkness of the unconscious, shaping something entirely new as a result.

The creative spirit is a force of nature growing within the human psyche that dreams of full-bodied expression. It moves through individuals, generations, and epochs. People gripped by the creative spirit are driven by an inner necessity to give outward form to what has taken hold of them within. Creative people offer themselves as instruments in service to the realization of this creative spirit.

All art, science, religion, and technology—everything that has ever been done, thought, imagined, or spoken—has its origin in the creative nature of our soul. Jungian psychologist and philosopher Erich Neumann comments, "The self-generating [creative] power of the soul is man's true and final secret, by virtue of which he is made in the likeness of God the creator."[6] Creative artists don't reproduce and imitate nature; rather, they produce in their own soul an analogous creative process that nature outwardly reflects. This fruitful creative center of the soul that is typically identified with the creative divinity is a never-ending source of renewal and rebirth upon which the continued existence of culture and civilization depends.

For Berdyaev, we stand at the threshold of the dawning of the "religious epoch of creativeness,"[7] which he considers to be a third, anthropological revelation, following and completing that of the Old and the New Testaments. There will be no holy scripture for this revelation, as it will take place and become lived and accomplished within humanity, thereby fulfilling the Christian revelation. The anthropological revelation of the creative epoch will disclose Christ in the life and workings of the world, such that Christ unites with humanity through our creative acts. Thus the etheric Christ emerges as a result of our creative activity, while in a life-creating feedback loop it endlessly inspires the very creativity that gives birth to it.

This new world epoch is the creative revelation of humanity, revealing the creativeness of being itself. To quote Berdyaev, "The creative secret is both hidden from man and revealed by man."[8] Berdyaev felt that our previous cultural attempts at creativity through both the arts and the sciences were preparatory—a hint, the palest reflection, a mere foreshadowing of the vast spiritually informed, grace-filled creativeness that lives within us in a state of potentiality. When we consciously access the spiritual source of creativity Berdyaev was of the opinion that we will realize not merely a more refined culture with more evolved arts and sciences, but a whole new dimension of our being altogether. All true art is a way to a new being.

Artistic creativity doesn't merely reflect the actuality of the world, it always adds to the world's reality something that has never been before. Through the creative act, in creating something new, we are playing our part in creating a new cosmos. By consciously participating in our own evolution, our internal transformation can't help but change the world in the process. According to Berdyaev, our present life is only transitioning to the true creative life instead of being creative life itself. To quote Berdyaev, "We have not yet known true creativity in the final and ultimate religious sense of the word."[9] The consciousness informing the—potentially—newly emerging religious creativeness has never before existed in the world; it is literally being born in our epoch. Creative expression is just as spiritual as prayer, meditation, or asceticism.

Being creative is a self-sufficient and self-validating experience that needs no external authorization. Creative expression is not something secondary or derivative; its roots go to the deepest depths of our being. Being creative is not just our right, it is our duty, a moral imperative, our calling. Berdyaev felt that the Fall of humanity had to do with the *objectification* of the world (thinking the world exists objectively), a process by which the spirit becomes enslaved to external things and its potential creativity becomes entombed within us. As Berdyaev says, "Creativeness more than anything else is reminiscent of man's vocation before the Fall."[10] Every act of the dawning of consciousness is a creative act.

Those of us who are not creatively active will, according to Berdyaev, never see Christ in his full glory and majesty (what Berdyaev calls "the integral Christ"). Berdyaev felt that if we are not connecting with our creativity, Christ will only show us his crucified and tortured face without ever revealing his glorified and transfigured body, which can only be recognized when we bring forth our own glory through the creative act. What Berdyaev calls "the epoch of redemption" (in contradistinction to "the epoch of creativeness"), where only the suffering, crucified Christ shows his face, will never end for those who don't allow their true nature to be revealed through creative activity. In Berdyaev's words, they will be stuck in "an evil endlessness in redemption itself, [having] resistance to the completion and the fullness and the end of redemption."[11] In essence, as they turn away from their calling to be free they are choosing not to step off of the cross and thus they are unwittingly colluding in their own crucifixion. They have become attached to and identified with and addicted to their own suffering, which is to be unwittingly colluding with evil.

Creatively bringing forth and giving form to what is within us helps us heal our suffering, as it breaks the curse of the unexpressed. As Nietzsche writes in *Thus Spake Zarathustra*, "Creation—that is the great redemption from suffering." It is as if the act of expressing ourselves creatively—expressing who we are—completes and actualizes the process of redemption. "Redemption, that is to say the greatest event in world history," says Berdyaev, "is the result of the existence of evil."[12] True redemption always leads beyond itself to a new birth, to a new creation, to "the creation of a new race of spiritual men."[13] We are mere shadows of ourselves until we consciously participate in the ongoing creation of ourselves. Redemption leads to a new race of spiritually awakened humanity, which will be the offspring of the dark forces. The question arises: Who do these dark forces work for?

"The ethics of creativeness," Berdyaev writes, "breaks with the herd-existence."[14] Being creative necessitates breaking free from the mass psychology of groupthink. Being creative comes with a cost: it involves being disobedient to the consensus way of viewing things and honoring one's own inner law. Being creative necessitates unsubscribing from our culture's unexamined assumptions about the collectively agreed-on way things are, as well as seeing through our limited ideas about what is possible. A creative person interfaces with the infinite, as the world is experienced as open, malleable, and plastic, with endless horizons to be explored and numberless possibilities of breaking through to other worlds and dimensions of experience. Berdyaev writes that the creative person "overcomes the nightmare of the finite from which there is no escape."[15]

Owning Our Creativity

It is noteworthy that the main gift that quantum physics—the wisdom tradition of modern times—is offering to the world is that it is revealing to us and activating our unconscious creativity. The revelations emerging from quantum physics are expanding the realm of the possible to previously unimaginable degrees, helping us wake up from "the nightmare of the finite." It is revealing that the world is open-ended and malleable, and that we have a hand in creating it. Quantum theorist Christopher Fuchs writes, "The real question is which point of view about quantum mechanics is the most ripe for leading to new things. . . . Understanding that the world is, at its core, malleable to our hands? I think that that will ultimately be the greatest gift this century [the twentieth] has to give to the next."[16] The mutability of the universe, which quantum physics has found to be one of the primary qualities of nature as well as our minds, says that nothing is absolute, nothing is so fundamental (particularly our state of consciousness) that it cannot change under certain circumstances. The revelations emerging from quantum physics are the magical elixir that heals the venom of the impossible.

Creative imagination is at the root of creative activity. Creative imagination calls forth and evokes something more grace-filled than our existing world, as it rises above reality. If we aren't actively imagining a better world, the question that naturally arises is, "Why not?" In a very real sense, says psychologist James Hillman, we must "imagine to discover reality, and dream to be awake."[17]

"The ethics of creativeness," Berdyaev writes, "alone overcomes the negative fixation of the spirit upon struggle with sin and evil and replaces it by the positive, i.e., by the creation of the valuable contents of life."[18] Instead of being overly fixated on struggling with evil, we can choose to invest our attention on creating positive value for the world, sponsoring a more loving and grace-filled world. What better thing is there for us to do?

It is important to note that it is extremely difficult—almost impossible—to overcome what Berdyaev calls "evil passions" negatively, through asceticism, suppression, or prohibition, which oftentimes, through our struggle against these passions, strengthens the seeming power of the evil impulses against which we are fighting. These evil passions, Berdyaev says, "can only be conquered positively, through awakening the positive and creative spiritual force opposed to them."[19] By being involved in creative activity, something positive and life-affirming captures our attention. Investing our psychic energy in something wholesome dispels the power of the dark forces, which feed off of our attention. When we are more interested in focusing on the positive, the negative loses its power over us. What more reason do we need to get creative?

Owning the creative gifts that are our natural inheritance is wetiko's worst nightmare. Connecting with our creativity helps us wake up from the spell of the nightmare mind-virus. Instead of being disempowered victims of an imposed creation separate from ourselves, once we realize that we ourselves are the creators of our experience, wetiko doesn't stand a chance. For once we connect with our calling, find our authentic voice, and express our creative nature, wetiko has no place to stand—just like the cartoon character Wile E. Coyote falling off the proverbial cliff.

8

Rebirth of the Self

At the present moment, our country and our world are insanely polarized. Wetiko is both an expression of and is at the root of this extreme polarization and dissociation in both the human psyche and the world at large. If humanity is seen as a single macro-organism, it is as if there is a fissure, a primordial dissociation—a split—deep within its very source. Just as an individual can suffer from a dissociation within their psyche, so can a nation and a people. Our species is suffering from what Jung calls a "sickness of dissociation,"[1] a state of fragmentation and incoherence deep within the collective unconscious (which Jung equates with God). This dissociation has seemingly spilled outside of our skulls and has taken the form of certain collective events playing out on the world stage. We are at a severe crisis point in our world, which, medically speaking tells us that our sickness is reaching a dangerous climax.

Neurosis

Jung calls humanity's "split consciousness," in which the right hand doesn't know what the left hand is doing, "the mental disorder of our day."[2] Playing out on the world stage, this dissociation has its source in the collective psyche of modern humanity. Suffering from a disunity with ourselves, we then identify with a partial aspect of ourselves and project our shadow onto the outside world. It is the face of our own unrealized shadow that glowers at us in the face of the enemy. The world then acts out our shadow, giving us all the evidence we need that the evil is to be found outside of us. Split in two, we become neurotic as hell.

We are living in the time of the splitting of the world. Our fragmented outer world is dissociated like the inner psyche of a neurotic. Lying behind our neurosis is concealed all of the genuine suffering that we have, for whatever reason, been unwilling to bear and unable to embrace. Theologian Dietrich Bonhoeffer observes, "Suffering willingly endured is stronger than evil, it spells death to evil."[3] We foreclose on the chance of real happiness if we refuse the genuine suffering that is sent our way as part of life. Jung famously writes, "Neurosis is always a substitute for legitimate suffering."[4] When we suppress the legitimate suffering that is ours to bear, we create a substitute form of neurotic suffering that can be more painful than the legitimate suffering.

Neurosis is not a localized illness that only affects a small, isolated part of us, but something that affects the whole human being on all levels. Because neurosis is only a symptom of a deeper imbalance, the focus of therapy should not be on what Jung calls "the fiction of neurosis," but rather, on the whole human being who is suffering from the neurosis. Neurosis splits us from our psychic wholeness. The outbreak of neurosis is not a matter of chance, it is usually the moment when a new psychological adaptation is demanded by life.

According to Jung, neurosis is the suffering of a soul that has not discovered its meaning. The absence of meaning, the "senselessness and aimlessness" of life can be thought of as the fundamental neurosis of our age. Neurosis oftentimes emerges when people content themselves with inadequate or wrong answers to the questions of life. As Jung realized, many neuroses are caused by people blinding themselves to their natural spiritual promptings. Neurosis is an attempt to escape from our inner voice and hence flee from our vocation and ultimately, from ourself. What Jung calls our "neurotic perversion" conceals our vocation, our destiny, and the full realization of our inherent will to life to actualize itself. The neurotic is someone who has fallen victim to their own illusions. Like a psychic barometer, neurosis can tell us when and where we are straying from our individual path and destiny.

People who have fallen neurotic are often potentially destined to be the bearers of new creative cultural ideals. We stay stuck in neurosis only as long as we remain obedient children who bow down before authority and refuse the freedom that is our destiny. Giving our power away to an external authority—which is to betray the powerful impulse of our nature to develop, express, and realize itself—simply strengthens the very forces that made us sick in the first place. As psychologist Otto Rank points out, the neurotic is a potential artist who, failing to access the creativity hidden within the powerful transpersonal energies from which they suffer, is unable to transform their inner conflicts into art. In their compulsive and self-destructive acting out, the person in a neurotic state can be compared to someone who is bewitched.

Our personal neuroses are reflections of the great problems of society and our times. Due to our interconnectedness with the whole of reality, our particular neurosis is an individual attempt, however unsuccessful, to resolve a universal problem. We are individual nodes of awareness in a vast, interactive, self-synchronizing, and reciprocally co-arising living network. We are all parts of the great stream of human history, which countless times has experienced conflicts and neurotic patterns that we each mistakenly use as evidence for our personal craziness. Recognizing the greater archetypal pattern that we are expressions of can take our neurosis out of the realm of pathology, dispel our feelings of isolation, and help us feel connected to all of humanity and more at one with ourselves.

The implications are clear: if we avoid the shadow, we ensure we will remain neurotic. And if we don't deal with our neurosis, we will be avoiding—and thus feeding—the shadow. We are mostly asleep to the iron curtain that splits the soul of humanity, and we need some form of a wake-up call to rectify our inner dissociation. All of the evil that is playing out in the world is a loud alarm clock letting us know that it's time to wake up and recognize our own hand—our complicity—in creating the dark shadow of evil that has enveloped our world.

Neurosis is by no means solely negative: it has a positive aspect that holds the key to accessing the wholeness of our psyche, the hidden part of ourself. If our neurosis could be plucked from us like a bad tooth, we would lose an essential means of accessing our wholeness, as if a part of our body had been amputated. Our neurosis signifies and contains an undeveloped and precious fragment of our psyche, without which we would be condemned to resignation, bitterness, despair, and depression and fall under the sway of wetiko.

So we should follow the way of our neurosis. In a sense it's the best thing we have ever produced. A neurosis can be viewed as a positive symptom, as it is a manifestation that something is not right in our present state, an expression that something within us wants to grow. Hidden within our neurosis lies a precious seed that if nurtured can help us grow beyond the neurosis into a more coherent and integrated version of ourself, and in ways that would be impossible without the gift of our neurosis. If this growth opportunity is not accepted, however, then our neurosis works against us.

We need to learn not simply how to get rid of our neurosis, but how to carry and bear it, to go into it so that it can reveal its deeper meaning. Our neurosis is teaching us something about ourself that we clearly haven't been able to learn any other way, so trying to get rid of it without uncovering its deeper meaning is analogous to attacking a fever in the belief that *it* is the noxious agent, rather than recognizing that the fever is an expression of the process of healing that is underway. Neurosis is nature's attempt to heal us. We so easily think of neurosis as being worthless, but contained within it in hidden form is the alchemical gold that we cannot find anywhere else. Neurosis is an attempt by the self-regulating nature of the psyche to restore balance to the overall psychic system, similar to how our night dreams compensate a one-sidedness in the dreamer.

A neurosis is only truly healed when it transforms a false attitude. We don't cure our neurosis—it cures us. Our neurosis is ultimately of numinous origin. "The core of the neuroses of our time," Jung's colleague Erich Neumann writes, is "the search for the self. In this sense neuroses . . . are a kind of sacred disease."[5] Though our neurosis strengthens and seems to feed into and off of our feelings of alienation, its origin is actually to be found in the wholeness-creating tendency of the Self. Paradoxically, neurosis splits us off from our psychic wholeness, while simultaneously being an expression of that very wholeness attempting to actualize itself through us. Where the process of neurosis feeds into evil is the loss of our relationship with our psychic totality. The cure for neurosis—as well as the alleviation of evil—involves reconnecting with our wholeness.

Neurosis is not a residue or hangover from the past. The source and solution of neurosis always lies in the present, since the neurosis only exists in the present. A neurosis is freshly made every day. And it is only in the present, not in the past, that it can be cured, just as it is for wetiko, whose origin and existence is ultimately to be found in the present moment.

The outer divisions in our world, with all of its myriad political, social, and military conflicts, are but an outer reflection of the dissociative neurotic split between the conscious and the unconscious minds of humanity. In a neurosis, two points of view are in complete opposition to each other, one of which is unconscious. When there are no open lines of communication between the seemingly opposing conscious and unconscious aspects of ourselves, it can become a very dangerous situation. The more one-sided, out of balance, dissociated, and out of touch with ourself we become, the more fearsome the unconscious contents that are struggling to restore our psychic wholeness will appear to us.

We neglect the ever-present forces of the unconscious at our own peril. The greater the gap between the conscious and the unconscious, the greater the probability for psychic infection and mass psychosis. In this overly rational and materialistic age we live in, we are profoundly out of touch with our souls, and as a result of our disconnection we unwittingly open ourselves up to being unconsciously possessed by the irrational parts of our psyche that we have marginalized. Possession by the unconscious means being torn apart into a multiplicity of selves, a *disiunctio** (and the opposite of the alchemical *coniunctio,* in which opposites become united). This disiunctio plays out both within the individual as well as collectively, where it is writ large in the greater body politic of humanity.

Jung was of the opinion that we would know where to begin to tackle the overwhelming polarization in our world if and only if we as a species realized that the world's overwhelming problems arise out of the splitting of the opposites in the psyche. When Jung was asked if a third world war could be avoided, he answered that it depended on how many people could reconcile these opposites within themselves, for it is the disjunction in our individual psyches that is the source out of which the outer conflicts that erupt in our world emerge.

A Period of Pregnancy

And yet, everything in our world has at least two sides, which is to say that our sickness of dissociation is not solely pathological. When dissociation happens within an individual psyche, it can be pathological or it can initiate a shamanic journey of healing so as to integrate the cause of the dissociation. How things turn out depends on how we, as a conscious human ego, are able to relate to the contents of the unconscious which are erupting both into our world and within our minds. As Jung says, "the sickness of dissociation in our world is at the same time a process of recovery, or rather, the climax of a period of pregnancy which heralds the throes of birth. A time of dissociation . . . is simultaneously an age of rebirth."[6] There are times—and ours might be one of them—

---

*An alchemical term that means "disconnection from" (in this case, the multiplicity of selves are disconnected from each other).

when the spirit has become completely obscured and darkened because it needs to be reborn in a new form.

Reflecting on this deep process of dissociation that is playing out in our world through a psychological lens can be illuminating. Dissociation, Jung points out, is related to birth. We can deepen our understanding of dissociation by shedding light on the archetypal process of birth as represented by the incarnation of Christ. Contemplating the West's prevailing myth of the birth of God, the Christ event, in psychological terms—which is to say symbolically, as if it were a dream of our species—might help us gain deeper insights into the cure for our sickness of dissociation. Jung points out that when we contemplate the Christ event—the incarnation of the Divine in a human form—symbolically, God, who can be thought of as the dreamer of the dream, can be seen to have fallen into an extreme dissociation. In *The Red Book,* Jung writes, "But I must say that God makes us sick. I experience the God in sickness. . . . But he appears as sickness, from which we must heal ourselves. We must heal ourselves from the God, since he is also our heaviest wound."[7] Here Jung is pointing at the numinous source of our wound of dissociation, both individually as well as collectively, as a species.

It is an archetypal idea that sickness is God's attempt to heal us. The idea that God "makes us sick . . . [and] appears as sickness" perfectly describes wetiko disease, whose source is beyond us. Jung asserts that the sickness of dissociation from which our species is suffering, which is none other than wetiko, is the disguised form that God takes "from which we must heal ourselves" (paradoxically, with God's help). Regarding God as "our heaviest wound" reminds us of the words of Jesus in the Round Dance "I will be wounded and I will wound."[8] The idea of God as a sickness or a wound that we are asked to heal, though radical and disorienting from a mainstream point of view, is a helpful recontextualization that is in alignment with actual experience.

In contemplating the incarnation of God symbolically, opposites became totally polarized—dissociated—in the figures of Christ and

Satan, with Christ as the incarnation of the light, and Satan the incarnation of evil. As soon as Christ shows up with an abundance of light on one side, it is no coincidence that Satan enters the scene with an infinitude of darkness on the other. Just like the way shadows belong to light, it's as if these light and dark figures are inseparable, reciprocally co-arising and interrelated aspects of a greater unity that includes both. Something deeper, of a higher order or dimension of our being, is revealed to us through their interplay.

We all consist of two sides—a front and a back, an inside and an outside, a light and a dark side. The Antichrist is the dark side, the shadow of Christ, yet they are one and the same being. This is to contemplate Christ/Satan symbolically, as if they *re-present* a deeper process within each one of us that maps onto our own light and dark sides; both of these, when seen together, represent our wholeness.

When these opposites materialize in a totally polarized way in our world, be it during the time of Christ over two thousand years ago or in the world today, this can be seen as the revelation of a radically holistic unity that informs, embraces, and transcends this pairing of seeming opposites. The polarization in our world can be likened to the shadow on the wall of Plato's cave being cast by something beyond itself. We should keep our eyes open for this deeper unifying opportunity that is announcing itself through the extreme polarization evident in our world today.

Jung refers to the "transconscious character"[9] of this pair of opposites, by which he means that the opposites don't belong to the ego, but are supraordinate to it in that they are an expression of the Self, of the wholeness of our true nature. When unleashed, like unrestrained wild animals, these opposites can become the warring elements of primeval chaos. This can be unconsciously and tragically lived out on the physical plane, through endless wars, for example. A new realization, however, can potentially be born out of the conflict between these primordial opposites. As Jung points out, if our conscious mind doesn't interfere with its "irritating rationality," the opposites, because they are in conflict, will gradually draw together. What looked like death and destruction then reveals itself to be the labor pains of something completely novel being birthed.

Becoming conscious of our distress is necessary in order to activate the archetype of unity and bring about healing. If we are unconscious of our dissociated state, the unifying forces of the psyche will not arise other than to reflect back to us our inner state of not being one with ourselves. Once we realize that the conflict is inside of us, though, we can understand that its tribulations are in fact a means to access our greatest wealth. Instead of squandering our riches by projecting our inner conflict externally and attacking others, we can "attack" the problem at its source, which is within ourself.

Christ and the Tension of the Opposites

It's as if we're a piece of iron that is situated between two magnetic poles that are pulling us in opposite directions. The danger is that we can split in two and fall into pieces. How we deal with our situation—splitting, dissociating, falling apart, or somehow finding the strength within to consciously carry the tremendous tension between the two poles— makes all the difference in the world. By integrating these opposing forces in a unique and coherent synthesis, we can become an undivided, whole person. This, according to Jung, is the process of individuation.

Christ on the cross is a symbol of this process, for as Jung points out, the Crucifixion—what he calls "that acute state of unredeemedness"— perfectly symbolizes consciously holding the tension of these opposites. As consciousness develops and differentiates, there comes an ever more acute awareness of the inner conflict within us, with its agonizing suspension between seemingly irreconcilable opposites. This is experienced as a veritable crucifixion of the ego. To understand this conflict psychologically, we can say that the unconscious longs to reach the light of consciousness, while at the same time recoiling against the light. This built-in dynamic of the unconscious is something that each one of us experiences in our own unique way. Being able to bear the painful tension of these opposites constellates the unconscious—and life—in its deepest sense. The crucifixion is a symbolic expression for the inner condition of being in a state of extreme conflict, where, to quote Jung, "one almost loses one's mind. Out of that condition grows the thing which is really fought for . . . the birth of the self."[10] The powers of the unconscious often put us—either individually or collectively—in a numinous situation where there is no rational solution for our conflict. Our ego-consciousness gets pushed up against the wall, such that anything we try to do is wrong—it either doesn't help or makes things worse. This can potentially undermine the superiority of the ego and dispel the illusion that the ego can solve the burning dilemma we're facing. Situations like these can be understood as having been orchestrated by transpersonal forces in order to humble and chasten the ego and its hubristic sense of power.

If we are ethical enough to suffer this defeat of the ego, this allows something beyond the ego—the Self, which we subjectively experience as grace—to emerge and start to guide our experience. The unconscious often produces a seemingly impossible situation in order to bring out the very best in the person that would not have been realized otherwise. Hence the unconscious, which after all is the dreamer of our dreams, covertly operates with the most amazing cunning, arranging potentially fatal situations in order to wake us up.

It is important to not get caught up in or overly react to the religious language; the same ideas can be expressed psychologically. In place of *God,* we can substitute *the collective unconscious;* instead of *Christ,* we can say *the Self;* instead of *incarnation,* we can say *integration of the unconscious;* in place of *salvation,* we can say *individuation; crucifixion* can translate as *realization of our wholeness.*

The deep suffering involved in an inner crucifixion experience is not a symptom of a disease of the mind, but rather it is a passion of the soul. Suffering is intrinsic to individuation. Life leads us through the path of crucifixion to the complete unfoldment of the Self. We need to cultivate the ability to withstand the pain of seeing and embracing both of the extreme opposites within us simultaneously, without splitting, losing awareness, or identifying with one or the other of the pair. Consciously experiencing pain can become a doorway to experiencing oneself in a deeper, more authentic way, potentially leading to the unfoldment of the Self, of our wholeness.

When Christ is nailed to the cross during the Crucifixion, it symbolically represents that it is through the experience of being bound and severely limited in the space-time continuum that introduces us to the transcendent part of us that is beyond the physical—our spiritual nature. Holding the tension of opposites and consciously experiencing our finite limitations becomes a doorway to the infinite part of ourselves. Consciously holding the tension of the opposites liberates us from identifying with our fixed and cherished perspectives. We transcend the notion of a privileged and correct point of view and become aperspectival as we see the relativity of *all* viewpoints—a way of seeing that is the metaperspective of the Self.

Christ modeled this process on our behalf. Because the opposites were utterly differentiated in him through the Passion of Christ so as to become conscious, he became the prototype, the incarnation of the archetype of the one who awakens himself and others. The essence of the Christian gnosis—the incarnation of God through humanity—can be understood as humanity's creative confrontation with the opposites of light and dark and their synthesis in the Self. Whenever the archetype of the Self becomes activated within us, the inevitable psychological result is a state of inner conflict symbolized by Christ's Crucifixion. Berdyaev writes, "Man is reborn into the new Adam only if he has had an immanent experience of the crucifixion."[11]

The crucifixion is symbolized by the cross, which represents both the union of opposites and the suffering Godhead that redeems humanity. This redemptive suffering would not have occurred, and would not have had any effect at all, had it not been for the existence of a power that was opposed to God (the AntiChrist). This is to say that the powers of evil play a crucial and mysterious role in the redemption and salvation of humanity. Christ is the embodiment of the human response to our existential situation. If God wants to unite with humankind, the *Goddessence* (a combination of the words *God, Goddess,* and *essence*) must suffer what it is to be human. It's as if the Divine realized that in order to get to the root of the problem facing humanity, it would have to become a human being. This is the cross that Christ had to bear. What Christ consciously passed through is the destiny of humanity, and we must partake of what he is symbolically revealing to us if we are to have any chance at realizing our true nature.

With the Christ event, an atemporal, higher-dimensional, formless archetypal process got literally and symbolically dreamed up in form in order to incarnate in the realm of linear time so as to potentially become conscious. The Crucifixion of Christ is an outer symbol that expresses and reflects a parallel psychic event that is taking place within us. Recognizing the symbolic nature of the Christ event constellates an analogous psychospiritual process within us.[*]

The Western materialistic worldview, with its emphasis on the outer world of objects, tends to relate to the ideal, Christ, in his outer, physical aspect, thus robbing it of its mysterious relation to our inner being. Modern Christianity has largely become superficial, not reaching into the depths of the soul. It is only a minority who have experienced the inner transformative meaning that is reflected through the Christ event as the most prized possession of our souls.

Seen symbolically, Christ both inspires and threatens something deep within the human psyche. A symbol really lives and enters life only when it is the best and highest expression of something divined but

---

[*]Jung uses the term "phenomena of assimilation" to denote the reactions in the unconscious psyche that are aroused by the appearance of the Christ figure. The symbols and archetypal images with which the unconscious responds to the figure of Christ demonstrate to what degree the meaning of the Christ figure has penetrated and become assimilated in the depths of the psyche (Jung, *Psychology and Religion*, 431, and *Symbolic Life*, 18, para. 1827–28).

not yet known to the conscious mind. A symbol compels the participation of the unconscious, thereby having a life-giving and life-enhancing effect. A symbol speaks to and potentially activates a deeper part of our unconscious.

We can escape the uncomfortable experience of recognizing the opposites by choosing to identify with the light and denying the darkness, up to a certain point. This is because ultimately there is no avoiding the darkness, for it is our destiny to come to terms with it. Trappist monk and mystic Thomas Merton says, "Every man is Christ on the Cross, whether he realizes it or not. But we, if we are Christians [and in a deeper symbolic sense we are all Christians], we must learn to realize it."[12] Realizing we are Christ on the cross *re-contextualizes* our suffering, transforming it from a deeply problematic personal situation to a more universal process in which we are all enlisted. Berdyaev confirms this: "But there was a tendency to forget that the cross had a universal significance and application. The Crucifixion awaits not only the individual man but also society as a whole, a State or a civilization."[13]

To carry our cross is to consciously face our dark side. Christ shows us how every one of us will be crucified just as he was, which is to say, forced to meet the demands of the incarnating Self. Christ didn't carry his cross so that we could escape carrying ours. The bill of the Christian era has come due. Our world is sundered in two; we are confronted with the real possibility of destroying ourselves, and there is no getting around the undeniable fact that it is our fate—written in heaven—to face our shadow. The cross is the symbol of the individuation process, which is to say that it is our destiny to individuate and become who we truly are and who we are meant to be as unique human beings.

When we consciously hold the tension of opposites, we are participating in Christ's Crucifixion such that ultimately something deeper—the resurrected body—can potentially emerge in the world via our expanded consciousness. Jung calls what emerges out of this creative tension the "reconciling symbol" or "transcendent function" (whose function is transcendence).[14] Opposites never unite at their own level; a supraordinate third element that partakes of each of the opposite pair but is the same as neither is always needed in order to synthesize them. Without the tension of opposites, no forward movement is possible, for life is born out of the friction and the resulting spark of opposites.

The real problems of life, the profound conflicts, cannot be solved by any technique or in any ready-made, prescribed way. There is no instruction manual. It is only when we are confronted with an insoluble conflict that we can become acquainted with how the Self operates. It is only when there is no way out and we are in desperate need of a solution that we experience the creative source within us that interfaces with something beyond us and resolves the tension and unites the opposites. Creatively and consciously confronting and suffering the tension of the opposites is to be serving something greater than ourselves. Our darker half—the shadow—is necessary for consciousness to arise, because it creates a division and concomitant tension between the spirit and its opposite. This polarization is necessary for the evolution of consciousness to take place. In this process we have become the instruments through which the creator becomes conscious of its creation.

Jung says that to be truly imitating Christ—*imitatio Christi*—is to be living our life as authentically as Christ lived his. To model our life after Christ involves embodying the meaning of life as we seek to be as true to our unique incarnation of Spirit as he was to his. We try to become Christ-like in our striving to find our own way to an inner spiritual source that is wholly and uniquely our own, while being impersonal/universal at the same time. This is radically different than simply trying to mimic Christ, or in Jung's words, "ape his stigmata,"[15] forgetting to make real our own deepest meaning, which is self-realization. It's no easy task to imitate the life of Christ, but it is unspeakably harder to live one's life with the integrity that Christ lived his. In his personal journals, it is clear that Jung was realizing that to be a true follower of Christ ultimately meant becoming Christ oneself.

The figure of Christ is a sacred symbol because it is the psychological exemplar of the truly meaningful life, which is a life that strives for the absolute and unconditional realization of its nature. In becoming an authentic self, we develop integrity and a self-consistency and fidelity to the laws that characterize our own uniqueness. We all secretly dream of individuation—of becoming who we are truly are—which is what sacred legends such as finding the Holy Grail are symbolically expressing.

Our age is calling for—and dreaming of—what Jung calls "the redeemer personality,"[16] as if we are projecting outside of ourselves, in the figure of Christ, the inner part of us that can emancipate us from the inescapable grip of the collective madness. Analogous to becoming a disciple of Christ ultimately means to become Christ, the one and only way of discovering the Grail is by becoming it—by alchemically becoming living philosopher's stones.

Genuinely imitating Christ is not for the faint of heart, as it invariably leads us to our own very real, Christ-like confrontation with darkness. Jung isn't merely talking about an encounter with our personal shadow, but with the archetypal shadow, the transpersonal forces of darkness, the powers and principalities of the Bible. These biblical powers and principalities are always present; there is no need to create them (as if we could). It falls on us to choose the master we will serve, instead of being mastered by "the other," whom we have not chosen. It is challenging to our ego to admit that we are dependent on "powers"—both light and dark—beyond our control. It is ultimately our decision, however, at whose altar we will worship and which forces we will serve.

It is Jung's opinion that most of humankind is in such an unconscious state that they should be protected from the overwhelming shock of what it means to genuinely imitate Christ. But as we become able to withstand the shock and over time reconnect with our true nature, we can realize that we have access to a heretofore unknown strength within us, which can revitalize us beyond belief. We not only endure the shock, but grow even stronger from the stress that this process necessarily entails.

Coming to terms with the fact that we are dependent on powers greater than our own ego requires us to develop a living connection with the wholeness of the psyche, the Self. Christ is the perfect symbol of the hidden immortal God who lives within mortal humanity. A symbol simultaneously reflects and effects the very mystery of which it is an emanation. A symbol such as Christ reconciles and unites God and humanity in one being. Christ's two seemingly contradictory natures— human and divine—interpenetrate each other so thoroughly that any attempt to separate them mutilates both.

Christ, when seen as a living symbol, effects this synthesis of the human and the Divine in a way that literal, traditional accounts fail to do. This failure has been the cause of innumerable schisms and conflicts throughout history, whereas recognizing Christ's symbolic nature could have averted innumerable instances of unnecessary suffering. Tragically, viewing Christ symbolically, with its immense reconciling power, has been generally banned and denounced as heretical by his literal-minded followers.

For traditional, literal-minded believers, Christ is anything but a symbol. And yet, Christ is a symbol by his very nature. He would never have made the impression he did on his followers—imprinting himself within their very souls—had he not embodied and reflected something unknown that is alive and at work in their unconscious. To say that Christ is a living symbol in no way is to say he didn't exist or wasn't the incarnation of God. Seeing Christ symbolically doesn't devalue him in the slightest, but rather, invests him with the highest value and is the highest praise. Seeing the symbolic nature of Christ opens us up to new pathways of revelation and insights into the mystery that he represents and to which he bears witness.

Seen symbolically, Christ exemplifies the archetype of the Self. One of Jung's favorite ways of explaining the notion of an archetype is the formation of a butterfly. If we cut open a butterfly pupa at a certain stage, all we will find is a milky liquid, but the whole gestalt of the butterfly is already functionally contained within the liquid—it possesses a *qualitas occulta* (a hidden quality) encoded within it.

Existing in the unconscious of humanity is a latent slumbering seed that corresponds to what Christ is embodying as a prototype. This seed becomes activated and starts to blossom once it recognizes itself in the seemingly outer figure of Christ. This is to say that there is a divine light within us that—because of its resonance with and connection to the figure of the Savior—enables us to see itself (and ourselves) reflected through the figure of Christ.

Spiritual renewal is not an alteration of consciousness, but rather a restoration of an original condition, an apocatastasis. There is an ever-present archetype of wholeness within us that may easily disappear from the purview of consciousness until we recognize our wholeness through a figure such as Christ, who embodies it and reflects it back to us. This brings to mind the gnostic conception of Christ, who was envisioned as a figure who entered our world to illuminate the stupidity, darkness, and unconsciousness of humanity and lead us back to our origins through self-knowledge.

Had there not been a magnetic attraction and affinity between the figure of Christ and certain contents in the unconscious, we never would have been able to recognize the light shining through him. The figure of Christ, as the living symbol of the wholeness of the Self, has a power that attracts that which belongs to his divine nature, thereby reconnecting these parts back to their divine nature. Our divinity lies slumbering within us in an unconscious state and is incarnated in (and projected on) the man Jesus so as to make itself visible. Just like our unconscious creates symbols in a dream, we have dreamed up the figure of Christ in order to reflect back our intrinsic wholeness/holiness so that we can recognize, actualize, and increasingly embody it.

As a symbol, Christ is an open portal into a deeper dimension of being. He's not just reflecting an unknown aspect of ourselves, he's also helping us actualize this part. He is pointing at the goal and is the way to reach it as well as the goal itself. If we want to extract the endless blessings that Christ freely offers us, we must interpret the Christ event as he himself taught us to interpret it. It warrants our highest attention that Christ, as we shall soon explore, apparently wants us to view the divine drama that played out through him symbolically, as if it were all a dream.

Symbols

Rudolf Steiner states, "The symbol prepares our soul to receive the truth from the spiritual world."[17] To say this differently: spirit approaches humanity in the form of symbols. Symbols participate in the reality to which they point. They clothe the formless mystery of being in forms that can draw us into direct participation in the numinous mystery of existence that they represent. Symbols come to us from beyond ourselves, speak to us of realities beyond ourselves, and can lead us beyond ourselves.

Through a symbol, the absolute can become present in the relative, the infinite in the finite, the unconditioned in the conditioned, the eternal in the temporal. Transcending the distinction between the inner and the outer, symbols are the sensually perceptible expression of an immaterial inner experience emerging in concrete shape in visible life. Symbols, by their very nature, synthesize what seems to be contradictory opposites into a higher unity. They give meaningful shape to life, and shape us as well.

Speaking of the union of the opposites within us, evil will do anything it can to prevent the union of opposites, for if we accomplish this union—the sacred marriage of alchemy—evil is out of business. The last thing the dark forces want is for us to synthesize opposites, as this would actualize our true nature. This is why they are always seeking to foment polarization, be it within our mind or in the external world, by creating social or political conflicts that keep people in conflict, fighting one another. The forces of darkness can make us overly identify with our rational intellect at the expense of our awareness of the meaning of symbols. When the intellect doesn't serve the symbolic life, it makes us neurotic and serves the powers of darkness.

A symbol is a bridge to all that is the most sublime in humanity. In a symbol, an inner spiritual experience wants to step into life and take visible form so as to be consciously lived and experienced. Deriving as much from the conscious as the unconscious, the symbol reconciles and unites them both. Symbols potentially release psychological energies that are compulsively bound up in struggling with the forces of darkness. Symbols can be described as compressed information, they can be likened to psychospiritual zip files; they are psychic energy transformers in that they potentially liberate blocked, unconscious energy, enabling it to be channeled creatively. The healing power of symbols indicates an intelligent agency at work in our unconscious that has our best interests at heart.

The determining factor as to whether something attains the esteemed status of a symbol is the attitude of the observing consciousness—for example, whether we regard something not merely as the thing in itself, but also as an expression of something unknown. Being, in Jung's words, "a living body," a symbol can't be chosen or constructed, but rather is a kind of revelation that carries with it a new way of seeing and imputing meaning to our experience. Like a baby gestating in its mother's womb, a symbol is produced organically by the unconscious. It is designed to be taken in and amplified by the conscious mind. A symbol is not solely derived from something else, but compels our participation as it seeks to become something other than how it appears.

The symbolic attitude only partially correlates to what is actually happening in the world; for the rest it depends on that part of us that assigns meaning to events in the world and endows them with meaning that has a greater value than the bare facts. This view of things is in contradistinction to the typical materialist viewpoint, which puts facts on the throne and subordinates meaning to them.

When we view the world literally, carnally, and empirically through what Jung calls "the cult of rationalism and realism,"[18] we become bound to and limited by the physical senses. When, however, we begin to see the symbolic dimension of existence, we are roused from our "dense materialistic slumbers,"[19] and our life force becomes free—in psychology-speak, "canalized"—to move in a more spiritual direction (which is to be reborn in and of Spirit). Regaining access to symbolic awareness is vitally important for the continuation of civilization. It serves us greatly to gain fluency, as if learning a foreign language, in the symbolic nature of our world. Recognizing the symbolic dimension of reality and becoming symbolically literate unlocks the door to the unconscious, helping us gain access to the healing energies that lie therein.

Interestingly, one thing that Jung and Christ have in common that is rarely pointed out is that they both spent their lives trying to awaken people to symbolic awareness, to see events in our world symbolically, *as if* life were a dream. There are a number of instances when Christ professes the importance of seeing things symbolically. For example, in speaking about rebirth, Jesus says to Nicodemus, "Except a man be born of water and of the Spirit, he cannot enter into the Kingdom of God. That which is born of flesh is flesh, and that which is born of the Spirit is spirit" (John 3:5). Jung points out that in this statement Christ is expressing "the problem of rebirth in symbolical terms."[20] The underlying meaning of Jesus's words, according to Jung, is: "Do not think carnally, or you will be flesh, but think symbolically, and then you will be spirit."[21] If Nicodemus were to continue to interpret his experience literally, just sticking with the facts, he would be strengthening his bondage to the senses and to the material world. Nicodemus would remain stuck in banalities if he did not step into seeing his situation through the eyes of symbolic awareness.

The reason why Jesus's words have such suggestive power is because they express the symbolic dimension of the human psyche. It's as if Jesus's words are symbolic utterances that resonate with—and thereby awaken—a deeper part of ourselves. Just as Jesus felt it was important to point out to Nicodemus the symbolical view of reality, so did Jung spend his whole life fighting for, in his words, "the reactivation of symbolic thinking."[22]

Just like the the way the higher intelligence that is intrinsic to our psyche continually deliberates on how to create suitable symbols that can be received by the state of the dreamer's unconscious psyche, Jesus was in a similar predicament. He, too, continually tried to come up with myriad ways to bear testament in order to transmit the living spiritual reality that he represented to his unconscious but potentially awakening followers.[23] This is why Jesus spoke in a multitude of similes, metaphors, analogies, and parables, saying, for example, that the Kingdom of Heaven is like a pearl, or a treasure, or a mustard seed, and so on. It is noteworthy that Jesus, himself a living symbol of the higher reality that he is pointing at, is speaking in symbolic terms while he was simultaneously attempting to activate symbolic awareness and illumine the symbolic nature of reality in his followers.

In the apocryphal Acts of John, Jesus appears during the Crucifixion in a vision to John, who had fled to the Mount of Olives, and instructed him to view the Crucifixion symbolically. He says, "John, for the multitude in Jerusalem I am being crucified and pierced with lances and staves, and vinegar and gall are given me to drink." Christ then shows John a "cross of light," saying, "this is not the cross of wood which you will see when you go down from here; neither am I he that is on the cross."[24] In other words, though Christ appears to the masses as being nailed to the cross, this is not who he really is. This is symbolic of when we are going through our own personal crucifixion experience—for example, being absorbed in pain as we are taken over by an unconscious complex—we can recognize that the part of us that is going through this is not who we ultimately are. This awareness can help us to step out of our unconscious identification with our complex while simultaneously connecting us with the witnessing part of us that's free of the complex.

With these words, Christ was giving John a transmission on how to see life symbolically and perceive all experiences as a reflective mirror, as a way of seeing that evokes a deeper sense of meaning. There are two radically different viewpoints for interpreting the Crucifixion of Christ. The first: perceiving the historical, material event through the

214 @ Angels, Demons, and Rebirth

five senses, in which case the cross is a wooden instrument of torture. From the visionary and spiritual point of view, however, the cross is seen to be a glorious, life-affirming symbol. After receiving Christ's transmission of the symbolic dimension of reality, John writes, "Holding fast this one thing to myself, that the Lord contrived all things symbolically and by a dispensation toward men, for their conversion and salvation."[25] This bears repeating: John's takeaway from his visionary encounter with God is that the Lord is arranging events in our world as a living symbol—just like a dream—so as to help us awaken to the dreamlike nature of our situation. We are simply asked to recognize this in order to receive the benefits.

Seen symbolically, the Crucifixion and the Resurrection (these two events go together and are part of a deeper process) is a revelation that depicts the relationship between dissociation and the birth of something new. On the cross, God (in the form of Christ) is seemingly abandoned by—dissociated from—himself, while at the same time, paradoxically, never being more himself. This is the moment where Christ is fully human, which paradoxically is also when he fully actualizes his divinity. Having been forsaken by God, as expressed by Christ's words on the cross, "My God, my God, why hast thou forsaken me?" (Mathew 27:46) is a crucial phase that we all have to pass through to realize the divine life. Seen symbolically, God's state of being dissociated from himself literally becomes the doorway for his re-birth—through us—into our world.

Creative Conflict

It is an archetypal idea that some form of conflict, destruction, or *dis-integration* is a prerequisite for individuation and for the birth of the Self. The Self has an antinomial character, which is to say it includes both conflict and unity. Our wholeness has a paradoxical nature, as it contains and embraces all kinds of opposites, conflict and unity being but one example. Jung's perspective removes conflict from the realm of

Rebirth of the Self ❀ 215

pathology into something potentially creative, as the wholeness of the Self emerges out of the conflict between opposites. When we encounter conflict between opposing parts of ourself, we are asked to find a center point between the opposing tendencies. Finding this center point supports our individuation in that it serves as the locus for the Self to emerge from the background of the unconscious and take living form.

Opposites are intrinsic to the nature of the Self, to our totality. In coming to terms with opposites, they invariably awaken and incarnate within us. We then become, in Jung's words, "a vessel filled with divine conflict."[26] The emergence of the Self out of this kind of conflict is mirrored in the fact that the founders of religions in both the East and the West had to endure a period of intense conflict prior to their revelations—for example, the Buddha struggled with Mara, the evil one, and Christ had it out with the devil.

Archetypal in nature, what Jung calls "the conflicting nature of God"[27] shows up in each of us in a unique way, as our conscious personality is brought face to face with the counter-position of the unconscious. To the extent that this inner conflict is not dealt with consciously in a creative confrontation with the opposites via the process of individuation, it will be fated to be unconsciously, destructively, and literally acted out via projection out into the world.

Stepping on the stage of the cosmic drama at the same time as Christ (which was no coincidence, but rather, a *co-incidence* of inter-related factors), Satan, when seen symbolically, represents the antithesis of the intolerable tension in the world psyche that Christ's advent signified. This is to interpret these theological events symbolically, as expressions of a process whose source is the collective unconscious of humanity. Similarly, the deep dissociation that is playing out on the world stage today can be seen as a reflection of the polarization that exists in the collective psyche and within each one of us.

Writing about "the neurotic sickness" that has befallen our species, Erich Neumann says that it is "an expression of the fact that the collective is not grappling with the problem of evil, which is actually clamoring for its attention."²⁸ We can no longer afford to ignore evil, for if we do we ensure that it will take its revenge on us in a way we don't even want to imagine. Evil is most dangerous when allowed to work in the dark. Humanity today needs to cultivate an awareness of the workings of evil, primarily within each of us. Our darker half has typically been projected onto others via our unconscious need to find a scapegoat to carry our own evil and feed the illusion that we are innocent. This unconscious mechanism results in the world being split into good and bad, an outer circumstance that mirrors the inner landscape of our dissociated psyche.

Recognizing the correlation between the inner and outer can be incredibly helpful. Instead of pathologizing oneself, identifying with and personalizing our inner conflict, which can lead to despair and depression, we can recontextualize our experience of the conflict, *re-cognizing* that the inner tension many of us are feeling is a reflection of a deeper archetypal process that pervades the nonlocal field. Addressing "the apparently unendurable conflict" that someone was inwardly going through, Jung writes that this is "proof of the rightness of your life."²⁹

This realization—that when we experience inner conflict we might be picking up something in the field—can also help us recognize that instead of being separate from the world, we are fundamentally plugged into it, a deeply interconnected expression of it. We shouldn't try to avoid the uncomfortableness of this conflict by stepping into a premature state of resolution, which would be to unconsciously provoke this very conflict in the outside world. Jung adds, "And that is of the devil."³⁰

By identifying with only one of the opposites and splitting off from and projecting out the other, we unconsciously "dream up" this inner conflict to get acted out in full-bodied form in the world. So in avoiding dealing with the conflict between the light and the dark within us, we are unwittingly colluding with the dark forces of death and destruction that are playing out all around us today. But by channeling and inwardly metabolizing the underlying conflict that pervades the greater field, we can become oracles, healers, and shamans for the world, depending on whether we're able to creatively and constructively express what is moving in and through us.

Cosmic Rebirth

Jung is not alone in pointing out the cosmic dissociative disorder from which God—by whatever name we call him/her/it—seems to be suffering. Philip K. Dick writes, "The Godhead is ipso facto divided and pitted against itself; it assumes an antithetical interaction with itself. . . . Hence the Godhead is in infinite crisis. . . . And this ur-paradox in the macrocosm has mirrored effects in every microform down throughout creation."[31] In a situation where the macrocosm mirrors the microcosm and vice versa, this dissociation in the godhead is reflected in every microform (that is, in each one of us). From the kabbalistic point of view, this cosmic dissociation, a seeming crisis in creation itself, is no accident or mistake; it is a necessary part of the evolution of the universe. So there is a divine "method to the madness" that is playing out.

Dick comments, "Thus the rupture in the Godhead was *necessary,* given its (the Godhead's) drive to complete itself as kosmos. It was driven inexorably to this schism; hence the one became two, and the dialectic came into existence, as it became increasingly aware."[32] Dick is pointing out the deeper teleology cloaked within God's dissociation: the split is the way, through a constantly evolving dialectic, that God is becoming increasingly aware, or conscious. And we humans find ourselves playing a key role in this cosmic process in which God requires humanity to resolve its antithetical nature and become whole.

Where did this sickness of dissociation come from? The germ of the *dis-ease* was implanted in our soul the moment we started to become conscious of ourselves and our world. The process of becoming conscious is symbolized in scripture when Adam and Eve ate the forbidden fruit of the Tree of Knowledge in the Garden of Eden, an act that gave humanity knowledge of the opposites of good and evil. This awareness shattered the primal state of unconscious identification and fusion with the world. This is the moment when one splits into two and self-consciousness was born. At that point we became aware of ourselves in such a way as to not feel at one with ourselves. This initiated the evolution of human consciousness. As part of the cosmic plan, this division into two was imperative in order to bring the one out of a state of potentiality into actuality.

Because the origin of this impersonal, universal, archetypal process is in consciousness itself, the cure for our sickness of dissociation is to be found—and can only ever be found—in the realm of consciousness. The current state of extreme polarization in our world is the womb in which the Self will be born within each of us, and collectively, in the world. By acccepting our mission, we will find our true selves and remember who we are in the process. We will discover that we play a crucial role—a role seemingly prepared for us since beginningless time—in what is the most archetypally creative process imaginable. How amazing is that!

9

Reflecting on
Jung's *Answer to Job*

As a psychiatrist, Jung considered himself to be a physician who was trying to heal the sickness that has afflicted humanity. In what may be considered his masterpiece, *Answer to Job,* Jung interpreted the Old Testament story of Job from a psychological perspective, as if it were humanity's dream, which is to see it as symbolizing the process of individuation as it has unfolded in the collective psyche of humanity. In trying to come to terms with the seemingly darker side of God that Job encountered, Jung was creatively pointing at wetiko in his own one-of-a-kind way. Understanding Jung's insights regarding humanity's relationship to evil as described in *Answer to Job* can help us better see and break the spell of wetiko.

Answer to Job was Jung's most inspired work in the sense that something beyond his ego and conscious personality was coming through him. Seventy-five years old and in the middle of a feverish illness at the time, Jung referred to this book as "a little essay."[1] Once he completed it his illness was over. Jung describes how *Answer to Job* came into being by means of a letter in which he said it was like "the spirit seizing one by the scruff of the neck."[2] When the book, in Jung's words, "came to me,"[3] he had the feeling that he was at a concert listening to a great composition—as if the text was a channeled work, dictated directly from the unconscious. Toward the end of his life, Jung commented that he wished he could rewrite all of his books, but he wouldn't change a word in *Answer to Job*. After writing it he wrote, "I have landed the great whale."[4] Jung felt that what he wrote about in this book was the unfoldment of "the divine consciousness in which I participate, like it or not."[5] Completing *Answer to Job* was, according to author and documentarian Catrine Clay, who has written about Jung's marriage to Emma Jung and the early years of psychoanalysis, the happiest moment of his life.[6]

To say *Answer to Job* is a controversial book is a vast understatement, for it goes directly against the traditional dogmatic view of theology and created a huge uproar when it was published in 1952. To this day it is widely misunderstood, even by many Jungians. In this amazing book, Jung interpreted the biblical story of Job, a wealthy man who is brought low by God after Satan challenges him, as symbolically representing an individual ego's encounter with the Self, both in its conscious and unconscious aspects.* As Jung points out, a person's individuation process is the vehicle for the Self's incarnation. As Jung articulated throughout his writings, when we start to develop conscious realization of the Self, becoming to whatever degree "self-realized," we are, in metaphysical terms, supporting God's incarnation.

The Book of Job is the pivotal point in the unfoldment of what Jung calls "a divine drama."[7] Job's experience represents the Bible transitioning from collective to individual psychology. The story of Job is the first part of the Bible where God, who in Jungian thinking symbolizes the Self, engages in a dialogue with an individual representing themselves rather than merely being a spokesperson for the collective. The underlying theme of the story is the relationship between humanity and God. Psychologically, this symbolizes the emergence of the continually unfolding relationship between the ego and the Self (the God within)—a dynamic that Jung refers to as the "ego-Self axis."[8] Jung realized that the story of Job symbolically expresses a new relationship between God

---

*In this discussion I'd like to acknowledge the work of Jungian analyst Edward F. Edinger.

and humanity that mirrors our ever-evolving individual relationship with our unconscious. As Jung tried to make clear, the Book of Job symbolizes a divine initiation process in which we're all enlisted, which can potentially expand our consciousness and introduce us to a radically new state of being.

In viewing the Job story symbolically, Jung realized that the ordeal that Job, a good, God-fearing and wealthy family man, went through was an outpicturing of an inner process that was taking place within God himself.* The events that unfold in the Job drama are symbolic of the transformative inner process going on deep within the collective unconscious of our species, which each one of us is participating in, whether we know it or not. Jung wrote so passionately about Job's encounter with the dark side of God because it mirrored his own personal encounter with the darkness of the unconscious. When asked how he could live with the knowledge he had recorded in *Answer to Job,* Jung replied, "I live in my deepest hell and from there I cannot fall any further."⁹

In *Answer to Job* Jung was trying to come to terms with the dark side of God, that is, evil. Jung wanted to know why Job was treated so badly—actually wounded—by God (who, as the Book of Job makes clear, was secretly in cahoots with Satan). He was attempting to show how we can connect with the light once we have fallen into the darkness. He realized that the story of Job expresses the psychospiritual dynamic of the human encounter with evil—a story that resonates today in the current dark times we're living through.

According to Jung, Job's ordeal was not an expression of his personal psychology, but rather was set in motion by deeper, transpersonal, archetypal forces. Job didn't interpret the darkness and suffering that overtook his life in a personal way, feeling like it was his fault, which would have invariably led to despair. Rather, Job viewed

---

*For consistency's sake, I have chosen to keep Jung's use of the masculine gender when referring to God throughout this chapter.

his situation—which is really our own—as potentially containing a deeper transpersonal meaning. This perspective makes all the difference in the world. In Jung's words, the events in the story of Job are such that "one cannot altogether suppress the suspicion of connivance in high places."[10] A higher-dimensional process was informing and potentially being revealed through the darkness that Job was personally living through. Jung counsels us to keep our eyes open so as to recognize the deeper dynamic that gave shape to Job's ordeal.

It is highly significant that in the story of Job it is Satan who initiates Job's ordeal. Breaking with traditional religious thinking, Jung pondered the disturbing fact that in the Book of Job, God allows himself to be bamboozled and hoodwinked by Satan. As Jung points out, Satan was the only one among the angels (considered the sons of God) who took the initiative to create obstacles, which, as Jung points out, were "necessary and indeed indispensable"[11] for the divine drama to be successfully accomplished. Though on one hand Satan is God's adversary, on a deeper level the two are intimately related—maybe, if we let our imagination run wild, even secretly conspiring with each other in order to accomplish the same goal.

Through his own personal encounter with evil, Jung became increasingly aware that evil itself, and humanity's relationship to it, plays a key role in the divine incarnation process. He realized that it clearly wasn't God's intention, if we could speak in such human terms, to spare humanity from experiencing evil. Jung was struck by how human beings have a strongly ingrained unconscious tendency to avoid even considering that in the power of evil, God might have hidden a special purpose, which is "most important for us to know."[12]

Jung realized that evil, if it doesn't destroy us in the process, actually activates the latent, unconscious impulse in us to individuate, to become who we are. In *Answer to Job*, he asks whether it was God himself "who egged Satan on"[13] for the ultimate purpose of glorifying and blessing Job. Jung suggests that the meaning of Job's seemingly undeserved suffering, the origin of which is actually Satan, was to catalyze Job so that he would develop a conscious relationship with—and realization of—the Self.

Job's ordeal symbolically represents God's attempt to bring to Job (who symbolizes the human ego) an awareness of God (that is, the Self). This is why in *Answer to Job* Jung describes Satan as "the godfather of man as a spiritual being."[14] It's as if evil is potentially helping humanity (in this case, in the person of Job) to realize its divinity. Of course, in true quantum style, whether evil potentially destroys us or awakens us is a function of whether or not we recognize what it is revealing to us.

In this book, Jung interprets world history as the dreaming process of a greater being (whom we call God), whose origin lies outside of time and yet manifests—and reveals itself—in, through, and over time. Secretly pervading all of humanity, God fashions humanity as the instrument by which he can incarnate and consciously realize himself. This is a timeless, eternal, archetypal event echoing in our world today, however, this time, instead of just one man, all of humanity has gotten drafted into participating in this process.

Jung emphasizes that it makes all the difference in the world if we *unconsciously* enact (as opposed to *consciously* recognizing) the deeper mythological and archetypal process in which we are all participating. The difference between these two "is tremendous,"[15] with consciousness being the determining factor. In reading the story of Job between the lines and interpreting it as the psyche's self-revelation, Jung is able to discern the deeper archetypal process that is symbolically being revealed to us through Job's ordeal.

Jung realized that the birth of a figure such as the Savior (archetype) typically takes place in our world when humanity has fallen into a time of darkness, confusion, and disorientation—exactly what we see in the world today. Viewing the Job story symbolically, Jung realized that atemporally, from a dimension outside of linear time, the birth of the Savior—who is none other than the Self—in and through humanity has already happened, and that this needs to be "perceived, recognized and declared" by humanity to make it real "in time."[16]

Becoming, in Jung's words, "baptized in"[17] (via our conscious recognition of) the deeper cosmic process that we are participating in is the crucial act that changes everything. Instead of merely being the recipient of a divine revelation, we become a conscious participant in the divine drama. Instead of observing this deeper cosmic process as a passive observer or as an intellectual idea, we find ourselves consciously playing a role in a mythic process, which can be a truly revelatory and transformative experience.

As Jung makes clear, if ever there was a time when psychological understanding is needed, it is now. That the deeper mythologem is actually coming to light and both literally and symbolically playing out in our world is so obvious that, according to Jung, "We must be deliberately blinding ourselves if we cannot see its symbolic nature and interpret it in symbolic terms."[18] Seeing the deeper mythic drama in which we are playing a central role transforms our vision of the events in our world from the literal to the symbolic. This process, in which we step into what Jung calls "symbolic awareness" involves seeing the dreamlike nature of the world and is, psychologically speaking, known as the individuation process.

Contemplating the incarnation of God through Christ as a dreaming process, Jung wonders: where did God's darkness go? In today's world we are being forced to find an answer to this fateful question. When God became human in the form of Christ (who, being the incarnation of the light, was spotless in his purity), all darkness and evil were carefully kept outside of God's chosen instrument of incarnation. Viewed psychologically, if God had self-reflected during his earthly incarnation as Christ, Jung points out that he, God, would have recognized what "a fearful dissociation"[19] he was acting out.

Is God Working Something Out through Us?

When the Christ event is interpreted symbolically, it's as if God is working something out in his unconscious through the collective dream/drama of humanity. God's inner opposites—his light and dark parts—had become totally polarized in the figures of Christ and Satan. Instead of manifesting through two adversarial figures like it did over two thousand years ago, today this polarization is manifesting not only within the individual human psyche, but in the collective unconscious and the body politic of humanity, which has become split into two warring camps.

As Jung makes clear, the source of all the conflict is ultimately to be found within God himself. Since humans share in God's nature, we discover, in Jung's words, "that God in his 'oppositeness' has taken possession of him, incarnated himself in him."[20] The paradoxical nature of God has a direct impact on our inner life—we are torn asunder into opposites and are left having to deal with a seemingly insoluble conflict, being challenged to reconcile these divinely sponsored opposites as they show up within our own unconscious. The darkness of the unconscious wants to reach the light and become conscious, while at the same time it continually thwarts itself as it would rather remain unconscious. Jung says, "God wants to become man, but not quite."[21] He recognizes that God acts out of the unconscious of humanity in order to unite these primordial opposites, whose origin is to be found within God himself.

As Jung recognized, God has eternally wanted to become human. To put this in psychological terms, everything dreams of individuation, of becoming who we truly are. Instead of choosing a pure, guiltless vessel (Christ) as his birthplace, God now wants to become, as Jung says, "wholly man"[22] and incarnate through the empirical, creaturely human being who unconsciously participates in the darkness of the world. As Jung points out, this "might well be a cause for anxiety."[23]

If God incarnates through ordinary, partly unconscious human beings, there is no avoiding or getting around the experience that each one of us are fated to face, which is to come to terms with the divine problem of reckoning with the opposite forces within us. Jung realized that the more intimate this bond between God and humanity becomes, the greater the danger of encountering evil. This metaperspective can help us gain a new perspective on the wetiko epidemic rampant in our world today, in which we are being forced to come to terms with evil in its greater cosmological context. Because God wants to become human, the uniting of the antinomies that are intrinsic to God's nature must take place in humanity, which is the role that we, as living, breathing, alchemical vessels, have been being prepared for since the beginning of our appearance on this planet.

In our current age, God has granted humanity an almost superhuman, godlike power to destroy ourselves with weapons of mass destruction that were unimaginable to our ancestors. This places a great responsibility on us, which, in Jung's words, "we can no longer wiggle out of"[24] based on our seeming helplessness. Our situation places an urgent demand on our species to step out of our unconscious blindness and consciously deepen the realization of something we are suffering from: in Jung's words, "a terrifying ignorance"[25] of our true nature. Since a godlike power has been placed in our hands, humanity "can no longer remain blind."[26] It should get our attention that again and again, Jung is pointing out the self-induced blindness of wetiko that is afflicting humanity.

Psychologically, the process of healing our blindness represents a level of development in which the human ego becomes relativized and realizes (opens its eyes) that it is subordinate—and in service—to the Self. The individuated ego, instead of being unconsciously inflated—in other words, unknowingly identified with and thus blind to the Self— finds itself in an ever-deepening conscious relationship with the Self, as our eyes become more and more open to who we are—and who we are related to.

As Jung concludes in *Answer to Job*, Job's newborn awareness of God's dark side requires, in turn, a response from God, resulting in God's incarnation through humanity. Job is a stand-in for the human ego, and God represents the Self, our wholeness. Our expanded awareness of darkness is not a passive moment, but has an effect on the deity. Jung considered Job's experience to be the precursor and catalyst for the incarnation of God through Christ. He realized that the real reason for God incarnating as a human being is to be found in God's earlier encounter with Job. Jung conceived of Christ as the prototype of a deeper primordial pattern that exists outside of time, as the first born who is succeeded by a continually expanding number of younger brother and sisters—us. He called this "the Christification of many."[27]

As Jung wrote in *Answer to Job*, due to our littleness and extreme vulnerability, there is one thing that humanity possesses that God, because of his omnipotence, doesn't possess: the need for self-reflection. In the human act of self-reflection, God becomes motivated to step off his throne, so to speak, and incarnate through humanity in order to obtain the uniquely precious jewel that humanity possesses via our self-reflection. The act of deepening our realization of the Self has an effect on the Self that we are realizing.

Jung says that God needs conscious reflection "in order to exist in reality."[28] This is analogous to how if light is not perceived, it is invisible and might as well not exist. The existence of light is as dependent on our perception of it as the act of perception depends on light. This brings to mind Christ's reference to his light-filled nature in the apocryphal Acts of John: "A lamp [light] am I to you that perceive me."[29] Our conscious perception is the key factor in the light that is symbolic of the Self, or God, fully realizing and actualizing its nature. Thus the Self is, for all intents and purposes, nonexistent unless it is consciously realized by us, hence the crucial importance of self- and Self-reflection.

In *Answer to Job*, Jung lays the groundwork for a new worldview, a new myth for modern humanity, and our place in the greater scheme of things. In this new way of seeing ourselves, we are invited to recognize that we have always been in a co-creative partnership with the Self, but *consciously* realizing this is a true game-changer. As Jung couldn't emphasize enough, individual self-reflection, which returns us to the deeper, darker ground of our light-filled nature, is the beginning of the cure for the blindness of wetiko.

PART III

The Quantum Synchronistic Field

This section elucidates the quantum nature of wetiko, showing how understanding wetiko's entangled wave/particle quantum nature helps us to come to grips with the tricksterlike nature of this mind-virus, as well as shedding light on the quantum nature of both the world and ourselves. Being quantum in nature, wetiko contains encoded within it both the deepest poison and its own vaccine, and how it actually manifests depends in a very real sense on how we dream it. We inquire into how the revelations emerging from quantum physics—provided we have the eyes to see— provide the medicine for healing wetiko. Because synchronicity is the internal corollary in human experience of the seemingly external quantum idea, this section concludes by doing a deep dive into the nature of synchronicity. Because wetiko can only be seen when we recognize that, just like a dream, the inner and outer worlds synchronistically reflect each other, our shedding light on the workings of synchronicity can help us illuminate and dispel the mind-virus that plagues our world.

10

Quantum Physics and Wetiko

One way of understanding wetiko is to understand its antidote, as both the illness and the cure co-arise as inseparable parts of a whole, quantum system. It is noteworthy that wetiko is a quantum phenomenon, for the revelations emerging from the field of quantum physics, now considered the crown jewel of the physical sciences, provide insight into the disease's cure.

Though discovered a bit over a century ago, we are still in the beginning stages of unpacking the meaning of quantum physics. Such an epochal and world-transforming discovery typically takes centuries to integrate into and transform our existing view of the world and our place in it. Perhaps a clue to the deeper meaning of quantum physics as well as the healing medicine for the mind-virus lies in its revelatory aspect.

Revelation

"Revelation," to quote Jung, "is an 'unveiling' of the depth of the human soul first and foremost, a 'laying bare'; hence it is an essentially psychological event, though this does not, of course, tell us what *else* it might be."[1] Even though we subjectively experience revelation as typically coming from outside of ourselves, revelation is a spiritual occurrence that takes place within us. The inner spiritual event of revelation can, and often does, take on external form and symbolize itself through outer events. To become a revelation, an outer historical event must be realized within us spiritually. Being a divine-human interaction, the nature of revelation is something in which humanity is inextricably involved. Revelation can remove our limitations, transform and re-shape our consciousness, and change our orientation towards life, the world, ourselves, and the realm of spirit.

The revelations emerging from quantum physics—which, being psychological, are inner, subjective events—are unveiling something deep within the depths of our souls. Quantum physics is a theory about our state of knowledge of the world, which is a subjective state, rather than being about objectively real states of a supposedly objective world. Quantum physics is therefore perfectly suited to addressing and reflecting back to us important features about our own psyche, which is the very domain where wetiko operates.

The quantum is itself a living revelation.* The great theoretical physicist John Archibald Wheeler (1911–2008) wanted to "jolt the world of physics into an understanding of the quantum because the quantum surely contains—when unraveled—the most wonderful insight we could ever hope to have on how this world operates, something equivalent in scope and power to the greatest discovery that science has yet yielded up."[2] Simply put, the quantum is the greatest scientific discovery in all of human history, and it offers insight into how wetiko operates.

It is as if the universe secreted a psychic vitamin to compensate for the extremely materialistic one-sidedness of our age inspired by the wetiko pathogen, and this immaterial medicinal supplement is quantum physics. Quantum physics can serve as the medicine that helps us correct the distortion that causes our materialist myopia. Similar to how

*As discussed in my book *The Quantum Revelation: A Radical Synthesis of Science and Spirituality.*

in an individual's process, the unconscious compensates a one-sidedness by sending us dreams (whose language are symbols) that can help bring us back into balance, quantum physics (also a symbolic process) can be seen to be something that humanity has dreamed up in order to find a new way to look at both the world and ourselves. In so doing, quantum physics is serving a similar compensatory function as our dreams, as it can bring us back to ourselves.

In the past, revelations of consciousness were the purview of contemplative spiritual traditions. Now an analogous revelation has insinuated itself into the physics lab. Many spiritual traditions throughout history have relied on divine revelations concealed within phenomena, which await discovery in order to initiate or continue to propagate the lineage's liberating gnosis. For example, the Nyingma lineage of Tibetan Buddhism, a tradition I am personally familiar with, has refined the revelatory experience of keeping their teachings fresh to an extraordinary extent, in a phenomenon known as *terma*. Terma are hidden treasures encoded within the fabric of the universe that are discovered during times of great need. The specific form that the hidden treasure takes speaks precisely to the particular need of the community. Though not exactly a form of Buddhist terma as it is known traditionally, quantum physics can be conceived as being a particularly unique, modern-day analogue of terma. Notably, terma are in fact quantum phenomena; they do not take a definitive and materialized form until their moment of revelation, which is a quantum-like process in which we are participating.

We should be extremely cautious when calling something an actual terma, which is a highly codified mystical treasure unique to the Nyingma school of Tibetan Buddhism. The terma tradition was created by the great eighth-century spiritual adept Padmasambhava for the benefit of future generations such as ourselves. Padmasambhava was the founder of Tibetan Buddhism and is considered the second Buddha as well as the Buddha of our age. In designing the terma tradition, Padmasambhava was—is—able to nonlocally engage with this world of ours in such a way as to transcend time and space in order to creatively conspire with us, in the present moment, in our own awakening. Padmasambhava mystically concealed many terma throughout the multiple dimensions of the universe, enlisting powerful elemental beings to be spiritual protectors of these terma so as to ensure that they would not be revealed until their appropriately prophesied time of discovery. Padmasambhava then appointed and empowered certain close disciples, called *tertons,* who are considered emanations of Padmasambhava, to discover and reveal the terma in future times whenever a specific treasure was most needed.

Sometimes the terma is an actual blessed object or teaching that is found in the environment. Other times there is a mnemonic cue in the environment that jogs the terton's memory to help them access the hidden treasure, which exists in the essential nature of their mind. Sometimes no external support is needed and the terton discovers the terma encoded within the recesses of their own mind when they are able to reaccess the pristine state of radiant light that they were in when they received their initial commission from Padmasambhava.

Because of the cultural context and very specific conditions that certify something to be a terma, we should be very careful about labeling something a terma in the traditional Tibetan Buddhist sense of the word. Of course, we could take an expansive view and consider that Padmasambhava, as the personification of the awakened state, is himself the source of and inspiration for quantum physics,* as well as all other revelations that emerge into our world. This is a perspective that would render the revelations emerging from quantum physics as being an actual terma, but it's a slippery slope to conflate all revelatory phenomena as being terma. This becomes particularly tricky when we realize the equivalence between our quantum nature and the Buddha nature (the awakened mind) that every terma is pointing at and of which they are an expression.

---

*Some researchers seriously consider the question of whether Padmasambhava was indeed the father of quantum physics.

With this in mind, we can conceive of the awakened mind, which is the origin of all terma, as enlisting quantum physics to be one of its more modern channels of transmission into our world. In honoring the very rigorous and specific circumstances that need to auspiciously coincide to bring about the revelation of a terma, however, I would prefer to say instead that quantum physics, in its revelatory aspect, is *terma-like*. In other words, with the terma tradition as my reference point and inspiration, I am pointing out that quantum physics, when seen as a living revelation, can be likened to a modern-day analogue of a Tibetan Buddhist terma.

Terma stir our memory, helping us remember something that we once knew—what is known as *anamnesis,* an "unforgetting," which is the antidote to the *amnesia* (the unconscious ignorance) from which our species is currently suffering. This unforgetting, an alchemical *re-membering,* is like a shamanic retrieval of a lost part or *member* of our soul. This memory is not recollected from past experiences of the senses from this mortal life. It is a remembering of the timeless, which has to do with who we are.

Originating from a timeless dimension, terma can be thought of as alarm clocks planted within the universe that are set to go off at exactly the right moment in time to help us awaken. In Buddhism, the basic source and essential nature of terma is considered to be the primordial awakened mind itself. Due to its deeper purpose of awakening humanity, hidden treasures are inexhaustible, continually arising in our world like spores from mushrooms. Ultimately, a treasure revelation is never really over until our species fully wakes up—in Buddhist thinking, until samsara, the endless, suffering-filled cycle of death and rebirth, is emptied. The very existence of terma is an expression that the universe we live in is an abundant treasure trove bursting—and birthing—at the seams.

Something within us resonates when we connect with a symbol in our dreams. Similarly, when quantum physics is contemplated in its symbolic, terma-like aspect, something deep within us can potentially open and become more alive. A novel, psychoactivating life form, terma enhance and revitalize whatever universe—or mind—they arise within. Like a key unlocking a door or like a charm that breaks a spell, terma have the power to unlock the mind to reveal its true timeless, changeless, unconditioned nature.

These hidden treasures are intended to be expressed and shared so as to fully unlock their nonlocal benefits and blessings. A novel form of language, these living revelations are a cipher of information that are thirsting to be deciphered and translated into a communicable and easily disseminated form. After all is said and done, the ineluctable destiny of a terma is that it is to be made public in one form or another. Whereas in the Buddhist terma tradition certain spiritual teachers are destined to discover, interpret, and translate the treasure to the community at large, might it be that in our present time those among us who grok what is being revealed through our universe when it is seen as a living revelation are being cast in this role?

When seen as a modern-day analogue of terma, quantum physics is reflecting back to us our creative partnership with the genius of the universe. The revelation that is quantum physics can be seen as a potential model for many other modern-day analogues of terma, all arising in a variety of channels. When an organism, be it an individual, a species, a biosphere, or a universe, gets off-balance and one-sided, the dreamlike nature of things becomes self-regulating through any and every means necessary. So we should keep our eyes, ears, and every other sense organ, both physical and nonphysical, open to such creative compensatory interventions from this dreamlike universe of ours. The universe is a continual theophany, an endlessly unfolding revelation, a living oracle thirsting for divination.

Similar to if we are open to the possibility of synchronistic phenomena, we will see synchronicities, the more we are open to the possibility of terma-like revelations in our world, the more revelatory our world becomes. As quantum physics reveals, the mirrorlike nature of the world simply reflects back to us the attitude of our mind, as the two, mind and world, are not separate, but are interconnected parts of one whole quantum system.

The awareness that we live in a universe in which synchronicities happen and hidden treasures are found helps us realize that we live in a magical universe. John Wheeler, one of the most rigorous thinkers of modern science, opines "There is some magic in this universe of ours."[3] Wheeler felt that when we finally discover what's at the bottom of what's really going on in our universe, we won't find a central mechanism, but rather, "magic may be the better description of the treasure that is waiting."[4] Quantum physics is revealing that we don't live in the mechanistic Cartesian world of classical physics, but rather we inhabit an enchanted world, a waking dream that is filled to the brim with magic. This brings to mind the words of anthropologist and mythologist Sir James Frazer at the end of his magnum opus, *The Golden Bough:* "In the last analysis, magic, religion, and science are nothing but theories of thought; and as science has supplanted its predecessors, so it may hereafter be itself superseded by some more perfect hypothesis. . . . The dreams of magic may one day be the waking realities of science."[5]

Jung was aware that this universe is a potential treasure trove waiting to be discovered and unlocked. He was frustrated at being a bit ahead of his time and thus was not able to transmit the profundity of what he had realized. As he was approaching death, in 1960 he wrote in a letter to Eugene Rolfe, "I was unable to make people see. . . I have failed in my foremost task, to open people's eyes—to the fact that man has a soul and there is a buried treasure in the field."[6] The real treasure is the creative essence of our soul—our very nature—which is hidden from view to the extent that we haven't opened our inner eyes. This is a recurring motif in world mythology: that we actually possess what we're looking for but don't know it.

The Physics of the Dream

Quantum physics is the physics of the dream. It points at the dreamlike nature of reality while simultaneously being an expression of that very dreamlike nature at which it is pointing. Wheeler wrote in a letter, "I would willingly give up an arm or a leg to understand 'How come the quantum?' or 'How come existence?'"[7]—which Wheeler felt was the same question.

The essence of the quantum nature of things is expressed in the well-established fact that light appears as either a wave or a particle depending on how it is observed. This reflects back to us that the way our universe manifests is in some mysterious way, just like a dream, a function of our consciousness, determined by how we observe it. Wetiko's quantum nature is similarly characterized by how it manifests—as a curse or a blessing—depending on whether we cognize what it is revealing to us, that is, how we dream it up.

In disclosing that just like a dream, our act of observing the universe influences the very universe we are observing, quantum physics is revealing that the act of observation is itself creative. This has always been the case, but it greatly behooves us to recognize and activate our quantum creativity so that we can consciously participate and have a say in our own evolution, both individually and collectively. When we fully take in the radically liberating and empowering insights that quantum physics, like mana from heaven, is freely offering us, it can't help but unlock the creative spirit within us.

Our universe is quantum on all scales, big and small; it is quantum through and through. Grappling for most of his life with the question of why our universe is quantum in the first place, Wheeler wrote, "My tentative answer is stated nowhere more compactly than in Act IV, Scene 1, of Shakespeare's *The Tempest,* 'We are such stuff as dreams are made on.'"[8] Wheeler is here reflecting on the undeniable insight that quantum physics had stumbled upon: that reality is dreamlike in nature. Not trained in such seemingly mystical matters, quantum physicists are still in the beginning stages of wrapping their minds around the profundity of this revelation.

Having a dream places an ethical responsibility on the dreamer to work (and play) with the dream so as to unlock its blessings. Similarly, for quantum physics to reveal the extent of its gifts necessitates our active engagement with its revelations, which point us toward the dreamlike nature of reality. Its medicinal effect is particularly unique, with its own mode of healing, which could be called *participatory medicine,* as in order to receive quantum physics' untold benefits we have to engage and participate in what it is revealing to us.

Just like the way a dream compensates for a one-sidedness and false attitude in the dreamer, quantum physics can only be fully appreciated when it is seen relative to the classical Newtonian physics mindset, with its overly rational, mechanistic, deterministic, materialistic, and reductionist way of viewing things. Just like a symbol in a dream compensates a one-sidedness in the dreamer, quantum theory arose out of the one-sided view of classical physics. To fully take in the world-transforming revelations offered by quantum physics, it behooves us to understand the Newtonian universe out of which quantum physics emerged, as quantum physics is truly a product of our times.

Newtonian Madness

The Newtonian worldview of pre-quantum, classical physics provides an ultimately false, limited, and low-resolution lens for understanding the universe, and this happens to be the very framework that empowers wetiko, thus enabling this mind-virus to more rapidly spread and propagate itself throughout the human world. Wetiko is supported and fed by the internal logic, seeming coherence, and spellbinding power of classical physics. This mechanistic worldview takes the heart, soul, and magic out of the world, relegating it to a dead, inanimate, and insensate domain.

The classical worldview is a masterful spell that has been cast over humanity, seriously misleading us about the fundamental nature of reality. Its power is all the more seductive and compelling due to the undeniable mastery over the physical world via the massive technological developments that classical physics has conferred upon us. Interestingly, the founding fathers of quantum physics, in struggling to characterize the dreamlike nature of the quantum realm they were beginning to access, used words like *evil spells* and *exorcism* (evoking the image of the wicked fairy in the fairy tale *Sleeping Beauty*). This shows the deeper archetypal energies of the human psyche that quantum physics had tapped into. The revelations emerging from quantum physics were truly—in true quantum style, potentially—beginning to break the spell of wetiko.

The Newtonian perspective, which sees the world as objectively existing outside of and separate from ourselves—an "independently existing objective universe,"—or IEOU—is based on scientific materialism, which has been the template for much of modern science, in addition to greatly influencing every aspect of our lives with its compelling but ultimately false worldview. This viewpoint is actually deluded, as it expresses an epistemological blind spot at the very center of the predominating scientific vision of the world. The vast majority of modern society is unaware of this pervasive psychic blindness—what Philip K. Dick calls "our materialist-atomist blindness."[9] Though more and more giving us the ability to dominate nature, the scientific materialist worldview of classical physics has not helped us control our own nature, which is to inevitably court a disaster of our own making.

The Newtonian perspective worked remarkably well when it came to dealing with the macroscopic world, enabling unprecedented levels of control to be exerted over the physical world. But in the process of obtaining mastery over the physical plane, an unseen cost was being incurred by the human spirit. In viewing life mechanistically, the very thing that makes life the sacred miracle that it is, consciousness, has been increasingly ignored, marginalized, even considered a mere illusion, a product of the physical brain instead of the other way around, as the data from quantum physics indicates. The materialistic worldview is potentially threatening to destroy the most precious essence of what makes human beings human in the first place. Jung refers to materialism as a "loathsome, stinking plant [that] is being grown in all the scientific institutions in the land . . . sowing the poisonous seed that fecundates confused minds."[10]

The Newtonian worldview was revolutionary in its power, yet it contained a subtle error—the thinking that the world objectively exists—that has solidified into a widespread delusion that has over time gone pandemic. This rigid and unquestioned ideology has profoundly enabled the collective madness in which our species is currently immersed. To think in terms of the one-sided, overly materialistic Newtonian point of view is, in Jung's words, "crazy in itself and has always engendered craziness whenever it was taken seriously."[11] The Newtonian worldview is not only crazy but crazy-making for all who subscribe to its viewpoint. Its way of viewing the world disables our highest evolutionary potential, as it is an inadequate and impoverished map of reality that we then can easily mistake for the real thing.

This craziness, however, tends to remain invisible to those afflicted, as this worldview provides a convincing interpretational lens that contextualizes everything it sees within the framework of its unquestioned assumptions. This induces a self-satisfied blindness in which the blindness is unrecognized by those suffering from it. Those afflicted with this blindness think they are seeing accurately, while the opposite is actually the case.

An essential feature of this madness is the severing between subject and object, or observer and observed. In looking at the world as existing separate from us, the scientific imagination thought that it wasn't part of, participating in, or affecting what it was investigating. Classical physicists pretend that they are not involved in their own experiments by maintaining the illusion of a scientific "objectivity."

The view that splits the world into observer and observed can be thought of as a sickness of epidemic proportions that has become a self-propagating idea; it's a way of viewing the world that has penetrated and made itself at home in the human mind. The scientific materialistic worldview has become infused into the core of our being by a kind of osmosis. Like a virus (sound familiar?), it spreads and seeps into our minds without being seen, until this psychic infection becomes the lens through which we naively interpret and place meaning on our world and our place in it. This dualistic worldview has been reified and mathematically formalized into an orthodox creed that has entranced us, holding us in a prison of our own making. There are no bars in our self-imposed prison, however; there is nothing stopping us from activating our quantum creativity except our own limited conception of things and lack of awareness that such an empowering option is even possible. This Newtonian prison is not even recognized as a prison, which is the most effective kind of prison, as the inmates—we the people—don't even suspect that we're in prison and actually believe that we are free.

As a result of this mistaken view, humanity has become entrained by the self-reinforcing fetters of scientific materialism, spellbound by its vision—or rather, hallucination—of the world as objectively existing separate from the observing subject, us. Speaking of the "distance between the observer and the observed," to quote spiritual teacher and philosopher Krishnamurti, who was aware of the revelations of quantum physics through his friendship with trailblazing quantum theorist David Bohm, "in that distance, the division between the seer and the thing seen, in that division the whole conflict of man exists."[12]

Due to the fact that our social and political institutions are still organized around an outdated materialist, reductionist Newtonian worldview, many of our collective problems today are essentially crises of perception, just as was true for physicists in the 1920s. Our classically induced habits of perception tend to freeze and concretize the fluidity of the world, not to mention our mind, thereby restricting the dynamic richness of it available to us at any given moment. This erroneous view began to be corrected in the first part of the twentieth century with the discovery of quantum physics, yet it is still, unfortunately, reigning as the dominant worldview. And this is why our social, political, and economic systems, which are expressions of this inaccurate and wrong-headed view, are breaking down, as we see all around us today.

Diseased Ideas

The accumulated and agreed-upon ideas we have about the nature of our world are inherited. This is analogous to the transmission of genetic traits from generation to generation. Instead of genes, however, it is ideas—memes—that are being inherited and propagated through human minds across multiple generations. And some of these ideas, such as the idea of an objectively existing reality, are simply mistaken.

An inherently existing, objective world, something that has its own nature, separate from something else, is an idea that only exists in the human imagination. An objective anything cannot actually exist in the infinitely interconnected universe that we inhabit. I recently had an experience that brought this insight to mind. I was trying to get on a website, and I had to prove that I wasn't a robot by picking out the boxes that had traffic lights in them. Some of the boxes clearly had what I thought they were looking for—the red, green, and yellow lights. Other boxes didn't have these lights but simply had the poles on which the actual lights were mounted, which threw me into a deep philosophical quandary. Weren't these poles also part of the traffic light? What about the ground that the poles were mounted on? What about the whole rest of the universe that ultimately isn't separate from the traffic light? The idea of a traffic light as intrinsically existing on its own is a construction of our mind; it has a certain utility, but when we get right down to it, it only exists as an idea in our mind.

Playing the game I found myself in, I decided to check the boxes that gave them the answers I imagined they were looking for, which allowed me to access the desired website. One of the weirdest parts of this whole experience is that if I were to answer the questions from a wholistic, awakened point of view that resonates with the revelations emerging from quantum physics, I would be seen as a robot and wouldn't have been able to successfully navigate consensus reality the way I wanted to.

The deluded notion of an objectively existing reality independent of us (an IEOU), an idea that has become imprinted on the quantum substratum of the collective unconscious, is both the cause of the plethora of problems facing our species today, as well as the reason why we can't solve them.

Recognizing that there is no objective world "out there" is an expression of wisdom, potentially helping us dispell wetiko. And yet, wetiko can easily usurp this realization for its own nefarious ends if we aren't careful. More and more people in modern society are using in a distorted way the idea that there is no objective reality to justify their outlandish and crazy beliefs. People think that if there is no objective world, this means that everything is subjective, which implies that all views are equally valid—which in turn makes it easy to start making false equivalencies between various perspectives about the world that are anything but equal. We should beware: wetiko can exploit something that is intrinsically true and good to serve its own dark agenda.

To learn, we must be free to make mistakes, for correcting our mistakes is how we evolve. But if our mistakes go undetected and uncorrected—such as the idea of the universe as objectively existing— we deviate from our nature, with potentially destructive consequences that threaten not only our own survival but our planet as well. Physicist and Nobel laureate Richard Feynman was of the opinion that this process of unconsciously transmitting ideas through the generations "had a disease in it."[13] This disease is none other than the wetiko mind-virus, one of whose main vectors of propagation is conceptual, that is, through the medium of concepts and ideas.

Quantum physics can teach us how certain unexamined and mistaken assumptions, such as that of an independently existing objective universe (IEOU), actually distort our thinking in subtle, hidden ways that hinder the realization of our full creative potential. Seeing the world as if it objectively exists separate from us is not simply an impotent and passive idea, but due to our powerful creative agency it actively draws the landscape of the world to manifest in our mind as if it *is* truly other than us. This then proves to us the rightness of our unexamined viewpoint, creating an endlessly self-generating, self-reinforcing feedback loop whose ultimate source is our own mind.

Just like how within a dream whatever viewpoint we are holding is reflected back to us by the forms appearing in the dream (which is itself nothing other than a reflection of our viewpoint), when such a fertile idea as an objective world gains enough traction among sufficient numbers of people it becomes self-evident in a collective, self-generating feedback loop, supplying all the needed "evidence" to prove and ratify the rightness of its perspective. The idea can develop a seeming life of its own, driving its own propagation, and is therefore self-replicating. If we are unconsciously in the grip of an unreflected-on idea such as an objectively existing world, then, like puppets on a string we become the idea's instruments for reproducing itself in the world and in people's minds. In this way the idea takes on a seeming realty. We are then unwittingly reinforcing the supposed truth of a false notion, while simultaneously strengthening the spell we're under, which gets reified with the world's cooperation. Ultimately speaking, we have cast this spell upon ourselves. Having forgotten that we have reality-shaping powers at our disposal, we have bewitched ourselves, putting ourselves in a self-induced trance via our own innate yet unrealized genius for co-creating reality. Because we don't *consciously* realize our own divine gift, we are using our power to create our world *unconsciously*, which is to say destructively.

The truth of our situation, simply put, is that we are creative geniuses with amnesia, as if we are suffering from a form of spiritual dementia. We have forgotten who we are, and in so doing we've disconnected from our vast creative powers for consciously shaping and co-creating reality. Our own creative powers then turn against us and haunt us in a way that shapes us, instead of us shaping them. It's like we're disoriented, deranged magicians who have created a world for ourselves that not only doesn't serve us, but is destroying us, all the while thinking that we're being victimized by an objective reality that we cannot change.

Richard Feynman comments, "Then a way of avoiding the disease was discovered. This is to doubt that what is being passed from the past is in fact true, and to try to find out *ab initio* [from the beginning], again from experience, what the situation is, rather than trusting the experience of the past in the form in which it was passed down."[14] In other words, instead of unthinkingly accepting other people's versions about the nature of our situation—not taking anybody's words, ideas, or opinions as sacrosanct—we can think for ourselves. If we're too lazy to think for ourselves and we outsource our thinking to others, however, we open ourselves up to being controlled by the influence of wetiko. That's why the nightmare mind-virus' worst nightmare is when we creatively think for ourselves.

This is why the Buddha's essential message to his followers was "don't take my word for it, do the experiment (look within your own mind) yourselves." The cure for the disease that afflicts our species entails each of us becoming an empiricist and simply inquiring directly into the nature of our present-moment experience, without giving credence to what any "authorities" may have told us. It is there that we will find ourselves.

Quantum Medicine

In a deceptive trick of our mind, the world we cognize occurs within and through the act of cognition, but we interpret our experience of the world *as if* it is separate from and external to our consciousness. When we view the seemingly external world phenomenologically, the one and only thing we are directly experiencing is not the world, but our mind perceiving the world. We then overlay on our direct, unmediated experience the idea that the world exists "out there," external to us—an unwarranted assumption if there ever was one. Dissociating from our direct experience, we forget that our experience of the world only arises within our awareness. In other words, our world is not as external as we have been conditioned to think it is. Though we experience within our mind a representation of the world, quantum physics points out that there is no external, objective world that corresponds to our inner impression.

This is similar to how within a dream a seemingly real world appears, but in actuality there is no objective, external world in the dream, but rather, there is just the inner experience of a seemingly real world within the mind of the dreamer. This is related to our experience of seeing a rainbow: though it is very convincing that the rainbow exists in the sky, there is no objective rainbow separate from the mind that is observing it, for our experience of the rainbow, when we get right down to it, is nothing other than an image in our mind. The highest teachings of Buddhism—in agreement with quantum physics—point out that our seemingly external world is similar to a rainbow in that it likewise doesn't exist *objectively,* separate from the *subjective* consciousness that is observing it.

The convincing experience of inhabiting and interacting with a seemingly real, objective world (an IEOU) allows us, as the dreamer, to experience our unconscious—and ourselves—in a way that we wouldn't have been able to if we had immediately recognized the dreamlike nature of our situation. This points to a potential evolutionary utility in falling into our mind's self-deception, as if in so doing we can consciously experience and live out our karma (our own actions, our own doing) in order to gradually purify, integrate, heal, and learn something about ourselves. This is another example of how encoded within the seeming obscuration is a gift, depending on whether we assimilate what is being revealed to us or not.

Quantum physics' universal insight that there is no independently existing objective universe (IEOU) separate from our consciousness of the universe is analogous to the personal insight that we have been unconsciously reacting to our projections as if they objectively exist in the world, rather than originating within our own mind. Quantum physics is pointing out that just like in a dream, we are participating— whether we know it or not—in creating our experience of the world and ourselves moment by moment.

Seeing the world as if it exists objectively—which is to mistake the appearance for the thing itself—reciprocally turns us into objects who are then *subject* to the world, killing our soul in the process by devaluing the central creative role that our consciousness plays in shaping the world in each moment. Berdyaev writes, "To separate oneself inwardly from the universe is inevitably to enslave one to it outwardly."[15]

The idea of an independently existing objective universe (IEOU) reciprocally co-arises with and simultaneously evokes and is evoked by an apparently independently existing inner reference point: we experience ourselves as seemingly separate and self-existing subjects. This false conception (or false imagination) about the seemingly objective nature of the universe in which we live feeds off of and into the interrelated notion that we exist in a way—as a separate self—that we simply do not. These two unexamined and erroneous assumptions—the idea of an IEOU and its reflexive corollary, the idea of our existing separately from the IEOU—mutually condition, reinforce, and generate each other, co-arising simultaneously.

Once we see through the illusory idea of there being an independent, objective universe, however, something amazing happens. We discover that who we thought we were—an independently existing separate subject (an IESS) relative to the defunct and debunked idea of an objective universe also comes into question. For if there is nothing objective to be subjects in relation to, what then happens to us as subjects? Once we recognize that there is no objective world out there separate from us, our experience of ourselves as subjects relative to the world instantaneously revises itself, changing according to our level of realization.

The belief in—and identification with—a false, independent, objectively real subject (experienced as a separate self) is considered in Buddhism to be the core illusion that is the root cause of all our delusions. In a circular process without end until seen through, this sense of being an inner subject continually self-generates, continually providing evidence for its own existence. Our sense of existing as a separate subject brings with it—and is not separate from—our experience of a seemingly objective world, which loops back into our minds so as to feed into and serve as evidence that confirms our belief that we exist as a separate self. This is the primordial feedback loop that is at the very root of our madness. Once we identify as being a separate self, our belief instantaneously—in *no time*—feeds back into the illusion of an inherently existing outer reality in an infinitely, self-perpetuating feedback loop whose source is our own mind. Physicist David Bohm calls this process "an illusion-generating illusion,"[16] which is to say one illusion can endlessly generate and be reinforced by another illusion. This intricate web of illusions has no substantial reality, but if the initial illusion is not seen through and instead is accepted as true, it can shape reality to both conform to and confirm the initial illusion, as well as feed a host of other illusions based on the initial illusion.

Quantum Physics as Spiritual Path

In discovering the fundamental cure for the psychospiritual illness that ails our species, quantum physics has promoted itself to the level of a spiritual wisdom tradition. Quantum physics uses reason and the intellect, combined with carefully gathered empirical data from experiments, in order to investigate the underlying essence of our physical world. It is thus a western, scientific type of jnana yoga, which is considered the path of the discriminative intellect. Jnana yoga engages and works with the mind so as to discriminate truth from falsehood as a way of going beyond the mind and discovering our true nature. Quantum physics is a scientific form of spiritual practice that like jnana yoga engages the conceptual mind and the rational intellect so as to surpass their conditioned limitations. Particularly suited to the western mind that has become entrained by the Newtonian worldview of classical physics, the practice of contemplating the revelations emerging from quantum physics is a deconditioning exercise, a mental detox that deconstructs the deeply imprinted habits of the mind inherited from the scientific materialist worldview.

The remedy for wetiko is to be found in our already-perfected indestructible nature, what Jung regards as the innermost foundation of our being, which is nothing other than our quantum nature. We already have the cure for wetiko within us—we literally *are* the remedy! It's just a matter of being able to recognize and remember it.

If we wish to address the problem of evil, we need self-knowledge—knowledge of the nature of the wholeness of the Self—more than anything. This self-knowledge is radically different from most people's limited conception of self-knowledge as simply being aware of their conscious ego personality and its intentions. Our self-knowledge needs to include the realm of the unconscious, with all its hidden agendas.

We are not just made of quantum entities, we are quantum beings in the flesh. Our quantum nature is the source of immense, seemingly never-ending creativity that when consciously accessed and wielded can be used for our betterment, instead of being used unconsciously for the destruction of our species. As any creative person knows from their own experience, there is a fine line between destructive and creative energies. It is not for nothing that wetiko tries to immobilize, disable, and kill our creativity. Becoming an authentic conduit for the creative spirit is what vanquishes wetiko. When we connect with other people who are also tapping into their quantum creativity, all bets are off regarding what is possible.

There is a world of difference between something being highly unlikely to happen and something being completely impossible. Quantum theory points out that an event of seemingly low probability, such as humanity collectively waking up to its quantum nature (and therefore evolving out of our unconscious state), is, out of the vast array of potentialities, possible. It can be realized "in reality." The revelations emerging from quantum physics open our mind to what is possible in a way that makes the possible more probable to becoming the actual. It is truly time for us to start to imagine and actively engage in bringing forth an expanded vision of what is possible. If we aren't doing this, what are we thinking?

A Fictive Personality

Wetiko—what years ago I initially called *malignant egophrenia,* or ME disease—is in essence a case of mistaken identity in which the convictions and ideas we have about who we are provide the most subtle obstacles to our individuation. In essence, to be afflicted with wetiko is to identify with a false self that doesn't exist, at least in the way we think it does. Wetiko feeds off of our misidentification of thinking we exist as a separate entity (to use Alan Watts's infamous term, "a skin-encapsulated ego"). This mistaken identity is not just food for wetiko, it is the very delusional dynamic that *is* wetiko.

Speaking about most people, the great healer and alchemist Paracelsus writes, "What he fancies himself to be has no worth."[17] This is because the fictitious identity that most of us cling to isn't real in any sense of the word except for the fact that it is an unreal product of a deranged imagination that we then take for being who we are. It is a forgery, a counterfeit (the counterfeiting spirit, aka wetiko), of no intrinsic value in and of itself.

We have become brainwashed into conceiving of ourselves in purely spatio-temporal terms, believing that we exist as a reference point in time and space, and proving this to ourselves, to use one example, by thinking we are deciding what food to eat, without questioning who is actually deciding. Is it us or the counterfeiting spirit, wetiko, impersonating us who is deciding? Are we nourishing ourselves or wetiko with the food we put in our bodies? We oftentimes imagine we have an agency that we don't have, while disassociating from our true agency, that which is intrinsic to our nature.

The false self that we identify with is an arbitrary and acquired personality made up of distorted beliefs about ourselves. In this perversion and diminishment of our true identity, we unnecessarily limit ourselves, hindering both our creative genius and the boundless wealth of potential compassion available within our true nature. A great danger facing humanity is to identify with what Jung calls our "fictive personality" and the corresponding abstract worldview rendered by scientific rationalism, which can't help but to alienate us from ourselves. It should be noted that suffering results from two causes: mistaking that which is not "I" as being who I am, combined with failing to recognize who I *really* am.

Speaking of identity, one arena in which wetiko has a field day is identity politics (which on one level has some beautiful intentions behind it as well as potentially profound value and merit). All of the identities at play in identity politics, however, are prone to being exploited by wetiko to serve its agenda of creating separation among us if we overly identify with whatever conditioned identity construct we've taken ourselves to be. This is because all of the identities that are engaging in identity politics are ultimately false identities.

When we get down to it, identity politics *is* wetiko politics, as it is the perfect arena for wetiko to run amok, creating endless conflict and division between all of the false identities, which are all busy "othering" one another. To the extent that we are overly identified with whatever identity we've taken on, we will endlessly protect, defend, and be offended by people who have different identities from us (who themselves also tend to be overly identified with their own false identity). To the degree that we identify with these false egoic identity constructs is the degree to which we are inviting wetiko into our lives and minds. Maintaining awareness of our true nature, therefore, is like having antiwetiko virus software installed on our human biocomputer.

If we identify with the fictive personality, we are then living someone else's life rather than our own, which is to say we are living a lie. We then proceed to live our lives within the false construct of a fragmented, compartmentalized, and encapsulated self that is separate from other seemingly separate selves. This error-ridden construct is the distorted foundation out of which the pernicious plague of wetiko springs. This self-justifying but unreflected-on assumption is the poisoned soil out of which the maleficent, stunted, twisted "tree" of wetiko grows (a diseased and toxic version of the Tree of Life). The tree of death that is wetiko bears the pestilential and fear-ridden fruit of unnecessary war, crime, disease, and poverty such as we see in the world today.

Imagine our situation: we are in a world whose nature we misapprehend, thinking it exists as something separate from ourselves, not realizing that we, through the act of observing the world, are influencing the world we then take to be other than ourselves. On top of this we misconstrue who we are and our place in a world whose reflective nature we don't recognize. Not knowing who we are, not understanding the nature of our world, and not comprehending our relationship to the world, we then try to find answers to our self-created problems that are the result of this disoriented viewpoint by looking outside of ourselves. This ignores and takes us away from both the source and solution of the problem, which is within ourselves. The whole thing is madness on an industrial scale. This benighted *project(ion)* is not just sponsored by wetiko, it is the revelation of wetiko for those whose hearts, minds, and inner vision have been opened.

What we perceive as seemingly separate, objective parts of the universe is a false appearance that occurs only within our minds, with no correlate in reality. The projections of our unconscious cast a false glamor over what appears to be reality, but is in actuality a barrier in seeing reality. To clarify: our projections don't exist superimposed on objects (as if overlaid onto an existing object), but rather, our projections appear *as* objects. Thinking of the universe as being composed of separate objects is the very activity that creates the false appearance of objects existing in their own right in the first place. We become victims of a self-created illusion in the process, unwittingly offering ourselves up as a vehicle for wetiko to use as its vessel of incarnation in our world in the process.

Who Are We?

Science, when we get down to it, is part of our endeavor to answer the great philosophical question "Who are we?" Taking in the revelations of quantum physics necessarily demands that we change our conception of who we are. Our idea of ourselves—who we think we are—is a primary driving force in human affairs, as who we imagine ourselves to be and how we think we fit into the greater scope of the universe powers the major currents of world history.

Going along with the idea of an IEOU is a shallow, limited, and impoverished conception of how humankind, seen as a material object existing within a mechanical universe, fits into such an apparently objective world. Both aspects of this view—that of ourselves and that of the world—are crude artifacts of a truncated and deficient worldview that is incapable of adequately representing the underlying wholeness of the universe. The revelations of quantum physics are pointing out that we, through our consciousness, are integral participants in nature's ongoing process of creation, a dynamic process that quantum physics is revealing to be filled with the utmost magic.

Jung was aware that the outworn ideas of scientific materialism were doing great damage to humanity. As if offering a prayer, Jung expressed the hope that the time is fast approaching when "this antiquated relic of ingrained and thoughtless materialism will be eradicated from the minds of our scientists."[18] In dispelling the unexamined illusion that forms the very basis of scientific materialism, quantum physics is thus playing a critical role in removing one of the greatest impediments to the evolution of human freedom.

To see that the world doesn't exist as an object out there, combined with seeing that we don't exist as an "objective" subject in here, is the doorway to the dreamlike nature of reality, and to ever-greater degrees of lucidity. This is what quantum physics is revealing to us, and it is precisely the central insight that can liberate our full human potential and dispel wetiko.

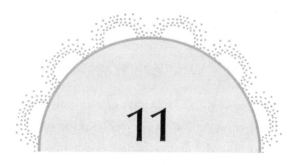

11

Catching the Bug of Synchronicity

Wetiko only has power over us to the extent that it is not seen. We begin to see wetiko when we recognize that what is happening in the world, like a dream, is synchronistically reflecting back to us what is happening deep within our psyche. Understanding how synchronicity works, therefore, can help us illumine and dispell wetiko.

Synchronicity was one of Jung's most profound yet least understood discoveries, in part because it cannot be appreciated until it's personally experienced. Because synchronicity is so radically discontinuous with our conventional notions of space, time, causality, and the nature of reality, to experience it can be so mind-blowing that Jung contemplated this phenomenon for over twenty years before he published his thinking on the subject.

Jung considered synchronicity to be the contact point between physics and psychology, where the two meet. It is the corollary in the inner human experience of the seemingly external quantum idea. In synchronicity, there is a peculiar interdependence between external events and the subjective, psychological state of the observer. Synchronicities are those moments of meaningful coincidence when the boundary dissolves between the inner and the outer so as to reveal their oneness, and as such they are a form of revelation. At the synchronistic moment, just like a dream, our internal, subjective state appears as if it is material-izing in the outside world.

Synchronistic experiences reflect back the fact that the human mind does not exist in isolation from the world, nor is it just passively aware of the world, but is somehow mysteriously linked to the world in a way that the mind can potentially become aware of. Our psyche is set up in accord with the structure of the universe; what is happening in the macrocosm of the universe is in some way connected to the deepest subjective reaches of the microcosm that is the individual psyche.

In a synchronicity, the conjunction of two cosmic principles, psyche and matter, takes place, and in the process a real exchange of attributes occurs as well: the psyche behaves as if it were material, and matter behaves as if it were an expression of the psyche. In synchronis-tic phenomena, the opposites of spirit and matter reciprocally inform and reflect each other. Uniting in a timeless embrace in a synchronistic moment in time, the opposites openly reveal their interconnectedness and inseparability. The mental and physical dimensions of life, like the form and content of experience, are revealed as only separable in thought, not in reality.

Instead of orienting ourselves one-sidedly, to the spiritual, to the exclusion of matter, or to material matters disconnected from the spiritual, Jung felt that the central psychospiritual task of our unique moment in history is to realize the unity of spirit and matter, which is what synchronistic events are all about. Instead of, or in addition to, spirit coming down from the heavens above, spirit's guidance is emerging and rising up from within matter and is waiting to be recognized.

Going to the heart of our being, synchronicities are moments in time when there is a fissure in the fabric of what we have taken for reality and there is a bleed-through from a higher dimension outside of time. Synchronistic phenomena are moments in time when the timeless, dreamlike nature of the universe shines forth its radiance and openly reveals itself to us, offering us an open doorway to lucidity. They are simultaneously pointing at and doorways into the very dreamlike nature of which they are expressions.

Just as causality describes the link between the sequence of events, synchronicity deals with the coincidence of events, one of which is psychic, what is happening inside our mind. Both outer events and inner psychic events are exponents of the same moment in time. Anything happening in the moment (including what is happening in our mind) belongs to and is an indispensable part and unmediated expression of that particular moment of time. Synchronistic occurrences show that whatever is happening in a specific moment in time isn't mere coincidence, but is connected through a sense of meaning that is related to what is going on within one's mind. Synchronistic phenomena, which are quantum in nature, and quantum physics do strange things to the notion of causality. Both invite us, in Philip K. Dick's words, "to discard the modem of causation,"[1] which is a fundamental structuring factor in our perception, which he felt was a major conceptual occlusion to seeing reality.

Jung realized that the causality principle—what he calls "one of our most sacred dogmas"[2]—is insufficient to explain certain manifestations of the unconscious. As an explanatory principle, causality is only one possible category of thought to describe the connection between events. In his idea of synchronicity, Jung proposed a new principle in nature by adding an acausal link. A synchronistic universe balances and complements the mechanistic world of linear causality with a realm that is outside of space, time, and causality. In a synchronicity, two heterogeneous world systems, the causal and acausal, interlock and interpenetrate each other for a moment in time, which is both an expression of and the vehicle through which our deeper wholeness is revealing itself.

Synchronicities are glimpses of transcendental unity, what in Latin is called the *unus mundus,* "the one world." The unus mundus is the unitary and unifying realm that underlies and pervades all dimensions of our experience. The unus mundus is a psycho-physical reality, a universe beyond time and outside of space, in which psyche and matter are inseparably joined as interconnected parts of a deeper unified field. The unus mundus is a world in which we have already woken up. It is a realm beyond duality, beyond opposites, beyond even the concept of beyond. In the unus mundus, opposites like matter and psyche form the outer and inner aspects of the same transcendental reality. Revealing its designs through events in the outer world as well as the psychic land-scape within, the unus mundus actualizes itself in time as we divine our wholeness through the synchronistic clues encoded within the fabric of experience itself.

The synchronistic universe is beginningless in that we are partici-pating in its creation right now. From this atemporal metaperspective, there is a single underlying event that appears to be spread throughout time and space. Jung calls synchronicities "acts of creation in time."[3] Notably, in quantum physics the act of observation is considered to be a unique and elementary act of creation in time. The resulting universe arises concomitant with our observation, which is an act of creation in time that unfolds continually from the singular "now" moment, gener-ating endlessly unique explications of itself that give rise to the appear-ance of sequential events happening over linear time.

If we aren't careful, however, we can easily become entranced by this display, imagining we live in a linear sequential world that is solely based on causality, which fails to recognize our participation in the one creative act in the eternal present. Our failure to recognize our partici-pation in the creation of our experience in each moment creates the space for the wetiko bug to germinate, which is to say that recogniz-ing the synchronistic matrix that underlies and informs our experience pulls the rug out from under the mind-virus.

Revisioning Jung's Idea of Synchronicity

Synchronicity is considered to be one of the most important ideas emerg-ing out of the twentieth century. Jung coined the term *synchronicity* to

258 ✦ The Quantum Synchronistic Field

describe a category of experience that defied and had an altogether different logic than the widely accepted and virtually unquestioned logic of linear sequential causality. The idea that a cause precedes an effect in linear time was generally thought to be the only kind of causality operating in the universe during Jung's time. Bringing forth the notion of synchronicity was thus a bold and heretical act by Jung; it was a radical departure and challenged the most inviolable, sacrosanct, and seemingly unassailable foundation of the modern scientific materialistic worldview. In his idea of synchronicity, Jung proposed a completely different kind of organizing principle at play in the universe, one that was quite alien to the widely accepted Western worldview of how the universe worked.

To distinguish synchronicity from the limiting logic of linear causality, Jung chose the word *acausal*. He called synchronicities an "acausal connecting principle"[4] in order to characterize how they didn't have to do with causality as it had been generally understood. There was an unforeseen problem, however, that had to do with Jung's choice of the word *acausal*—and what he meant by this—which has created conflict and confusion among a number of theorists, researchers, scientists, and psychologists in their accepting his idea of synchroncity. Some people have even dismissed Jung's work on synchronicity, thinking his conception is incoherent or flawed.*

The dictionary definition of the word *acausal* is "not involving causation or arising from a cause; not causal. Synonym: *noncausal*." An acausal connecting principle therefore implies that there is no causality operating in a synchronicity.† Jung was of the opinion that it is

---

*To cite one example, J. B. Rhine, widely considered to be the father of parapsychology and one of Jung's inspirations for his work on synchronicity, couldn't accept Jung's idea of synchronicity being acausal, so he rejected Jung's entire theory of synchronicity. Jung therefore lost an important potential ally in helping him bring forth his concept of synchronicity to the world.

†For example, in describing synchronicity, Jung writes that it is "a modality without a cause, an 'acausal orderedness'" (Jung, *Structure*, vol. 8, para. 965).

our strongly "ingrained belief in the sovereign power of causality" that makes it seem unthinkable that "causeless events" could ever happen. But if events without a cause actually do exist, Jung regarded them as "creative acts" that are "not derivable from any known antecedents."[5] The type of causation we are dealing with in synchronicities was totally unknown to the prevailing Western scientific mindset in Jung's day. In his theory of synchronicity, Jung was articulating a radically new vision of reality—a new worldview—that was completely out of the box and off the radar of the existing scientific materialistic paradigm.

In his conception of synchronicity as being acausal, it is conceivable that Jung was way ahead of his time and was tapping into and pointing at the underlying unified quantum field, which from our spatio-temporal and dualistic perception, is openly hidden in the midst of our physical world. In this unified nonlocal field there is no separation whatsoever, as there are no independent things that interact with and hence have causal effects on one another. These seemingly separate parts are merely mental constructs, ideas in our mind, human overlays or projections of our own inner state of fragmentation onto an ultimately indivisible field of reality, which we then mistakenly take to be made up of separate things. In an undivided realm such as this, which is simultaneously immanent and transcendent, there can be no causality because causality implies separate entities that influence and have effects on one another.

To illustrate this, quantum theorist David Bohm uses the following example: imagine a fish swimming in a fish tank, with two video cameras at right angles to each other filming the fish's movements, which are then transmitted to and shown on two different monitors in another room in a way that makes us think we are looking at two different fish. The fish's movements on these two screens clearly seem related to each other, but we can't say that the fish's movement on one of the screens caused or influenced in any way the corresponding movement on the other screen. This is because the different images on the two screens are not pictures of independently existing entities that are interacting, but are in reality two images (from different perspectives) of one and the same entity. It would be an error to try to establish a causal relationship between these two images, as the notion of causality simply does not apply in this circumstance. It would therefore make sense to say that the connecting principle between the two different images of this single fish (representing the deeper, indivisible nature of reality) is acausal. Thus, in describing the nature of a quantum universe such as ours, Bohm characterizes it as having a noncausal connection between its elements.

Jung's use of the word *acausal* may have been intentional, referring to this intrinsically unified field that admits no separation. In any case, his choice of the word *acausal* has nevertheless created a lot of misunderstanding that persists up to the present, and this needs to be remedied.

Do synchronicities arise, as Jung seems to suggest, without a cause? Or, is there in synchronistic experiences an unfamiliar kind of causality that operates in the world, in which cause and effect are not taking place over linear sequential time, maybe not even taking place within time itself? If it does exist, how is this unknown type of causality a connecting principle between the inner and outer dimensions of our experience?

To address this problem, I propose coining a new word, *simulcausality,* to more accurately describe the kind of atemporal causality that might be happening in synchronicities. The notion of simulcausality remedies the confusion around the word *acausal* by acknowledging—rather than a linear sequential or temporal form of causality or no causality at all—that a new and different kind of simultaneous causality that acts as a connecting principle takes place in synchronicities.

This unfamiliar kind of causality that mysteriously links the inner and outer contents of our experience together is brought into focus through the notion of simulcausality. In synchronicities, these two realms, the inner (subjective) and the outer (objective), are connected in a way that is not sequentially causal but simulcausal. These two realms, the internal and the external, are connected through synchronicity, which acts like a bridge between the two. Simulcausality implies that there is a different kind of causality operating than we are accustomed to, but this other kind of causality occurs between the two seemingly distinct realms of mind and matter, while taking place outside of time, in no time—that is, simultaneously.

Introducing the word *simulcausal* involves, of course, more than the mere changing of a word. Replacing the word *acausal* with *simulcausal* is symbolic of shifting into a new, more expansive mode of seeing that previously was unavailable to us because of our unconscious conditioning. With this new kind of vision comes a new way of understanding ourselves and the world; we can now see how our self-reflecting and potentially self-reflective universe actually operates, rather than how we have been thinking it operates while being conditioned by the spell of linear time and its natural correlate, linear causality.

We can now redefine synchronicity as a simulcausal connecting principle in which causality happens vertically (simultaneously) in addition to horizontally (over linear time). Vertical causality refers to a kind of causality that occurs between different dimensions or domains of our experience that are inseparably embedded and internested within one another in the same moment. This perfectly describes the interdimensional relationship between the subjective world within us, which takes place in a *higher* dimension (*in* is *up* dimensionally), compared to the *lower* dimensions of the seemingly outer 3D world of matter, time, and our physical sense perceptions (commonly known as the space-time continuum).

The higher dimension and the lower dimension of our experience interpenetrate each other so fully such that there's an intrinsic connectivity between them through the simulcausal connecting principle, which allows these two realms to instantaneously influence each other interdimensionally in literally no time at all. Because this is an interdimensional connection, this process happens simultaneously—in the present "now" moment, without time being involved whatsoever. Mind and matter are thus connected through a simulcausal interdimensional communication link that takes place outside of and independent of linear time.

The different dimensions of mind and matter that are conceived as influencing each other interdimensionally are ultimately not two separate dimensions that are interacting with each other, but rather a multidimensional continuum that is inseparably one. To recognize this is to begin to see the dreamlike nature of our universe, where just like our dreams at night, the physical world we experience is not separate or separable from our consciousness.

Synchronicities thus operate through an instantaneous simulcausal resonance or interdimensional coordination between the contents of our inner (higher dimensional) life—our mind—and the outer events taking place in the (lower dimensional) 3D physical universe. These two domains, our inner subjective and outer objective life, are conventionally thought to be distinct and noninteracting, but are in fact inseparably interconnected parts of a unified multidimensional whole system. The two domains of mind and matter, which since Descartes have been traditionally understood in the West to be operating independently and separately from each other, are, in synchronicities, revealed to have a mysterious correlation that clearly defies the strict Cartesian dualism that requires mind and matter, the subjective and objective, to be separate and noninteracting.

The coordination between these realms takes place instantaneously in the implicit interdimensional simulcausal dynamics constituting each and every moment of our experience. This accounts for the uncanny correspondences between the inner and the outer worlds that are the most notable feature of synchronistic phenomena. Because simulcausality operates instantly, outside of time—in the realm of no time—its very existence is easy to miss, which is one of the reasons why it is omitted from the Western scientific materialistic worldview, which is more outwardly focused and not as introspective as the Eastern worldview. Understanding simulcausality is the key to understanding the physics of synchronicity.

From the materialistic point of view, synchronicities are inexplicable not only because their cause is unknown, but because (presupposing three-dimensional space and time as being objectively real) their cause, to quote Jung, is "unthinkable." This is to say that we can't comprehend the unfamiliar type of causality involved in synchronicity if we are stuck in our thinking mind, as this phenomenon forces us out of our cognitive, conceptualizing mind.

Our experience of the world, which is composed of a combination of both linear causality and simulcausality, can be represented by a symmetrical cross that we'll call "the cross of linear and simultaneous causality/simulcausality (see diagram). In this image, the horizontal X axis of the cross represents the realm of linear time and linear causality in which cause precedes effect; this then becomes the cause of a subsequent effect, and so on. This is the conventionally understood sequential timeline that moves from the past on the left to the future on the right, moment by moment. The vertical Y axis represents the timeless "now" moment in which no linear sequential time occurs, but rather, is the domain in which a timelessly operating simulcausality is at work in each and every moment in a way that connects the inner (mind) and outer (matter) dimensions through a kind of instantaneous interdimensional resonance. The intersection of these two axes at any given moment in time corresponds to the interface of the timeless dimension of our unconscious inner subjective life with the seemingly objective side of our experience in space-time. These two modes of causality, the linear causal and the simulcausal, coexist and interpenetrate each other in an elegantly integrated harmony that is an expression of the wholeness of our universe, as well as a reflection of our own intrinsic wholeness as multidimensional beings.

In proposing the notion of simulcausality I am offering what is possibly a new way of contemplating the nature of synchronistic phenomena. The concept has some novel features and some significant

Cross of Linear and Simultaneous Causality
(Simulcausality)

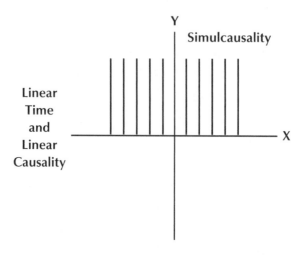

Each point on the horizontal timeline of linear sequential causality has a vertical line that can be drawn perpendicular to it. (Not all of these vertical lines are drawn in the diagram as there are an infinite number of them, each one corresponding to one of the infinite number of points or moments on the horizontal timeline.) The region of the diagram above the horizontal X-axis represents an ascending sequence of higher dimensions beyond the space-time continuum. The domain that's relevant to our discussion is the X-axis and above. Each and every point of intersection between the two axes represents a specific moment in linear time that is being influenced by and is an expression of the simulcausal connection between the inner (higher) and the outer (lower) dimensions of our experience.

conceptual advantages that bypass the problems that Jung's notion of acausality and "acausal orderedness" brought with them. The principle of simulcausality enables us to describe the way that synchronicities operate in a new way that opens up fresh possibilities for us to envision the nature of our universe, as well as our own nature.

One of the key features of this revisioning of our scientific conception of reality is the recognition that reality as a whole is a profoundly nonlinear affair, with linear dynamics only comprising a small subset of the total dynamics that make up the cosmos. Since Jung introduced the concept of synchronicity there has been an explosion of new scientific theories and creative maps and models of reality that push our understanding far beyond the logic of linear causality. These new insights have moved the scientific imagination into vast new realms of nonlinearity that are now recognized as fundamental and essential features of nature, of the universe, and of reality itself. For example, nonlinear whole-systems sciences like chaos theory—more accurately described as the science of nonlinear order—and complexity theory have made many groundbreaking inroads into the nonlinear frontier that have changed the scientific picture of our world and our understanding of reality in profound and fundamental ways.

Simulcausality is, however, not really anything new at all. It has been recognized by esoteric wisdom traditions across the world throughout recorded history. For example, simulcausality is equivalent to what in Buddhism is known as the simultaneity of cause and effect. At the very heart of the Buddha's teachings, the simultaneity of cause and effect points to the dynamic in which we are creating our experience of the seemingly outer world (which is not separate from us), while at the same time being influenced by our creation, in a reciprocally co-creative feedback loop. Contrary to linear cybernetics, in which feedback loops take place through space and over time, simulcausality is characterized by a process of *synchronistic* cybernetics in which the feedback loops are beginningless, circular, instantaneous, and timeless.

The principle of simulcausality does not negate the possibility of linear causality, nor does linear causality disallow simulcausality. These two fundamentally different types of causality naturally coexist. This is reflected in the Buddhist understanding of how the simultaneity of cause and effect (instant karma) does not negate, but harmoniously coexists with linear cause and effect (karma that unfolds over time). Their coexistence produces a much more complete view of reality.

The Buddhist teaching known as "As Viewed, So Appears"[6]* is another example of simulcausality. As Viewed, So Appears can be thought of as a mystic law or mystic equation describing how we formulate and co-create reality instantaneously within and with our dreamlike universe. Think about the nature of a night dream: it is a reflection, a projection of the mind that is observing it. In a dream, the very moment we connect the dots on the inkblot of the dream, interpreting and placing meaning on it, the dream has no choice but to instantaneously (in no time) reflect back to us our perception/interpretation (for a dream is nothing other than a reflection of the mind that is dreaming). This then confirms to us the seeming objective truth of whatever we happen to be seeing, as we now have all the evidence we need to prove that what we are seeing is true.

This becomes a self-confirming and potentially never-ending instantaneous feedback loop that is self-referential and self-generated by our own mind, which, since it is happening in no time and unfolding over time simultaneously, continually feeds back into itself until it is seen through. Not seeing how simulcausality operates in our moment-to-moment life is one of the main reasons why we are prone to getting stuck in insidiously self-reinforcing feedback loops that seemingly trap us in all sorts of self-limiting double-binds, self-bewitching spells, infinite regressions, and dead-ends within our own minds. Becoming conscious of the simulcausality principle that is continually at work crafting our experience of both ourself and the world can prevent us from falling under these maddening self-created spells, while at the same time immediately puts immeasurable and otherwise unavailable creativity at our disposal. In essence, we have bewitched ourselves—putting ourselves under a spell—through our own creative genius. This dynamic teaches us something about how simulcausality

---

*The full expression is "As a thing is viewed, so it appears." This teaching is a terma, a hidden treasure. As Viewed, So Appears is as all-pervasive and universal a law in the realm of consciousness as gravity is in the physical dimension.

acts as a connecting principle between the inner and outer dimensions of our experience and is intrinsic both to how we dream up our sleeping dreams and how we create our waking life as well.

In our universe, everything is simultaneously *intercausing* (causing and being caused by) everything else in a cybernetic chain that recursively loops back on itself in no time. This means that everything that manifests is reciprocally co-arising with everything else in a nonlinear and nonlocally coordinated way in the one singular and eternal "now" moment. In Buddhism, this principle of intercausality (a third type of causality) is called *dependent co-arising* (also known as *interdependent co-origination*) and it is considered the fundamental dynamic by which empirical reality is continually reconstituted in each and every moment. Basically, this principle says that everything is interconnected. Everything affects everything else. Everything that is, is because other things are. What is happening now is part of what happened before, and is part of what will happen next.

Being the heart of the Buddha's realization, the principle of dependent co-arising helps us awaken from the spell of linear causality and enables us to see how our experience of the world and ourself actually arises in the present "now" moment, while at the same time giving the very convincing appearance that it is unfolding in a linear, sequential way. Each new configuration of the outer universe as well as our inner subjective life in each moment (which is always happening in the same eternal "now" moment) is thought to be and subjectively experienced as another (separate) moment. This gives birth to the notion of a linear sequence of distinct moments that arise one after the other, like a conveyor belt. Emerging out of this way of looking at things is our illusory conception of linear sequential time, which as quantum physics has pointed out is nothing other than a *construct(ion)*—a creation—of our mind.* In fact, based on our experience, we always find ourselves in

---

*Jung suggests that what happens successively in linear time could be conceived as occurring simultaneously in the mind of God.

the one and the same singular, unchanging "now" moment, which is a realization that can't help but transform the very consciousness that has realized this.

An expression of the interconnectedness, interdependence, and undivided wholeness of the universe, where there is no separate self to be found and no separate things of any sort, dependent co-arising operates throughout space at any given moment in time as well as in each moment. Simulcausality, on the other hand, operates in a realm outside of time in that it connects the different dimensions of our experience, such as inner (mind) and the outer (matter), in a way that does not take place over time.* Transcending linear causality, both intercausality (happening throughout space in any and every moment in time) and simulcausality (happening outside of time altogether) mysteriously come together in a timeless embrace, as they reveal themselves in a singular synchronistic moment in time.

Bringing more and more consciousness to the experience of simulcausality enables us to deepen our understanding of how we play a key role in creating ourselves and our experience of the universe in each and every "now" moment. This process is similar to how a dream in which the seemingly inner and outer realities are unified is constructed. Dreams reveal that the primary dynamic of how we co-create the reality we experience is simulcausal in nature. Sequential (linear) causation can be recognized to be a secondary dynamic that builds on, extends, and transforms over time, that which has already—and always is—being instantaneously and simulcausally created.

The tragic and unnecessary confinement of our minds to a

---

*There are a number of phenomena that seem to defy our ordinary sense of spacetime logic, such as nonlocality (quantum entanglement), dependent co-arising (intercausality), simulcausality, synchronistic phenomena, and psi phenomena. Because they all appear to violate the third-dimensional laws of space and time, these phenomena tend to be mistakenly conflated as being equivalent, which has resulted in confusion and misunderstanding. They are all somehow related, as they are interconnected aspects of the sentient dreamlike universe that we inhabit, but exactly how they are related has yet to be fully established.

linear-sequential logic can be seen as a reflection of what has happened to much of humanity in its fall into the overly rationalistic scientific materialist paradigm. Although granting humanity immense power over the physical universe, our entrainment in scientific materialism has sadly atrophied our immensely powerful inner psychic and spiritual faculties, changing many of us into misshapen, one-sided, unbalanced creatures.

Similar to how the unconscious compensates for a one-sidedness in us by sending us dreams, Jung considered synchronicity to be an indispensable counterpart to linear causality that is compensatory in nature. As a connecting principle, synchronicity can thus help us connect with ourselves and our own creative power. The compensation for the one-sidedness of humanity as a whole must come through the reawakening of these atrophied and dormant inner faculties of the mind.

Bugging Out on Synchronicity

To illustrate what he meant by synchronicity, Jung brings up an experience he shared with a patient of his. She was stuck, trapped in the self-created prison of her own mind, and the analysis was seemingly going nowhere. Jung realized there was nothing he could do. He was resigned to hoping that something unexpected and irrational would show up in their sessions, something that would, in his words, "burst the intellectual retort"[7] in which she had imprisoned herself. Then she had an impressive dream in which someone offered her a golden scarab, a valuable piece of jewelry. At the moment she was telling Jung the dream, there was a tapping on the office window. Jung opened up the window and a scarabaeoid beetle, whose golden green color closely resembles that of a golden scarab, flew into the room. Jung caught the beetle in his hand, handed it to her, and said, "Here is your scarab."

The shock of recognition in this synchronistic moment in which Jung's patient realized her dream of the previous night was being both literally and symbolically enacted in her waking life pierced through her resistance and cracked her defensive shell wide open. At the moment of synchronistic transmission, a fundamental shift in perception took place in her that inwardly transformed her and made her receptive in a new way. From that point on, Jung wrote that her treatment was able to successfully continue toward healing.

There was no conventional linear causal link between the patient's dream and the beetle tapping on the window. But there was clearly an equivalence and meaningful connection between the two related events, which were not based on linear causality, but rather, on simulcausality. The patient, as an active, egoic agent in space and time, didn't cause or create the synchronicity, which in that sense was acausal in that it happened of its own accord. And yet in some mysterious way, the beetle tapping on the window was intimately related to her.

Synchronicities are cystallizations in linear time of a nonlinear, acausal, atemporal process, windows into the realm beyond time and space. Synchronicities are acute outbreaks of the archetypal collective mind field that have crystallized into our personal sphere through the third-dimensional medium of time and space. Synchronicities are both timeless and temporal, which is to say they are possessed of a double nature with regard to time. Genuine wake-up calls from the awakened part of oneself, synchronicities can be conceived as being emanations of the timeless, already awakened part of oneself projecting itself into the dimension of time so as to help us further wake up.

Being unmediated manifestations of the dreamlike nature of reality, we can interpret synchronicities just like we would interpret a dream. Mythologically, a scarab is an archetypal symbol that in ancient Egypt represented death, rebirth, and transformation, while gold represents the highest value. When Jung's patient was offered a golden scarab in both her night and waking dreams she was experiencing a form of synchronistic notarization by the archetype, highlighting its arrival on the scene. Like the underlying, invisible axial system of an emerging crystal, an archetype of the collective unconscious is an informational field of influence that acts as a blueprint, *in-forming* and patterning the workings of our psyche, which in turn shapes our experience of the world around us and how we experience ourself. Catapulting Jung's patient out of the limited frame of reference of her conceptual mind, the synchronistic moment helped her access a deeper part of herself as well as reconnecting her to the universe in which she lived.

The synchronicity was an expression of—as well as the doorway through which—Jung's patient was personally enacting the archetypal process of the renewal of consciousness. The synchronicity bore the stamp of the activated archetype, revealing to her and making real in time that she was actually taking part in a timeless, mythic drama of death and rebirth. Her conscious realization of the heretofore unconscious archetypal process that she was involved in kick-started the archetype into high gear. An archetype synchronistically revealing itself in the outside world is a reflection that this same condition is in the process of being inwardly realized; recognizing this deepens our inner realization of the archetype. The outer, synchronistic materialization of the inner archetypal process is itself the vehicle through which the archetypal process both actualizes itself in space and time and is inwardly realized.

In a synchronicity, an outer object—sometimes animate like the beetle, other times inanimate—behaves as if it is evoked by and expressing an activated archetype. When the beetle tried to get into the room, it was as if it was fulfilling its mythological role as a symbol of rebirth in a deeper archetypal drama.

What I call the *deeper dreaming Self* (analogous to Jung's *Self*) is that part of us that is the dreamer of both our night and our waking dreams. Being nonlocal, meaning not bound by the conventional laws of space and time, as well as being multidimensional, the deeper dreaming Self can simultaneously express itself through inner experiences such as inspirations and dreams as well as by attracting events in the seemingly outer world so as to crystallize itself in embodied form.

The deeper dreaming Self was simultaneously the dreamer of the patient's golden scarab night dream; the inspiration for her to tell Jung the dream in their session; the source of the beetle that was tapping on the window at exactly the right moment; the impulse that animated Jung to open the window, catch the beetle, offer it to his patient, and say what he said; as well as the patient's inner, revelatory experience of transformation that was the result. Being multifaceted and multi-channeled, the deeper dreaming Self nonlocally arranged all these dimensions enfolded within the field into a singular psycho-physical experiential gestalt, in which the oneness of spirit and matter became visible.

Interestingly, this synchronicity noted by Jung was an experience in which Jung himself played an active participatory role. As the synchronistic moment was erupting into time, he found himself dreamed up by his patient to pick up and play out a role in her dreaming process. At the moment of synchronicity, Jung went from passively sitting in the audience hearing about her process, to being drafted into the act and stepping into a scene in the play of his patient's mind. Not merely witnessing his patient's synchronicity, he found himself spontaneously enacting it with her, playing his part and saying his line perfectly.

If Jung hadn't opened the window, caught the beetle, handed it to his patient while saying his line, the synchronicity wouldn't have happened. Imagine, as the beetle was outside tapping on the window, if both Jung and his patient ignored it instead. Here was an insectoid emissary of potential healing that was trying to enter their space—literally knocking on their doors of perception—and they would have been too asleep to notice how the nonlocal field was responding to what they were working on. Or imagine if Jung would have opened the window and as the beetle flew in, Jung and his patient didn't recognize the correlation between what was flying around in the room with what was buzzing around in the patient's mind. Once again, no synchronicity would have occurred.

The potential synchronicity was not just happening to Jung and his patient *objectively;* for it to be notarized and take on full-fledged reality as a synchronicity it required the participation of their *subjective* awareness. This is to say that they needed to recognize that a synchronicity was in the process of unfolding. The synchronistic moment needed to speak to them and activate a deeper sense of meaning within their minds for its full effect to be realized. In other words, the synchronicity was not just objectively happening to Jung and his patient as passive observers; they were active participants who were involved in creating it in time. I imagine that having Jung bear witness to his patient's synchronicity made its impact and its reality even stronger in her.

Jung's words, "Here is your scarab," fell into his head similar to how his patient's dream fell into her head the night before. The question naturally arises: from where did these thoughtforms and dreams arise? The point is that all of these seemingly random and disconnected events were somehow connected and expressed something deeper, something healing, that was potentially emerging into form and being created through their interactions. The connection that had developed between Jung and his patient had activated the field between them to precipitate healing.

To say this differently, there was a deeper process of healing that was ready to happen for Jung's patient, and Jung, being open and receptive to what was happening in the moment, willingly stepped into a key role in her process that helped midwife the deeper process of healing that was wanting to happen in the field. In offering her the precious jewel of a golden scarab symbolizing death and rebirth, Jung spontaneously found himself being an open instrument for the synchronistic universe, which is filled with healing, to manifest through him into material form and express itself in the world.

The synchronicity was not monopolized by Jung's patient, as it didn't belong only to her. Participating in his patient's synchronicity, Jung was at the same time having a living experience of his own synchronicity. We can only imagine how having a front-row seat while simultaneously being cast in a key role in his patient's synchronicity affected Jung's psyche. Even though the synchronicity was a reflection of his patient's inner landscape, it was simultaneously a synchronistic reflection of a deeper process taking place within Jung's psyche, too.

Jung's patient's synchronicity clearly made a profound impact on him. In introducing his work on synchronicity to the world, he chose to use this patient's synchronicity as the example. And God only knows how those of us who are writing (me) or reading (you) are being affected deep within our respective psyches by contemplating this synchronicity in the present moment, since we are all connected in this quantum universe of ours, throughout time and space.

To see the whole picture is to realize that Jung and his patient were reciprocally and interdependently collaborating in co-creating or dreaming up their shared synchronistic event. For Jung to be hearing a patient's dream of a golden scarab and to have a golden scarab fly into his office was an externalized, synchronistic reflection of the archetypal, universal, impersonal process of death and rebirth, not just within his patient, but in him as well—and potentially in all of us. It is noteworthy that a synchronistic event can collectively reflect and be mutually shared by more than one person in both similar, different, and singularly unique ways.

Jung's patient's synchronicity can be seen as a symbol of the deeper potential for healing encoded within the fabric of the universe that is available to us in each and every moment. Contemplated symbolically as if it were a dream, this synchronicity reveals how any one of us, at any moment, if we are open to the healing that wants to happen in the field, can become an instrument for this healing to actualize itself in real life. Jung didn't do anything other than just allow the field to speak through him; he became receptive to the deeper healing that was in the process of happening, such that it used him to implement that healing.

Imbued with a deeper fragrance of meaning, a synchronistic event is a revelation that contains within it a potency to insinuate itself into our very being and alter us from within, transforming us on a cellular level. Potentially changing us down to our core, a synchronicity transforms our perception of the universe we live in, as this universe of ours has widened to accommodate the possibility of synchronicities taking place. No one could have convinced Jung's patient—not to mention Jung—that her synchronistic experience should be dismissed as a mere coincidence, as she had an inner knowing of its meaningfulness due to how it transformed her. She no longer lived in a disenchanted universe.

Jung and his patient's shared synchronistic event was a living experience of being connected to something greater than themselves. Being numinous, synchronicities have a strong feeling component and emotional charge, oftentimes being deeply religious and mystical experiences, as they potentially expand our sense of who we imagine we are and transform our intimate relationship with ourself. Synchronistic moments can feel like grace, inducing the feeling that we're right where we're supposed to be.

Paradoxically, a synchronicity is a living, unmediated materialization of our unconscious, while also being a nonlocalized manifestation of that part of us that's waking up into a more expanded consciousness. A genuine symbol, a synchronicity is an utterance of the soul, as it contains, is an expression of, and unites opposites. Synchronicities are soul-making in action.

An Impossible Situation

It is noteworthy that right at the moment that Jung's patient was deadlocked in her therapy was the moment when a deeper archetypal dynamic within her psyche became activated and expressed itself nonlocally as a synchronicity in her outer world. It is typically when we find ourselves in an impossible situation that constellates the deeper archetypal dimension to become visible. It is when the deeper, archetypal dimension of the psyche gets activated that synchronistic phenomena tend to manifest. What is true individually is also true collectively; when we, as a species, find ourselves in an impossible situation with no exit, it is this very kind of dilemma that constellates the healing and revelatory archetypal realm to become synchronistically activated.

Synchronicities occur at times of deep archetypal excitation in the field—moments of crisis, transition, creative tension, and dynamic intensity. Periods of disturbance in our world are both a manifestation of and a trigger for a corresponding archetype in the collective unconscious of humanity to draw to itself everything it needs to synchronistically render itself visible in form. Such times of distress catalyze a deeper, self-regulating healing process to awaken both within individuals and in the collective.

When an archetype gets activated within us, due to its nonlocal nature it constellates itself outwardly in the world. An activated archetype's force field organizes the entire field to synchronistically rearrange itself so as to embody the archetype "in form."* When a formless archetype of the collective unconscious is at the point of becoming conscious and incarnating, it has an energetic charge that will seize people, get them in its grip, and compel them to act it out so as to give shape and form to it.

An activated archetype can possess individuals, groups, whole nations, and even an entire species. When a formless archetype takes over a person or community of people, they can be said to be the incarnation—or revelation—of the the archetype in human form, as they synchronistically embody and mirror back to us this archetypal dynamic which exists deep inside of all of us. Recognizing the archetypal dimension as it plays out in the world can awaken the archetypal dimension inside each of us, such that we snap out of viewing the

---

*Jung emphasized that the archetypes are not themselves the cause of synchronicities. Rather, the archetypes "take on form" such that deeper archetypal patterns appear and become visible in the form of synchronicities.

world in a literal way, through a personal, reductive lens, and as if finding ourselves living in a mythic realm that speaks to us symbolically, we experience an expansion of consciousness. When the archetypal realm takes on form, something of the eternal, imperishable dimension synchronistically reveals itself to us as it enters the realm of time and embodiment.

Subjectively, synchronistic phenomena evoke in us the feeling that we are not alone, that there is a silent partner that we share our lives with who is dreaming with us. It's as if there's an autonomous factor deep within us arranging our experiences so as to help us wake up. Part and parcel of a synchronistic event's numinosity is its ability to help us deepen our acquaintance with this mysterious inner figure who shapes our lives. Paradoxically, through synchronicities we connect with our true self by being introduced to that part of us that is other than who we imagine ourselves to be.

Form and Formless Synchronicities

Synchronicities are those moments of revelation that show us that the same correspondence between the inner and outer realms that is true in our dreams is also true in our waking life. Our seemingly mundane world is synchronistic at its core in the sense that the outer world does not simply reflect our inner reality occasionally; it is *always* manifesting synchronistically, for being a dream, how can it be otherwise? At certain synchronistic moments, however, this correlation becomes acutely obvious.

Generally, we can distinguish two types of synchronicities. Traditional synchronicities, where an acausal, meaningful correlation manifests in form between the inner and outer domains of experience, we can call *form synchronicities*. This contrasts with what we can refer to as *formless* (or *empty*) *synchronicities*. Our entire lives are lived within the context of one continual formless synchronicity, in which the inner and outer domains of experience are always in an inseparable correspondence. The difference between these two kinds of synchronicity reflect the fundamental correlation between form and formlessness (or emptiness) that is the essence of the Buddhist Heart Sutra. In the Heart Sutra, just as form and emptiness are considered one ("Form is Emptiness. Emptiness is Form. Form is none other than Emptiness. Emptiness is none other than Form."), form and formless synchronicities are inseparable, yet at the same time they are distinct.

Because formless synchronicities are always happening, as they are the underlying substrate that informs our dreamlike universe, this mirroring correspondence (which is the doorway to recognizing the dreamlike nature of the universe) is generally missed, so it takes the irruption of *form(al)*, meaning-rich synchronicities to jolt people out of their trance of nonlucidity and draw their attention to the true nature of their experience, to the seemingly (from a nonlucid perspective) uncanny correlation between the inner and the outer realms. Formal synchronicities serve as indicators that wake us up to the implicit correspondence between the outer and inner realms of experience and clue us in to the existence of the underlying formless synchronistic continuum in which we live.

One of the hallmarks of conventional, dichotomized, nonlucid, ordinary waking consciousness is the assumption—and consequent experience—that subjective and objective experiences are categorically separate and distinct from each other. Synchronicities reveal that the split between the *subject-ive* domain of our inner life and the *object-ive* domain of the outer physical world is an illusion that never existed in the first place. This illusion is the mistaken premise that synchronicities are potentially helping us to see through and overcome. The fact is that this dichotomy between one's inner and outer life doesn't actually exist except within a dualistic mindset. The illusory distinction between the inner and the outer is merely an artifact of a chronic fragmentation within us that is projected out into the field of our experience, thereby producing—due to the dreamlike nature of reality—the immediate and convincing *appearance* of this ultimately nonexistent duality. The world manifests as if this duality actually inheres within its structure—which it most decidedly does not.

This assumption of a distinct bifurcation between one's inner and outer life is the consequence of the projection of the seemingly objective existence of space and time. Providing the underlying framework for our physical perceptions, neither space nor time exists objectively; these concepts are constructs that have been created by our consciousness. Though the concepts of space and time have utility in the everyday macroscopic world of classical physics, in a thoroughly quantum universe such as ours they ultimately have neither meaning, application, nor existence separate from the mind that created them. This was recognized by philosopher Immanuel Kant, who pointed out that space and time do not exist objectively, outside of us, but are what he called "pure forms of intuition,"[8] projections of our own mind onto our experience so as to order and make sense of things. As Einstein points out, space and time are modes by which we think, not objectively existing conditions in which we live. Space and time are like the underlying grammar, the elements of a language used by us to make sense of and describe our environment, enabling us to communicate our experience. The projected structure of space and time is the lens and perceptual framework through which we interpret, place meaning on, organize, and contextualize our experience, providing us with the perfectly designed stage set, if we are so inclined, for us to experience the inner and outer domains of our experience to appear as distinctly separate.

Wetiko is able to prey on us—and play us—through our spatio-temporalizing and dichotomizing tendencies. The degree to which we can see through, overcome, and transcend these inveterate tendencies is the degree to which we will slip free of wetiko's grasp and become impervious to its malign influence over us.

The original singularity* of our being always and already exists beyond and ontologically prior to our construction and projection of a spatial-temporal structure onto our experience. The primal timeless singularity that is intrinsic to our true nature is not in any way limited or altered by the synthetic overlay of a spatio-temporal structure and the corresponding projection of a false subject-object dichotomy. The true singular and whole nature of our being is always present, and thus potentially available to experience directly in each and every moment.

Wetiko can only influence and prey on that which we are not. Wetiko can only manipulate an ersatz us; it can never touch the real thing, for who we are is not a thing. Wetiko can only interact and have intercourse with our false, inauthentic self. We are truly "fallen" when we believe wetiko's fictitious version of ourselves. But if we don't identify with its replica of who we are, we divest ourselves of wetiko's power over us and this mind-virus then has no purchase on us. From the undivided wholeness of our authentic self, wetiko has no existence whatsoever and never did—a realization that renders us invulnerable to wetiko's harmful effects.

This understanding can help us to come to terms with the age-old religious questions of whether evil actually exists. If we haven't realized our original nature, evil is a power that needs to be taken seriously in the relative reality we are navigating. If we haven't realized our true nature, to simply think evil doesn't exist is to unwittingly offer ourselves into its hands. From the point of view of realizing our true nature, however, evil is recognized to have no intrinsic, independent existence. A quantum phenomenon, evil both exists and doesn't

---

*The word *singularity* is used here not in the mathematical or physics sense (in which it connotes the center of a black hole), but refers to our original state of undivided awareness. I am using the word *singularity* to point to the underlying experience of inseparability that is the singular and indivisible primordial sentient experience at the core of our being, prior to the structuring of the space-time construct and prior to the division of our experience into inner and outer, subjective and objective.

exist, depending on our viewpoint. To say something both exists and doesn't exist is a perspective that makes no sense from the logic of the dualistic mind, but it makes all the sense in the world when we have seen through and stepped out of our conditioned, dualistic mind and realized the true essence of who we are, which exists beyond the mind.

Synchronicities are moments of disclosure that can, if we are paying careful attention, reveal a preexisting fundamental reality: the realm of formless synchronicity in which both inner and outer domains perfectly coincide, existing as an indivisible singularity. Synchronicities can introduce us to the primal singularity of our being—our wholeness—in which our inner schism never existed in the first place. Contacting this already whole place within us can unify, heal, and reintegrate back into our wholeness our conditioned, split-off, traumatized parts. We can then recognize our inseparable oneness with the entire universe.

There is always a perfect correspondence and coincidence of all aspects and elements of our experience, both inner and outer, because they ultimately coarise and coexist within the same transspatial and atemporal sphere of the primal singularity that is the true, original nature of our being. When we discover our essential Self, which exists in a dimension that we have forever known but have temporarily forgotten, we are forever beyond wetiko's grasp. This is a realm we can recognize because it is intimately familiar to us, it truly belongs to us, for it IS us.

Dreamlike

It's no wonder Jung described physical reality as dreamlike, for synchronicities are expressions of the dreamlike nature of reality. The spirit that animates synchronicities, if we can speak of such immaterial matters, is the same spirit that inspires our dreams at night. To the extent that we recognize the dreamlike nature of our waking life is the degree to which our life is experienced as synchronistic.

Synchronicities, just like symbols in a dream, are not separate from the dreamer, which is us. To say this a bit differently: just like symbols in a dream, synchronicities do not exist objectively, separate from our own psyche. Synchronicities openly point to the fact that the psyche is not separate from the world—the world is imbued with psyche through and through.

Just like it was with Jung's patient, our night dreams can oftentimes take on form and manifest both literally and symbolically in the outer world of our waking life. In a night dream there is an instantaneous correspondence between the inner and outer worlds, not because they are two separate dimensions that are communicating faster than the speed of light, but because they are inseparably united as one seamless, unified continuum. The same is true in our waking dream.

Just like a dream, whatever we are unconscious of gets dreamed up and acted out in our waking dreamscape. What plays out in one person's night dream is a reflection of their inner process; similarly, what is getting dreamed up by all eight billion of us on the world stage is a reflection of a process going on deep within the collective unconscious of humanity—which is to say inside each one of us. The key is to find and notice this correlation between the macro and the micro. Recognizing that there is a connection between what is happening in the greater body of the world and what is taking place within our own mind opens a hidden portal that leads beyond our particular personal psychological issues, empowering us to deal with the truly important and fundamental problems of our time.

Being initiatory rites of passage, synchronistic events empower us to view all of life synchronistically. Seeing through synchronistic eyes has nothing to do with overlaying a fabricated or arbitrary interpretation on events to make them appear *as if* they are synchronistic. I have coined the term *over-synchronicity stimulation* (acronym OSS) to point to how when we get in touch with the synchronistic dimension of our experience, we tend to overdo it, seeing synchronicities everywhere—

in license plates, street signs, phrases in books, comments people make, and so forth. Realizing the underlying synchronistic matrix that is informing our universe can initially be a bit destabilizing for the unprepared mind. We can easily become overwhelmed by the majesty of our realization and get off-balance, reading more than is warranted into things. This can be symptomatic of the manic behavior of so-called bipolar disorder, which oftentimes is simply the beginning of recognizing the synchronistic nature of the universe, but not having integrated it yet, being swept away by it.

Seeing synchronistically involves recognizing the underlying synchronistic web that is always weaving itself through our experience. The more we are open for synchronicities to happen, the more they happen. This is analogous to how being inside a night dream and viewing the dream as if it were a dream has the instantaneous effect of allowing the dream to more strikingly manifest its dreamlike nature. Changing our perspective within a dream doesn't cause the dream to become a dream—the dream has always been a dream, we just didn't recognized it before. Similarly, we live in a synchronistic universe, and by recognizing this we allow the universe to manifest more synchronistically. Seeing that every moment is synchronistic is not a fabrication, a game of make-believe, but is actually seeing the true nature of our situation. Seeing synchronistically is to realize that instead of being out of our mind, as in crazy, we are, just like a dream, inside of our mind.

Synchronistic awareness can only be developed through our receptive and active engagement with synchronicities. The more synchronicities we experience, the more our synchronistic eyes open, and the more our synchronistic eyes open, the more synchronicities we are able to perceive in a synchronicity-generating positive feedback loop that changes everything, including ourselves. Once our synchronistic vision goes online, it changes not only the way the world appears to our mind, but reorients our mind as well, which can't help but transform our experience of the world we live in.

Realizing we live in a synchronistic universe where mind-blowing synchronicities are a real thing and actually take place can inform and expand our ideas about the nature of the magical world we inhabit. This dreamlike, synchronistic universe we live in is overflowing with hidden treasures that are woven into the fabric of existence, custom-designed by the deeper dreaming Self to help us awaken to our true, authentic nature. The magic inherent in the universe isn't sufficient by itself, however; what's needed, in Wheeler's words, is "magic plus the prepared mind."[10] We must cultivate a mind that is able to recognize and receive the universe's untold magic as it manifests in our seemingly ordinary, everyday lives. The image comes to mind of fishing in the deep ocean, which represents the unconscious: we need something—the prepared mind, which acts like a net—to catch and then "land," or integrate, the magical creatures that live in the depths.

Synchronicities are like cultures from another dimension that create and enrich our own culture. To use another metaphor, the synchronistic mindset can be likened to an antibody secreted by our psychic immune system that neutralizes the pathogenic effect of the wetiko virus. Like a bug in the system, synchronicities are cultures that propagate virally through the field of consciousness, which means that synchronistic awareness is contagious. The "bug" of synchronistic awareness, the lucid consciousness that recognizes the synchronistic nature of the universe in the dream of life, is something we can turn each other onto and catch from one another. Just like Jung, we can help each other catch the "bug" of synchronicity. We can cultivate a network of allies who creatively collaborate in bringing forth the precious jewel of synchronicity. The archetypal field becomes greatly potentiated for synchronicities when we get in sync with other people who are also waking up through the shared open heart of synchronistic awareness. When cooperatively engaged, synchronistic awareness activates our collective genius and creates true culture in that it effortlessly, endlessly, nonlocally, and virally transmits and fractally reiterates itself throughout time and space. Shared synchronistic awareness magnetically draws and attracts the universe into itself, materializing through life itself, creating a revelatory universe in the process.

Cultivating synchronistic awareness is to be continually opening to the intertwining and oneness of our outer and inner worlds. Recognizing the synchronistic dimension of our experience dissolves the materialistic lens that rigidifies our naturally fluid universe into something solid, liberating it so as to allow it to resume its naturally revelatory function. Then and only then can we fully receive its freely offered gifts. In our realization of synchronicity, the pernicious effects of wetiko are naturally dissolved back into the emptiness out of which they arose as a matter of course. Then there's nothing else to do but creatively express and celebrate our true nature in the name of serving others, who are recognized to be none other than "other" parts of ourselves.

PART IV

The Self as Revelation

Being that wetiko is a form of psychic blindness, this section starts off by contemplating the nature of our blindness and how we can begin to see it. Seeing the underlying unconscious dynamics that fuel our blindness helps us realize how we can help open other people's eyes as well. We then explore the nature of wetiko as a disguised form of revelation. The source of the greatest evil imaginable, wetiko contains encoded within it a hidden revelation that when brought to light, becomes its own medicine. Wetiko is a particularly unique form of revelation, however, in that it needs our conscious recognition of what it is revealing to us in order to effect its transformation and bring forth its positive healing aspect. This section concludes by contemplating the reflective, mirrorlike nature of the Self. It points out that the best medicine for the wetiko mind-virus is to connect with the presence and light of our true nature, by stepping into who we truly are.

12

The Disease of Not Seeing

We live in a time when the dark forces of the universe are coming out of hiding and are visible for all who have eyes to see. This is not to say that everyone sees these dark forces—many people are turning a blind eye, which only feeds the evil aspect of wetiko. Of course there is disagreement about where these dark forces are to be found—the Republicans, the Democrats, the atheists, the fundamentalists, the terrorists, the Left, the Right, the liberals, the conservatives, the pro-vaxxers, the anti-vaxxers, the Illuminati, the globalists, and on and on. It's always some form of "the other." Some people even have the temerity to suggest the radical idea that these dark forces are ultimately to be found within our own minds, a perspective that gets closer to the mark than any other perspective. I imagine that one thing we can all agree on is that there is something truly evil playing out in our world. So the question naturally arises: what is to be done about these dark forces, which comes down to the age-old question of how do we deal with evil?

As I've pointed out in my previous work on wetiko, Jung was tracking this mind-virus, not calling it wetiko, but mainly referring to it as the "totalitarian psychosis."[1] Wetiko, after all, is an inner disease of the soul that somehow is able to extend itself out into the world and express the inner state of the person under its thrall through the pattern of events occurring in the outer world in which they live. What if the entire human species is under its spell? The fascist, totalitarian forces that are insidiously making their moves and creeping all over our world today are but an outer reflection of the inner state of the collective human psyche, which has been taken over by these dark forces.

Totalitarianism in today's world is the merging of corporate economic power, including the media, with the political power of the state. The result is a corporate tyranny whose main goal is absolute power and control over people. The rigidity of thinking, lack of self-reflection, and absence of creativity that characterizes the totalitarian mindset, combined with its lack of compassion, is a psychological and spiritual problem. The core disability in the realm of heart and mind—a sclerosis of consciousness—that has produced the horrific nightmare of totalitarianism in the world today is mirroring (and hence revealing) the inner psychological blindness of wetiko that hardens our hearts. However, the totalitarian psychosis that is running rampant in our world can also help us see the heretofore invisible wetiko virus that is to be found hidden within our own minds.

The twentieth-century form of totalitarianism that we're familiar with has become outdated—it's so yesterday. It once tried, as if in the Stone Age, to implement its heavy-handed dictatorial agenda through outright military force. This old form of fascism was mainly political and nationalistic, and was typically centered around an ideologue. Today's form of fascism that is being incorporated into our world is depoliticized in that it is more supranational, with no specific underlying ideology that can be easily pointed out. This gives it cover, making it much harder to identify and thus defend ourselves against. The only ideology of this mutant form of totalitarianism is whatever is expedient to advance the agenda of strengthening and consolidating power and control of its system over the masses. Though it's in our face, this novel, anomalous form of totalitarianism is faceless and thereby hard to see and directly confront. The kind of authoritarianism we're dealing with today is perfectly captured in political theorist Hannah Arendt's words: "tyranny without a tyrant."[2]

Totalitarianism is not a fixed thing, a pattern that always or reliably shows up in a similar, recognizable, easily identifiable form; it is instead highly mutable as it shape-shifts and adapts to the circumstances and psychosocial conditions of a particular time and place. As such, totalitarianism—itself an expression of the wetiko mind-virus—has a viruslike nature. To survive and perpetuate itself, it must camouflage itself and constantly create novel variants, mutating into new hybrid forms that are unrecognizable as totalitarianism so as to avoid being detected by the "immune system" of society.

Totalitarianism is a political system that can only assume power through the disorienting and destabilizing effects it has on people's minds. Like a dark cloud that has come over our world, the totalitarian virus that is wreaking havoc throughout the world today has clouded our eyes, muddled our thinking, and hardened our hearts. Cardiologist Peter McCullough points out that the assaults on our freedoms that are taking place during the global pandemic are not about Covid: "It's about some type of mental contagion, it's about some type of mental psychosis, some type of neurosis. Some type of totalitarian takeover that's occurred all over the world. Something very dark is going on."[3] McCullough is precisely describing the wetiko mind-virus, a contagious mental psychosis.

A totalitarian regime must deceive people into thinking and feeling that it is improving their lives, providing them with safety or security from an imminent danger. Its implementation is greatly assisted by the accompanying presence of some form of major menace or peril that makes its adoption even easier—in fact, seemingly necessary—in order to protect against the threat. If the virus of totalitarianism successfully mutates into a new, unrecognizable variant, it appears in a form that most people are not only *not* threatened by, they even welcome it with open arms. In this way the new mutant form of the totalitarian psychosis can implant itself and spread its roots deeply into the hearts and minds of a population, enabling a significant rearrangement of society to take place before sufficient numbers of its members wake up and recognize that the "cure" proposed by the state is far worse than the alleged threat. Meanwhile, the whole society has been unknowingly altered and infected to a frightening degree as it becomes increasingly under the control of the new, harder to see form of totalitarianism.

A totalitarian system of governance promotes never-ending lies upon lies, the effect of which is to falsify reality, such that the distinction between reality and fiction becomes harder and harder to discern. Such a state has devolved from being a political organization to being a mind-control operation that continually manages our perception of reality. The systemic institutionalization of lies muddles our minds and disconnects us from our discernment, which destroys our ability to distinguish truth from fiction, and anesthetizing our soul. If we participate in the totalitarian state's lies, we invariably internalize them, which feeds into the process of lying to ourselves. We then become split in two, dissociated from our authentic selves and disconnected from our intrinsic creative power. This makes us much easier to control.

This is why the power of people living the truth, of not going along with the lies of the totalitarian system, is the greatest obstacle and the greatest threat to totalitarianism. Authentic spontaneity and the creativity that is the result of it is the most powerful solvent for the totalitarian calcification of our consciousness. As Nobel laureate Aleksandr Solzhenitsyn reminded us, even one person who refuses to participate in this lying could bring down the whole totalitarian system! This is the domino effect in action.

The totalitarianism that is stealthily encroaching into the global body politic today is the living revelation of how the wetiko virus is colonizing our individual minds. This totalitarian virus has been invisibly pushing boundaries, getting away with whatever it can as it slowly and surreptitiously extends its reach out into the world. This mental virus is slowly creeping and potentially taking over our global body politic as it puts its roots down all over the planet, as well as within our minds. We could call this insidious process "the totalitarian lockstep." The dictionary definition of *lockstep* refers to a rigid, mindless conformity that minimizes individuality, spontaneity, and creativity—the

292 ⊕ The Self as Revelation

perfect description of the underlying mindset of this aberrant pathology. Naming something unknown and invisible objectifies it, which helps us see it. Finding the moniker for an external process also helps us see the inner process that it is reflecting, how totalitarianism, a result of the wetiko virus, operates within our own minds. If we don't see the totalitarianism that's spreading throughout our body politic today, we won't be able to deal with it until it's too late. The totalitarian virus is not a thing, but an ever-changing *process,* with both inner and outer expressions. This deadly germ can only fully incarnate in our world if it is not seen—which is why it's so important that we *see* it.

Meet the New Boss, Same as the Old Boss

The same evil force that has animated past atrocities in our species' history, as if reincarnating itself in a new form, is enlivening the global evil that is trying to assert dominance over the planet today. The evil that is being acted out in our world today is the same spirit of evil—it has been called "the dark side of God"—that has been enacted throughout history in many different guises, all shadows of the same seemingly evil entity. Originating in the same archetypal dimension that exists within the collective unconscious of humanity, all of these manifestations of evil throughout time are variations on the same sordid and horrific theme, informed by the same deeper archetypal pattern; it is only their scale, strategy, and scope of operations that are different. The same evil that in the past has possessed human beings or large groups of people is manifesting in today's world in a much harder-to-see and therefore insidious form.

The evil that is getting enacted today, though working through individuals as its instruments, is spreading and incorporating itself throughout the collective body politic as if it's a systemic disease. As a result of this it seems that we are moving towards a newly emerging, global supranational technocratic control system that has an anti-life logic built into its very fabric. We live in a world where many corporations have more sway in the political process than governments do, and unelected people who do not have our best interests at heart are making decisions that affect all of our lives. This systemic evil is operating both underground, where it is hard to see, and more and more above ground as well, where it is harder to deny. Instead of being a solely national phenomenon, happening within particular sovereign nation-states, evil is now manifesting on a global scale, attempting to assert its dominance by centralizing power and control over everyone and everything. To not see this is to be blind.

The same deeper psychospiritual malady—of disconnecting from our human hearts, not feeling our interconnectedness with other human beings or the whole of life, combined with projecting our own darkness onto others (scapegoating)—that has *in-formed* and given shape to all sorts of evil acts in the past is still at work in today's world. The systemic evil that is incorporating itself on a global scale dehumanizes people, seeing human beings as merely collateral damage that can be easily discarded in order to attain dreams of power. This is what happens when, to use Nietzsche's term, "the will to power" of the human shadow splits off from our wholeness and goes rogue. This dark energy, unhinged from our humanity and not mediated by human conscience, consciousness, or compassion literally takes over and possesses human beings to become its purveyors in our world.

It's not just people in positions of power who are conduits for evil. It could be normal, everyday good-hearted people like you and me who might unwittingly be cogs in the wheel of a destructive system (aka "the machine"). We might, to use a very innocent seeming example, be a secretary at a corporation that is harming the environment. Though just doing their job in order to pay their rent, and not *directly* enacting evil, there is no way around the fact that this secretary is playing a role, to whatever small degree, in being complicit in the evil being perpetrated by whoever is paying their salary.

As psychiatrist Robert Jay Lifton explored in his book *The Nazi Doctors,* the Nazi physicians in the concentration camps whose job it was to decide who lives and who gets murdered would come home to their families at night and be loving husbands and fathers. As Lifton points out, it was as if these doctors had split in two, creating a double of themselves that was disconnected from their soul. Their dissociation allowed them to enact full-blown evil in their day job, but sleep guilt-free at night. This shows us that evil is able to be enacted through us when we become alienated from ourselves. Moreover, evil is a disintegrating energy that when encountered can easily split us in two, thereby preparing us to be one of its instruments if we don't become aware of, come to terms with, and assimilate what within us has fissured off from our wholeness. Is a similar process, on a smaller scale, at work deep in the psyche of that secretary at the environment-harming corporation? And is a similar psychogical process happening in all of us who are forced to participate in a corrupt system?

If life is seen as a play, as living theater, it's as if (to personify the formless archetype) the figure of evil, which has made its appearance in previous acts throughout the play of human history in both subtle and not so subtle ways, is striding across the global stage in a way that's impossible to deny or ignore (though some people are doing exactly that). This evil figure, instead of having fangs, horns, and blood dripping out of its mouth, is wearing a costume to disguise itself, maybe even wearing a tailor-fitted business suit, such that many people don't recognize its malicious intent. This figure claims that, in its beneficence, its overriding intent is our well-being, whereas the overwhelming evidence, based not on its words but on its actions, points to the exact opposite. We are all seeing and registering this fact, consciously or unconsciously. Some of us turn a blind eye and just try to make the best of it. Others of us feel drawn to a creative response.

Unlike Nazi Germany, where the inhuman and inhumane forces of evil goose-stepped their unimaginably murderous ways into our consciousness in a way that was impossible to miss, what the great spiritual teacher Sri Aurobindo calls "the hostile forces"[4] are using much more subtle and covert means today in order to conceal and thereby effectively accomplish their nefarious agenda. The same archetypal, impersonal evil forces that have animated unthinkable horrors throughout human history have now shape-shifted and changed their strategy in order to fit into our modern world in a hybrid form that we haven't yet sufficiently recognized.

It's as if the dark powers have realized that they could never get away with overt militaristic acts of aggression in today's worldwide court of public opinion, so they have cloaked themselves in a more benevolent form in order to carry out the same sinister agenda. They have shifted their tactics from the battlefield to the domain of the human mind, from military control to mind control. Modern-day evil, though blatant and hard to miss on the one hand, bypasses our mind's radar due to its underhanded and clandestine nature. This ensures that it will go unrecognized by the masses.

In a process known as *regulatory capture,* the dark forces have more and more insinuated themselves into and captured the very regulatory agencies whose job it is to monitor these very same dark forces. Like the proverbial fox guarding the henhouse, instead of keeping the dark forces in check, the very organizations that are supposed to oversee them have been co-opted by these same sinister forces to serve their evil agenda. This real-world situation reflects what happens when the wetiko mind-virus takes over and colonizes people's minds. The psychospiritual self-monitoring immune system within our mind— our internal regulatory agency—is fooled by the very pathogenic tendencies that it is supposed to monitor and keep at bay. In this way we are co-opted by wetiko.

As spiritually awakened figures throughout history have taught, it is critically important to recognize evil and call it by its right name. Historically, times of great spiritual realization were also times when the dark forces were clearly and widely recognized for what they were. The periods when the powers of darkness weren't consciously registered, however, were the times when the most unspeakable human-created destruction occurred in our world. As spiritual wisdom traditions the world over have pointed out, evil derives its seeming power over us only because it is not recognized.

The fact that the same deeper archetypal pattern of collective insanity and brutality—we can call it the wetiko archetype—that is playing out in today's world has been acted out over and over again throughout human history is revealing an underlying dynamic that exists within the collective unconscious of humanity. The terrible tragedies of the past include countless massacres, wanton cruelty, extreme inhumanity, and episodes of genocide and mass murder that fill the historical record. All of these terrible human-created horrors are manifestations of one and the same timeless archetypal pattern and are far too numerous to list here. Some notable examples include the massive slaughter by Genghis Khan and his Mongol hordes, the vast genocides and enslavement of indigenous people in Africa, North and South America as well as the more recent genocides that took place in Armenia, Rwanda, Stalin's Russia, Mao Zedong's China, Hitler's Germany, Pol Pot's Cambodia, and the list goes on. It greatly behooves us to shed light on the underlying psychospiritual dynamic that *in-forms* all of these atrocities, including the ones taking place right now.

There is a real edge to even broach the topic of evil in our planetary dialogue, as if to directly discuss the topic has become taboo. It is as if evil has dumbed us down, as we have become unable to carry on intelligent conversations about the subject. Evil doesn't easily lend itself to language; in a sense it is "unspeakable." The age we live in is truly suffering from the presence of the unspeakable. The very fact that there is something unspeakable in our world is an expression of the black magic we are dealing with. In trying to deal with evil, our words fail in their function of transmitting meaning, oftentimes obscuring, rather than illuminating the evil that we are trying to shed light on. In trying to point at evil, our words can easily become psychic flypaper that attracts other people's projections and misunderstandings.

It is a weird situation we find ourselves in: everyone has a felt sense of the evil that is being enacted in our world, yet it is practically verboten to do a deep dive and get to the bottom of what is driving it. It is important to point out that there is indeed something to be pointed at, something to be seen. Our turning a blind eye from what is demanding to be seen doesn't just feed wetiko, it *is* wetiko.

There is a way of talking about and shedding light on evil where we aren't simply projecting our own shadow (which would be to unwittingly offer ourselves into evil's hands), but are actually feeding the light that dispells wetiko. To not be able to talk about evil, and to be accused by the thought police of all sorts of unsavory things if we do, is itself part and parcel of the very evil we are up against. In our heavily propagandized and mind-controlled world, we are programmed and conditioned, not only on how and what to see, but what *not* to see, let alone talk about.

In trying to silence the people who are shedding light on the evil that is happening in our world on a global scale, the gatekeepers of our planetary dialogue are strengthening the power of evil by keeping it in the dark. In righteously attacking (often with the best of intentions) those who are trying to illumine the darkness, these guardians of what we're allowed to talk about are becoming instruments of the very evil against which they believe they are fighting. This common but utterly insane dynamic should open our eyes to how the dark genius of wetiko "plays us" for all we're worth. I'd like to name this process *duped into unwittingly supporting the opposite,* DUSO, or *duped into unwittingly supporting evil* (DUSE). When people have fallen under the spell of DUSO or DUSE, wetiko is enlisting the very population it seeks to control to become its unwitting agents of their own enslavement.

To see wetiko, it can be helpful to inquire into what goes on in the process of *not* seeing wetiko. The form of blindness that turns a blind-eye to evil can be called *not see disease* (acronym NSD), which it should be pointed out is pronounced the same as "Nazi disease." It is as if the extent of evil that is being enacted is so dark that it feeds into an undertow in people's unconscious, which induces them to look away, to see and hear no evil; meanwhile, looking away turns us into becoming instruments for the very evil we are looking away from. It greatly serves our best interests to overcome our unconscious proclivity for putting our head in the sand when we encounter things we'd rather not see.

It's understandable and even makes sense why so many people deny the reality of the evil that's currently incarnating in our world. It can be overwhelming to see the face of evil operating through individuals and in society at large. In today's upside-down world it is considered a mark of sanity to be able to repress one's knowledge of and sensitivity to the world's cruelty, so as to not let it dampen one's state of inner peace. Clinging to one's precarious state of inner peace by repressing and looking away from anything that threatens it will not lead to enlightenment, however, whereas an enlightened person will not be brought down by the horrors of the world, but will use the darkness they see to deepen their inspiration as they continue to persevere in the path of truth.

Ironically, if we refuse to repress and compartmentalize our knowledge of the world's evil, in our crazy world we are considered sick. But people who see the cruelty in our world are only sick in the sense that they have lost some of the underlying psychological defenses that many use to keep the terrifying reality of our world out of sight and mind. In essence, they are more in touch with reality than most, as they are seeing clearly a reality that most people deny. Those who are awake and aware no longer invest in the "normal" illusions that protect us from reality and bestow a façade of sanity in a world gone mad, a madness in which we are all, to varying degrees, complicit. Similar to how recognizing trauma is a sane response to an insane situation, are people who are unable to *not* see the evil that's happening in our world the sick ones, or the truly sane? Are they blessed or cursed? The answer depends on how they carry the horror of what they have realized.

There are some people who are totally tracking the deeper systemic evil that is playing out through the global body politic. Instead of being ignorant, asleep, dissociated, or in denial, their eyes are wide open as they try to understand and figure out how to deal with the evil they see being played out all over the globe. And yet, these same people can't make the leap to realize that the source of the evil they see being acted out in the world is a mind-virus that is to be found within the human psyche. Many of these people are brilliant scholars. It's as if they are too steeped in academia, in the scientific, materialist worldview, a perspective which doesn't allow them to see something that doesn't seem to exist in the third dimension of space and time, unable to see something that is immaterial such that it can't be quantified or measured. Tragically, their academic training, though having great merit and utility on one level, doesn't allow them to see the dreamlike nature of their experience. As if having perceptual blinders on, they are only seeing a limited flat cross-section of the full multi-dimensional territory in which wetiko operates and does its dirty work.

I've seen some of the most intellectually brilliant people on the planet get unknowingly played by wetiko like a fiddle. This shows us that seeing wetiko is not a function of the intellect, but has to do with developing our deeper intuitive, psychic, and visionary capacities. It also involves and even requires developing a deep familiarity with the inner landscape of our own heart, mind, and soul.

The results of this modern-day, aberrant form of totalitarianism are, when we get right down to it, the same as the old form of totalitarianism (in the words of English rock band The Who, "Don't get fooled again. . . . Meet the new boss, same as the old boss"): centralized power and control, the removal of constitutional and human rights, outright censorship, and criminalization of those who express a viewpoint that questions the mainstream narrative, to name but a few. And let us not forget that all forms of totalitarianism give license to the people controlling the levers of power to literally get away with murder. If we turn the blind eye of wetiko to what could not be more obvious, we become enablers of our own demise, investing in our own genocide. This would be truly tragic, as it is potentially avoidable—if only we open our eyes, our hearts, and our minds to see what is happening all around us.

Techno-virus

In our world today there exists a unique factor that has never existed before, having to do with the remarkable advances in technology that have taken place in recent decades. Unprecedentedly powerful tools such as the internet, social media, computers, artificial intelligence, biotechnology as well as ever more sophisticated surveillance and mind-control technology make our age radically different from any other time in our recorded history. These new technologies can be used for tremendous good or for terrible evil depending on the level of conscious evolution and ethical development of the people that are controlling them. If these technological tools, which bestow practically superhuman powers on their possessors fall into the wrong hands, that is, into the hands of people who have become taken over by the wetiko archetype, we will find ourselves under an existential threat unlike anything we've ever seen before.

Though the advances in technology bring incredible benefits, it is important to realize that these breakthrough technologies not only have the potential for, but are being presently used in order to guide, shape, manipulate, and control people's opinions and perceptions of what is happening in the world in ways that are to the advantage of the wetiko-ridden controlling powers-that-be. Many of these technologies that could be used for honestly informing us about what is happening in our world in ways that would empower all of us are unfortunately being weaponized to deceive us on a mass scale (weapons of mass deception). These new technologies are also being used to create polarization and division among people so as to foment conflict instead of unity throughout our modern-day electronically interconnected global village.

Technology in the wrong hands can become a powerful amplifier and superspreader of wetiko. These new technologies open up novel means for wetiko to potentially colonize our minds in ways that were previously unimaginable. This isn't a conspiracy theory, but rather, a conspiracy fact that can be seen by anyone who has open eyes. Before we can even begin to learn how to deal with this sci-fi situation that we are confronted with, we have to acknowledge the nature of the technological beast we are dealing with. It all comes down to decolonizing our own minds.

Wetiko, like any virus, is continually mutating. Wetiko itself can be thought of as being analogous to a particular type of computer program that constrains what is possible such that it acts like a psychic form of *mal-ware* in our minds. When we become infected by wetiko, our creativity gets crippled, we lose our humanity, and we become programmed by its wetiko logic in such a way that we become part of the machine, like zombies, robots, or automatons.

Technology is a creation of our minds that can genuinely help us in many ways but, tragically, a significant amount of our technology is being used in ways that are destroying us. This is reflecting the inner situation of the psyche where instead of using our creativity to lessen suffering and liberate all beings, we are using our creative genius to destroy ourselves. Why are we doing this? And how do we stop doing this to ourselves? And what is this revealing to us about ourselves?

All of this has to do with a battle for the human soul. Shadow projection, the underlying psychological dynamic that fuels wetiko, is based on dehumanizing people. Scientific materialism, the underlying self-worldview that feeds wetiko, marginalizes the role that humanity plays in the universe. The newly emerging technologically empowered variant of the mind-virus threatens to take away our humanity. The totalitarian psychosis is all about destroying whatever it is that makes us human. This is why stepping into becoming a human being with an open heart filled with compassion who is connected with their soul, and by extension, with the soul of humanity, is the way to meet this challenge.

It is in our best interest to become wetiko-literate and conversant in the nonlocal ways of wetiko so as to have a chance of receiving the empowering wisdom that comes from seeing—and seeing through—the covert psychological operations of wetiko, thereby accessing the medicine for transforming our current world crisis. We are entering uncharted, dangerous waters that demand that we wake up from our slumber and step into the highest and best parts of ourselves. We are presented with an opportunity for an unprecedented evolutionary leap in individual and collective consciousness, wisdom, and understanding. Let us have the courage to meet this challenge. May the (nonlocal) force be with us.

13

The Art of Seeing

It's important that we get our language right. When we see people who have fallen under the spell of wetiko, it's very tempting to think of them in any number of ways—they're ignorant, crazy, or maybe somewhat evil themselves. But this would be a mistake. Many people under wetiko's thrall can be quite brilliant, sane in many ways, and are genuinely good people with the best of intentions. To mischaracterize them is to not see them accurately (remember, wetiko is a form of blindness). This furthers the separation, polarization, and misunderstandings, and hence not only feeds wetiko, but *is* wetiko in action.

An Eye-Opening Experience

Wetiko can wreak havoc in our relationships with one another. To only see one aspect of a person, be it good or bad, and to solidify that as being who they are, is to fall under the spell of wetiko. To judge someone this way is a reflection that we are in a solidified (as compared to fluid) state ourselves, which only furthers the dominion of wetiko in the collective field. On the other hand, to be awake is to notice this part of the person, and instead of concretizing and reducing them to merely one or two qualities, we can realize that whatever characteristic they are manifesting in the moment is simply one ephemeral aspect of their fluid, multidimensional nature. By not holding them in such a particularized and limited way, we energetically create space for them to step out of whatever identity pattern they may be stuck in. To not concretize who we think they are is to simultaneously *de-solidify* ourselves as well. This not only gets us more in touch with the fluidity of our own nature, but can introduce us to the open-ended, creative spirit in all our interactions.

However, in order to help us understand what happens to people who come under wetiko's sway it is helpful to try and describe the process: in a "fallen state," they have fallen into their unconscious and are (nonlucidly) dreaming. Having fallen asleep to the truth of who they are, it's as if they have fallen under a spell and have become blind in a way that might not be obvious at first glance. Similar to how in a myth or fairy tale the would-be hero has to discover the right name of the demon, we have to find the correct name of the syndrome that has afflicted our species, which has to do with a type of blindness related to ignorance.

If we want to help people who have been stricken with this malady to wake up and "see," we have to understand the nature of the universal affliction that is potentially blinding all of us. We are susceptible to the same condition as those we see who have fallen blind—which is to say that the way to understand this affliction is not solely by studying how it manifests in others, but recognizing how it operates within ourselves as well. So recognizing it in others can, via our ability to self-reflect, help us get a handle on how it manifests in ourselves.

Wetiko is a form of psychic blindness. At a certain point in time we chose to look away—to blind ourselves—so as to avoid being in relationship to a part of ourselves. Our turning away *is* wetiko. This is to say that our blindness is, on one level, a willful blindness—a choice— that becomes habitual and is rendered unconscious so that we don't even notice that we are looking away from something. Seeing can only happen when we are present, both with what we are seeing "out there" and what we are seeing—what it brings up—"in here" (within us), in the "now" moment. Seeing cannot happen when we *split*, which has two meanings—to dissociate, and to leave (that is, to not be present). Being fully present is kryptonite to wetiko. The radiant presence of our true nature effortlessly dissolves wetiko on the spot, just like the darkness of night can't fight against or stand up to sunlight, but instantaneously disappears as if it never existed in the first place.

It isn't beneficial to preach the light to people whose eyes can't see it—this indicates that we too are partially blind. It's a much better strategy to teach people the art of seeing. How do we do this? Most people have become so accustomed to their blindness that they don't know they are blind. It's as if people don't even know that their eyes are capable of seeing. What does it mean and what would it look like to teach people how to see? What would we be teaching them to see?

Those who are attached to their version of reality oftentimes refuse to even consider evidence that might contradict their viewpoint. This is the modern-day equivalent of the Church refusing to look through Galileo's telescope, which would have proven that their ideas about the universe were flat-out wrong. So how do we get people to look through Galileo's telescope with an open mind, such that they are able to take in evidence that can correct their unconscious viewpoint and expand their minds? The answer is to be found within the psyche.

These questions bring to mind something that quantum physicist Christopher Fuchs wrote:

> One of my greatest eye-opening experiences was in learning that when the Japanese look at the moon they see a rabbit pounding rice cakes. Ever since being told that, I've been able to see it too. It's plain as day. Thirty-three years of not seeing it once, and then, boom, someone tells me of it and I see it all the time. Likewise, I'll bet the next big step in physics will only require that we see something right here in front of us. It'll be something no big multi-billion dollar particle accelerator will be needed for. We just have to figure out how to take note of it. I'm banking that a hint is already written down in the quantum.[1]

Instead of seeing the conventional image of "the man in the moon" that we in the West grew up with, in Fuchs's "eye-opening" experience he snapped out of his habitual, conditioned way of seeing things and saw the world, and the moon, through a different lens. The Japanese image of a rabbit pounding rice cakes, like the image of the man in the moon, doesn't exist objectively, separate from the observer, and yet either way of looking at the moon, as a man or a rabbit, were there all along in potential, staring him—and all of us—in the face.

Some of the most mind-blowing ideas are so obvious they're right in front of our noses, and this is why no one notices them. This is exactly how Tibetan Buddhism describes our true nature: it's like those childhood puzzles with multiple faces hidden in the picture in plain sight; we don't have to draw the faces, they're literally right in front of us. We just have to recognize them.

Visionary physicist John Wheeler was convinced that at the bottom of the universe, so to speak, is not a mathematical equation, but a simple idea: he was of the opinion that until we realize this basic idea that underlies the quantum, we have not fully understood the quantum principle, the universe, or our place in it, and ourselves as well. Since we live in a thoroughly quantum universe, our task—the next big step in physics—becomes that of uncovering the simple idea that demands the quantum. When we finally do see the simple idea that informs our quantum universe, Wheeler suggests that it will have been so obvious that we will wonder how we could have been blind for so long.

The Polarizing Lens of Our Mind

The metaphor of a lens with a polarizing filter—a lens that is also a polarizer—can help us understand how the mind-blindness of wetiko functions. A lens is something that we look through that controls the nature of what we see, either by distorting our vision of the world or bringing it into better focus. There is an important difference, however, between a lens and a filter. A lens usually lets in all of the light impinging on it, whereas a polarizing filter (think of polarized sunglasses) selectively blocks out some of the light from passing through it so that aspects of the light that are polarized differently from the filter never reach the eye of the viewer, thereby never even registering in the viewer's awareness.

A polarizing filter only admits light that is similarly polarized as itself. In an interesting choice of words that maps onto our current political reality, the polarization of photons that make up light is what quantum physicists call *spin*. If the spin (think of our "narrative bias") of the incoming light aligns with that of the polarizing filter, it will allow the light to pass through the filter. If the incoming photons have a different spin than the polarizer, the polarizer will not admit the light and will block it from being registered.

A worldview that's different from ours is often automatically and unconsciously rejected depending on the axiomatic settings of the lens and polarizing filters of our mind. In other words, the "polarizing filter" built into the "lens" of the mind will not accept any information that is not in agreement with its spin, due to the built-in bias of the polarizing filter. In this metaphor, the polarizing lens of the mind is the means by which we experience, place meaning on, make sense of, and interpret the world.

This metaphor highlights the fact that there are two different forms of blindness operating in a mind afflicted with wetiko, and they are both self-reinforcing. One type of blindness is caused by the lens of the mind distorting what is seen, such that our world is not perceived accurately, but rather, is overlaid with our inner projections that are then taken to exist out in the world. The second type of blindness is where some of the incoming information in our world is selectively blocked out by our inner polarizing filter, thereby never reaching the sense-making apparatus of the mind.

These two processes are not separate, but work together in concert in a way that compounds the blinding effect that we unconsciously impose on our view of reality. The polarizing lens of our mind only allows a limited subset of available information to be registered in our awareness, thereby diminishing the quality of the picture of reality that we see, while the distortions in our mental lens further deform this already impoverished picture of reality. We then become convinced that our distorted version of reality is objectively true, a conviction that feeds back into and further strengthens the fixed nature of the polarization settings of our inner filter. These two blinding factors work together compounding each other in such a way that not having a clear and unadulterated view as a reference point, we become completely unaware of just how slanted our vision of reality is.

We can easily hypnotize ourselves via the creative power of our own mind to think that the falsified version of reality we are seeing is the real thing, thus falling prey to wetiko. Add to this the fact that there are institutionalized powers in our society whose intention is to obfuscate and falsify what is happening in our world, and the challenge we all face in refining our vision in order to see clearly becomes all the more evident. The mind never suspects that it is not receiving all of the information that is available, and makes the mistake—a mistake that is key to the workings of wetiko—of assuming that it is seeing clearly and fully. We then become blind to the fact that our perspective is only one among many perspectives, and instead mistakenly assume that our perspective is the only correct way of seeing things.

A result of this filtering by the mind is that we tend to naively believe that what we are seeing is objectively true, which strengthens the mistaken belief that what we are perceiving is not just true for us, but is universally true for all others. This can easily lead to fanaticism and crusades of one sort or another to convert the unbelievers, as we see in the world today in both subtle and not so subtle ways. Wetiko is given cover and thereby greatly enhanced, protected, and strengthened within the mind that is overconfidently and unquestioningly convinced of its own rightness.

It can be helpful to remember that when one person sees a rainbow, another person is not seeing the same rainbow. There are as many rainbows as there are observers—each observer is seeing their own private rainbow. There is no objective rainbow out there that each one of us is seeing, but rather, the rainbow we perceive is nothing other than an image in our own individual mind. Quantum physics and Buddhism make the point that, in the very same way, our physical world is rainbowlike in nature.

So many conflicts in our world, both big and small, consist of people fighting over the belief that their version of reality is the correct one. Quantum physics says there is no one objective reality, but similar to how there is no singular rainbow, there are as many "realities" as there are observers. So many, if not all of our conflicts arise due to a breakdown of communication between different people with different realities. Realizing the deeper quantum (and dreamlike) nature of our universe can help us build bridges that connect the multiple realities that seemingly separate us.

That our mind has a built-in polarizing lens means that we are each prone to seeing reality in a distorted, biased, or partial way. This realization can make us question and possibly "put in brackets" the veracity and reliability of our own perceptual and sense-making abilities, such that we become open and more willing to changing our viewpoint when new evidence presents itself. His Holiness the Dalai Lama says the same thing about Buddhism when he points out that if new evidence is discovered that proves that some aspect of the accepted wisdom in Buddhism is wrong, that Buddhism should change to include this new understanding.

Realizing that we each see the world through the polarizing lens of our mind's eye offers a deeper context and puts a more expansive spin on our understanding of the extreme polarization in the world today. A belief system and worldview that differs from ours not only tends to be automatically rejected, but there is an unconscious built-in tendency within us to conflate such views with the people holding them. We then reject and create separation from those who hold a different perspective from our own, seeing them as "others" who not only threaten our view of the world, but our very sense of self.

We are much more prone to falling prey to wetiko when we are blind to the fact that our mind has blinders built into its operating system. When we are blind to the blinding filters of our mind, we become dangerously blind. Our lack of insight into our blindness ensures that we will unconsciously act out this blindness in ways that ultimately do not serve, and even hinder the highest good for both ourselves and the world at large.

We begin to learn the art of seeing by recognizing our unconscious tendency to be blind, and then taking this into account so that we can gradually overcome this tendency. A sincere disposition of humility is thus a powerful wetiko-neutralizer that will dramatically diminish and weaken the grip that wetiko has on us. Staying ever mindful of our potential for self-deception can help inoculate us from falling under wetiko's thrall. Wetiko cannot survive in a psyche that is truly, sincerely, and humbly committed to consistent self-examination.

Omniperspectival Vision

Recognizing that the overwhelming majority of people are unaware of the polarizing lens within—and intrinsic to—their own mind can change our perspective on how we can more compassionately relate to their blindness. The first step in teaching people the art of seeing is showing them—opening their eyes to—the fact that they are blind. The part of us that sees our blindness is the part of us that is beginning to see.

Part of seeing our blindness is recognizing how we've been brainwashed. To see involves seeing that part of us that is in denial. And not just seeing the part of us that's in denial, but then no longer denying what we're in denial about. This liberates enormous psychic energy that was bound up in denial.

Once we begin to embrace our moment-by-moment experience, we can recognize that there's nothing in particular that we need to see as an object "out there." Recognizing that there's nothing to recognize is when our eyes have opened and we are seeing through the very act of looking. In other words, this is when we realize that seeing is itself a creative act. The way we see affects what we see. Then and only then can we consciously start to create the world we want to live in.

As members of society, we've all been programmed as to how to see, what to see, and what not to see. Philip K. Dick coined the term *negative hallucination,* by which he means that, unlike in a typical hallucination (where we are seeing what is *not* there), we cannot see what *is* there. Not being able to see what's right in front of our eyes is a form of the psychic blindness that is wetiko.

Ideas are the means by which we see the world. Maybe what we need to help people see isn't simply new ideas (as objects), but rather, as if giving people a new pair of eyeglasses, we can show them how to subjectively see the world *through* new ideas, new ways of looking at the world. Jung points out that when it is a question of mass psychosis such as wetiko, nothing but new symbolic ideas that can help us see in a new way can save us from our self-created collective nightmare. The nightmare mind-virus of wetiko enlists us to dream up our own worst nightmare in waking life. What can be thought of as a *saving* idea, an idea that brings a new way of seeing, can rescue us from becoming entrenched in a fixed, limited, one-sided perspective. A salvific idea can awaken us to the ultimate relativity of all ideas and perspectives, a metaperspective that creates an openness in our mind and a space in our heart for love, compassion, and empathy to find their place.

How do we do this? What would introducing a new idea, a new way of looking at the world, look like? Cultivating the art of seeing involves self-reflectively turning our awareness onto the process of seeing itself. It's not a particular perspective that we need to teach people to see, but more of a sense that whatever we're seeing isn't written in stone (the moon being a rock), but is malleable and a function of our mind. The way we see the world and what we are seeing in it reflects something unknown in ourselves that has to do with our creative power. Whatever viewpoint we are seeing through is simply one of a vast range of possible perspectives. Maybe teaching people the art of seeing involves showing them how getting fixed in a particular (and thereby partial) viewpoint doesn't serve them or anyone, as it hinders our intrinsic creative genius to constructively forge our experience of both ourselves and the world around us.

I have coined the phrase *massively uninformed smug certainty syndrome,* or MUSCS, to describe a situation when someone who has hardly done any research on a topic other than imbibing the mainstream (or alternative) media's propaganda then develops the absolute conviction that they are in possession of the truth. If questioned on the origin of their certainty, it oftentimes comes down to having read an article or heard someone on a podcast. We can practically smell someone who is acting out MUSCS, as this condition has an aroma all its own.

If someone is shedding light on the darkness playing out in our world, the dark powers, for example, might set up "fact-checking" sites or create hit pieces to attack the truth-teller and what they're saying. The search engines, whose algorithms are highly influenced by these same dark forces, make sure that the sites that draw people away from what is being illumined come up first when we search online about what the truth-teller is trying to expose.

If we are not awake to this modus operandi, we can easily fall under the spell of believing a lie to be the truth and the truth to be a lie (hence one of the monikers of wetiko, "the counterfeiting spirit"). It never seems to occur to people who regularly fall for this ruse that the sources that claim they possess the truth (and are deceptively pointing out that the truth-tellers are giving misinformation). When we try to open people's eyes to this they typically think we're either crazy, paranoid, overly suggestible, or a conspiracy theorist. Their reaction shields them from having to look at the depth of evil we're dealing with in the world, as well as their own unconscious complicity in this evil (as a result of denying that it exists). They might even accuse us of having a smug certainty about what we're pointing at, even though, instead of being "massively uninformed," we've done voluminous amounts of research. This is one of the ways how wetiko propagates itself in our world and in our minds.

I can speak from my own personal experience. It is very triggering, even maddening, when I encounter people who are afflicted with MUSCS. I take it as part of my spiritual training to not unconsciously react to them by trying to convince them of the wrongness of their viewpoint. Rather, I try as best I can to skillfully and consciously relate to them in a way that I can maintain my own integrity and still be helpful to them. I've noticed that if I try to convince someone of something, any attempt to do so, however well-intentioned, is almost always doomed to fail.

Seeing in a more wholistic way involves recognizing that it serves us to view something from as many angles—omniperspectivally—as we can imagine. Part of seeing wholistically is stepping out of our own perspective as we enter into another person's point of view, particularly if they see differently than us, and then trying to entertain how they are seeing things. What do they see that we aren't seeing? What are their blind spots? How does their vision—as well as their blindness—help us further our own vision and more deeply illumine and alleviate our own blindness? A deepening of empathy is likely to be the result.

It is a mistake, however, to overly identify with a more expansive metaperspective that holds all possibilities as true if in so doing we marginalize, ignore, or disregard what is actually happening, i.e. what is true. Seeing omniperspectivally and not taking sides, though *seemingly* enlightened (and it *is* enlightened under certain circumstances), can easily be usurped by the wetiko mind-virus to serve its agenda, through the seemingly awakened justification of not wanting to become fixed in a particular viewpoint.

Holding the creative tension that is required to see omniperspectivally does not preclude the possibility that one point of view might actually be true. This would mean that the other point of view is false. Viewing our world from this more expansive perspective does not preclude taking a particular viewpoint as being true. At certain points it literally demands that we do so.

Seeing wetiko necessarily involves cultivating a wholistic vision that sees—as quantum physics points out—how everything is interconnected with everything else. There are so many major crises converging in our world right now that it's easy to not recognize the deeper underlying dynamic that connects them all. Realizing that all of these seemingly disparate processes are interwoven parts of a single unified tapestry being generated by the same underlying dynamic demands a change in focus, such that we develop a more comprehensive and wholistic vision. Instead of becoming entranced by any of the seemingly separate parts or processes, viewing from a whole-systems point of view becomes the doorway to seeing how the wetiko mind-virus is threaded throughout the parts so as to make up the whole.

What is the simple idea that underlies all of quantum physics? Concerning "the next big step in physics" I agree with Fuchs when he says that "a hint is already written down in the quantum."[2] In showing us that the universe, just like our experience of the moon, isn't separate from our perception of it, quantum physics is revealing the dreamlike nature of reality. Our perception of the universe is a part of the universe that is happening through us. Just like a dream, our perception affects the universe we are observing, a universe of which we are simultaneously both an insignificant and a key part.

No physicist worth his salt disagrees with the fact that quantum physics is the greatest discovery in the history of science. What is controversial is how to interpret the revelations emerging from quantum physics. Classical physicists are not only not trained to realize that quantum physics is revealing this dreamlike nature, they are actively indoctrinated by the academy and the corporate state to not recognize this. They have literally fallen blind, as if put under a spell, by scientific materialism, and have been conditioned to think that things and people exist in a way that they simply do not.

Wheeler felt that if we really understood the simple idea that is at the root of quantum physics, we could express our realization in one sentence, short enough to put on a T-shirt, a bumper sticker, or a tweet, such that even a child could understand. In light of this, Wheeler once proposed a challenge: describe the essence of the quantum gnosis in five words or fewer. My answer: Life is but a dream.

Life is not a dream in the sense that it's a meaningless illusion; it's a dream in a much more profound sense: the universe doesn't exist as something separate from us, and we are both created by the universe as well as its co-creators—in my parlance we are "dreaming it up." The question, which feels like the right question, then becomes how do we stabilize this realization and help other people—the other dream characters (interconnected, inseparable aspects of ourselves)—become lucid in the dream of life, such that we can connect with one another through our shared realization, unlock our creative genius and dream a dream that's more in alignment with who we're discovering ourselves to be? We can dream, can't we?

14

Wetiko as Revelation

Revelations are interesting things. They are not something that our ego creates, but in a very real sense they are given to us. We have this one word, *revelation,* for a phenomenon with many degrees of subtlety, nuance, and profundity. Revelation is of a higher order than mere insight. With a revelation it's as if something entirely new, often unexpected, comes our way. In its full-blown form, revelation has a biblical flavor, bringing to mind the archetypal figure of the prophet. But a prophet isn't so much a foreteller of the future, but rather, is someone who discerns the deeper unconscious pattern that has given shape to the past and, to the extent that it remains unconscious, is informing the present. The prophet is able to shed light on and creatively express this unconscious pattern in a new way that, if their revelation is able to be sufficiently communicated to others, can potentially transform the future.

In our overly rationalistic and materialistic culture, people who claim to have revelations that can help the world are often seen as mad. Many such people populate the back wards of psychiatric hospitals. To have a revelatory experience and identify with it such that it feeds our self-importance is easy to do if we haven't developed a strong enough sense of self. Instead of recognizing that we're just an instrument for something to reveal itself through us, we then become inflated, thinking we're special—a not uncommon form of pathology. It's typically considered okay to have a revelation concerning one's own life, but God forbid if someone has a revelation that they claim has relevance for humanity—they will likely be thought of as having taken leave of their senses. For this I have coined the term *revelation denigration syndrome,* or RDS.

For the majority of card-carrying members of consensus reality it is out of the realm of possibility that an ordinary person can have a world-transforming revelation. Having internalized the unreflected-on and limited assumptions of our culture, many people don't even recognize their own revelatory experiences. And yet, in these very dark times we are living through it makes all the sense in the world that we should be on the lookout for revelatory experiences for guidance, be they out in the world, within our own mind, or in the interface between the two.

Oftentimes revelations show up in the most unexpected of ways. Sometimes we have mind-blowing and life-transforming revelations and don't even realize the profundity of what has been shown to us. Revelations often contain encoded within themselves multiple levels of teachings and gifts that can take years, maybe even decades, to decipher and consciously realize and bring into one's life. It is only after we are able to take in and integrate what the revelation is showing us that we are able to embody it in our lives, thereby creatively transmitting it to others in our own unique way.

The hidden treasures embedded in a revelation are meant to be shared with others. Once the revelation takes hold within others' minds, it only increases the revelation's potency. Stemming from the universal, impersonal substrate of mind itself, revelations have a contagious nature that can go viral if they "touch" enough people. The universe and our very lives, after all is said and done, are living revelations, ever pulsating with unrealized potentialities, an unsurpassed and unsurpassable revelatory experience of the highest order. Being by nature visionary beings, we just need to cultivate the requisite vision. As sacred scriptures throughout the ages have reminded us, if we don't develop our inner spiritual vision, we are complicit in our own demise.

Surely Some Revelation Is at Hand

When someone becomes fixed and one-sided in their viewpoint, a counterposition will invariably grow in their unconscious. Once it gains enough energy, it can erupt into consciousness as a revelation. Revelations (arche)typically occur during times of extreme creative tension, oftentimes as the direct result of the person's unconscious being disturbed, as if something is emerging in the unconscious that threatens the prevailing attitude of the conscious mind. Might this same process be true not just on the individual level, but collectively, on a species level, as well?

This dreamlike world of ours, inseparable from the psyche, is, like the psyche, compensatory in its actions. When we disconnect from our true nature and get off-center, the psyche sends us dreams that simultaneously express and reveal the contents of our unconscious so as to help us reestablish conscious connection with our authentic self. Similarly, but writ large on the global stage, our world is being collectively dreamed up by us to play out—and reveal—the contents of the collective unconscious. Everything depends on whether we comprehend what is being revealed to us.

This compensatory, dreamlike nature of our world is intimated in William Butler Yeats's famous poem "The Second Coming": "Things fall apart; the centre cannot hold; Mere anarchy is loosed upon the world, The blood-dimmed tide is loosed. . . . Surely some revelation is at hand." Yeats was intuitively giving voice to the idea that when our world is coming apart at the seams, we should keep our eyes open for a revelation that can potentially bring us back to our center. These two events—the world falling apart and revelation—are not separate and unrelated, but rather, they reciprocally co-arise, as they are ultimately indistinguishable parts of a greater process.

This is similar to how a symbol that arises in a dream, and the mind of the dreamer that recognizes and is transformed by what the symbol is revealing, are not two separate things interacting, but rather, are inseparable parts of a greater quantum system, which is the psyche of the person dreaming. As soon as the person takes in and is changed by what the symbol is revealing, the unconscious (the dreamer of the dream) instantaneously registers this expansion of consciousness and recalibrates itself, reflecting back to the dreamer new symbols that reflect the dreamer's more integrated state. This process happens in no time—outside of time, in fact—and over linear time as well.

This dynamic can be creatively symbolized by the image of an enlightened deity splitting itself into two and giving itself a teaching. As the part of the deity that is receiving the teaching takes in and receives the gnosis that is being transmitted by its awakened other half, it gradually becomes assimilated into the part of the deity that is giving the teaching. As this process imaginatively unfolds, these two split-off parts of the deity merge and become one, which was their original condition in the first place. But in this new state of integration, the deity has now become self-reflectively aware in a way that it wasn't prior to its dissociation. This process expresses the nature of our situation, as the awakened part of us that is consciously engaging with us in dreaming the dream is continually sending us wake-up calls through the endless variety of means at its disposal. Wetiko is the source of the greatest evil imaginable. And yet, at one and the same time it is a revelation, showing us the very thing we need to know at this dangerous moment in time in order to save ourselves. Woven within the warp and woof of all of the multiple dimensions of wetiko is a hidden revelation. It is a full-blown revelation that is anything but hidden, as it is not just in front of our face, but *in* it, or rather, in our minds. We typically associate revelations as being filled with love and light, but some revelations are transmitted through the darkness and are truly horrifying. The wetiko revelation is physically materializing in our world while at the same time it is reflected in our minds. The disease's revelatory aspect is available to be seen for those who recognize the inseparability of our inner and outer realities.

That something causes suffering doesn't preclude that it can also contain a transformative revelation, maybe even being the necessary catalyst to transfigure individuals, societies, and potentially our entire species. Isn't this the deeper meaning of the Christian myth—that we can't have the Resurrection without the Crucifixion and the descent into the underworld? That there is a potential revelation hidden within our suffering, showing us how we create our own suffering and revealing how to end this suffering, is the basis of the whole Buddhist path.

Being a dreaming phenomenon, like any dream, wetiko has many perspectives built into its fabric, as well as multiple levels of meaning. Wetiko psychosis is something that we—all of us—are collectively dreaming up each and every moment. Being that we are dreaming up wetiko, we have the capacity to *un-dream* wetiko (similar to dissolving a self-created apparition). As if we possess a magic wand that we haven't learned how to use responsibly, we're like sorcerer's apprentices who are suffering and being destroyed by our own conjurations.

Why are we dreaming up wetiko in the first place? It is indisputable: we are dreaming up this deadly pathogenic mind-virus because we don't know how *not* to! This is evidenced by the fact that if we knew how not to dream up wetiko, we would. However, secretly encoded within wetiko's manifestation is the very teaching we need to realize how not to dream it up.

Just like the the way the forms in a dream reflect and compensate for an unconscious one-sidedness in the dreamer (which in this case is us), the wetiko epidemic in our world is both an expression of and compensation for something within us that we are asleep to. We won't be able to un-dream wetiko until we learn what it is trying to teach us about ourselves. We just can't wish a recurring dream to go away because we don't like it. Recurring dreams stop happening when we get their message. Wetiko, in slapping us upside (and inside) the head, is ultimately revealing that we ourselves are the co-dreamers of the dream.

The wetiko psychosis that is running rampant in our world is an expression that we are not consciously in touch with our immense, practically unimaginable creative powers that are part and parcel of our human nature. To the extent that we are asleep to our true nature as creative beings is the extent to which our creativity is rendered unconscious and outsourced, such that other people—not to mention the powers-that-be of the corporate state—will gladly pick up our disowned creative agency and use it against us in a way that can only be described as a nightmare. The point is, to the extent that we have disconnected from and not consciously realized our creative spirit, we ourselves are colluding with our oppressors. Wetiko is freely revealing this to us, provided we have an open mind.

Being a quantum phenomenon, wetiko is the source of the most toxic poison as well as the greatest potential wake-up call we could ever imagine. Due to its quantum nature, wetiko is both and neither of these things, for it has no objective existence separate from our own minds, which is to say that how wetiko manifests, as a world destroyer or an awakener of humanity, depends on nothing other than how we dream it, and whether we recognize what it is revealing to us.

Wetiko is not a static entity but a dynamic, ever-changing, continually evolving *process* that initially manifests in its evil aspect but potentially transmutes itself so as to reveal its good side. As a quantum phenomenon, wetiko is a particularly unique form of revelation—a special type of hidden treasure—that needs our conscious participation in order to effect its transformation and bring forth its positive aspect. In true quantum style, wetiko is a participatory revelation in that it is a potential revelation waiting to unfold its gifts, but needs us to actively partake in what it is offering or it will withhold its blessings. If we don't step up and engage with it at the level it requires (which is to apprehend what it is revealing to us, and then act out of this realization), it will continue, as if programmed by a robotic intelligence, to manifest its destructive aspect. If left unrecognized, wetiko's potentially medicinal effects turn into the poison of all poisons. Recognizing wetiko as a revelation and taking into ourselves what it is showing us disables its malevolent aspect and alchemically transfigures it, and us. It should get our attention that Mercurius, the alchemical equivalent of the spirit of wetiko, is, among many other things, the god of revelation.

The concept of wetiko, a nonlocal mind-virus whose origin is within the psyche yet has the ability to manifest physically through events in the outer world, helps us get a handle on the madness and evil that is happening in our world (as well as within each of us) in a new way that helps us to more effectively deal with it. Being a revelation, wetiko can potentially stimulate our lucidity, as it expands our consciousness, while at the very same time entertaining the idea of wetiko is itself an expression of an expanded consciousness.

Like a volcano, the dark forces of the unconscious—the powers of the underworld—are erupting into our world. To the extent that we are enamored of and identified with scientific materialism, with its overemphasis on the rationalism of the intellect, we have become disoriented (not to mention deranged), and this has put us at the mercy of the psychic underworld.

Instead of manifesting through the light, the divinely sanctioned wetiko revelation is emerging from the depths of the underworld. True revelation includes, embraces, and is linked to its opposite, as revelation serves the uniting of the opposites, which exist relative and in relation to each other. The light isn't simply revealing the darkness, it is revealing itself *through* the darkness. Just as darkness is only known through light, it is a kabbalistic idea that light issues forth and is known through darkness.

The powers of darkness are coming up—the *Deus Absconditus,* the dark or hidden God—and we need to come to terms with what these powers are revealing to us or suffer the consequences. Humanity is making a collective shamanic descent into the underworld of the unconscious. As mythologies the world over have pointed out, this darkness is the place where the sacred treasure—the creative soul of humanity—is to be found and realized.

There is light that is hidden, imprisoned and held captive within the darkness, and it is our job to recognize and liberate this hidden light. This insight is expressed in various ways in alchemy, gnosticism, the Kabbalah, and many other wisdom traditions. The darkness can't be rejected, avoided, marginalized, or ignored, for it is essential to the revelation and illumination of the light. The revelation of darkness— and the revelation hidden within that darkness—is an unavoidable and critically important part of the next stage of humanity's collective psychospiritual evolution.

Our universe is a treasure trove overflowing with a nearly infinite variety of treasures, wetiko being one, quantum physics being another. We shouldn't limit our conception of the nature of these hidden treasures or the forms they can potentially take, for the entire universe is itself a continuous living revelation, offering us everything we need in order to wake up—if only we have the eyes to see.

We should be grateful for wetiko. When seen as the revelation that it is, wetiko can be recognized as a precious gift that, based on how things appear on the surface, is presenting itself as anything but. And yet, wetiko's endowments are legion. When recognized as a revelation, we can realize that wetiko is showing us our own unimagined darkness and not-yet-realized light. Wetiko is making sure that we make the best use of our divine endowment. Wetiko is a peculiar form of mind-blindness that contains its own cure. This virus of the mind is disclosing to us the dreamlike nature of our situation. It is showing us our place in the world. It is potentially unlocking the creative spirit within us. It is divulging to us our interconnectedness with one another. And, as an added bonus, it is laying bare and revealing who we are. Not bad for something we initially thought of as a curse. Not bad at all.

15

The Self as Mirror

When we get right down to it, the greatest protection from and medicine for wetiko is to recognize and connect with our true, original nature, which wetiko both obscures and reveals, depending on whether we can identify within ourselves what it is showing us.

One of the traditional Buddhist symbols of our true nature is the spacious sky. Like space, the nature of mind has no limit or center, is not defined by restrictions, nor can it be constrained or reified in a particular form. Unlike the contents of our mind, which are like ever-changing clouds, the awareness of our true nature, like the cloudless sky, never changes. Like space, our true nature is an uninterrupted, unceasing, expansive, unbounded openness and evenness that isn't affected by external factors. As we discover the spacelike quality of our true nature, we naturally open up and extend ourselves out to the entire universe, dropping the compulsive need to self-protect. Our nature is naturally radiant and intrinsically lucid, possessing a cognitive aspect, a luminous faculty of self-knowing.

The purity of our true nature, like the spacious sky that has room for everything, is never tainted or stained by any cloud, no matter how dark, just like the purity of our mind is not corrupted by the vilest thoughtform. Our open, skylike nature is incorruptible—it can't be contaminated. On the one hand, the clouds (representing the conceptual mind) are not separate from the sky, for they come out of the sky, abide in the sky, and dissolve back into the emptiness of the sky. The true, essential, empty nature of clouds is not separate from, will always return to, and is one with the emptiness of the sky. If the sky is seen as symbolizing primordial awareness, the clouds (our thoughtforms) are its display, like the sun displaying itself as its rays. The clouds are the expressions and ornaments of the sky—they are the sky's adornment.

The clouds arising in the sky depend on the sky for their existence, as clouds never exist except within the sky. This is similar to how reflections in a mirror depend on the mirror for their existence, as reflections do not exist except in a mirror. The sky and the mirror, symbols of our true nature, don't depend for their existence on either clouds or reflections. Like the sky, primordial awareness—our true nature—is always spontaneously present as the basic space and ground of all phenomena.

Though the clouds are supported by, depend on, and are not separate from the sky, the clouds and the sky never touch or become parts of each other, for they exist in two entirely different dimensions. This is a paradox: not separate from the sky by even one iota, the clouds are at the same time separate from the sky. The spacelike nature of the sky is the most fundamental quality of all of the other elements of the universe (earth, water, fire, and wind), for it is the element out of which all of the other elements arise and into which they are absorbed. Whereas all four elements arise and eventually cease to be, the element of space, like our innate true nature, is beyond arising and ceasing, beyond birth and death. Our true nature is not a product of causes and conditions, existing in a realm transcendent to causal factors, a realm that is forever untouched by wetiko.

The Mirrorlike Nature of the Mind

Our true nature is like a mirror in that it remains unaffected by the objects it reflects, the reflections themselves, as well as the act of perceiving the reflections. The essence of a mirror, just like the Self, always remains imperturbably and unwaveringly the same: a presence of pristine clarity. The reflections, though seemingly obscuring the silvered surface of the mirror, simultaneously reveal it, for we would never notice the mirror without the reflections, which inform us of the existence of the mirror. A polished mirror is open and receptive to the world, invisible by itself were it not for the world outside that is reflected in it. The philosopher's stone of alchemy—the healing panacea for what ails humanity—is said to be as clear and translucent as a diamond or crystal, considered invisible to normal vision, a *lapis invisibilitatus*.*

A clear mirror is empty of all qualities except its ability to reflect. Yet it cannot reflect itself, just like the pure state of awareness that underlies and precedes every state of ordinary cognition can itself never be the object of such cognition. If left to its own devices, the mirror would never enter our experiential reality; it needs something seemingly outside of itself for it to be revealed.

The reflections in a mirror are inseparable from the mirror, and yet the reflections are not the mirror. As if an emanation from a higher dimension, the reflections don't originate in the mineral substance of the mirror. The image of the reflections is not derived from the mirror, but from something beyond it. The reflections are the energy and pristine presence of the formless mirror manifesting and being expressed in form.

The forms of the reflections are imbued with the pristine purity of the mirror, yet if we overly focus on the forms without noticing the mirror that contains them and in which they are suspended, we will tend to not perceive the mirrorlike purity of the forms. The source of this process, which is analogous to not seeing the mirrorlike purity of the mind's expressions, is not to be found in either the mirror or the reflections, but within our own mind.

We can think of the reflections in the mirror as representing thoughtforms that arise within the empty, mirrorlike nature of our mind. When we have a thought, awareness itself is appearing as the

---

*The lapis is one of the symbols for the philosopher's stone.

thought, just as the mirror appears as whatever it is reflecting. The experience of the thought is not happening to awareness, as if thought and awareness are distinct entities; the experience of the thought is itself how awareness is manifesting to itself at that particular moment. This is similar to how the reflections aren't happening *to* the mirror, as if they are two separate things; rather, the reflections are how the mirror is manifesting at that moment. Just like how reflections are an expression of the nature of the mirror, thoughts are simply the expression of awareness, and not necessarily problematic in and of themselves.

The emptiness of the mirror can take on all possible reflections, similar to how awareness is empty of intrinsic, independent existence and yet can appear as anything. A thought never takes on a separate existence independent of the empty awareness in which, and to which, it appears. Similar to how we can't separate the surface of the mirror from its reflections, naturally occurring timeless awareness (the mirror-like nature of our mind) is not separate from, but rather, is identical with its manifestations, our thoughts.

This is similar to how dreams experienced at night are not separate from the awareness that experiences them. Apart from this awareness, our dreams have no existence. Dreams do not happen to the dreamer's mind as if they were separate from the mind, like two separate entities meeting; they are the unmediated manifestations of the mind appearing to itself. There seems to be a duality between a dream image and the person perceiving it, but this difference is only an apparent duality not actually existing.

Whatever reality is, there is one indisputable fact: we can only *experience* it. Experience is a fundamental feature of the world. As quantum physics has revealed, there is no objective world separate from our awareness of it; our awareness of the world is a key component of the very world we are experiencing. The world, and our experience of it, is never found without awareness being part of the equation, as our experience of the world necessarily arises within awareness. The reality of our world is only something we experience. It is the in-our-face obviousness of this realization that makes it so hard to see. Experience is such a constant, pervasive, implicit feature of being alive that it's easy to ignore and disregard.

The teachings of the Buddha reveal that there is no experiencer who is separate from experience, no isolatable self who is having an experience. This "I" is a construct, a convenient abstraction, a convention of popular speech. This is similar to when we say "it rains," we do not mean that something external to the rain is raining. The Buddha didn't deny the subjectivity of our experience; rather, he denied the ability to isolate and set apart the subject who was having the experience from the experience itself.

Similar to awareness appearing in the form of a thought when we are thinking (or a feeling when we are feeling), when we experience the seemingly outside world, awareness itself is appearing as the world we are experiencing. The highest teachings of Buddhism point out that all phenomena, both inner and outer, are a magical display of pure awareness. Both our inner and outer experiences are not happening to awareness, but rather, these experiences *are* awareness. The observer *is* the observed, and there is truly no separation between subject and object.

Our sensory experiences are often mistakenly interpreted as being evidence for a real, objective, independently existing world "out there." It is the light of awareness (our true nature) however, that gives the world color and sound; our experience of the world is brought to us through our five senses and then neurologically remixed within our mind into a convincing experience of a seemingly solid, external, material world. The idea of a real physical external world is just that—an idea. The idea of an *independently existing objective universe* (the aforementioned IEOU) is an unwarranted assumption, a projection that we overlay onto our direct experience that we assume to be true; this is how we entrance ourselves.

Appearances of whatever sort—not just our inner landscape of thoughts, feelings, dreams, and visions, but the sensory experiences of the seemingly outer world—are all manifestations of the basic ground of uncontrived awareness. Whatever appearances we are experiencing are not separate from our awareness, as the two, awareness and appearances, are always one. Just like how we can never find a reflection without a mirror, we can never have an experience of the world without awareness.

All wisdom teachings the world over have pointed out in their own way that there is nothing other than naturally occurring, naked, timeless awareness. This timeless, pristine, pellucid, limpid awareness is identical with its manifestation as appearances, and despite the seeming modifications to awareness, it can never become anything other than itself. This is to recognize that we are living inside our psyche, which is both within us and all around us in the guise of the world as it reflects back to us through both the inner and outer worlds. Our world is a psychical experience, meaning it can only be experienced through the psyche. This is to awaken to the dreamlike nature of life and become lucid in the waking dream.

The empty, pristine nature of awareness permeates whatever thoughtforms arise as water pervades waves in the ocean. Waves appear simultaneously along with the ocean. Waves are never separate from, but always remain within the ocean throughout their rising, billowing, and falling. Waves are not happening *to* the ocean, they *are* the ocean. The fundamental nature of the water is not altered in any way by the shape of the waves. In the same way, though the outer appearance of the mirror is superficially altered, the fundamental nature of the mirror is not affected by its reflections, nor is the true, essential nature of our mind changed or bound by any of the thought forms that arise within it.

Each thoughtform is like a dream in the sense that it brings with it a corresponding universe and sense of identity. We typically identify with some thoughtforms, contract against and react to others, dissociate from some, judge ones we don't like, become fascinated with a few, and become conditioned by them—all forms of grasping. In all these cases our thoughtforms seem to wield power over us. This is analogous to thinking that—and reacting to—the reflections in the mirror as separate from us.

Our thoughtforms have great creative power to conjure up our experience of both the world and ourselves, depending on our relationship to them. Some people experience their thoughts as problematic, as obscurations to their true nature. Others recognize that like the reflections in a mirror are not separate from, but actually reveal the underlying mirror, our thoughts are actually the unmediated display of our true nature. How we relate to the contents passing through our mind—as obscurations or revelations—determines not only how these contents actually manifest in our experience, but is a major determining factor in how our life unfolds.

Many of us tend to focus our attention on the reflections—the contents of our mind, our thoughtforms—without noticing the formless, mirrorlike awareness that underlies and sustains the thoughtforms. We can become so distracted by the reflections that we forget about and fail to register the fact that the mirror is their source. If we need to clean the mirror, however, we have to change our focus so that we can see the clear glass of the mirror instead of solely focusing on the reflections. The Self as a mirror is difficult to understand, not because of its obscurity—it is literally staring us in the face—but rather, because of our unfamiliarity with a dimension of our experience that is practically invisible because of its obviousness.

Similarly, we can change our focus, and instead of being entranced by the myriad appearances (reflections), we can re-cognize our condition (the mirror). We can begin to put our attention on what it is within us that notices the contents of our mind. We can begin to recognize the always-present, naked awareness that is the open, spacious, self-cognizant, observing aspect of awareness. This clear, changeless awareness that mirrors and witnesses whatever is within us is not locked up in, but rather is transcendent to and hence free of whatever arises as the contents of the mind.

The mirror is a way of characterizing the open-ended freedom and invulnerability of our awareness, our presence, and true nature. In each moment that a thoughtform arises, we have a choice: whether to grasp onto it and identify with it, which keeps us caught in our self-generated prison (thereby feeding wetiko); or recognize that the arising of the thoughtform is revealing the mirrorlike, unconditioned nature of our mind. If we recognize that the thoughtform arising in our mind is an empty display of its mirrorlike nature, we then are no longer unwittingly carried away by our thoughts (like a baby left unprotected on the street might be taken away by a stranger), but can choose to intentionally create with our thoughts.

The Edge of the Mirror Metaphor

Once we attain mirrorlike wisdom, we no longer need identify with, react to, or become conditioned by our thoughtforms. Instead, we become like the mirror, which cannot be thrown off-balance by any of its transitory reflections. These reflections, which are our thoughtforms, have no effect on our intrinsically pure nature, which is always above and beyond the fray while ironically always right in the center of the action. As if in a different dimension, the unchangeable essence of the mirror of pure awareness is untouched and untainted by any of the reflections. Recognizing the mirrorlike nature of the Self renders the thoughtforms that arise within it totally harmless. The situation is then like a thief coming into an empty house—there's nothing to steal.

This shift in perspective is like looking at our reflection in the mirror and then finding ourself not only in the mirror, but discovering that we are the mirror itself looking outward—our own nature thereby meets itself in self-recognition. This experience of integrating our intrinsic nature is like space dissolving into space. For example, when a clay pot is broken, there are no longer two seemingly separate spaces, the space inside the pot and the space outside; there is only one space. Yet space has in no way been changed or modified. Our true nature is always the same; it's simply a question of whether we recognize it or not.

It is helpful to remember that the mirror is merely a metaphor. A mirror is a two-dimensional flat surface, whereas our mirrorlike true nature possesses dimensions without limit. So the mirror metaphor only goes so far in describing the mirrorlike nature of our mind. The true nature of our mind is *unlike* a mirror as well, in that the world of physical objects that is the basis of the mirror's reflections exist outside of the flat surface of the mirror, whereas the world that is reflected through the mirrorlike nature of the mind is not external to nor separate from the mind in which it is reflected.

Whereas a mirror is an object existing in space, the mirrorlike nature of consciousness is not an object existing in space, but rather is co-extensive with and equivalent to space. The mirrorlike nature of the mind is also spacelike in that it pervades, contains, and is one with all that arises within it. The mirrorlike nature of the mind is not a flat, two-dimensional surface; we and the world are both in the mirror— more precisely, we *are* the mirror. Due to the intrinsic openness, emptiness, and lack of limitation of our true nature, it is the source and medium for all potential manifestations, just as a mirror possesses the potential to reflect all possible objects and reflections. Thus perhaps an even more accurate symbol of our true nature might be a multidimensional, crystalline, holographic mirror that possesses infinite reflective surfaces.

The mirrorlike nature of the mind is not solely passive in its reflective ability, merely reflecting back an objective external, or subjective internal world. The mirror of the mind is not reflecting a world, be it inside or outside ourself, which we are passively witnessing; rather, as quantum physics has revealed, the very act of observing the world instantaneously affects how the world reflectively *re-presents* itself within our mind each and every moment. This is to say that the magic mirror of consciousness is not solely a reflector of forms, but rather, being a creative mirror, it is participating in creating the very forms it is reflecting. The mirrorlike nature of consciousness is therefore, by its very nature, simultaneously active and passive, thus embracing and resolving the conventional notion of duality between these seeming opposites.

The reflections resulting from the mirrorlike nature of our mind synthesize and couple with what seems to be an objective world outside of ourself and a subjective world inside of ourself into what convincingly appears to be a real world that is other than ourself. This apparently "real" world can only be experienced subjectively (within ourself) but appears to exist objectively (outside ourself).

If we don't recognize how these two realms—the inner subjective world of experience and the seemingly outer objective world—are reflectively linked together, the inevitable result is that we create the illusion of seeing ourself as being a *(subject)ive* ego that is separate from the seemingly objective world. We have then split the world, which is intrinsically whole, into two seemingly separate parts. Severing an ultimately indivisible unity into separate parts is a primordial form of madness (wetiko at work!) that is at the very root of the myriad interconnected problems we are facing today.

In actuality, we are actively participating in the creation of these mirrored reflections in such a way that the reflections manifest as if we aren't involved in their creation. This process, if left unseen, tricks us out of our right mind. Instead of recognizing that we are the mirror, we think we're separate from the mirror, thinking that its reflections are outside of us as well. The mirrorlike nature of our mind will then instantaneously reflect back our subjective thinking that we are other than and separate from the mirror and its reflections, thereby offering us all the proof we need to confirm the seeming rightness of our deluded viewpoint.

When we have a self-validating experience such as this, no one can talk us out of our conviction that we are seeing clearly. As our conclusion that we're seeing "reality" is based on our direct experience, we have all the information we need to convince ourself of the rightness of our point of view. And yet, via the creative power of our mind to influence how reality manifests, we have hypnotized ourself. This entire process takes place atemporally, in no time—outside of time—and yet it is experienced as unfolding over time, a combination that renders this

334 ⊕ The Self as Revelation

creative dynamic invisible to us. Ensnared by the power of delusion, we then heap delusion on delusion in a never-ending process. This endless process is simultaneously beginingless too, in that it does not originate in linear time, but continually reoccurs in the eternal "now" moment.

If not recognized, this process continually reinforces and perpetuates itself, making us, in our delusion, think that we're simply relating to the "real" world as it is. In Buddhism, this consensual reality is pure illusion; it is known as samsara, or cyclic existence, the endless round of death and rebirth, the world of never-ending delusion and its consequence, suffering. The revelation of the Buddha is, in its very essence, that we hold the key to unlocking this process by recognizing how we are complicit in conjuring it up in the first place, a realization that can only be had in the present moment.

The Miracle of Self-Reflection

Etymologically, the word *mirror* means "the holder of the shadow." Isn't it interesting that the holder of the shadow, the mirror, is at the same time a symbol for the Self? This points to the intimate connection between the shadow and the wholeness of our true nature. Humanity is in the collective role of the mirror that God holds up to become self-aware. It's as if human beings are the sense organs in the mystical body of the Divine, through which God becomes familiar with his/her/its own nature. So not only is a mirror a symbol of the Self, humanity is the mirror through which God—the Self—becomes aware, as we realize who we truly are.

It is helpful to recall Jung's cautionary words about the need for us to self-reflect as the "absolutely necessary and only right thing"[1] for us to do in our present day and age. Self-reflection, which Jung equates with "the urge to individuation,"[2] is the one act that might save us from the impending catastrophe that we are collectively creating. Instead of blindly living our experience, acting out and being puppeteered by the mythical, symbolic, and archetypal dimension of our experience without knowing it, self-reflection requires self-awareness such that we reflect upon and see what we're experiencing. In this way we broaden and deepen our understanding of both our experiences and ourselves. The act of self-reflection catalyzes a process of transformation in the archetypal realm of the collective unconscious, giving birth to the light of consciousness intrinsic to the Self within the unconscious. The Self is revealed and brought into incarnation through the human act of reflection.

The act of self-reflection, however, is one of the most abhorrent and repulsive things there is for humanity, as there seems to be a built-in dread in us for seeing the less than savory aspects of ourselves. We could call this automatic compulsive reaction *knee jerk reflectophobia* (KJR), which is an expression of the pervasive human *dread of seeing ourselves* (DOSO) as we are. In addition to being seen as a phobia, KJR can also be viewed as something like an allergic reaction to self-reflection. Similar to how the treatment for a physical allergy is to introduce a miniscule amount of the allergen into one's system, the treatment for KJR is to encourage minute amounts of self-reflection that can take root and grow over time.

Self-reflection and the more expanded awareness of oneself that comes from it are the prerequisite for basic sanity; whereas the lack of self-refletion is a recipe for insanity. The real leaders and heroes of humanity are the ones who overcome this instinctual inertia and resistance and have the courage to self-reflect. There is a strong correlation between being unable to self-reflect and being blind to the darkness that is playing out in the external world.

Self-reflection is a recollection and remembering of all of the split-off and projected parts of ourself in order for them to be integrated back into the wholeness of our true nature. It is shamanic soul retrieval in its most fundamental form. In gathering together the dissociated parts of ourselves into a unity, individuation is a revelation of the wholeness of the Self which existed prior to the ego and is actually the ego's creator. Though we as an ego need to voluntarily choose to self-reflect in order to participate in our own process of individuation, the impulse to self-reflect is inspired by the Self. The impulse to avoid self-reflection, on the other hand, is inspired by wetiko.

The self-realization that comes through self-reflection is mirrored back to us in our external relations with the world. The more we see ourselves in the world and deepen our ability to self-reflect, the more we see the light of the Self shining through other people and the world at large. Self-reflection helps us see through the illusion that we are separate from one another, as we recognize that we are all mirroring to one another parts of ourselves that we may not recognize, a realization that expands our sense of self and deepens our compassion. Connecting us with ourselves and one another, genuine self-reflection provides us with the antidote for what Hannah Arendt considers the elementary building block of the totalitarian state—the atomized, isolated individual (aka the separate self), which also happens to be the fundamental component of wetiko.

Through our ability to self-reflect, we have been drafted to play a key role in the cosmic process of the incarnation of God—that is, the Self—into the world. Through the intervention of our self-reflective consciousness, we are the second creators of the world, indispensable to the completion of creation, what Jung refers to as "the second cosmogony."[3] In essence, humanity is the aperture through which God—by whatever we call him/her/it—makes itself known and real in time. We are the eyes through which God sees itself, thereby becoming conscious of itself as we become conscious of ourselves. We are the conduit through which the universe, in becoming conscious and aware of itself through us, is waking up.

It should get our highest attention that wetiko necessitates and is the catalyst and inspiration for our self-reflection. If wetiko didn't exist, we'd have to invent it in order to evolve. Maybe this is actually what has happened: we have already unconsciously created the wetiko epidemic in order to evolve, and we simply have to recognize this to—*abracadabra!*—make it so.

As Jung has reminded us, the savior is already born within us and our role is simply to recognize it—to bear witness—in order to make its birth real in space and time. Our realizing this is the paradoxical part we play in liberating an already self-liberated universe. This is, alchemically speaking, to free the spirit that has been seemingly imprisoned in matter. It's as if the evolutionary process has been conspiring to bring us right up to this very crucial point. Do we recognize the nature of our situation? Do we see the part we are playing in creating our experience of both ourselves and the world in this very moment? Do we connect with our God-given agency, or do we continue to feel helpless and victimized by the world?

Solving the Puzzle

Symbols, which are the language of dreams, originally had to do with a missing piece of an object that had been broken in two, which, when reunited with its missing partner, reconstituted the original object in its wholeness. The newly recreated object symbolically embodies and transmits this energy of wholeness that it *re-presents*. A living symbol, where two seemingly separate pieces that ultimately belong together find each other, creates something greater than either one can on its own. This brings to mind a jigsaw puzzle. It's as if all this time we've been holding one small piece of a jigsaw puzzle, and we've had to wait for the other pieces of the puzzle to come together before we can possibly know where to put the one little puzzle piece that is ours. Having fit together all the other pieces, we're now left holding the last piece of the puzzle, a piece that we may not have even realized was a piece of a larger puzzle. It has now become crystal clear what to do with it.

Playing our part in the divine drama, we are being asked to simply be who we are as we step into the role that has been prepared for us since the beginning of time. The essence of wetiko is to mistakenly identify with a fictitious identity, a false version of ourself, so it makes perfect sense that its antidote would be for us to connect with who we really are. We can only make a difference in the world if we are truly ourself; if we are living someone else's idea of who we are, how can we possibly benefit anyone? We can't even benefit ourself! Only what truly belongs to us—what is truly ourself—has the power to heal. Paradoxically, while connecting with our true Self is the only way to heal, healing comes only from what leads us beyond our self.

To find the place for the last puzzle piece is symbolic of finding our place in the universe, which is to discover our mission, our vocation. The original meaning of the word *vocation* has to do with being addressed by a voice. Finding our calling, what we are here to do, involves connecting with both our inner and outer voices. When we have the courage to creatively give living shape and outer form to the promptings of our inner voice, it is our own unique, subjective personhood that we are manifesting, while simultaneously expressing the deeper, universal ground of immediate and unmediated shared human experience. Going beyond the merely personal aspect of ourself and tapping into the archetypal, impersonal, universal dimension of our experience can't help but resonate with and potentially enliven this same dimension within everyone else, as this is the dimension where we're all connected. When we speak from such a deep place within, we cease to belong to ourself alone, for in speaking our true voice we connect with, call forth, and become a channel for the life-affirming energy enfolded throughout all time and space and beyond.

In creatively expressing what outwardly moves us, moves within us, and stops us from moving, we make it possible to find our way back to the deepest springs of life. Our soul, with its wild and passionate dreams of freedom and liberation, is beckoning to us to become the one person that only we can authentically be. Let us have the courage to fly on the wings of an unfettered creative imagination so as to become who we truly are. Who we are is both beyond, and to be found within, our wildest dreams, visions, and imagination. For the truly creative person, be they poet, writer, dancer, painter, or anyone who engages in creative work, is that courageous someone who gives living form to not only what they are personally feeling, sensing, and envisioning, but touches and becomes the instrument for the universal substrate that informs all of our experience to shine through.

Being interdependent, we all hold pieces of the puzzle for one another. When any of us discovers our mission, connects with our voice, and steps into who we are in the great scheme of things—in other words, when we realize where to place our puzzle piece—we might be helping someone else to complete their puzzle for themselves such that they then know where to put their piece of the puzzle, which in turn might help another person, and so on, ad infinitum. When we all put our puzzle pieces together, they no longer exist as separate pieces, but as interrelated aspects of a larger whole that each piece is co-creating along with the others.

Maybe that "someone" is the unknown part of ourselves. Maybe that "someone else" is the rest of the universe. Maybe that "someone else" *is* us.

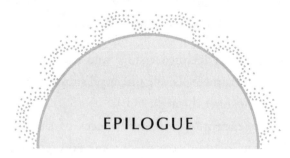

All You Have to Do to See Is Open Your Eyes and Look

Concerning wetiko, the diagnosis (and prognosis) of the malady that humanity is suffering from has been found. To say this is big news is an understatement—it should be on front pages all over the world. This diagnosis is historic. But this diagnosis is meaningless and will give us no traction in dealing with this disease unless a sufficient number of us realize the profundity of what the diagnosis is revealing to us about the participatory role we are playing in the creation of our collective sickness.

As I've repeatedly said in all my writings, wetiko is a form of psychospiritual blindness. In a very real sense, humanity has fallen blind, and we don't even realize that we are blind. More precisely, we suffer from a form of hysterical blindness that we ourselves are inducing and maintaining, not knowing that our inner eyes can see.

At the start of my spiritual awakening in May 1981 I had a seemingly miraculous experience that changed my life's trajectory.* This experience happened within the first minute of being brought to a

---

*If you want to read the story in greater detail, I've written about it in the afterword of my book *Dispelling Wetiko*.

psychiatric hospital for the first time. It involved an interaction I had with a blind woman that resulted in her sight being restored. To say I cured her of her blindness would not be accurate, as I didn't do anything other than simply be myself while playing a role in a deeper process. The key part of the encounter was that while looking in her sightless eyes, I was inspired to repeat the words that had spontaneously fallen into my head: "All you have to do to see is open your eyes and look." After I repeated these words a handful of times, her diseased eyes miraculously transformed into healthy, seeing eyes right in front of my very eyes.

During this literal eye-opening experience, I had the meta-awareness that my close friend who had brought me to the hospital (who was standing off to the side observing my interaction with the blind woman) didn't see—was blind to—what had just happened with the now formerly blind woman. I'm sure he just saw my histrionics—speaking to a complete stranger in such a seemingly strange way—as part of my "insanity." His perception was validated by what happened a moment after the blind woman's sight was restored: I was led to another room in the hospital, where I was tied up to a bed, which is where I spent the night. My friend's view of me as having had a psychotic break was further solidified by psychiatry, which, crazily enough, was more than happy to affirm that my life-transforming experience (which was so off their radar of what was possible that not only was it not recognized, it was pathologized) was further proof of my newly diagnosed mental illness. In retrospect it seems no accident that my initial face-to-face encounter with psychic blindness taking physical form took place in the hallowed—and maddening—halls of psychiatry.

Another benefit of this experience with the blind woman is that it saved my life. Once I fell into the clutches of the psychiatric system I was consistently pathologized and constantly met with the reflection that I had a mental illness that I would have to deal with for the rest of my life. Refusing to accept this diagnosis (the diagnosis itself being what was pathological), I was further diagnosed as being in denial about my illness—which is to say I had fallen into a topsy-turvy world in which my *(mis)treatment* would be deemed a success if I were to disso-ciate from what my own experience was unequivocally showing me and instead subscribe to someone else's version of me as being mentally ill. The whole thing was crazy beyond belief. The experience with the blind woman was of such a different order of experience—self-authenticating by its very nature—that it instilled in me a certainty about the spiritual nature of what I was going through. This ensured that I would never buy into psychiatry's deluded and pathological version of who I am.

Encoded within the experience with the blind woman was a revela-tion that has taken me years—make that decades—to decode. Here I am, more than forty years later, and I am still in the process of decoding what happened that night, as if the revelation has a built-in time-release quality that is only fully disclosed when I am psychologically and spir-itually ready to receive it. The revelation was an epiphany taking on material, physical form, clothed in both the blind and the sighted part of myself. The blind woman and I were both contained within and expressions of a higher-dimensional, unified—and unifying—process that was revealing itself through our interplay. Like a hidden treasure, the revelation was a cipher filled with catalytic information and trans-formative insights that needed to be deciphered in order to unlock its hidden blessings and teachings. This is a process that is still ongoing.

In this experience I wasn't just *having* a revelation as if I was merely a passive witness; I was somehow playing a key role in bringing forth the revelation. I was enacting—living out—a revelation that the awak-ened part of me, by arranging events in my outer life as well as coor-dinating my inner reactions to these events, was showing me a less conscious part of myself. The coming together of the blind woman and I in that unique moment in time way back when was an auspicious, synchronistic coincidence of factors that revealed a universe overflow-ing with magic and grace. The revelation was quantum in nature in that like the way quantum physics reveals the fundamental participa-tory nature of our universe, I was actively participating in acting out and thereby helping to create the revelation. It wasn't something outside of me that was being revealed to me, however, but rather, an archetypal, universal process that exists not only deep within me individually, but deep within the collective psyche of humanity that—both literally and symbolically—was being shown to me as well.

Upon reflection over the decades it has occurred to me that it is not an accident that the contents of this revelation involved healing blindness. Encrypted within this revelatory experience, in both a hidden and yet completely obvious way, is both the pathology and the cure of the psychic blindness of wetiko that afflicts not only myself, but our entire species. Like the way a fragment of a dream can contain our whole process or a piece of a hologram contains the whole hologram, encoded within this vignette with the blind woman was the hidden inner dynamic that underlies our collective madness, as well as its cure. This revelation was a perfectly dreamlike symbolic expression of what was to become the main focus of my life and work. It was a prophetic premonition, presaging and foreshadowing my life's work of shedding light on the mind-blindness that afflicts our species.

Seen as a dreaming process in which every character in a dream is an aspect of oneself, the blind woman symbolically represented a part of me—and a part of all of us—that refuses to look and is hence blinding oneself. Turning a blind eye is an active act of contracting against oneself, which in essence is avoiding relationship with oneself. Looking away—choosing to not see when we are able to see—feeds wetiko while also being its effect. Notably, the Bible consistently uses eyes to symbolize consciousness, and correlates eyes that are blind (mind-blindness) to possession by dark forces. Our looking away is wetiko in action.

The blind woman's restoration of her ability to see didn't entail her having to "do" something, but rather consisted of her *not* doing something that was obscuring her vision. Her blindness was not exogenous—there was nothing external to her that was causing her blindness. Her lack of vision was endogenous in nature—it originated from within herself. She was complicit in creating her own blindness by closing her inner eyes and refusing to look, an activity that, once it becomes chronic, easily gets rendered into the unconscious. Unbeknownst to her she had the power to heal her blindness within herself. My utterance, like an incantation, was the seemingly magic words that at that exact moment she needed to hear, and that helped her break her self-created spell, dispelling her blindness.

Speaking of this mind-blindness, Christ says, "They have shut their eyes, otherwise they might see with their eyes . . . and I would heal them" (Matthew 13:15–16). The blind woman's inability to see was draining her creative life force; it needed an investment of energy on her part to maintain itself moment by moment. Her blindness was healed once she stopped closing her inner eyes, which restored the natural function of her physical eyes. Her inner blindness, like a mirror, was reflected through her outer blindness. As Christ intimated, once we open our eyes—which symbolizes opening up to the healing power of life itself— he, Christ, the embodiment of life itself, can heal us.

The deeper process I'm describing in this example of the blind woman is not just one person's process; it points to the impersonal and universal process that underlies, informs, and gives shape to the mind-blindness from which we all are suffering. My experience with the blind woman reveals that we already possess everything we need in order to heal our psychic blindness, all we have to do is consciously realize this.

My friend who was there in the hospital with me but didn't "see," as well as psychiatry, when seen as dream characters in the waking dream I was having, can be recognized as aspects of myself that are blind. It is noteworthy that as the blindness in the woman was healed, it showed up in other people throughout the field. This shows that psychic blindness is not a local phenomenon that exists in individuals, but rather, it pervades and is distributed throughout the nonlocal field of consciousness—which is to say that it exists in potential in varying degrees within all of us. Quantum physics confirms that how this world is observed influences how it actually manifests. It is interesting that during this life-transforming experience I was having, the observers of the experience—my friend and psychiatry in general—were both blind to what was happening. It makes me wonder how things would have unfolded differently in my life if they had been able to see what was taking place. I can dream, can't I?

In this dreamlike experience I had gotten drafted into picking up a role so as to play out a symbolic enactment of healing the mind-blindness of wetiko that ails our species. I was having a lived, embodied experience of the very moment when we step out of our self-created blindness and open our eyes, and instead of seeing ourselves as we imagine others see us, we look out of our own eyes and see the world—and ourselves—anew. This experience was not just healing for the blind woman, it was profoundly healing for me as well. Unable to heal in isolation, the two of us were collaboratively helping each other conjure up our own healing. What we acted out between us is a prototype for what is available to us collectively as a species.

In this experience with the blind woman I was simply available for the healing that was wanting to happen, very naturally just stepping into a role that was getting dreamed up by the field in order to help and support this to happen, just like when Jung and his patient collaboratively dreamed up the golden scarab. I was simply open, allowing the universe to move through me so that the field could become more coherent and in phase with itself. What I did is something that is possible for everyone when we step out of our narcissistic self-absorption and false sense of separateness. Like the blind woman and I, we can all get in sync with one another, come together in the spirit of serving the whole, and cooperatively help one another heal our psychic blindness. What a radical idea!

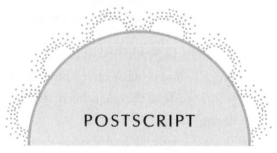

Dreaming
Ourselves Awake

In reading my work on wetiko it can be helpful to have a bit of context for how I can write about such weighty matters with such authority. Not part of the academy, I am certainly no scholar, though I am a bit of a nerd when it comes to stuff that interests me, particularly information that helps alleviate my suffering. I like to think of myself as an independent researcher. Not having an external boss, I am fortunate enough to have the freedom to follow my own intuition and curiosity. When I write about wetiko, I am not drawing from book knowledge, but rather, from my own lived experience.

Without going into the story (I've written a book about this, *Awakened by Darkness*), wetiko entered the petri dish of my family, ravaging it—destroying it, actually—to the point where I haven't had a family for a bit over twenty years. During this nightmarish process I forcibly received a direct transfusion of the wetiko virus into the very core of my being. Like "catching" a cold, I had "caught" wetiko in the sense of becoming infected by it. Practically overnight I went from being a happy, healthy person to someone who was overwhelmed with deep, soul-crushing suffering.

Though I didn't understand or have words for what I was going through at the time, I had been introduced to something uncanny—

practically supernatural—that would radically alter the course of my entire life. As a result I have fallen into a decades-long, creative, shamanlike sickness from which I am still in recovery. Like the universe itself, I am a work in process.

I have been fortunate, however. I count my blessings every day. My "close encounters of the wetiko kind" was an initiatory ordeal that has taught me something that I evidently needed to learn. I have found myself living out the deeper archetypal pattern of the wounded healer in that over time I've gradually been able to alchemically transform my own woundedness and trauma in the crucible of my being into medicine that hopefully can be helpful to others. I like to think of my ever-increasing ability to access new insights into the nature of wetiko as being the gift—compensation pay, so to speak—for having gone through such a horrific ordeal. Little did I realize at the time that the darkness I was going through was in fact the beginning of a revelation.

When I write about wetiko I am writing about it from two points of view at the same time. On the one hand, I am describing it as something that I witnessed playing out in my family (and, once psychiatry became involved, the entire mental health system as well). Since becoming so intimately acquainted with wetiko—we're on a first-name basis—my vision has expanded such that I see wetiko acting out, both covertly and overtly, throughout the human realm on all scales.

On the other hand, I was infected with this deadly and crazy-making germ too. Because it's an "inside job," I have also been able to bear witness to how wetiko, which has a transpersonal and impersonal aspect, covertly works not just within my own mind, but within human minds in general. I'm not writing as a detached intellectual observer sitting in the audience who is not involved or participating in my subject matter. On the contrary, it is due to my full immersion in the topic (and its full immersion in me) that enables me to author my books about wetiko with such intimate familiarity and authority.

It's a total trip—truly psychedelic in nature, without having to take a drug—to be authoring books on the very mind-virus that, unrecognized, is currently wreaking unspeakable havoc and unnecessary suffering in our world. When any of us goes deeply enough into our personal process we can potentially discover that our individual lives are reflecting, in condensed form, the impersonal, archetypal, universal process that our species is playing out collectively on the world stage. Realizing the correlation between the micro and the macro snaps us out of taking our experience of wetiko personally, helps us realize our interconnectedness, and dissolves the illusion that we exist as separate selves. It also introduces us to the dreamlike nature of reality, wherein the outer and inner realities reflect each other. These realizations, when taken together, help us dispell the poisonous aspects of wetiko, turning them to our advantage.

Shedding light on wetiko has become central to my own healing, as creatively articulating how this elusive mind-virus works helps free me from its negative effects. Writing these books on how wetiko plays out has become a focus of my spiritual practice as well, as it has helped me discover my calling, connect me with my voice, and allow me to know who I am. Like Jacob wrestling with the dark angel, I've been forced to have it out with the wetiko virus within myself on a daily basis in order to wrest free its blessings and gifts. Through this experience I've had to confront and come to terms with "the other" in myself—my darker half.

It is such a weird—and weirdly satisfying—experience, as I'm encountering the manifestation of wetiko in my own process in this very moment, to read what I've previously written about this mind-virus and realize that the words I chose in the past directly address the very process I'm going through right now. It's as if my past self is sending a message to my future self, whose time has now come in the present moment.

This reminds me of those experiences that I imagine all of us have probably had, of finding a book that synchronistically speaks to our exact situation in the present, but in this case *I* am the author of the book. As I write these words, I find myself wondering if maybe I am communicating in this very moment with my future self? From another angle, is my future self reaching backward in time to inspire me to choose these very words, as these are the thoughtforms that I and maybe others need to reflect on in the future? As quantum physics points out, being that we live in a nonlocal universe that transcends conventional limitations of space and time, are my past, present, and future selves (which are ultimately not separate) all interacting and conspiring in the present moment so as to help me potentially realize who I am? Time gets turned on its head in the process, as does my own mind.

We can view our current situation simultaneously from what seems like two mutually exclusive points of view—the past and the future influencing the present. Seeing from this meta-perspective seemingly collapses the difference between the past and future, such that, as quantum physics elucidates, both the past and future seem to meet and give shape to the present moment. In a sense there is no time, as there truly is no time like—and other than—the present, which is our true home, the only place we can ever be.

In any case, it makes me wonder whether knowingly or unknowingly we all have planted time-release clues and reminders in our waking dreams (what I call *lucidity stimulators*) that, like an alarm clock, go off at exactly the right moment in order to help wake us up. A simple, mundane example: say if when I leave the house tomorrow I want to not forget to bring my notebook. I might put a pillow against the front door such that it blocks my ability to open the door, which will be the prompt to remind me to bring my notebook. The next day, I'm about to leave my house and I see the pillow blocking the front door, which, because I've invested this scenario with meaning (bring the notebook!), helps me to remember to bring my desired notebook. Note that in this example, I set up a seeming obstacle (the pillow), which served a greater function—to help me to remember something. My past self (the one putting the pillow against the front door) planted a signal that will communicate to my future self (the one who is leaving the house the next day), reminding me to do the desired task (bring the notebook). Is the deeper part of us, the dreamer of our life, doing something similar—planting clues throughout and within the fabric of our waking dream? Are there things happening in our current life—maybe even right now—that were designed to trigger an anamnesis (an overcoming of amnesia), helping us remember what we are here to do? As if conspiring with our own awakening process, these hidden treasures, which we ourselves have planted, only serve their desired function to wake us up if we consciously register what they are speaking to within ourselves and get their message.

This dynamic is illustrated in the gnostic Hymn of the Soul (also called Hymn of the Pearl, found in the apocryphal Acts of Thomas[1]), in which the son of the king is sent forth by his parents to a foreign land, Egypt, to recover a precious pearl that had fallen from the king's crown down a deep well, where it is guarded by a deadly dragon. The son sets out to fetch the jewel, but, like spirit becoming imprisoned in matter as it incarnates in form, becomes absorbed in—and bound by—the seductions of the material world. Falling asleep as if under a spell, the son forgets his royal origins as well as his appointed task, and instead follows the beguiling appearances of mundane life. In response, the king sends a letter to his son that speaks to—and awakens—what was inscribed in his son's heart, reminding him who he is, as well as helping the son recall his mission, which he then returns to and successfully accomplishes.

Interpreted as a dream (in which all the characters are parts of oneself), the Hymn of the Soul beautifully symbolizes how through the process of incarnating in our world, with all of its distractions and temptations, we easily forget our divine purpose, not to mention ourself. Fortunately, as the myth reveals, a wiser, more conscious part of ourself sends messages to help us awaken from our slumber. The more awakened part of us is continually reaching out to us when we fall asleep, through both our night dreams as well as various events in our waking dream. We simply need to learn to be receptive to its promptings and become fluent in its symbolic language, dreamspeak, in order to "read" its messages.

Have you, dear reader, dreamed up these very words so as to transmit a new idea—a new way of looking at the world—into your mind so as to awaken you? As writer and reader, it is as if we are connecting with each other through our particular present moment in time in such a way that collapses and transcends time, as if we are meeting in a place that exists outside of time. In a collaborative venture taking place outside of the third-dimensional space-time continuum, I find myself imagining the possibility that you have dreamed me up (for, after all, we are ultimately interconnected) to write these very words because these are the thoughtforms you need to read in this moment so as to help you to remember the dreamlike nature of reality and wake up to who you are.

Being a dream, however, if you realize that these very words are your own mind appearing within and to your own mind in order to help you awaken to the dreamlike nature of reality, then—*abracadabra!*—this is exactly the way your experience will manifest. You will have then, in my language, "dreamed yourself awake." In a radical conspiracy that is no mere theory, you will have found yourself conspiring with both yourself and the seemingly outer world so as to inspire you to wake up. In a real sense, and as quantum physics has revealed, you have then tapped into the fact that the dreamlike universe we live in is overflowing with the utmost magic.

Glossary
of Acronyms

In dealing with the serious topic of evil, it's important to not take ourselves too seriously. Wetiko hates humor, it detests "making light" of anything, as it wants nothing more than to keep us in the dark. In the spirit of play I have created a bunch of new phrases, names, and acronyms in order to help the reader see what I'm pointing at in my books.* It's because wetiko is a creativity destroyer by its very nature that it is so important for us to make use of the creativity that is such an essential part of our nature. All of these acronyms can potentially help us become more aware of the various aspects of wetiko, which, when seen together, assist us in getting into focus and more clearly seeing this heretofore invisible virus of the mind.

Finding the name for something gives us a handle on how to comprehend and thereby skillfully navigate a process that has previously escaped the reach of our language and, therefore, our conscious awareness. As myths and fairy tales from around the world have shown us, finding the name of the offending demon takes away its power over us, while at the same time empowering us. Language is never a static, finished product, but is always in need of being creatively refreshed in order to keep pace

---

*Some of these acronyms are to be found in my previous books as well. This list is a compilation of most of the relevant acronyms that I have created throughout my writings.

with our ever-changing perceptions, insights, and experiences. The creation of language is a dynamic process that requires that our words, as well as ourselves, be continually born anew. Hopefully, many of these acronyms will give us a new vocabulary to describe previously unnamed wetiko dynamics that most of us are intimately familiar with and know all too well from our own experience, but that we previously didn't have the words for. This is by no means an exhaustive list—I encourage the reader to mobilize your own creativity and add to the list.

2V²: *two-valued virus* (pronounced "2Vsquared"). Compared to the four-valued logic of Buddhism, which is the logic that characterizes the interdependence and unity of all things—(this is also the logic of both quantum physics and dreaming)—two-valued logic is when something is either true or false (compared to four-valued logic, where something can both be true and false at the same time). Though two-valued logic has a definite utility, it limits our thinking (and hence our mind) and stultifies our intrinsic creative brilliance. As such, two-valued logic can itself be conceived of as being a virus. 2V² is the underlying structural grammar that allows wetiko to flourish.

AAIFA: *articulating abuse induces further abuse* (or RARHA, *replicating abuse in response to hearing about abuse*). In trying to express to others our experience of abuse, they unconsciously get dreamed up to enact with us the very abuse we are trying to get across to them. For example, say our abuse (that is, an encounter with wetiko) consisted of our creative self-expression being pathologized—maybe even shut down—by someone in a position of authority. In sharing this with, for example, a therapist, who is an authority figure, instead of understanding what we're trying to communicate, they pathologize us, which is to be unwittingly recreating a more subtle iteration of the very abuse we are sharing with them.

ACRS: *acronym creation resistance syndrome* (pronounced "acres"). When presented with the possibility of creating new acronyms, a spontaneous antipathy, judgment, and resistance to creating them arises, which itself is a psychological dynamic that people with AMS (see below) will naturally create an acronym for (as is evidenced by this acronym).

ADS: *aparticipatory delusional syndrome.* Based on the deluded assumption that we are not participating in co-creating our experience of the outside world (as well as our experience of ourselves). In ADS, we react to and become conditioned by our perceptions of the world, thinking they inherently, independently, and objectively exist outside of ourself (see IEOU), imagining they have nothing to do with how we are interpreting them. We then feel victimized by circumstances, without realizing our complicity in creating the experience we are having. ADS is one of the primary dynamics or "engines" that fuels the malignant aspect of wetiko (aka, malignant egophrenia; see ME disease).

AMS: *acronym mania syndrome.* An inability to restrain oneself from creating new acronyms that capture various psychological processes that have yet to be named. The author of this book might be suffering from this.

CSD: *candor suppression dynamic.* An interpersonal dynamic that arises when we get a clear sense that it's not okay, and may even be dangerous, to simply be and express oneself candidly. The presence of CSD is a clear sign that wetiko is active in the field of our interpersonal relationships.

CSS: *creativity suppression syndrome.* When people who typically aren't in touch with their own creativity encounter another person's creativity, they tend to compulsively judge and put down the other person's creative expression, maybe even trying (if they're in a position to do so) to shut down and potentially destroy the other person's creative spirit. I've been on the receiving end of this myself—for example, being judged for using my creativity to make up these acronyms.

DCDS: *dismissing content due to source.* When we won't read or watch an important article or podcast that would expand our viewpoint because it's on a website from the "other" side, be it the Right or the Left, Christian or atheist, from a country or person who is deemed to be "bad," and so forth. Overly identified with our personal narrative bias, we stay within the bubble of our comfortable echo chamber, thereby continuing to tragically miss important information that could truly inform and expand our view of what is actually happening in the world.

DOSO: *dread of seeing ourselves.* An unconscious tendency seemingly built within the human psyche that avoids seeing certain shadow-infused parts of ourselves. This propensity feeds wetiko and is something we have to learn to overcome within ourselves (related to KJR).

DTR: *disregarding a triggered reflection.* Say someone is triggered by us, and in their triggered state they offer us a reflection of something that is unconscious in ourself. There's a tendency to disregard the reflection they're giving us because we can see that they're triggered, therefore assuming that what they're reflecting to us has no value. This is a mistake, however, and potentially a missed opportunity for us to grow. Just because someone is triggered—and therefore in their unconscious—doesn't mean that they might not be seeing an unconscious part of us that we can't see. It behooves us to at least consider their reflection, whether they're triggered or not.

DUSO: *duped into unwittingly supporting the opposite* (or DUSE, duped into unwittingly supporting evil). When we think we're on the side of good but unknowingly support the adversary we believe we're fighting against. For example, when we're identified with the light (and are hence split off from and unaware of our own darkness) and attack people who are reflecting back to us the very darkness we are denying while we unconsciously act it out. In doing so, we are unwittingly aligning with and empowering the very dark forces that oppose our light.

EUQuaG: *erroneous use of quantum gnosis* (pronounced "you quag"). Dismissing an inconvenient fact that you don't want to look at by invoking quantum physics; for example, thinking that things are both true and not true as a way of not facing the darker, painful reality of what is actually happening.

FAAWADS: *false appearance of agreement while actually disagreeing syndrome.* For example, if I write that evil is playing out in the body politic of the United States, both Democrats and Republicans would agree. What appears on the surface to be a point of agreement between these two parties is anything but, however, as the Democrats see the evil playing out in the Republicans, while the Republicans see it playing out in the Democrats.

FOS: *fake ownership syndrome.* Presenting oneself as taking in and owning other people's reflections of us while we are merely saying the words they want to hear. Instead of signifying that we recognize and are integrating the reflection being offered to us, we are actually hiding (both from ourself and others) as we deflect the reflection.

IEOU: *independently existing objective universe.* Quantum physics has discovered and empirically proven that the notion of an independently existing objective universe (separate from consciousness) is a mistaken conception with no correlate in reality and only exists as an idea in our minds. This "known to be false" idea is at the root of—and reciprocally feeds into—our misconception of our own nature, in a self-reinforcing feedback loop that helps to perpetuate wetiko.

IESS: *independently existing separate subject* (pronounced "ice"). This refers to our sense of existing as a separate self, as a reference point in time and space. Our sense of existing in this way feeds into (and off of) our idea that the universe exists in an objective fashion, separate from us. An IESS and IEOU (see above) reciprocally co-arise together and reinforce each other's seeming reality. Not existing separately from each other, they should be thought of as expressions of a deeper unified process that is revealing itself through their interplay.

KJR: *knee jerk reflectophobia.* A conditioned, yet seemingly instinctual response to resist seeing the painful parts of ourselves that contain our shadow and unhealed trauma (related to DOSO).

ME disease: *malignant egophrenia.* ME disease was my original name for what I later discovered the Native Americans called *wetiko.* ME disease, or wetiko, in its essence comes down to a misidentification with who we think we are, which is to say a mistaken or distorted sense of *me.*

MUSCS: *massively uninformed smug certainty syndrome.* When we have done hardly any research on a topic at all other than simply imbibing the mainstream (or the alternative) media's propaganda, and then develop an absolute conviction that we're in possession of the truth. If questioned on the origin of our certainty, it often comes down to having read an article or heard someone express an idea on a podcast. Having not done our own research, we have outsourced our thinking and sensemaking, allowing others to think for us.

NSD: *not see disease* (pronounced "Nazi disease"). A form of blindness in which we turn a blind eye to evil, whether the evil is within us or out in the world, a process that not only disables our ability to deal with evil, but opens the door for us to unwittingly become instruments for the very evil we are denying. NSD is an unconscious process that gives rise to and helps to continually feed and perpetuate wetiko.

OSS: *over synchronicity stimulation.* When we begin to experience synchronicities, there is an unconscious tendency to overdo our newfound realization by seeing them everywhere, including situations where they might not exist. The synchronicities we think we're seeing might be more an expression of our own inner imbalance than a revelation of the underlying synchronistic matrix, a dynamic that unfortunately blocks our ability to experience genuine synchronicities. OSS can be made into a verb, such as "He is OSSing."

PaTCWATS: *partial truth conflated with absolute truth syndrome* (pronounced "patsee watts"). This is when someone sees a partial, relative aspect of truth (be it in an event or a person) and imagines they are seeing the whole, inviolable, absolute truth.

PBD: *pathologizing by default.* When hearing someone else's out-of-the-ordinary, nonconsensus reality experience, we immediately judge it as being abnormal, pathologizing them by default instead of being open and curious as to what the other person might be tapping into. Related to RDS.

PCD: *premature comprehension delusion.* This has to do with briefly learning about a subtle yet profound multidimensional concept (wetiko being but one example) and quickly assuming that we understand and have fully grasped the whole idea, a process that disables our curiosity and shuts down further inquiry into the subject, hence making sure that we don't understand what we think we understand.

PKAE: *presuming knowledge of another's experience* (pronounced "PK or pee kay."). This is a deluded state in which we arrogantly assume we know someone else's experience better than they do, even though they're the one actually having the experience.

QPIT: *quantum physics induced trauma.* Shattering our view of the universe we live in, the revelation that is quantum physics is so discontinuous with our accepted (classical) notions of how the world works that it induces a form of trauma that can make us contract against and turn away from quantum physics (the agent of the trauma). If the shock from the encounter with what quantum physics is revealing to us is reflected on and consciously integrated, however, this unique form of trauma can potentially heal the more fundamental trauma of the separate self.

RDS: *revelation denigration syndrome.* When someone has a genuine revelation, insight, or new idea that is not just beneficial for them, but could be truly helpful for the world, and therefore should be shared more widely, but when it is offered to others it is denigrated, and the person having the revelation is pathologized and seen as inflated, crazy, or unhinged.

RTSE: *revelation through suppressing exposure* (pronounced "ritzee"). When someone sheds light on the dark forces, and the dark forces respond by suppressing and possibly even trying to destroy the person who is exposing them. Paradoxically, in trying to hide their darkness by attacking the one who is illuminating it, the dark forces are unwittingly revealing the very evil they are trying to conceal, thereby offering evidence confirming what the person who is shining light on the darkness is pointing at.

SACFA: *small agreement conflated with full agreement.* When we have a small area of agreement between what we think on a particular issue and what another person or group thinks (oftentimes for completely different reasons), it is often assumed that we agree with everything else they think.

SRIDJAS: *self-righteous informationally deficient judgmental arrogant syndrome.* When we have very little information about a situation but arrogantly think we understand what's happening better than those who actually are experiencing—and know—what's happening. A simple way of describing someone with SRIDJAS is to say they're being arrogant and don't know what they're talking about. SRIDJAS is related to, and a variation of, both PKAE and MUSCS.

TMDS: *traumatized messenger dismissal syndrome.* Say, for example, we have had a direct encounter with wetiko that has opened our eyes to the reality of evil. Oftentimes this experience can shake us up and completely shatter our ideas of the familiar world we thought we lived in, and this, by its very nature, can be traumatic; depending on its intensity, such an encounter can potentially take years, even a life-time, to fully integrate. If we then try to communicate the depth of what we have seen to others in order to help them see wetiko as well, because we're still in the process of assimilating the trauma of what we have experienced in our "close encounters of the wetiko kind" (and therefore might have an emotional charge around what we're trying to communicate), we might be written off and not taken seriously. I personally can relate to this syndrome based on my own life experiences over the last forty-plus years.

WFP: *wetiko fleeing process.* If we haven't developed a strong enough sense of self to self-reflectively look at the darkness within us, when the outer world reflects an aspect of ourself that is unknowingly acting out wetiko, the part of us that is taken over by and unconsciously identified with wetiko will make sure to remove us from this situation (flee) as quickly as possible. This dynamic ensures that we can continue to avoid dealing with the shadow of wetiko within ourself.

AFTERWORD

Paul Levy's Conversion
of First Nations Cannibalism
to Global Sociopathy

By Richard Grossinger

I have had the honor—responsibility, privilege, pleasure—of twice introducing Paul Levy and his wetiko teaching to new readers. First, as over-
seer of North Atlantic Books, a press that my wife, Lindy Hough, and I
founded in 1974 as a successor to our journal *Io,* I published *Dispelling
Wetiko: Breaking the Curse of Evil* in January 2013. Paul developed and
wrote the material for that book in 2011–12. That *Io* came out of over-
lapping literary and psychospiritual traditions of the first counterculture
in the 1960s made it apt that the person who called my attention to Paul
was Michael Brownstein, a poet and novelist from the *Io* world. Michael
said, in essence, "You should publish this guy; his work is prophetic."

The profundity of Paul's clarion trope was elusive to me at first
glance. As an anthropologist in graduate school in the 1960s pursuing
a North American specialty, I had read about wetiko and windigo, the
name of the mythological yeti-like humanoid spirit of Plains and Great
Plains native peoples. It caught my attention because it was so quirky—
an indigenous (ethnomedical or, more specifically, ethnopsychiatric)
term in a trans-Algonquian tongue.

Here's the specific trail I followed later to Paul: In 1979 I wrote about both practical and spiritual ethnomedicine in my book *Planet Medicine: From Stone Age Shamanism to Post-Industrial Healing.* Practical ethnomedicine included the use of herbs, animal products, rocks, sticks, thorns, water (cold and hot, ice and steam, running and still), and forerunners of pharmacy, osteopathy, acupuncture, and surgery. Spiritual and energetic ethnomedicine consisted of shamanism, vision quests, faith healing, divination, vitalistic chemistry (or alchemy), and ceremonies like the Navaho sand-painting journey and Australian Aboriginal initiation rites by quartz crystals. Other than wetiko and windigo, I did not encounter any overt psychiatric category. Coming from a culture that was liminally spirit-based in all regards, it was not psychiatric in a Western, but in a shamanic sense. While astutely emotional and cognitive, it was also innately magical and ghost—or *tcipayak*-based—too.

Under my umbrella of energy medicine, I blended magic, shamanism, ethnobotany, homeopathy, faith healing, and psychoanalysis, which led me to the esoteric source of all diseases and cures and the symbolic and sociocultural basis of healing itself. Though I did not address the subject of wetiko per se—I don't remember why—the term stayed with me as the epitome of a non-Western ethnopsychiatric category.

I came away from researching and writing *Planet Medicine* with the belief that natural immunity, subtle energies, and embryogenic fields are senior to the most advanced technological and pharmaceutical interventions. The vital force described before the Common Era by Greek physicians, the Chinese Yellow Emperor, and the Cree shaman with his medicine bundle is still our once and future hope, especially since the medical establishment lieged itself to computer science and biotech. It is in this vortex that Paul rediscovered wetiko, and I rediscovered it through Paul, and then I discovered Paul, who brought his own *weltanschauung,* or worldview, and transformed wetiko through Buddhist, Jungian, and Western political views into an entire philosophy, phenomenology, and cosmology of its own.

That insight didn't all come at once. Though I was intrigued by Paul's manuscript, submitted upon request, I didn't initially get the radical angle at which he approached his topic. I was dubious about a white dude elucidating a Native American concept. More than that, though, Paul was creatively repurposing a specific loan word from an uncommon source language and making it newly concrete in a Western contemporary context while assimilating it into his own heart-mind teaching. Over time, and at a deeper level as a result of writing this afterword, I have come to understand the true power of Paul's "appropriation." So my afterword is an active one of deepening recognition rather than an *ex post facto* trumpeting of the book. I am continuing to rediscover what Paul has done and how it is persistently not what it looks like, nor can it easily be valorized by the bandwagon of neo-wetiko enthusiasts or dismissed by identity-politics critics.

First of all, you have to realize that Paul is unusual in his journey and approach. He has cultivated a very wide, independent view of reality from years of Jungian study and Buddhist practice, without becoming either a card-carrying Jungian or a conventional Buddhist. Before wetiko, his skill set had already encompassed a nonsectarian, cross-cultural perspective on social and psychological phenomena and an ability to read energy from sound, nuance, and oracle. He entered the cross-cultural and ethnographic wetiko field more like a wetiko channel and Cassandra than an indigenous ethnographer or colonizer. Creatively flouting conventional cultural and linguistic boundaries, he made his own esoteric bond with the term and then recoded and released it into the collective consciousness of humanity.

I think of "Levy's wetiko" as something like a spontaneous calling by wise guides who use the semes of language and etymology on this plane like wind chimes to tell stories. A message geocached across tribes was being downloaded through different vision quests, dreamings, song lines, and skries. Then Paul came along with his unique glossolalia.

However pronounced, wetiko ("wet-tee-ko," Paul's preference, or "wet-tick-ko," as Western Algonquian linguists propose) makes a primal onomatopoeia. Turtle Island speakers didn't use the same phonetic palette, so neither version is precisely Algonquian, Cree, or Powhatan. Likewise, Paul didn't have to rederive the term's wisdom tradition or the applications that it developed in pre-Columbian cultures, because he received it as an archetype, a calling from an inner plane as well as a neo-Platonic form. On that basis—trickster, shadow, self—he took the indigenous term and inducted it straight into English, Gaia's current Esperanto, and through her midwifery into all of Earth's tongues.

That was quite an achievement in its own right. Paul became something like an all-star word scout and wordsmith, rendering a concept not quite available in his own tongue from a foreign lexeme. For instance, set his conscript alongside the Yiddish *mensch,* which has no precise English correlate, or the Australian Aboriginal *alcheringa,* which transmits the idea of a unique and universal Dreamtime.

To come at it from a different angle, wetiko is a pathology diagnosed by First Nations clans but pretty much ignored by later diagnosticians of the Western manual. In it, a swath of indigenous cultures not only saw psychological aberrations of human nature but discerned aspects of spirit war: nonphysical forces impinging and operating on our plane and blending with our emotional disturbances. They interpreted it without making a passage through Platonic philosophy, proto-neurology, Sigmund Freud, psychoanalysis, behavior modification, and psychopharmacology. Instead, they had shamans, medicine bundles, and herbs. With different ways of viewing not only pathologies but crimes (and their relationship), they developed a "hospital" or lodge for diseases and malfeasances of spirit, soul, and psyche.

Because indigenous "doctors" and "lawyers" don't closet their diagnoses like us in separate domains of therapeutics and jurisprudence, they approached matters of protection, justice, and cure along broader psychospiritual parameters that have been ignored in our allopathic clinics and courts of Anglo-Saxon law.

The way wetiko functions in the context of invisible entities is in keeping with Jungian symbols of transformation and the nonlocality and uncertainty states of quantum physics rather than Oedipal complexes and fifty-minute hours. Jung once remarked that the gods on Olympus had become the diseases of modern man. For Turtle Island clans, the equivalents of Hesiod's Titans in his *Theogony* were already theriomorphs, were-beasts, tricksters, heyokas, and mind-possessing spirits. They possessed humans through wetiko madness. In a sense, Paul re-recognized Jung's miasms of modern civilization in Algonquian totem-spirits.

I was alerted to Paul a second time by my friend, crystal alchemist Robert Simmons. After that, I published Paul under my new Inner Traditions imprint, Sacred Planet Books, beginning with his second volume on the topic, *Wetiko: Healing the Mind-Virus That Plagues Our World,* and now this third folio, *Undreaming Wetiko.* In the process, I have come to accept Paul as a polymath: a freelance philosopher, independent clinician and healer, Jungian grimoirist, and Buddhist-oriented teacher. In his spiritual journey he has gone from assimilating Carl Jung and Buddhist meditation practice, to developing a Dzogchen-inspired, archetypally informed teaching that he calls "Awaken in the Dream." This in itself falls somewhere between an esoteric mystery school, a psychic group, group therapy, and a shamanic lodge.

In Awaken in the Dream groups, Paul posits that if more of us recognized that this so-called physical reality is actually a shared dream state, a fluid, ever-shifting matrix of our combined inner states of consciousness (one of many), we could together help one another further awaken and more deeply grasp our actual condition, both individually and collectively. What is primarily psychic is a function or re-rendering of our consciousness through understanding itself as also a transpersonal thoughtform. This version of wetiko also dovetails with traditional Dzogchen meditations for awakening us to *rigpa,* our original, true essence, purity, and heart reality.

In Paul's system, we are transmitters and receivers of mindstreams and thoughtforms, as we are creative agents navigating the bardo of waking life, which, for being a bardo, is merely another dream or journey among multiple realities that are all dreamlike. Prior researchers—anthropologists, social workers, priests—have noted wetiko and its psychospiritual impact in indigenous societies where it was identified, but they missed its Dreamtime and bardo equivalences. Paul, as an oneirologist, caught that at once: wetiko's meta-dimensionality. He tracked and articulated its role in an intensifying world crisis. He incorporated it in the modern zeitgeist as part of a wisdom tradition, supported by new vision quests and herbal allies and resembling what was conducted in the Eastern woodlands and on the Great Plains until colonials imposed their own worldview and laws.

Before Columbus, Cabot, and the *Mayflower,* privations of Turtle Island winters had led to metamorphoses combining cannibalism, selfishness, greed, sadism, and sociopathic narcissism in tribal contexts, creating a crisis in which a borderline person and his or her tribe could no longer hold or be held by one another, that is, could no longer maintain a healthy and reciprocal relationship. The person ceased being a socially responsible, caring member of the group and ran amok, exhibiting a mix of cannibal, thief, and loner: a sociopath. Indigenous philosophers and psychologists tried to diagnose imbalance and restore social and spiritual harmony, developing their own methods for recovering the homeostasis of nature, psyche, and culture within spirit realms.

In that sense, I think of wetiko as a sort of "true" sorcery like that mythologized in Ursula Le Guin's Earthsea realm. In Earthsea, first a thing had to be named. It had to be named and known and "said" before it could be triaged, treated, contained, and cured.

Do shadow archetypes emerge from the unconscious minds of trauma victims, or do they arise from an exogenous demonic force attaching to a person under borderline psychological conditions? Exorcists question whether there is even a difference or if the distinction matters. Psychologist M. Scott Peck interrogated diabolic entities and disembodied evil in his book *People of the Lie.* He described patients whose neurotic or psychotic behavior he could not cure or improve with therapy. They were angry, vindictive, and routinely wrecked the lives of those around them. When, however, confronted with the cross or Christ's spoken name, these people changed voices: they hissed, cursed, and writhed, screaming things outside their personality or frame of reference. Everyone in the room had the conviction that they were in the presence of evil personified. This was a wake-up call for Peck: the devil is real. One doesn't have to adopt Peck's Christian iconography to accept his clinical hermeneutics. He was viewing diabolic possession.

Meanwhile *demonic* possession, or wetiko, is a category in a hypothetical First Nations folk manual that encompasses a number of Northern tribes, extending a bit into the Southern cult, as the mound-builders were hypostatized by archaeologists. The surprise—to early anthropologists, then to Paul—was that it contained a precognitive vision of modern madness. A psychic disease discerned and articulated by indigenous shamans and ethnopsychologists became a diagnostic representation of a swiftly masting miasm that would afflict humanity at large.

Insofar as we are in a true wetiko dilemma now as a species, the indigenous Turtle Island disease provides an opportunity for calling out, diagnosing, and addressing our plight. That's where Paul comes in. The unnamed miasm and madness needed a namer. Paul's skill set and unique past let him see that the mind-virus possessing the world *already* had a name. That he borrowed a prescient indigenous term is neither here nor there in the greater wind tunnel of sound and glottochronological drift from some Ur Gaian hominid tongue. Yes, he "appropriated." But then, using the wisdom traditions of Buddhism, analytical psychology, anthroposophy, and quantum physics, he translated and transmitted the skrying from its native woodlands and plains. In its own phonemics, a strange owl-like *tcipayak,* or ghost, hooted "wetiko . . . wetiko . . . wetiko . . . windigo . . ." loud and clear.

Wetiko's subsequent planetarization made a clinical outlier like Paul a new sort of global psycholinguist and psychotherapist, and an exception to "paleface" appropriation. He came to wetiko innately through his Awaken in the Dream sangha, projecting cures by witnessing, *truing* (to coin a term combining *truth* and *reconciling*), individuation, and active shadow work. As our wetiko guide, Paul emerged from a Portland, Oregon office to warn Earth of its plight. Lexeme and therapist met in a blend of insight and transference.

The Algonquian language group evolved out of a proto-Algonquian/Wiyot/Yurok ancestral glossary that is characterized by the fusion of what we consider verbs and nouns into single units: polysemes, bound morphemes, and other polysemic and polysynthetic elements. These single-unit words constitute entire sentences and rubrics. Midtwentieth-century linguist Benjamin Lee Whorf demonstrated that many Native American languages also contain cryptotypes, words that hide subtle, covert, or unmarked meanings, as well as evoke alterations of time, space, relationship, and gender that are foreign to Newtonian mechanics and Indo-European social organization. The term *wetiko* arises in a fluid psycho-linguistic context, drifting by phonemes and across subgroups, many of them extinct and unknown to us. The shifting relativistic basis of First Nations lexemes contributed to a system that became known academically as the Whorf hypothesis—that the framing of thought and belief are influenced by sound and syntax. This may not be perfect physics or linguistics by contemporary standards, nonetheless, all worded systems are veils—symbolically encoded phonemics and deep syntax, through which concepts take on meaning and interpretation.

Wetiko morphophonemically drifts into *windigo* in the Ojibwa dialect and into *wintiko* in Eastern Powhatan. Its proto-Algonquian root, *wi-nteko-wa,* shares a source with a bird, probably an owl, perhaps for its nightly predation and ghostlike presentation. *Wetiko* and *windigo* variations stretched from the eastern forests of Nova Scotia to the Great Lakes and Wisconsin and, in different forms, west, where it was widely recognized as *windigoo, widjigo, weejigo, wentiko,* and *wintsigo,* with a plural of *windegoag* or *windikouk. Windegoag* reeked of winter, famine, starvation, and the north wind. Their weird moans and squeals allied them with Plains Cree ghosts, or *tcipayaks.*

In all its derivations, wetiko is an insatiable hunger and greed with cannibal and necrophiliac overtones—an appetite that can never be sated, consumption without boundary or moral compass, ceaseless clash with a goal of amplifying chaos, obsessive compulsion, cruelty, and a touch of *schadenfreude*, the joy of witnessing and causing the pain, downfall, and humiliation of others. An unnamed shaman quoted online put it this way: "Anything beyond what we need is poison. It can be power, laziness, food, ego, ambition, vanity, fear, anger, or whatever." Poison is a characteristic feature of the wetiko state.

Stated clinically, wetiko blends inconsolable rage and desire for revenge with continual grasping and constriction of old traumas that activate new tantrums; it combines psychic desolation with recreational rape directed against other clans, tribes, species, and nature itself, and finally against the perpetrator's own humanity.

The Cree and a few other tribes depicted giants that grew with each human meal, so they were simultaneously huge and emaciated, driven both by excess and insatiable appetite, searching desperately for their next victim. Wetiko was also described as a monster with human characteristics; a giant with a heart of ice; a skeleton missing flesh, lips, and toes; and a walking, treelike human with an overly large tongue, yellowed fangs, sallow skin, jagged teeth, matted hair, bloody footprints, and the psychic ability to disrupt weather and move unseen among humans. It was also of the vampire class. Those it didn't eat or suck dry, it took a bite out of, thereby turning them into a fellow vampiric entity. It especially enjoyed feasting on the flesh of those it once loved. We have seen plenty of that around these parts in current times.

You could say it's not real, it's a metaphor, an exaggeration, a fantastic legend like the European Cropsey Maniac, Mothman, and Rip Van Winkle of the same Eastern woodlands. I would say yes, of course, but also that it's real on an energetic level, much as dragons drawn in oracle decks are real and can be seen at large by dragon aficionados.

On this plane, wetiko can be understood as energy fields, totemic bricolage, and psychic waves. Where shamans travel, to middle and upper heavens, the possessed likely look exactly like the nightmarish descriptions, for their bodies, shaped by imaginal perception, karma, and the hermeneutic flames of a Dantean inferno, take on the proscribed appearance of their auras more than their bodies. According to *The Jesuit Relations* (ca. 1681), which chronicles the travels of Jesuit missions in "New France" (the areas of North America colonized by France, ranging from Newfoundland, Quebec, and the Great Lakes, all the way to the Gulf of Mexico):

> They are afflicted with neither lunacy, hypochondria, nor frenzy; but have a combination of all these species of disease, which affects their imaginations and causes them a more than canine hunger. This makes them so ravenous for human flesh that they pounce upon women, children, and even upon men, like veritable werewolves, and devour them voraciously, without being able to appease or glut their appetite—ever seeking fresh prey, and the more greedily, the more they eat. This ailment attacked our deputies, and, as death is the sole remedy among those simple people for checking such acts of murder, they were slain in order to stay the course of their madness.[1]

Ojibwe author, linguist, and storyteller Basil H. Johnston offers another vivid description:

> The Wendigo was gaunt to the point of emaciation, its desiccated skin pulled tightly over its bones. With its bones pushing out against its skin, its complexion the ash-gray of death, and its eyes pushed back deep into their sockets, the Wendigo looked like a gaunt skeleton recently disinterred from the grave. What lips it had were tattered and bloody. . . . Unclean and suffering from suppuration of the flesh, the Wendigo gave off a strange and eerie odor of decay and decomposition, of death and corruption.[2]

Because wetiko is viral, it is part of a transpersonal spirit microbiome. Its etheric DNA, with all its mutations and variants, permeates our minds and bodies. French philosopher Paul Virilio writes, "Interactivity keeps the world in a kind of tetanic trance, at once inert and overexcited, sleepwalking on a planetary scale."[3]

Since wetiko is no longer extractable, it has to be fundamentally transformed as what it is. Paul has offered a civilizational diagnosis in his previous books, and in *Undreaming Wetiko,* he offers a cure: the transformation of cannibal psychosis by engaging the shadow to make what is unconscious, conscious.

For Paul, wetiko isn't a mere theory or an abstract idea. He had a living encounter with what he calls "archetypal evil," which he says almost killed him and destroyed his entire family. Early interaction with the shadow altered the course of his life, wounding him so deeply he was forced—fated—to come to terms with the malevolent force he had encountered and illuminate it in order to survive. His work emerged out of this life-and-death struggle and has become a general alchemy for transmuting evil, as well as a warning, a witnessing, and a potential healing for others.

Our own deep "winter" is manifesting as the planet's untethered climate. Our biome is overridden by an increasingly dissonant and dehumanized *tcipayak,* a ghostlike technosphere, with its empowered robots, algorithms, and supply chains. Our psyche is projected through and cheapened by a transnational *mercado,* or global market, with its "vampire squid wrapped around the face of humanity, relentlessly jamming its blood funnel into anything that smells like money,"[4] to quote journalist Matt Taibbi (these days, add cryptocurrency and nonfungible tokens to the stench). It is no mere infected owl or tick anymore. Wetiko wants to disseminate and profit from corporate, GMO-ridden pseudoconsciousness and, like Gollum of Tolkien's Middle Earth lore, claim the binding ring, the genetic basis of life as its own—it literally wants the God code, too! It needs to satisfy its insatiable desire for control by intellectually and economically manipulating and consuming life down to the molecular and genetic level. This use of biotech is *wetiko, windigo,* and the rest of the Algonquian cannibal array in spades.

In this modern disease state, individuals, societies, institutions, political parties, nations, and the human species excuse or even valorize their own cannibalistic, narcissistic tendencies at the price of the destruction of the planet and the web of life. Blowing up coral beds to get at fish is about as wetiko as you can get. In Indonesian waters now, colored plastics mimic the creatures they have replaced. Meanwhile, as I write, Russian tanks bombard Ukrainian cities. Myriad other examples haunt our wetiko-infested world.

The Western diagnostic manual will not and cannot recognize a condition that pervades and overrides not only its encapsulated disease categories, medically approved complexes, and commoditized illness states, but also its own sanctioned means to treat them. The bloodthirsty giant honors no boundary, nor do we know how to avoid possession, contamination, and vampiric enlistment by a self-created golem. It emanates simultaneously throughout Prison Industrial, Military Industrial, Medical Industrial, Surveillance Industrial, and educational and religious complexes. Having taken on the form of civilization at large, it now affects doctors as well as their patients, good guys as well as baddies.

In the 1990s, Jungian homeopath Edward Whitmont, in his book *The Alchemy of Healing,* proposed a dynamic field in which doctors unconsciously and inadvertently converted cures into hexes, furthering the disease they were purporting to cure, but also (when awakened) could convert hexes and curses and even the shadow itself into cures. That is our best current prognosis and plan. Like any good virus, wetiko has numbed its victims to its presence. Wetiko has become the ultimate colonialist, conquistador, and hexer, posing wealth and power as goals of existence while leading people into the wetiko sickness of greed with a concomitant deadening of the heart that brings an incapacity to feel love, grief, or empathy. That is what we have to molt and transform.

Many sick people are not innately sick; they are being made sick by adapting or being forced to adapt to systemic wetiko. Their ostensible shrinks and healers are often just as possessed and wetiko-ridden as they are. Throw in opiate merchants, bought politicians, and overt criminals and crooks spreading and force-feeding wetiko serums to the masses, and you begin to comprehend the magnitude of the infection.

I believe that Paul is successful at what he does because he doesn't carry clinical baggage or credentials granted to him by an already wetiko-infested system. Instead, he brings a socially and spiritually active, ecological viewpoint that focuses beyond individual subneuroses, on an overarching psychosis that encompasses much of what passes for illness in conventional psychiatry. He views most psychological ailments as distortions caused by trying to live under wetiko as it manifests pandemically and spreads like an egregore.

Our civilization as a whole needs a new diagnostic manual and diagnosis. All its individual malaises—the depressions, anxieties, schizophrenias, and autisms—must be reexamined and revisioned to reflect the degree to which the corporate pharmaceutical, medical, and psychiatric complex is already infected by wetiko and therefore holds a skewed view of reality. The society and its institutions are what's sick, and it is crazy-making to be forced to live under their "treatments." While in search of true modes of transference and abreaction, the "patient" (meaning just about everyone) needs first to experience the cannibal shadow, acknowledge it, own it, see it for what it is—the inner werewolves and windegoag—and convert it into something that is free of distortion: our own true nature. Paul's ethnopsychology is a first step toward awakening in the dream and calibrating our collective psychosis into collective sanity.

Medical intuitive Laura Aversano received the following message from Spirit as part of a larger psychic download, which remains unpublished otherwise. It is a spot-on description of how to undream wetiko:

> We desire to know what evil is and why it exists. In looking for these answers, we must reflect deeply upon our relationship to the Divine, the relationship we have to others, and primarily, the relationship

we have with ourselves. If we are looking to define evil by searching externally, we are missing the opportunity to fully understand and embrace its nature. When we begin to explore these precepts, we will acquire the knowledge necessary to interpret the nature of evil differently than we have been. We will begin to see how both the light and the darkness of God work co-creatively to support human potential and spiritual growth. . . .

When held in the threshold of the Divine, any darkness can serve a higher purpose as it allows one to return to the Light if they are willing to surrender and learn from it. My prayer is that we all create a space for the darkness to birth a new way of seeing, sensing, feeling, and relating. May our darkness find the balance it needs to serve humanity as opposed to igniting chaos. May we stop projecting our sense of powerlessness and feeding that place inside of us that feels bound to a reality which we continually create with our fears. May we respect the teachings of the Masters within us; our thoughts and emotions, with a humility that births creation and not destruction. Darkness can perpetually serve the darkness, or it can evolve to serve the Light of God. Which path do you choose?

Paul's naming of wetiko provides a clue to a pancultural diagnosis and treatment.

RICHARD GROSSINGER is the curator of Sacred Planet Books at Inner Traditions and the cofounder and former publisher of North Atlantic Books with his wife, Lindy Hough. He has a Ph.D. in ecological anthropology and has written more than 40 books on alternative medicine, cosmology, embryology, and consciousness, including *Dark Pool of Light: Reality and Consciousness*, *The Night Sky: Soul and Cosmos*, *Bottoming Out the Universe*, and *Dreamtimes and Thoughtforms*.

Notes

Introduction.
A Thumbnail Sketch of Wetiko

1. Ouspensky, *In Search of the Miraculous,* vol. 5, para. 203.

Chapter 1.
Human Family Curse

1. Jensen, *Listening to the Lord,* 274.
2. Jung, *The Collected Works,* vol. 17, para. 88.
3. Jung, *The Collected Works,* vol. 17, para. 217.
4. Jung, *The Collected Works,* vol. 5, para. 203.
5. Jung, *The Collected Works,* vol. 17, para. 154.
6. Jung, *Letters,* vol. 1, 488.

Chapter 2.
Wetiko in Relationships

1. Forbes, *Columbus and Other Cannibals,* xix.

Chapter 3.
Wilhelm Reich's *Murder of Christ*

1. Reich, *Murder,* 4.
2. Reich, *Murder,* 221.
3. Reich, *Murder,* 1.
4. Reich, *Murder,* 6.
5. Reich, *Murder,* 17.
6. Reich, *Murder,* 142.
7. Reich, *Murder,* 103.

Chapter 4.
Shamans to the Rescue

1. Nicholson, *Shamanism*, 7.
2. Eliade, *Shamanism*, 508.
3. Mindell, *Shaman's Body*, 8.
4. Mindell, *Shaman's Body*, 8.
5. Nicholson, *Shamanism*, 16.
6. Jung, *The Collected Works*, vol. 16, para. 163.
7. Jung, *The Collected Works*, vol. 2, para. 861.
8. Jung, *The Collected Works*, vol. 10, para. 14.
9. Halifax, *Shamanic Voices*, 18.
10. Kerényi, *Asklepios*, 99.
11. Meier, *Ancient Incubation*, 5.
12. Jung, *The Collected Works*, vol. 11, para. 562.
13. Eliade, *Shamanism*, 63.
14. Jung, *Letters*, 377.
15. Sandner, *Navaho Symbols*, 138.
16. Jung, *The Collected Works*, vol. 10, para. 586.
17. Einstein, Condolence Letter to Robert S. Marcus, Feb, 1950.
18. Jung, *The Collected Works*, vol. 9i, para. 457.
19. Stevenson, *The Poems of William Blake*, plate 5.
20. Jung, *The Collected Works*, vol. 17, para. 309.
21. Jung, *The Collected Works*, vol. 17, para. 319.
22. Jung, *The Collected Works*, vol. 13, para. 300.

Chapter 5.
The Battle for Our Angel

1. Cheetham, *All the World an Icon*, 33.
2. Jung, *The Collected Works*, vol. 10, para. 151.
3. Corbin, *L'homme et son ange*, 81.
4. Corbin, *Avicenna*, 28.
5. Corbin, *Avicenna*, 31.
6. Cheetham, *All the World*, 103.
7. Corbin, *Avicenna*, 20.
8. Corbin, *Man of Light*, 7.

9. Jung, *Dream Symbols,* 188.

10. Corbin, *Man of Light,* 8.

11. Mallasz, *Talking with Angels,* v.

12. Mallasz, *Talking with Angels,* vi.

13. Wheelwright, *The Reality of the Psyche.*

14. Corbin, *Cyclical Time,* 52.

15. Corbin, *Cyclical Time,* fn. 89.

16. Corbin, *Cyclical Time,* fn. 89.

17. Corbin, *Man of Light,* 84.

18. Corbin, *Man of Light,* 17.

19. Corbin, *Alone,* 114.

20. Corbin, *Man of Light,* 22.

21. Corbin, *Voyage,* LV.

22. Walshe, *The Complete Mystical Works of Meister Eckhart,* Sermon 57, 298.

23. Corbin, *Man of Light,* 91.

24. Corbin, *Man of Light,* 21.

25. Corbin, *Cyclical Time,* 49.

26. Ruland, *Lexicon alchemiae* (1612).

27. Corbin, *Man of Light,* 18.

28. Corbin, *Avicenna,* 159.

29. Corbin, *Swedenborg,* chapter 1.

30. Corbin, *Alone,* 359, note 7.

31. Corbin, *Alone,* 248.

32. Corbin, *Alone,* 119.

33. Corbin, *Alone,* 248.

34. Raine, *Blake and Tradition,* 196.

35. Raine, *Blake and Tradition,* 189.

36. Corbin, *Avicenna,* 29.

37. Corbin, *Cyclical Time,* 60.

38. James, *New Testament Apocrypha,* 321.

39. *Commentaria in Malthaeum,* quoted with reference to parallel texts in Joseph Barbel, *Christos Angelos,* 292, n. 459.

40. Corbin, *Man of Light,* 92.

41. Corbin, *Avicenna,* 32.

42. Corbin, *Man of Light,* 92.

Chapter 6.
Rudolf Steiner on the Greatest
Spiritual Event of Our Time

1. Steiner, "Christ at the Time."
2. Steiner, "Reappearance of Christ."
3. Steiner, "Reappearance of Christ."
4. Steiner. "Christ at the Time."
5. Steiner, "Reappearance of Christ."
6. Steiner, "Reappearance of Christ."
7. Giersch, Harold. *Rudolf Steiner,* 110.
8. Shantideva, *Way of the Bodhisattva,* 58.
9. Steiner, "From Symptom to Reality."
10. Steiner, "From Symptom to Reality."
11. Steiner, "Fifth Gospel."
12. Steiner, "Christ Impulse."
13. Steiner, "Building Stones."
14. Steiner, "Christ Impulse."
15. Steiner, "From Symptom to Reality."
16. McDermott, *Essential Steiner,* 264.
17. Wilmer and Woodruff, *Facing Evil,* 12.
18. Steiner, "Christ Impulse."
19. Steiner lecture in Heidelberg, January 27, 1910, GA 118.
20. James, *New Testament Apocrypha,* 253–54.
21. Steiner, *Truth and Knowledge.*
22. Steiner, lecture in Zürich, November 13, 1917, GA 178.
23. Steiner, "Fifth Gospel."
24. Ben-Aharon, *New Experience,* 46.
25. Jung, *Red Book,* 167.
26. Jung, *Red Book,* 356.
27. Jung, *Two Essays,* 4.
28. Steiner, lecture in Stuttgart, on August 29, 1906, GA 95.
29. Steiner, lecture in Donarch, on April 2, 1921, GA 204.
30. Steiner, "Christ Impulse."

Chapter 7.
Nicolas Berdyaev's Epoch of Creativeness

1. Jung, *Nietzsche's Zarathustra*, vol. 1, 653–55.
2. Berdyaev, *Destiny*, 127.
3. Berdyaev, *Meaning*, 99.
4. Berdyaev, *Meaning*, 335.
5. Berdyaev, *Meaning*, 107.
6. Neumann, *Origins*, 210–11.
7. Berdyaev, *Meaning*, 108.
8. Berdyaev, *Meaning*, 100.
9. Berdyaev, *Meaning*, 337.
10. Berdyaev, *Destiny*, 131.
11. Berdyaev, *Meaning*, 336.
12. Berdyaev, *Freedom*, 184.
13. Berdyaev, *Freedom*, 184.
14. Berdyaev, *Freedom*, 143.
15. Berdyaev, *Freedom*, 133.
16. Fuchs, *Coming of Age*, 176.
17. Hillman, *Mythic Figures*.
18. Berdyaev, *Destiny*, 133.
19. Berdyaev, *Destiny*, 137.

Chapter 8.
Rebirth of the Self

1. Jung, *The Collected Works*, vol. 10, para. 290–93.
2. Jung, *The Collected Works*, vol. 10, para. 552.
3. Bonhoeffer, *Cost of Discipleship*, 159.
4. Jung, *The Collected Works*, vol. 11, para. 129.
5. Neumann, *Art and the Creative*, 132.
6. Jung, *The Collected Works*, vol. 10, para. 293.
7. Jung, *Red Book*, 480–81.
8. James, *New Testament Apocrypha*, 253.
9. Jung, *The Collected Works*, vol. 14, para. 4.

10. Jung, *Nietzsche's Zarathustra*, vol. 1, 449.

11. Berdyaev, *Meaning*, 98.

12. Merton, *Conjectures of a Guilty Bystander*, 219.

13. Berdyaev, *Spirit*, 151.

14. Jung, *The Collected Works*, vol. 8, Ch. The Transcendent Function.

15. Jung, *The Collected Works*, vol. 11, para. 522.

16. Jung, *The Collected Works*, vol. 17, para. 303.

17. Steiner, "Building Stones."

18. Jung, *The Collected Works*, vol. 5, para. 336.

19. Jung, *The Collected Works*, vol. 5, para. 333.

20. Jung, *The Collected Works*, vol. 5, para. 335.

21. Jung, *The Collected Works*, vol. 5, para. 335.

22. Jung, *Letters*, vol. 2, 8.

23. Jung, *Dream Symbols*, 277.

24. James, *New Testament Apocrypha*, 254–55.

25. James, *New Testament Apocrypha*, 256.

26. Jung, *The Collected Works*, vol. 11, para. 659.

27. Jung and Neumann, *Analytical Psychology*, 369.

28. Neumann, *Depth Psychology*, 31.

29. Jung, *Letters*, vol. 1, 375.

30. Jung, *Letters*, vol. 1, 353.

31. Jackson and Lethem, *Exegesis of Philip K. Dick*, 578–79.

32. Jackson and Lethem, *Exegesis of Philip K. Dick*, 579.

Chapter 9.
Reflecting on Jung's *Answer to Job*

1. Jung, *Letters*, vol. 2, 21.

2. Jung, *Letters*, vol. 2, 20.

3. Jung, *Letters*, vol. 2, 116.

4. Jung, *Letters*, vol. 2, 17-18

5. Jung, *Letters*, vol. 2, 112.

6. Clay, *Emma Jung*, 339–40.

7. Jung, *The Collected Works*, vol. 11, para. 677.

8. Edinger, *The Ego-Self Axis and the Psychic Life Cycle*, Chapter 1.

9. von Franz, *C. G. Jung: His Myth in Our Time*, 174.

10. Jung, *The Collected Works*, vol. 11, para. 582.

11. Jung, *The Collected Works,* vol. 11, para. 639.
12. Jung, *The Collected Works,* vol. 11, para. 36.
13. Jung, *The Collected Works,* vol. 11, para. 585.
14. Jung, *The Collected Works,* vol. 11, para. 600.
15. Jung, *The Collected Works,* vol. 11, para. 756.
16. Jung, *The Collected Works,* vol. 11, para. 748.
17. Jung, *The Collected Works,* vol. 11, para. 677.
18. Jung, *The Collected Works,* vol. 11, para. 754.
19. Jung, *The Collected Works,* vol. 11, para. 694.
20. Jung, *The Collected Works,* vol. 11, para. 659.
21. Jung, *The Collected Works,* vol. 11, para. 740.
22. Jung, *The Collected Works,* vol. 11, para. 741.
23. Jung, *The Collected Works,* vol. 11, para. 693.
24. Jung, *The Collected Works,* vol. 11, para. 747.
25. Jung, *The Collected Works,* vol. 11, para. 746.
26. Jung, *The Collected Works,* vol. 11, para. 747.
27. Jung, *The Collected Works,* vol. 11, para. 758.
28. Jung, *The Collected Works,* vol. 11, para. 575.
29. Jung, *The Collected Works,* vol. 11, para. 415.

Chapter 10.
Quantum Physics and Wetiko

1. Jung, *The Collected Works,* vol. 11, para. 127.
2. Fuchs, *Coming of Age,* 526.
3. Buckley and Peat, *A Question of Physics: Conversations in Physics and Biology,* 59.
4. Herbert, *Quantum Reality,* 29.
5. Frazer, *The Golden Bough,* 826.
6. Jung, Letter to Eugene Rolfe, 1960.
7. Fuchs, *Coming of Age,* 527.
8. Fuchs, *Coming of Age,* 527.
9. Jackson and Lethem, *Exegesis of Philip K. Dick,* 103.
10. Jung, *Zofingia Lectures,* 109.
11. Jung, *The Collected Works,* vol. 8, para. 529.
12. Krishnamurti, *Talks,* 50.
13. Michelle Feynman, *Quotable Feynman,* 75.

14. Richard Feynman, "What is Science?" April 1966.
15. Berdyaev, *Meaning*, 153.
16. Nichol, *The Essential David Bohm*, 232.
17. Jacobi, *Paracelsus*, 267.
18. Jung, *The Collected Works*, vol. 8, para. 529.

Chapter 11.
Catching the Bug of Synchronicity

1. Jackson and Lethem, *Exegesis of Philip K. Dick*, 706–7.
2. Jung, *The Collected Works*, vol. 10, para. 113.
3. Jung, *The Collected Works*, vol. 8, para. 965.
4. Jung, *The Collected Works*, vol. 8, part VII, "Synchronicity."
5. Jung, *The Collected Works*, vol. 8, para. 967.
6. Evans-Wentz, *Tibetan Book*, 232.
7. Jung, *The Collected Works*, vol. 8, para. 982.
8. Kant, *The Critique of Pure Reason*, 7.
9. Wheeler, *At Home in the Universe*, 15.

Chapter 12.
The Disease of Not Seeing

1. Jung, *The Collected Works*, vol. 16, para. 442.
2. Arendt, *On Violence*, 81.
3. "Dr. Peter McCullogh Urges Unbreakable Resistance," Lifesitenews website.
4. Aurobindo, *Letters on Yoga*, 1733.

Chapter 13. The Art of Seeing

1. Fuchs, "My Struggles with the Block Universe," Researchgate website, 34.
2. Fuchs, "My Struggles with the Block Universe," Researchgate website, 34.

Chapter 15. The Self as Mirror

1. Jung, *The Collected Works*, vol. 7, para. 4.
2. Jung, *The Collected Works*, vol. 11, para. 401.
3. Jung, *Memories, Dreams, Reflections*, 371–372.

Postscript.
Dreaming Ourselves Awake

1. James, *New Testament Apocrypha*, 411–15.

Afterword
by Richard Grossinger

1. Thwaites, *The Jesuit Relations and Allied Documents*, vol. 46, 263.
2. Johnston, *The Manitous: The Supernatural World of the Ojibwe*, 221.
3. Virilio, quoted in Hickman, "Paul Virilio: The Anti-City," onscene.weebly .com, September 9, 2017.
4. Taibbi, "The Great American Bubble Machine," *Rolling Stone*, April 5, 2010.

Bibliography

Adler, Gerhard, and Aniela Jaffé. *C. G. Jung Letters,* vol. 1, London: Routledge & Kegan Paul, 1975.

Adler, Gerhard, and Aniela Jaffé. *C. G. Jung Letters,* vol. 2, Bollingen Series XVI. Princeton, N.J.: Princeton University Press, 1975.

Arendt, Hannah. *On Violence.*

Aurobindo, Sri. *Letters on Yoga.* Charlottesville, Va.: University of Virginia, Sri Aurobindo Birth Centenary Library, 1970 (digitized 2010).

Barbel, Joseph. *Commentaria in Malthaeum,* in *Christos Angelos.*

Ben-Aharon, Jesaiah. *The New Experience of the Supersensible.* East Sussex, UK: Temple Lodge Publishing, 2007.

———. *The Spiritual Event of the Twentieth Century.* London: Temple Lodge Publishing, 2001.

Berdyaev, Nicolas. *The Destiny of Man.* San Rafael, Calif.: Semantron Press, 2009.

———. *Freedom and the Spirit* San Rafael, Calif.: Semantron Press, 2009.

———. *The Meaning of the Creative Act.* San Rafael, Calif.: Semantron Press, 2008.

———. *Spirit and Reality.* San Rafael, Calif.: Semantron Press, 2009.

Bonhoeffer, Dietrich. *The Cost of Discipleship.* New York: Macmillan Company, 1969.

Cheetham, Tom. *All the World an Icon: Henry Corbin and the Angelic Function of Beings.* Berkeley, Calif.: North Atlantic Books, 2012.

Clay, Catrine. *Labyrinths: Emma Jung, Her Marriage to Carl, and the Early Years of Psychoanalysis.* New York: HarperCollins, 2016.

Corbin, Henry. *Alone with the Alone: Creative Imagination in the Sufism of Ibn 'Arabi.* Princeton, N.J.: Princeton University Press, 1997.

———. *Avicenna and the Visionary Recital.* Irving, Tex.: Spring Publications.

———. *Cyclical Time and Ismaili Gnosis.* London: Kegan Paul International, 1983.

———. *Harmonia Abrahamic.*

———. *L'homme et son ange: initiation et chevalerie spirituelle.* Paris: Fayard, 1983.

———. *The Man of Light in Iranian Sufism.* New Lebanon, N.Y.: Omega Publications, 1971.

———. *Swedenborg and Esoteric Islam.*

———. *The Voyage and the Messenger: Iran and Philosophy.* Berkeley, Calif.: North Atlantic Books, 1998.

Eliade, Mircea. *Shamanism: Archaic Techniques of Ecstasy.*

Evans-Wentz, W. Y. *The Tibetan Book of the Great Liberation.* London: Oxford University Press, 1954.

Feynman, Michelle, ed. *The Quotable Feynman.* Princeton, N.J.: Princeton University Press, 2015.

Feynman, Richard. National Science Teachers Association Fourteenth Convention lecture, "What Is Science?" April 1966.

Forbes, Jack D. *Columbus and Other Cannibals: The Wetiko Disease of Exploitation, Imperialism, and Terrorism.* New York: Seven Stories Press, 1979.

Frazer, James George. *The Golden Bough: A Study in Magic and Religion.* New York: Simon and Schuster, 1996.

Fuchs, Christopher. *Coming of Age with Quantum Information.* Cambridge, UK: Cambridge University Press, 2011.

Giersch, Harold. *Rudolf Steiner uber die Wiederkunft Christi,* Dornach 1991.

Guggenbuhl-Craig, Adolf. *Power in the Helping Professions.* Putnam, Conn.: Spring Publications, 1998.

Halifax, Joan. *Shamanic Voices.* New York: Dutton, 1979.

Hickman, Steven Craig. "Paul Virilio: The Anti-City." onscene.weebly.com, 2017.

Hillman, James. *Mythic Figures.* Putnam, Conn.: Spring Publications, 2007.

Jackson, Pamela, and Jonathan Lethem, eds. *The Exegesis of Philip K. Dick.* New York: Houghton Mifflin Harcourt, 2011.

Jacobi, Jolande, ed. *Paracelsus: Selected Writings.* Archive.org website.

James, M. R., ed. *The New Testament Apocrypha.* Berkeley, Calif.: Apocryphile Press, 2004.

Jensen, Derrick, ed. *Listening to the Land.* New York: Context Books, 2002.

Johnston, Basil, *The Manitous: The Supernatural World of the Ojibwe.* New York: Harper Collins, 1995.

Jung, C.G. *The Collected Works of C. G. Jung.* Translated by R. F. C. Hull, Gerard Adler, and Sir Herbert Read. Edited by Gerard Adler, R. F. C. Hull, Lisa Ress, William McGuire, Michael Fordham. 20 vols. Princeton, N.J.: Princeton, 1961–89.

———. *Dream Symbols of the Individuation Process: Notes of C. G. Jung's Seminars on Wolfgang Pauli's Dreams.*

———. *Nietzsche's Zarathustra,* vol. 1. Princeton: Princeton University Press, 1988.

———. Psychology of Religion: West and East, vol. 11 (Princeton, NJ: Princeton University Press, 1973), *Answer to Job,* p. 355

———. *The Red Book: Liber Novus—A Reader's Edition.* New York: W. W. Norton, 2009.

———. *The Zofingia Lectures.* Princeton, N.J.: Princeton University Press, 1983.

———. and Erich Neumann. *Analytical Psychology in Exile: The Correspondence of C. G. Jung and Erich Neumann,* Martin Liebscher, ed. Princeton, N.J.: Princeton University Press, 2015.

Kant, Immanuel. *Critique of Pure Reason.* Cambridge: Cambridge University Press, 1998.

Kerényi, Carl. *Asklepios: Archetypal Image of the Physician's Existence.* New York: Pantheon Books, 1959.

Krishnamurti, Jiddu. *Talks in Europe 1968.* Netherlands: Service/Wassenaar, 1969.

Levy, Paul. *Awakened by Darkness: When Evil Becomes Your Father.* Awaken in the Dream Publishing, Portland, Oreg. 2015.

———. *Dispelling Wetiko: Breaking the Curse of Evil.* Berkeley, Calif.: North Atlantic Books, 2013.

———. *The Quantum Revelation: A Radical Synthesis of Science and Spirituality.* New York: SelectBooks, 2018.

———. *Wetiko: Healing the Mind-Virus That Plagues Our World.* Rochester, Vt.: Inner Traditions, 2021.

Mallasz, Gitta. *Talking with Angels.* Einsiedeln, Switzerland: Daimon Verlag, 1988.

McDermott, Robert A., ed. *The Essential Steiner.* San Francisco, Calif.: Harper and Row, 1984.

Meier, Carl A. *Ancient Incubation and Modern Psychotherapy.* Evanston, Ill.: Northwestern University Press, 1967.

Merton, Thomas. *Conjectures of a Guilty Bystander.*

Mindell, Arny. *The Shaman's Body.* San Francisco, Calif.: HarperCollins, 1993.

Neumann, Erich. *Art and the Creative Unconscious.* New York: Pantheon Books, 1959.

———. *Depth Psychology and a New Ethic.* New York: G. P. Putnam's Sons, 1969.

———. *The Origins and History of Consciousness.* New York: Pantheon Books, 1964.

Nichol, Lee, ed. The *Essential David Bohm.* London: Routledge, 2008.

Nicholson, Shirley, ed. *Shamanism.* Wheaton, Ill.: Quest Books, 1987.

Nicolaus, Georg. *C. G. Jung and Nikolai Berdyaev: Individuation and the Person.* London: Routledge, 2011.

Otto, Rudolf. *The Idea of the Holy.*

Ouspensky, P. D. *In Search of the Miraculous: Fragments of an Unknown Teaching.* San Diego: Harcourt Brace, 1949.

Raine, Kathleen. *Blake and Tradition:* Volume 2, Princeton, NJ: Princeton University Press, 1968.

Reich, Wilhelm. *The Murder of Christ.* New York: Farrar, Straus and Giroux, 1971.

Ruland, *Lexicon alchemiae.*

Sandner, Donald. *Navaho Symbols of Healing: A Jungian Exploration of Ritual, Image, and Medicine.* Rochester, Vt.: Healing Arts Press, 1991.

Shantideva. *The Way of the Bodhisattva,* edited by the Padmakara Translation Group. Boston: Shambhala Publishers, 1997.

Steiner, Rudolf. "Building Stones for an Understanding of the Mystery of Golgotha." London: Rudolf Steiner Press, 1972. Rsarchives website.

———. "The Christ Impulse and Development of the Ego-Consciousness." London: The Anthroposophical Publishing Co., 1926. Rsarchives website.

———. "Christ at the Time of the Mystery of Golgotha and Christ in the Twentieth Century." In: *Occult Science & Occult Development,* GA 152,

2 May 1913. London: Rudolf Steiner Press, 1966. Rsarchive website.

———. "The Fifth Gospel." Bristol, UK: Rudolf Steiner Press, 1992. Rsarchives website.

———. "From Symptom to Reality in Modern History, lecture 4. Rudolf Steiner Press, 1976. Rsarchives website.

———. "The Reappearance of Christ in the Etheric." Massachusetts: Steiner Books, 2003. Rsarchives website.

———. *Truth and Knowledge* (doctoral dissertation, 1892). Rsarchives website.

Stevenson, D. H., ed. *The Poems of William Blake.*

Taibbi, Matt. "The Great American Bubble Machine." *Rolling Stone,* April 5, 2010.

Thwaites, Reuben Gold. *The Jesuit Relations and Allied Documents,* vol. 46. London: Forgotten Books, 2019.

Tradowsky, Peter. *Christ and AntiChrist: Understanding the Events of Our Time and Recognizing Our Tasks.* East Sussex, UK: Temple Lodge Publishing, 2010.

von Franz, Marie Louise. *C. G. Jung: His Myth in Our Time.* G. P. Putnam's Sons, New York, for the C. G. Jung Foundation for Analytical Psychology, 1975.

Walshe, Maurice. *The Complete Mystical Works of Meister Eckhart.* New York: Crossroad Publishing Company, 2009.

Wheeler, John Archibald. *At Home in the Universe.* Woodbury, N.Y.: The American Institute of Physics, 1994.

Wheelwright, Joseph. *The Reality of the Psyche.* New York: C. G. Jung Foundation, 1968.

Wilmer, Harry A., and Paul B. Woodruff. *Facing Evil: Light at the Core of Darkness.* La Salle, Ill.: Open Court, 1988.

About the Author

A creative artist, Paul Levy was born in 1956 and grew up in Yonkers, New York. In the midseventies he attended the State University of New York at Binghamton (now called Binghamton University), receiving degrees in economics and studio art. While an undergraduate he was hired by Princeton University to do research in economics. In 1981, catalyzed by an intense trauma, Paul had a life-changing spiritual awakening in which he began to recognize the dreamlike nature of reality. During the first year of his spiritual emergence, he was hospitalized a number of times and was told he was having a severe psychotic break from reality and was (mis)diagnosed as having a chemical imbalance. He was informed that he had what was then called *manic depression* (now called *bipolar disorder*), and that he would have to live with his illness for the rest of his life and would need to take medication until his dying breath. Little did the doctors realize, however, that he was taking part in a spiritual awakening and shamanic initiation, which at times mimicked psychosis but in actuality was a spiritual experience of a far different order, one that was completely off the map of the psychiatric system. Fortunately, over time he was able to extricate himself from the psychiatric establishment so that he could continue to unfold his inner process of awakening.

After the trauma of his shamanic breakdown/breakthrough, Paul became a certified art teacher and taught both painting and drawing for a handful of years to people of all ages. Intensely interested in the work of C. G. Jung, in 1988 he became the manager of the C. G. Jung Foundation Book Service in New York, as well as the advertising manager for the Jungian journal *Quadrant*.

In 1990, Paul moved to Portland, Oregon. In 1993, after a dozen years of working on himself so as to integrate his nonordinary experiences, he started to openly share his insights about the dreamlike nature of reality by giving talks and facilitating groups based on the way life is a shared waking dream that we are all co-creating and dreaming together. A pioneer in the field of spiritual emergence, Paul is a wounded healer in private practice, helping others who are also awakening to the dreamlike nature of reality. He is the founder of the Awaken in the Dream community in Portland, Oregon.

This is Paul's sixth book (three of which are on wetiko). A Tibetan Buddhist practitioner for close to forty years, Paul has closely studied with some of the greatest spiritual masters of Tibet and Burma. He was the coordinator of the Portland chapter of the Padmasambhava Buddhist Center for over twenty years. He is on the faculty of The Shift Network. His website is www.awakeninthedream.com; his email is paul@awakeninthedream.com.

Index

manifestation of the universe and, 237
mirrorlike nature of, 332
of our state, 11
shamanic shift in, 108–12
simulcausality and, 268
split, 193–94
subjective and objective, 246
control system, 31
Corbin, Henry, 124–26, 129–30, 132–33,
  139–45, 150–52, 155, 158–59
cosmic rebirth, 217–18
countertransference, 98–100
Course in Miracles, A, 138
creative conflict, 214–17
creative suppression syndrome (CSS), 354
creativity
  about, 183–84
  artistic, 188
  Berdyaev's ideas on, 184
  coming Christ and, 185–86
  connecting with, 191–92
  dis-ease and, 186
  divinely inspired, 186–87
  ethics of, 190, 191
  evil and, 186
  image of God and, 185
  as obstructing shadow, 183–84
  owning, 190–92
  redemption and, 189–90
  religious epoch of, 187–88
Crucifixion, 67, 69, 175–76, 178, 204,
  213–14, 320
cyclic existence, 61–62

daemon, 117–18, 147
darkness. *See also* evil
  about, xii

of chaos, 10–11
daemonic energy and, 147, 148
in demon of sickness, 89
distinguishing ourselves from, 148–49
hiding the light in, 174–82
illumination of, 13
light and, 36, 322–23
passing through, 148
shamanism and, 77
death and rebirth experience, 74
demon of sickness
  about, 80–83
  conscious dis-identifying with, 94
  darkness encoded in, 89
  personal experience of, 120
  recognition of, 94–95
  relating to, 93
  shaman and, 106–7
dependent co-arising, 267
Descartes, René, 12–13
de-solidifying ourselves, 304
Dick, Philip K., 217, 239, 256
discernment, 14, 59, 170, 291
disease
  bearing, 88
  creativity and, 186
  nature of, 83
  of not seeing, 288–302
  revelatory aspect, 319
  in soul, 217
dis-figuring, 148
disharmony, 58
dis-identification, 93–94
dis-integration, 81, 214
dismemberment, shamanic, 95
dismissing content due to source
  (DCDS), 355